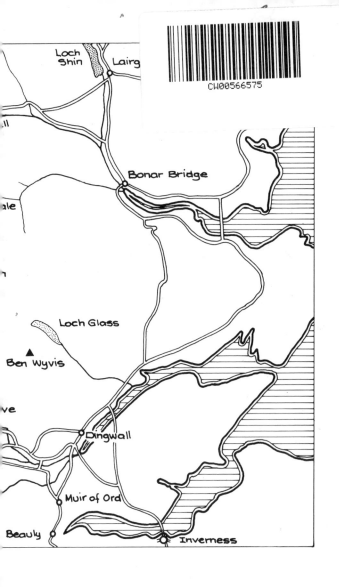

Loch Shin

Lairg

Bonar Bridge

Loch Glass

Ben Wyvis

Dingwall

Muir of Ord

Beauly

Inverness

This guidebook is compiled from the most recent information and experience provided by members of the Scottish Mountaineering Club and other contributors. The book is published by the Scottish Mountaineering Trust, which is a charitable trust.

Revenue from the sale of books published by the Trust is used for the continuation of its publishing programme and for charitable purposes associated with Scottish mountains and mountaineering.

Northern Highlands

Rock and Ice Climbs

VOLUME 2

Strathfarrar to Shetland

*With contributions from Geoff Cohen,
Andy Cunningham, Rob Christie,
Andy Long, John Mackenzie,
Andy Nisbet, Tom Prentice
and others*

Edited by Roger Everett

SCOTTISH MOUNTAINEERING CLUB
CLIMBERS' GUIDE

Published in Great Britain by the Scottish Mountaineering Trust, 1993

British Library Cataloguing in Publication Data
Cohen, G.
Northern Highlands Rock and Ice Climbs.
Vol. 2   2 Rev ed
I. Title II. Everett, R.
796.5
ISBN 0-907521-40-1

Maps and diagrams drawn by Jim Renny, Mary Benstead, Andy Cunningham, John Mackenzie, Donald Bennet, Kevin Howett and Jenny Mackenzie-Ross
Production by Donald Bennet and Peter Hodgkiss
Typeset by Elliot Robertson, Westec, North Connel
Colour separations and graphic work by Par Graphics, Kirkcaldy; Advanced Outlook, East Kilbride; and Elliot Robertson, Westec, North Connel
Printed by St Edmundsbury Press, Bury St Edmunds
Bound by Hunter and Foulis, Edinburgh

Distributed by Cordee, 3a DeMontfort Street, Leicester, LE1 7HD

Suilven

Contents

List of Illustrations

List of Diagrams and Maps

The Climber and the Mountain Environment

With increasing numbers of walkers and climbers going to the Scottish hills, it is important that all of us who do so should recognise our responsibilities to those who live and work among the hills and glens, to our fellow climbers and to the mountain environment in which we find our pleasure and recreation.

The Scottish Mountaineering Club and Trust, who jointly produce this and other guidebooks, wish to impress on all who avail themselves of the information in these books that it is essential at times to consider the sporting and proprietory rights of landowners and farmers. The description of a climbing, walking or skiing route in any of these books does not imply that a right of way exists, and it is the responsibility of all climbers to ascertain the position before setting out. In cases of doubt it is best to enquire locally.

During stalking and shooting seasons in particular, much harm can be done in deer forests and on grouse moors by people walking through them. Normally the deer stalking season is from 1st July to 20th October, when stag shooting ends. Hinds may continue to be culled until 15th February. The grouse shooting season is from 12th August until 10th December. These are not merely sporting activities, but are essential for the economy of many Highland estates. During these seasons, therefore, especial care should be taken to consult the local landowner, factor or keeper before taking to the hills.

Climbers and hillwalkers are recommended to consult the book HEADING FOR THE SCOTTISH HILLS, published by the Scottish Mountaineering Trust on behalf of the Mountaineering Council of Scotland and the Scottish Landowners Federation, which gives the names and addresses of factors and keepers who may be contacted for information regarding access to the hills.

It is important to avoid disturbance to sheep, particularly during the lambing season between March and May. Dogs should not be taken onto the hills at this time, and should always be kept under control.

Always try to follow a path or track through cultivated land and forests,and avoid causing damage to fences, dykes and gates by climbing over them carelessly. Do not leave litter anywhere, but take it down from the hill in your rucksack.

The number of walkers and climbers on the hills is leading to increased, and in some cases very unsightly erosion of footpaths and hillsides. Some of the revenue from the sale of this and other SMC guidebooks is used by the Trust to assist financially the work being carried out to repair and maintain hill paths in Scotland. However, it is important for all of us to recognise our responsibility to minimise the erosive effect of our passage over the hills so that the enjoyment of future climbers is not spoiled by landscape damage.

As a general rule, where a path exists walkers should follow it and even where it is wet and muddy should avoid walking along its edges, the effect of which is to extend erosion sideways. Do not take short-cuts at the corners of zigzag paths. Remember that the worst effects of erosion are likely to be caused during or soon after prolonged wet weather when the ground is soft and waterlogged. A route on a stony or rocky hillside is likely to cause less erosion than on a grassy one at such times.

Although the use of bicycles can often be very helpful for reaching remote crags and hills, the erosion damage that can be caused by them when used 'off road' on soft footpaths and open hillsides is such that their use on such terrain must cause concern. It is the editorial policy of the Scottish Mountaineering Club that the use of bicycles in hill country may be recommended on hard roads such as forest roads or private roads following rights of way, but it is not recommended on footpaths or open hillsides where the environmental damage that they cause may be considerable. Readers are asked to bear these points in mind, particularly when the ground is wet and soft after rain.

The proliferation of cairns on hills detracts from the feeling of wildness, and may be confusing rather than helpful as regards route-finding. The indiscriminate building of cairns on the hills is therefore discouraged.

Climbers are reminded that they should not drive along private estate roads without permission, and when parking their cars should avoid blocking access to private roads and land, and should avoid causing any hazard to other road users.

Finally, the Scottish Mountaineering Club and the Scottish Mountaineering Trust can accept no liability for damage to property nor for personal injury resulting from the use of any route described in their publications.

The Mountaineering Council of Scotland is the representative body for climbers and walkers in Scotland. One of its primary concerns is the continued free access to the hills and crags that we now enjoy. Information about bird restrictions, stalking and general access issues can be obtained from the National Officer of the MCofS. Should any climber or walker encounter problems regarding access they should contact the National Officer of the MCofS, whose current address is published in CLIMBER AND HILLWALKER magazine.

Acknowledgements

A great many people have contributed to this guide over many years. Although some of the areas covered in this book have never before been included in an SMC Climbers' Guide, acknowledgement is due to the authors of previous guidebooks whose work provided the foundation for this guide. Principally these were: Alistair Park and Philip Tranter, authors of the Corriemulzie MC's *Interim Guide to Easter Ross* and its *Foinaven Supplement* (published in 1966); Ian Rowe, author of Volume 1 of the SMC *Climber's Guide to the Northern Highlands* (1969); Tom Strang, author of the SMC *Northern Highlands District Guide*; and Hamish MacInnes and Kev Howett, whose excellent selective guides have overlaps with this area.

Various authors have compiled or made large contributions to substantial parts of the text. Principally these were:
John Mackenzie – Strathfarrar, Strathconon, Strathpeffer and Ben Wyvis; Andy Cunningham – Rhue and Reiff; Allen Fyffe – Ardmair; Tom Prentice – Stac Pollaidh; Andy Nisbet – Sheigra and Foinaven; Rob Christie – The East Caithness Coast; Andy Long – Shetland.

Other uncredited sections were initially compiled by Geoff Cohen, and the content has been kept up to date by Roger Everett with the assistance of a large number of correspondents, among whom Andy Nisbet deserves special mention.

Many other climbers have contributed their knowledge and advice by providing drafts, or specialist sections of the text or photographs. The contributions of the following have been particularly important:
Dave Butterfield, Ross Chapman, John Fowler, Mick Fowler, Dave Jenkins, Crag Jones, Paul Nunn, Simon Richardson, Mungo Ross, Andy Tibbs and Noel Williams.

The photodiagrams were contributed by Grahame Nicoll and Andy Nisbet, and the many excellent crag drawings were produced by Mary Benstead, John Mackenzie, Jenny Mackenzie-Ross and Kev Howett. The maps of Jim Renny deserve special mention. Finally, Donald Bennet's meticulous care in the final stages of preparation of this Volume, and the preceding Volume 1, has made a substantial contribution to their quality.

Introduction

Such has been the pace of development of climbing in the Northern Highlands of Scotland that the original concept of including all the routes in one volume proved impossible. This book provides a comprehensive coverage of the summer and winter climbing to be found in the northernmost corners of the British Isles. Starting with the accessible crags near Inverness, we proceed north via the Fannaichs and the lonely Freevater Forest, through Assynt and Coigach to the north and far north-east coasts of the mainland. The often adventurous climbing on Orkney and Shetland has also been included.

The title of this volume is slightly misleading. Although many high mountain crags are described, much of the climbing is on low-lying inland crags. Developed relatively recently, many of these provide excellent climbing on a variety of rock types. Some catch most of the sunshine that frequently blesses this area in spring, providing quick-drying quality routes that are the equal of many on the more crowded crags further south. The coasts of the mainland, Orkney and Shetland provide many excellent sea-cliffs, with Reiff in particular being outstanding. There are also the very best of those particularly enticing entities, the sea-stacks.

The rapidly improving road network provides surprisingly rapid access to most of the areas in this guide. Ullapool is little more than four hours away from the central belt, with the low-lying crags of Ardmair and the mountain walls of Stac Pollaidh, Sgurr an Fhidhleir and Beinn Dearg near at hand. Even the most northern mountains and sea-cliffs can be reached for a weekend's climbing, although it may be better to take a short holiday to savour their varied delights. Of course, Orkney and Shetland require a greater commitment of time and energy, but those with an exploratory urge will be amply rewarded.

Some of the detail in a minority of the chapters in this guide may be found, shall we say, a little speculative. But at a time when so much of our world can be described so accurately, it is surely refreshing and healthy for the inquisitive mountaineer to have the opportunity to explore an area where much remains to be discovered, and where the locations and details of some of the climbs that have been found in the past remain uncertain. We have done our best to be as helpful as possible; we hope that anyone finding deficiencies in some of the descriptions will have enjoyed their adventure and will value a similar sense of discovery that the first ascensionists must have experienced.

At one time it was (and probably still is) felt by some people that the Northern Highlands should be left as an uncharted wilderness, where climbers and mountaineers could venture without the hindrance of a guide book. Personally, I think that those who wish to do this still can; they can refrain from buying this edition. But experience has shown that many with this view actually had access to all the existing information in journals, magazines and personal files. We have merely pulled all this information together, to allow those whose life styles or inclinations limit their time for the research necessary to get the best from all too infrequent visits to these marvellous places.

There is something for everyone in this guide: climbs of all grades on small crags both near and far from the road; classic mountaineering excursions on summer rock and winter ice; modern mixed winter climbs of the highest calibre; long hard climbs on some of the most serious cliffs in Britain; sea-stacks with all the novelty of approach by boat, Tyrolean or swim. It has been a pleasure to help to bring all this together during long hours of 'theoretical climbing' on the word processor, but especially during memorable climbing weekends inspired by the descriptions of these very special places. On behalf of the SMC Publications Sub-Committee, I hope the users of this guide will have every bit as much enjoyment.

Roger Everett. March 1993.

Geology

Much of the special character of the climbing in the North-west Highlands is associated with the unique variety of rocks that occur there. Only five main types of rock are present, but they are all remarkably different from the igneous rocks, the granites and lavas, which are found in the classic climbing areas of Glen Coe, Glen Etive, Ben Nevis and the Cairngorms.

Lewisian Gneiss

The rock at the bottom of the pile is a coarsely crystalline metamorphic rock known as Lewisian gneiss. It is one of the oldest rocks in Europe, and can be regarded as the foundation on which the later rocks have been built. At least two major episodes of metamorphism can be recognised in the group, dated at 2800 and 1700 million years ago. The rock occurs extensively in the far north-west, and tends to be confined to the lower ground. However it is generally very rough sound rock, and where it does form crags it offers superb quality climbing. Possibly the two most notable crags of Lewisian gneiss are at Carnmore and Diabaig.

Torridonian Sandstone

Resting on the Lewisian gneiss is a very old, well-stratified sedimentary rock called Torridonian sandstone. It is one of the most distinctive rocks in the north-west because it forms much of the high ground. The rock is commonly dark red in colour and is more or less flat-lying. Its total thickness has been estimated at more than seven kilometres. Torridonian sandstone is some 800 million years old, which means that it is much too old to contain readily recognisable fossils (which did not start to appear until about 600 million years ago). It is thought that the original Torridonian sediments were deposited by rivers draining from a mountainous region which lay further north-west. The conspicuous pebbles present in some beds have been linked with rocks now found in south-east Greenland. Despite its great age, Torridonian sandstone has survived more or less unchanged since it first formed. In other words, it has not been metamorphosed and so must have remained outwith any mountain building areas.

There are not as many long mountain routes on Torridonian sandstone as might be imagined from the amount of exposed rock. This is because the bigger mountain faces tend to be broken up too frequently by terraces. However there are some fine long rock routes such as the Cioch Nose in Applecross and major winter routes in the corries of Beinn Bhan. As well as the countless short routes on the sea-cliffs near Reiff there are several sea-stacks, such as the Old Man of Stoer and Am Buachaille, which offer the jaded climber something a bit out of the ordinary, and on the oldest sedimentary rock in Britain at that.

Cambrian Quartzite

Lying on top of the Torridonian sandstone is another sedimentary sequence of contrasting character. It consists largely of a pure quartz sandstone referred to as Cambrian quartzite. This forms a very distinctive capping on many Torridonian peaks, including Beinn Eighe. The rock is white or grey in colour and tends to break into sharp angular fragments. It is badly shattered in places, but where it is sound it provides first rate climbing, for example on the ramparts and buttresses of Beinn Eighe. One particular type of bed is known as Pipe Rock because of the conspicuous markings it contains. These markings represent the vertical burrows left by organisms that lived in the sediment on the sea floor.

The quartzite beds dip towards the south-east and cut across the Torridonian strata. The Cambrian quartzite must therefore have been deposited much later than the Torridonian sandstone, after that rock had been tilted and eroded. The quartzite beds are dated at about 550 million years old.

Moine Schists

The deposits which started with the Cambrian quartzite continued with the Durness limestone. Then a major mountain-building episode began that culminated in the formation of the massive Caledonian Mountain chain. This chain was formed when two 'plates' collided with each other head on. The sediments in the ocean between the two plates were squeezed and heated during the collision, and produced a series of metamorphic rocks. As a result of the squeezing most of the metamorphic rocks were overfolded on a huge scale. In the north-west Highlands an extraordinary structure called the Moine Thrust zone developed as the pile of metamorphic rocks was pushed up and over the block of rocks that remained undeformed to the north-west. This stable block comprised the three main rock types described above, the Lewisian gneiss, Torridonian sandstone and Cambrian quartzite.

The Moine Thrust runs from Whiten Head on the north coast down to Loch Alsh on the west coast, from where it continues onto the Sleat peninsula of Skye. The Moine schists make up most of the Highlands lying to the east and south of this thrust. They originated as marine sediments, some possibly being contemporaneous with the Torridonian rocks. A great pile of schists was eventually transported several tens of kilometres north-westwards along the plane of the Moine Thrust, and came to rest on top of the younger Cambrian quartzite. Some 16 km south of Inchnadamph, at Knockan cliff, there is a Nature Trail, which visits an excellent exposure of this remarkable feature. This is a must for anyone interested in seeing this structure at first hand.

The Moine schists are a less interesting group of rocks from a climbing point of view, being rather vegetated on the whole. However, they do offer winter climbing opportunities, on Ladhar Bheinn for example.

Old Red Sandstone

Some 400 million years ago, after the Caledonian mountain building episode had passed its climax, a further group of freshwater sediments began to accumulate. These deposits are now well represented among the rocks of Caithness and Orkney. They comprise flaggy, red sandstones and contain fossil fish. Many spectacular sea-cliffs such as those on Hoy are formed from this rock. The Old Man of Hoy is set on a plinth of volcanic ash and basalt. Lesser but very scenic cliffs occur around Duncansby Head.

The final moulding of all these various rocks was brought about largely by the action of the huge ice sheets and glaciers which built up and melted down many times during the Ice Ages of the last two million years. At times the whole of Scotland was covered by ice, with the possible exception of the highest mountain summits. The last main ice-maximum occurred 17,000 years ago. In the north-west Highlands glaciers flowed both east and west, carving out the characteristic U-shaped valleys, corries and aretes, depositing moraines and sculpting the 'scarred and silent' landscapes in which we climb today.

History

STRATHCONON AND STRATHFARRAR

The development of what essentially is an outcrop area, with a few good mountain crags thrown in, happened over two distinct phases. These were prior to 1980, and post 1989, and they involved more or less the same group of climbers. Due to the helpful and diverse geology of the area, the pioneering sod-busters discovered that not only was each crag quite different from even a near neighbour, but that the numerous varieties of undifferentiated schists gave excellent and sound climbing material that varied from near gritstone-type cracks and roughness to slate-smooth slabs. In between these two there were several crags that offered vertical walls with or without holds, and climbing styles are thus diverse. This accident of geology was the main factor that encouraged exploration on such an enthusiastic scale. The quick regrowth of various lichens caused confusion when routes were occasionally 're-discovered' and claimed, but it is hoped that the majority of crags which are now clean will attract sufficient traffic to remain that way. Though the area is undoubtedly a pleasant backwater, the above qualities coupled with quick-drying accessibility mean that the crags were developed rapidly by the same group of friends claiming their own lines without fear of invasion from outside groups, the maxim being that he who cleaned it, climbed it.

The long and lonely private road that winds up Strathfarrar has not helped in the development of the winter crags that lie tucked into recesses on Sgurr na Lapaich and Sgurr na Muice. The majority of lines were climbed by John Mackenzie, Tom Anderson, Jerry Smith and Duncan McCallum in 1978 on the accessible Sgurr na Muice and Sgurr na Fearstaig's south top. Of these, three lines stand out: the icefall lines of Streaky and Best Back and the short but good gully of Enchanter's Nightshade. The earliest recorded route, Spindrift Gully on An Riabachan by D.Smith and J.S.Stewart, is also worthwhile if rather remote. More recently Nisbet and Lyall's much harder route on Sgurr na Lapaich, Lapland Buttress, points to some of the gems tucked away at the end of a long walk. Certainly the hills here attract a lot of snow, and despite the access difficulties they would probably reward a visit by those with an open mind.

Of all the developments, Strathconon has attracted the most interest due to its accessibility and pleasant surroundings. The lower glen contains all the outcrops, whilst the upper glen contains the mountain crags. Of the outcrops, Glenmarksie is overall the nicest and most open, being up on a sunny hillside. It was first climbed on by the late Ian Ruscoe, who opened the crag up with Greased Lightning; a second enthusiastic ascent by Richard McHardy led to a determined siege by Mackenzie, David Butterfield (Dave the Hat), Mike Birch, Dave Gilbert and McCallum in 1979. Proteus was the best of the routes done in this era, with Hiroshima Grooves being a close second. A brief wave of exploration by Butterfield and Brian McDermott in 1982 found lines now taken by Callisto, Sickle Moon and Selene, all good routes which became totally overgrown before the main second wave of exploration took place between 1989 and 1991. During this period, Robert Brown, Graham Cullen and Mackenzie cleaned and climbed the remaining lines, including the routes done by McDermott and Butterfield, albeit by more direct lines. The technical advance on the crag then jumped from HVS to E4 with Mackenzie's appropriately named Strategic Arms Limitation in the summer of 1989, a route which took such a striking line on the 1 in 4 overhang of the Brown Wall. Developments concentrated more on the fine walls to the left and perhaps the best of these are Phobos and Deimos, at a more reasonable E2, and Brown's stretchy Dynamite Direct. Undoubtedly the crag's most popular lines remain Callisto, with its puzzling traverse start, and the delightful two-pitch Sea of Tranquillity. The equally good Selene, which was climbed direct by Cullen, remains less frequented though it probably offers the best HVS on the crag.

Meig and Aspen crags on the north-facing side of the glen offered quite different styles on steep rock. Undoubtedly the two main lines on Meig offer climbs as good as any on Glenmarksie. The first, The Birch, an overhanging but absolutely safe crack that splits a blank wall was climbed by Mackenzie. The second, a bold affair climbed by Martin Hind in the summer of 1992, is the aptly named Yellow Streak which climbs the not too technical but thinly protected overhanging groove in the centre of the main wall. Hind made several productive forays onto this crag, discovering the delectable but rarely dry brown slab at the left end, which offers two really good VS lines as well as the bold Dancing in the Rain, another line where a fall is unthinkable.

Aspen Crag saw a sudden blitz of activity in 1991 and 1992 on overhanging rock littered with generous incut holds. Hind, Brown and Mackenzie were responsible for most of the routes. This, the nearest crag to the road and the most nearly worked out, saw some bold solos by Hind and more conventional ascents that culminated in Brown and Mackenzie's route Gobstopper, an unlikely-looking line taking the biggest roof at its widest point and one of the few lines not well endowed with protection. The most popular route remains the first, the bold but enticing line of Meridian, which encapsulates all that this crag has to offer.

A host of minor crags were also discovered during the years 1990 to 1993, and these offered the same team of climbers some very pleasant routes on the quick-drying southern slopes of the glen. Dam Crag offers the stealthy Gulf Crisis and the Upper Scatwell slabs some medium grade lines up the centre, but harder and delectably micro-precision (and protected!) lines up to the right. The much bigger but slatier River Slabs, the scene of one of Joe Brown's TV fishing exploits, has McDermott's exciting VS, Grand Central, well positioned above the deep black pool below. The future offers precarious lines up the blank slabs, but development has so far been inhibited by the fissile rock.

High up on the sunny southern slopes above the trees lies the best of the minor crags, Hidden Crag, which offered on its quartz-sharp rock some bold solo lines to Hind as well as the two best lines, Chinese Eyes to Brown and the well named Barker to Mackenzie. Scoop Crag up to the right offers a smooth contrast in the shape of the Scoop, marginally reminiscent of Hammer's scoop on the Etive Slabs. One of the boldest lines in the area, another Hind creation, takes the wall just left of the right arete; Brass Monkey will probably not see many takers.

The mountain crag that offers the most is the weird and wonderful Creag Ghlas, unique in its unsettling geology and ambience, offering quick drying and long routes. The more amenable, rambling and longer crag, the East Buttress, saw initial development by J.Rennie and M.Strong in 1967 with Oh Dear at Mild VS. An easier variation was soloed by Tom Patey a little later, with the suggested name of Oh! once he had discovered the previous ascent. Better things were in store when Mackenzie and Birch took the equally artificial but fun right edge of the crag at VS, Boulder and Bolder, and the more direct HVS of Whoops in 1991 by Cullen and Mackenzie. Pleasant though the East Buttress was, the real challenge was on the shorter but infinitely sterner West Buttress, sometimes compared to a steeper and more unfriendly Etive Slabs. It has the feel of a slate crag, despite being a sound schist. No matter how good the climber is, the routes always feel awkward due to the holds slanting to the right. Climbing here has all the attributes of the proverbial pimple on an elephant's backside, with protection usually behind exfoliation flakes. Despite the bald look and feel, surprising holds turned up on practically all the routes, giving hope when none should have existed. The audacious Lizard, climbed in 1967 by Dave Bathgate and Robin Campbell, left an indelible impression on Campbell and subsequent lines have remained memorable. The late Mark Selwood's fine on-sight lead of the excellent Loop Pitch on the Lizard, in the summer of 1990, was a direct attack on the bald arete to the right of the parent route's second pitch and was particularly bold with the crux moves many metres above the sole Friend Zero runner.

Possibly the best line so far, Glass Slipper, the combined product of Brown and Mackenzie in the summer of 1992, took the steepest rib at an easier grade than expected at sustained HVS. This benefitted from a dose of commonsense rather than a sense of adventure with a prior clean of the fine almost invisible lichen that makes such a difference between success and failure. Hind did a typically bold solo of the Wandering Minstrel the same day. The equally imposing Evening Arete fell to an on-sight lead to Brown and Mackenzie, Brown being forced to lead the desperate-looking second pitch in a thunderstorm, the crux coinciding with the heaviest rain. This was somehow typical of the place and equally typical that the 'desperate' pitch turned out to be pleasant VS. There are undoubtedly some fine and memorable routes still to be climbed here.

In Glen Orrin, the enigmatic crag noted by both the Creag Dhu and Robin Campbell had an indifferent skirmish by Mackenzie and Brown, 'The Curates Egg' in the autumn of 1989. Though good in parts, the sudden ability of holds to snap and the almost total absence of protection rather put off the pioneers as regards summer routes, though there are fine and stern-looking walls that may be perfectly sound. The highlight of the crag was the freezing of the central waterfall, which gave the 200m icefall of Ghlastail GTX to Cullen and Mackenzie in the winter of 1990, a crescendo of steepening ice pitches.

STRATHPEFFER AND BEN WYVIS

The biggest, blackest, steepest and mossiest of all the Strathpeffer outcrops is Raven's Rock, which received all its development in the years 1978 to 1980 after the original line (the ever-loose Raven's

Squawk) had been climbed in 1970. Much cleaning revealed excellent rock and protection and the combined forces of Mackenzie, Butterfield, Birch, Brown and McCallum accounted for most of the lines. With routes up to 90m which are very accessible, the best lines were undoubtedly Obituary, Tombstone Buttress, The Sting and Jacobite Wall. All these and many more on the right-hand side of the crag could be cleaned again without too much effort, and but for the rather gloomy north-facing and midge-infested atmosphere probably would be. Of all the outcrops, Raven's has the greatest potential for hard routes but considerable work would be needed to clean them.

Moy Rock, an even more esoteric crag, is the home of well-watched peregrine falcons. Composed of conglomerate, the protection is usually long weighted slings around the bigger 'pebbles'. An early and unrecorded history of climbing by Ian Rowe and later developements by Mackenzie, Birch and McHardy in 1978 led to the ascent of the impressive Magnificrack and the equally impressive posse of police, birdwatchers and assorted multitudes below who were unaware that the climbers were unaware of the peregrine, the least disturbed of any of the participants on that day. Moy Rock is perhaps best left to the birds and the two rather good low-level bouldering traverses can easily be climbed out of season.

Of the two main corries of Ben Wyvis, Coire Mor saw winter development in 1986 with Alan Winton and D.Bond climbing both the Waterfall (probably climbed earlier by Brown in the late 60s) and the impressive-looking Slab Smear Left-Hand, the mountain's first hard route. The unusual slabs set at an angle gave a few simple summer soloes to Mackenzie but the future within this corrie has to be in winter.

Coire na Feola has the biggest and best-defined of the crags and the ice-streaked Creag Coire na Feola had been noticed by several climbers. The winter of 1993 saw Dave Broadhead, Cullen, Hind and Mackenzie making the long approach and several fine mixed and ice routes were discovered, the hardest being Walking On Air. A feature of the place has been both the drudgery of the walk-in and the incessant wind, which seems to be created by the topography and ensures that whatever the wind's general direction, it will always be blowing directly in your face! The crag was, wind aside, an important discovery and is capable of producing ice in copious quantities as well as harbouring some epicurean-quality turf.

THE FANNAICHS

No climbs appear to have been recorded in this area before 1960. An unrecorded visit in that year by R.H.Sellers and Jerry Smith, and their untimely death a few months later, inspired Tom Patey and his colleagues to record the first two 'summer' climbs on Sgurr nan Clach Geala. This was followed by winter exploration by the Corriemulzie Club, whose fulsome descriptions in the 1966 Interim Guide spoke of 'a noble cluster of six magnificent buttresses up to 800 feet high'. The 1970s and early 80s saw a slow but steady flow of further excellent Aberdonian contributions to the winter climbing on the Geala crags. Skyscraper Buttress was probably the finest climb, and the source of a little rivalry, before falling to a powerful foursome on a perfect winter's day. Thorough mopping-up operations by Dougie Dinwoodie added two new difficult starts to this route and the well-named Destitution Road.

Meanwhile, after early climbs in Garbh Coire Mor in the south-east Fannaichs by Clive Rowland and his friends, the late 70s and early 80s saw intensive development of this area by a Dingwall-based group led by John Mackenzie. Although easy of access in the days before usage of the Fannich Lodge road became restricted, this corrie remained relatively unvisited by other climbers for many years. Mackenzie also produced several climbs on the north face of Sgurr Mor, among which The Resurrection, formidably described in *Cold Climbs*, provided something of an enigma to climbers viewing the face from the distant road. Finally the steep cliffs of Carn na Criche, whose potential was first demonstrated by Des Rubens in 1984, gained more good routes in the early 1990s. It offers an attractive venue, though it is rarely in good condition.

BEINN DEARG

Of Coire Ghranda, George Sang wrote in 1915, 'dark and frowning on the left, close from the water's edge, in awesome slope and airy leap, tower the mural escarpments of the great Beinn, the lower slabs still bearing on their repellent faces the writing of the age when ice held dominion in these lands . . . Their ascent is not lightly to be accomplished by even the most experienced cragsmen. Great masses of stone, held only to the mountain face by ropes of heather and padding of moss, await dislodgement, and the climber must use every care and all his skill to avoid weaning these children of destruction from their parent mount.' Not until 1946 was this challenge taken up by the redoubtable Dr and Mrs Bell, and it is quite possible that their climb has not been repeated in the ensuing half a century.

The initial exploration of the Gleann na Sguaib side of Beinn Dearg was instigated by Tom Patey, for whom it offered the most accessible winter sport from his Ullapool home. Two rock climbs in 1962 were followed in 1964 by the classic Penguin Gully, with Bill Murray and Norman Tennent. He maintained a bothy adjacent to his house and passing climbers were generously inspired (between copious drams and cigarettes) to go out and attack the myriad unclimbed routes. The easier lines fell to an Edinburgh Squirrels team, whose naming of The Reverend Ian Paisley Memorial Gully will no doubt set future climbing historians wondering. While Patey soloed many of the most obvious lines he gifted perhaps the finest of them, Emerald Gully, to Paul Nunn and his friends, who climbed it shortly before Patey's tragic death. In the 1970s the buttresses between the Gleann na Sguaib gullies were crossed with a network of interesting lines, while the impressive Ice Hose on the huge west face of Beinn Dearg fell to Ian Dalley and party. The most significant development of the 1980s was Mick Fowler's ventures onto the remote upper cliff of Coire Ghranda. Body Freeze apparently recorded an ascent completed in appalling conditions, while Ice Bomb was a typically audacious Fowler feat, whose difficulties remain unrecognised only because of their remotenesss.

The most recent route on the mountain is Jewel in the Crown, the much-eyed line of icicles left of Emerald Gully. An attempt by Simon Richardson and Roger Everett, in atrocious weather on a day when avalanches elsewhere caused several serious accidents, was thwarted by lack of ice. They climbed the interesting line of Archway as a consolation. Despite taking a circuitous detour to avoid the all too obvious avalanche risk, the party narrowly escaped being swept down the easy slopes in lower Gleann na Squaib. Richardson returned three years later with Chris Cartwright, who forced the icicle fringe on a day when even the ever-optimistic Richardson thought that the thawing conditions at the foot of the route dictated retreat.

CORRIEMULZIE AND ALLADALE

In the early 1960s, while Tom Patey was ranging far and wide, another group of young climbers coalesced around the charismatic figure of Philip Tranter. The Corriemulzie Club, many of whom were ex-St

Andrews, included Alistair Park, John Wedderburn, Will Fraser and Blyth Wright among its members, with Ian Rowe and Peter Macdonald slightly later associates. Their watering holes were the Loch Laggan Inn and the lonely Inveroykel Lodge, from where sallies were made into the wild hinterland. Aided by Tranter's ability to endure phenomenally long drives, they produced a clutch of summer and winter climbs on Seana Bhraigh, Glenbeg, the Alladale slabs and Foinaven. While not of great technical difficulty, these were true exploratory ventures carried out with huge enthusiasm, which culminated in the publication of Park and Tranter's 1966 *Interim Guide to Easter Ross* and the *Foinaven Supplement*. The sad death of both protagonists within the space of a few months initiated the dispersal of the Club, but in the late 1960s and early 70s the belayless Alladale slabs maintained sufficient reputation to attract climbers in search of harder routes. These included Kenny Spence and Pete Whillance, while Dougie Dinwoodie added two more challenging winter climbs in Luchd Coire. For the last decade, these areas have again fallen out of the limelight, and apart from the occasional inquisitive climbers prepared to take on leagues of heather and bog, they now remain largely the preserve of 'bothyers' and 'sportsmen'.

COIGACH

The beautiful mountains of Coigach were naturally an attraction to the early SMC. Stac Pollaidh, likened by Professor Heddle to 'a porcupine in a state of extreme irascibility', afforded a sporting climb up the western cliff to Dr, Mrs and Miss Inglis Clark in the company of C.W.Walker. It was reported that 'the climb was of unusual difficulty from the very bottom, and consisted almost entirely of pure rock pitches and chimneys, quite unclimbable but for the rough surface of the rock. ... A few hitches were indeed met with, but balanced so warily that a touch with the finger set them rocking. ... It was no easy matter to dispose of two ladies, two rucksacks and the writer on the meagre ledges of the face.' Ling made another route here in 1907 as well as a brave attempt on the Nose of Sgurr an Fhidhleir, where he and Sang were repulsed by holdless slabs. Until recently this climb still harboured ironmongery of considerable vintage. It was finally subdued by Drasdo and Dixon in 1962, a success which spurred Patey to develop two lines on the eastern flank of the Nose. Enigma Grooves on Stac Pollaidh was another typical Patey route, requiring a vigorous approach. Two more good routes were added to this cliff in the 1960s, Jack the Ripper by Anderson and Mair and Felo de Se by Carrington and McLean.

In the 1970s Richard McHardy, climbing with Dave Jenkins and Peter Macdonald, found two further interesting lines on the flank of Sgurr an Fhidhleir, and then in 1979 John Mackenzie added a Direct Finish to the Nose route, whose spine-chilling description must have reflected a protectionless near-death experience. The same year Aberdonians Norman Keir and Bob Smith finally achieved a fine winter ascent of the Nose, albeit not quite on the crest. This was rectified some years later by Wilson Moir and Chris Forrest who reported a superb climb up the summer line, mainly on frozen turf. A second ascent by Everett and Richardson in 1991 confirmed the quality of the route as surely one of the very best in Scotland.

The second half of the 1980s saw an explosion of new routes on Stac Pollaidh, principally on the beautiful, compact east flank of the western cliff, but also on No.2 Buttress and the smaller buttresses to its right. As is sometimes the way in climbing history, improvements in climbing standards and technology (small flexible Friends, specialist rock boots) offer at best a partial explanation for this sudden wave of advance onto steep blank sandstone walls. Following several new routes by A.Fraser in 1985, Tom Prentice, Simon Richardson and Rab Anderson formed the vanguard of the assault in 1988, with Expecting to Fly, Walking on Air and Mid Flight Crisis being perhaps their best routes. Walking on Air required several attempts, with Prentice making the long drive repeatedly, and succeeding only after considerable flight time had been logged. During this phase of exploration, Felo de Se was freed and Jack the Ripper straightened out to provide two excellent climbs at more amenable grades.

In the same period Anderson also joined forces with the Glenmore Lodge climbers in an intensive development of the Ardmair crags, first climbed on by Alex Taylor and Fraser Fotheringham in 1986. Allen Fyffe, Richard Mansfield and Andy Cunningham were the other leading lights here, producing some very hard climbs such as the wonderful prow of Burning Desire and the technical Neart nan Gaidheal, as well as an avalanche of excellent routes in the HVS to E2 range. Like Reiff further west, this development of sandstone outcrop climbing provided a very welcome (some would say overdue) addition to the climbing menu in the Ullapool area. Unfortunately Ardmair's greater accesssibilty as compared with Reiff is balanced by a considerably greater population of midges.

ASSYNT

The west face of Caisteal Liath on Suilven offered an obvious challenge to the early explorers and it succumbed in 1892 to the skills of Charles Pilkington and Horace Walker (known for their deeds in Skye and elsewhere). Three years later Professor Ramsay, having been baffled in an attempted descent of the route, returned armed with a 'stout clothes-line doubled'. Despite torrential rain and a wind which 'made merry with our kilts, blowing them anywhere but where they ought to be', he succeeeded in repeating the ascent in the company of his young son. Nevertheless A.E.Robertson, describing the climb up the shallow gully in the south-west angle of Caisteal Liath, warned of 'holds .... somewhat of the vegetable order'; while Sang some years later referred to 'a herbage scramble of the worst sort' and 'long loose heather with poor roots'. From men as accomplished as these in the arts of summer 'mixed' climbing in the Highlands such warnings are not to be taken lightly!

The Barrel Buttress of Quinag was first climbed at Easter 1907 by Raeburn, Ling and Mackay. Some twenty years later, writing after Raeburn's funeral, Mackay still vividly recalled the experiences of that first ascent. They had at first been repulsed and reached the top 'by a side route', but descending once more they rejoined the original line which Raeburn now forced in magnificent style. Mackay apparently liked bridging whereas Ling, 'a sinuous being', climbed 'close to the rock corner' as Raeburn commanded. Mackay insisted on his own way 'feet spread, finding far out counter-pushes, hands not used as hooks from which a heavy body hangs pendant, but balancing, distributing, controlling'. It would be hard to better this description of bridging, yet it must not have solved all the problems for he writes, 'if you, my reader, have felt a humble midge kicking futilely in an ethereal blue universe, then you felt like me'.

The orotund prose of the Edwardian era gave way in due course to the scientific detachment of the 1950s, when the description of Rose Route on Caisteal Liath (SMCJ 1958) was adorned with coordinates accurate to a tenth of an inch for reference to the photograph. Though Suilven has now been left free of new routes for a further quarter of a century, scope remains on the southern flanks for climbs 'in the modern idiom'. In the 1960s we find Tom Patey exploring both the Barrel Buttress and the long, loose western cliffs of Quinag. After him comes another lull until the first winter climbs were achieved by Dinwoodie and the insatiable Andy Nisbet. The latter, with Andy

Cunningham, also swept up the ascent of the semi-frozen Eas a' Chual Aluinn waterfall in passing.

REIFF

Talk to the local lads in the Am Fuaran bar in Altandhu, and after a few whiskies they will have laid claim to all the climbs at Reiff or, if not, will know someone who 'climbed there years ago'. Climbers visited the area over a number of years before the first recorded routes appeared in the SMCJ of 1987. Aberdeen climber Brian Lawrie was the main activist throughout the early period, having soloed many routes during 'family holidays' spanning well over a decade, then returning with ropes and various partners in the early 1980s to produce some superb climbs. Brian specialised in hard bouldering, with the dubious security of the platforms below. He also adopted a policy of not recording first ascensionists, which seemed in keeping with the general atmosphere of the area. This practice has continued, so this section will shed some light on the development of the Reiff sea-cliffs.

In 1987 Brian Lawrie submitted a record of about 110 routes to the SMCJ. These included climbs at the Pinnacle Area, Bouldering Cliff and Black Rocks at Roinn a' Mhill, at the Seal Song area and the Bay of Pigs of An Stiuir, and at the Golden Walls, Slab Inlet, Platform Walls and the Rampant Wall of Rubha Coigeach. Brian soloed the vast majority of the routes recorded at Roinn a' Mhill in the 1970s, with some fine gems including Tangle of the Isles (Hard Severe), Moonjelly (Very Difficult) on The Pinnacle; Earth Shaker (E2 6a; named due to the number of thundering jumps onto the platform below), White Horses (E2 6a), Golden Eyes (E1 5b), Romancing the Stone (E3 6b; a prolonged series of attempts finally matured in 1984), The Hand Traverse (HVS 5a), Hole in the Wall (E2 6a) and The Grooves (Severe). He teamed up with Neil Morrison and Martin Forsyth to climb, among others: Channering Worm (E3 5c), Sip from the Wine (HVS 5a), Westering Home (E1 5b) and with John Cunningham in May 1982 the desperate Leaning Meanie (E2 6a), using a secret hold! Partners Rick Allen and Greg Strange climbed the steep crack of Rick's Route (E1 5b). In July 1985 Brian and Neil returned to climb the excellent Tystie Slab (Very Difficult) and Black Gold (VS 4c), whilst the stunning Crack of Desire (E3 5c/6a) was climbed by Dougie Dinwoodie on the second attempt.

Around the same time Murray Hamilton and Rab Anderson climbed the amazing corner of Wyatt Earp. Murray soloed the very difficult variation start to the Crack of Desire (E3 6a) and also a superb crack line around Monster Breaker, an area which later suffered a huge rockfall during the storms of the following winter.

An Stiuir provided some fine solooes for Brian Lawrie during the 70s with Skullsmasher (VS 4c), Where Green Ants Dream (E1 5c/6a), Vision of Blue (E1 5b) and The Kraken (E2 6a). However, it was a trip in July 1985 with Neil Morrison and Kevin Murphy that produced the better of the harder routes. Neil led the excellent Seal Song (E3 5c), Kevin climbed Gussetbuster (E1 5b/c), Clam Jam (E1 5b) and Brian led Razor's Edge (E1 5b) and The Executioner (E2 5b), where a second fell off on a finger jam and had to be rushed to the nearest medical centre. Brian also climbed Sexcrementalism (E1 5b) with Ron Kerr. In 1986 Brian visited with Andy Nisbet to climb the superb Elastic Collision (E4 6a) but Alasdair 'Plod' Ross on the second ascent uncovered a huge jug after some 'heavy cleaning', reducing the grade to the present E3 5c.

Out at Rubha Coigeach a few of the shorter routes on the Golden Walls were soloed by Brian Lawrie early on, and Greg Strange climbed Strange Crack (HVS 5b) in May 1982. Brian and Neil Morrison returned in 1984 to climb the very good Black Magic (VS 4c) but it was on a trip in 1985, camping at Faochag, that Brian, Dougie Dinwoodie and Kevin Murphy realised the potential of the Golden Walls. Three out of the four cracks on the Golden Wall proper were climbed; Moronic Inferno, Crann Tarra and The Rite of Spring (all E3 5c). Dougie led Shades of Night (E2 5c), Horripilation (E2 5c), Carnival of Folly (E1/2 5b) and soloed the first major route on the Slab Inlet - Eas Dubh (HVS 5a). Kevin Murphy climbed Saint Vitus gets on Down (E2 5c), Halcyon Daze (HVS 5b) and Spasticus Autisticus (E1 5b), while Brian produced the hard Road to Nowhere (E4 6a), Dragons of Eden (E2 5c), and the superb corner of Necronomican (E1 5b). Kevin returned later with Doug Hawthorne and climbed Skid Row (E2 5c), and explored further along the coast to follow the impressive and exposed Spaced Out Rockers on the Road to Oblivion (E2 5c,5b).

In the summer of 1986 Brian Lawrie and Andy Nisbet climbed all the routes on the Rampant Wall with Andy winning on the overhanging Atlantic Crack (E3 5c) and Brian claiming The Ali Shuffle (VS 5a), the wall of Break Dance (E2 5b) and Autumn Sonata (E4 6a).

By the time Andy Cunningham produced a private guide to the Reiff sea-cliffs in March 1990 the total number of routes had more than trebled. This included a number of previously unclimbed areas such as the Stone Pig Cliff, the Orange Wall area of Black Rocks, the Sea Cliff, Pooh Cliff and the fine Leaning Block Cliff. Andy was responsible for the majority of the flood of new climbs with partners Jenny Pickering and Keith Geddes. However, in May 1987 Monster Breaker (HVS 5a) was recorded on the 'new' rock of the Bouldering Cliff by A.Matthewson and A.Tibbs, while S.Steer with A.Fraser climbed Street Surfer (E1 5b). Brian Lawrie returned to the Golden Walls early in June 1987 with Wilson Moir and Andy Nisbet to climb Bubblyjock (E2 5c) and Wilson led on Ruben Tadpole (E1 5b). In August 1987, SMCJ in hand, Andy Cunningham and Keith Geddes paid the first of many visits recording the routes on The Sea Cliff, Minch Wall and Bay of Pigs with climbs such as Walk Like an Egyptian (E4 6a; describing the crux moves), Social Democrat (E1 5b) and Parabolic Head (E1 5c), while Keith led Jim Nastic (VS 4c), Friends for Life (HVS 5a/b) and Blackadder (HVS 5a). Graeme Livingston joined in the action to climb Modern Thinking (E4 6a; the obvious route on the wall), Awesome (E5 6b) and completed Andy's much tried line of The Thistle (E5 6b); a prickly finish! Andy returned later in the month with Jenny Pickering to find the Pooh Cliff, a short crag with some 'fine wee classics'. Finally, Andy Nisbet succeeded in climbing the final superb crack of the four on the Golden Wall with Niall Ritchie and Stevie 'B' Blagborough - Split Personality (E4 5c). In September, A. Fraser and W. Faulkner climbed Wendy's Flying Circus (HVS 5a).

Over 1988-89 new routes concentrated on the harder unclimbed lines and easier filler-in climbs on existing cliffs, together with the development of Orange Wall, Stone Pig Cliff and Leaning Block Cliff. Andy Cunningham with Keith Geddes climbed A Walk Across the Rooftops (E3 5c), Yellow Dogs (E3/4 5c; too much fear resulted in too many falls!), Kurgan (E4 6a), Immaculate Desception (E1 5b), and with Jenny Pickering, Power Siezure (E3 5c/6a), Fly By Wire (E2 5c), An Dobhran Mara (E3 6a), Shootin' the Tube (HVS 5a). Andy and Jenny also climbed the routes of Orange Wall, the remainder of the climbs on Black Rocks such as Hourglass Groove (HVS 5a), Batman (HVS 5a), Black Pig (VS 4c), and Great Black Back (E3 6a). In October 1988, with Stevie Blagborough, they discovered the Stone Pig Cliff and climbed the routes on the non-tidal eastern section on the first visit. Also in October 1988, the lines between the Sea Cliff and An Stiuir promontory were recorded by combinations of Allen Fyffe, Blair Fyffe, Keith Geddes, Jenny Pickering and Andy Cunningham.

The good summer of 1989 started early in May with the harder routes at the Stone Pig Cliff being climbed by Andy Cunningham and Jenny Pickering; these include Wirly Girly (E1 5b) and Tinsel Town (E2 5c). In June, Keith Geddes climbed the fine crack of Strongbow (E2 5c) and Aquatic Jambouree (E1 5c). Keith moved to the Bouldering Cliff to complete Excellence by Design (E2 6a) a product of determined cleaning! Attention focused once more on the Golden Walls in mid-summer with Stevie Blagborough climbing Goldie Horn (E2 5b), Klondyke (VS 4c), Keith Geddes found Andrew the Milkman (HVS 5a), and Andy Cunningham climbed 49'ers (HVS 5b) and Sammy Seal (E1 5c). Significant ascents were made by Wilson Moir and Colin MacLean, who climbed the striking diagonal crack at the Bay of Pigs - Free Base (E5 6a/b), and the bold Eddy Current (E3 5c). Richard Mansfield scored with the short Storm in a Tea Cup (E2 5c). Dougie Dinwoodie, Brian Lawrie and Mungo Ross explored the coast line past the Spaced Out Rockers Cliff producing the first route on the Leaning Block with Dougie's very good Losgaidh (E3 5c). Dougie also climbed a hard E4 6a on the Golden Walls (after much consideration placing an in situ peg for protection on a serious runnout). Brian returned in July 1989 with fellow Aberdeen climbers Niall Ritchie, Colin MacLean and Wilson Moir to put the Leaning Block Cliff firmly on record with 10 routes, including Brian's Caoraich Mhor (E2 5c), Niall's excellent Wall of Silence (E3 5c), Sunshine on Reiff (E1 5a/b) and the aptly named Aroofoeryerheid (HVS 5a), with Colin climbing Golden Fleece (HVS 5b) and Wilson's Hand Jive (E1 5b) and Waigwa (HVS 5a).

After the release of Andy Cunninghams guide, many routes had repeat ascents confirming the good quality of climbing and gaining a concensus on grades. Over the following three summers activity centered on further development of Rubha Coigeach and some hard eliminates on existing cliffs. For example, Roinn a' Mhill gained Strangeways (E4 6b) in June 1990 from Richard Mansfield; Wilson Moir and Brian Lawrie sunburned on the thin Totally Tropical (E4 6b) in 1991. On the Bouldering Cliff in July 1990 Andy Cunningham climbed straight up on Toad in the Hole (E5 6a), Desire Direct (E4 6a) and with Niall Ritchie, the girdle of No Picnic at Hanging Rocks (E3/4 5b,5c). Allen Fyffe added Trout Mask Replica (HVS 5a) to the Seal Song area in October 1990 and on the Minch Wall Mark Charlton cashed in on Bank of Scotland (E3 5c) in May 1990. Pete Whillance and Cliff Fanshaw visited Reiff in 1990 recording half a dozen routes, including Scavenger (E1 5b/c), Making Bacon (E4/5 6a) and Reiff Encounter (E3 6b) in the Bay of Pigs, with a peg runner being placed on each climb. Concern was voiced as to the necessity of the in situ protection as the crux of Reiff Encounter had earlier been bouldered out and the peg on Making Bacon had previously been reached solo. In the same area in 1991, Wilson Moir and Brian Lawrie climbed Cleopatra's Asp (E5 6a) and Andy Cunningham added Sea Shanty (E2 5c).

Rubha Coigeach saw most new developments, particularly from the Leaning Block Cliff onwards. However, the Golden Walls had the attention of Martin Burrows-Smith, Allen Fyffe and Andy Cunningham in November 1990 with Martin's Break Off (E3 5c) and Verushka (E3 5c). In 1991, Richard Mansfield and David Etherington climbed Sniffing the Frog (E2 5c) and the brave traverse of Mad Dogs and Englishman (E3 5c) at the head of Rampant Wall. The Leaning Block Cliff was visited by Andy Cunningham, Richard Mansfield, Jenny Pickering and Niall Ritchie during July 1990. They climbed the remainder of the routes there to produce one of the best areas at Reiff for middle grade climbing, with many starred routes such as Richard's stunning arete on the block; The Gift (E5 6a) or Cross Eyed (E2 5b) and Brave Heart (E3 5c); Andy's The Screamer (E4 6a), Empty on Endorphins (E1 5b), Play it Again (E3 6a/b), Cyclops (E2 5c), The Africaan Problem (E1 5b) and Olympus (E2 5b/c) and Niall's Van Hoover's Awa (E1 5b) and Blind Bandit (HVS 5a). Andy and Jenny Climbed An Sulaire (E1 5b), a good route on Amphitheatre Bay but avoiding the main issue of the bay!

Jigsaw Wall Point and Rubha Ploytach were developed by Andy Cunningham, Jenny Pickering, Allen Fyffe and Blair Fyffe with various visits in August and September 1990, producing a fine concentration of routes in the lower grades and significant ascents of Ros Bhan (HVS 5a) by Jenny, Going Hypo (E1 5b) from Allen and The Toaster, Clansman, Claymore (E2 5c), Lilidh (E2 6a) from Andy.

THE SUTHERLAND MOUNTAINS

As usual the story starts with Ling and Glover who made early climbs on both Foinaven and Ben Hope in 1910. Their interest had been stimulated by the significant remark in the guidebook, 'no climbs recorded'. 'Like the henpecked sailor, the only thing for us to do was to go and see'.

The only climbing event of the inter-war years appears to have been JHB Bell's exploration of the north-west face of Ben Hope, where he found 'excellent rock with airy and occasionally difficult situations'.

The history of Creag Urbhard up to the mid 1970s was ably delineated by Peter Macdonald in SMCJ xxxi (1977) where fuller details will be found. In the early 1950s Tom Weir, Len Lovat and A.D.S.Macpherson climbed three long routes on Creag Urbhard and A'Cheir Ghorm, while D.Haworth was the first to record a climb on Creag Shomhairle. Later in the decade D.D.Stewart forced Priest's Rake on the awkward south-west face of Sgorr a'Chleirich on Ben Loyal; climbers from the Kinloss Mountain Rescue Team found several new routes on Creag Urbhard, and the first climb on the Dionard Buttresses was recorded. On Creag Shomhairle the Caithness MC produced a route of high quality, The Roost, in 1962.

As throughout this part of the Highlands, Tom Patey, the Corriemulzie Club and the Squirrels were the main players in the mid 1960s. Patey made a bold solo ascent of Fingal, a Severe near the second waterfall of Creag Urbhard; Tranter climbed two fine obvious lines - Chicken Run with Rowe and Fishmonger on Lord Reay's Seat with Fraser; while the Squirrels produced KWH and Crawlie Mouzie (for etymology see P.Macdonald, op. cit.). Tragically Alistair Park was killed in a fall on the crag that now bears his name.

In 1969 Les Brown climbed the long and difficult Marathon Corner on Ben Loyal, and more significantly for the future, the Sheffield-based climbers Paul Nunn, Clive Rowland, Tony Howard and their friends began a long association with the area. In this first year they produced several fine climbs on the First Dionard Buttress, including Cengalo and Dialectic which, even with aid, was much harder than any preceding route on the mountain. Unfortunately some other routes, such as The Veterans on Creag Urbhard and Gritstoner's Revenge on the Fifth Dionard Buttress, proved hard for later climbers to locate.

In 1971 Paul Nunn and Bob Toogood began their investigation of Cnoc a'Mhadaidh, Foinaven's most accessible crag, with Quergang which found a way past the large roof with some aid. The same year Peter Macdonald and Alan North climbed the splendid Pobble on Lord Reay's Seat, and on Creag Shomhairle the extremely strenuous Land of the Dancing Dead fell to Chris Jackson and Tom Proctor. In the following years Martin Boysen joined in the exploration, contributing Pilastre and Marble Corner with Nunn and Gog on Ben Loyal with Mike Kosterlitz. The latter, reputedly an excellent climb on an awesomely forbidding crag, awaits a second ascent.

A few Scots such as Arthur Paul, Des Rubens and Derek Jamieson produced interesting new climbs in the late 1970s, but the next really important event was the visit of Andrew Nisbet and a group of Aberdeen climbers in February 1979. Staying for a week in excellent conditions they climbed no less than ten routes and reported water-ice climbing of a quality to match any in Scotland. The 1980s saw a continuation of the trends of the 70s but with some harder rock climbs being found. Nunn and Livesey climbed the very fine Millennium in 1982, and four years later Murray Hamilton disposed with ease of the slender crack right of Land of the Dancing Dead - the area's first E6. More typically there was a slow flow of worthwhile new climbs in the 'middle' grades (these days around E1) – the Direct Finish to Pobble, Bardo Thodol and Look North being good examples. Nisbet returned in winter too, and although he failed to obtain such good weather as before, the Third and Fourth Waterfalls were climbed.

As will be apparent from the briefest perusal of the text, there remain many new climbs to do on Foinaven and much research would be required before its definitive history could be written.

SEA-CLIFFS

The history of sea-cliff climbing in Northern Scotland comes in three distinct phases. The first, included for the sake of completeness, is the 'working' phase of the last century (and into the early part of this century on St Kilda), when climbs were made purely for the purpose of collecting seabirds' eggs. The 'ascent' of the Great Stack of Handa by Donald Macdonald in 1876 has been ably described by Hamish Brown in SMCJ xxxiii (1984). In the middle of the 1960s the second phase was initiated by (as usual) Tom Patey. The Old Man of Stoer was the first to fall, in June 1966, but only after several attempts had been repulsed by tides. Various means of access including ladders, swimming and Tyrolean traverses were employed. The Old Man of Hoy, a much longer and more serious climb, followed a month later, and was revealed to the rest of the world in the famous television broadcast of July 1967 when two more new routes were climbed by Brown, McNaught-Davis, Crew and Haston. Am Buachaille, near Sandwood Bay, succumbed a few weeks later, and 1969 saw not only two climbs on the Great Stack of Handa but also a three-day televised ascent of St John's Head on Hoy, one of the highest sea-cliffs in the British Isles. The same year the Caithness Mountaineering Club made an extensive exploration of Dwarwick Head, east of Thurso. Around this time attempts were also made on the huge cliffs of Clo Mor at Cape Wrath, but they were defeated by bad rock and bird life, or maybe by the baleful influence of the monster Cu-Saeng, thought to wander in this region.

The end of the second phase was marked by Patey's tragic death descending from the Maiden stacks off Whiten Head, and by Ward-Drummond and Hill's epic ascent of Longhope Route on St John's Head. The initial descent of this cliff alone took two days and the subsequent ascent a further five days, enlivened by a 30m 'Vile Crack' and some desperate skyhooking.

The third phase began in the late 1980s, there having been only brief interruptions to the quiescence of the previous 17 years. One was in 1984 when the Old Man of Hoy was subjected to another television interview. For this occasion Murray Hamilton and Pete Whillance spent a full seven days preparing their make-up. On the big day a free ascent of the previously artificial south-east arete was climbed, and fittingly named A Fistful of Dollars to commemorate that mercenary decade. A month later the same pair returned with Paul Braithwaite to climb perhaps the best route on the Old Man – A Few Dollars More, on the north face. The proper commencement of the third phase is marked by two good climbs on the Old Man of Stoer in 1987. The following year Mick Fowler and his colleagues began to develop their expertise at seaward access. In May they climbed four new routes on The Maiden and later excelled themselves with the appallingly impressive Big John, the first time St John's Head had been climbed in a day. Over 400m in length, with a Fowler grade of 'XS' and several 5c/6a pitches, it seems unlikely that this will be often repeated.

Back at Cape Wrath, in 1989 Fowler returned with Chris Watts to climb Clo Mor Crack, the first party to succeed on this hugely daunting cliff. They also teamed up with Simon Richardson and Guy Muhlemann to climb some of the Cape Wrath stacks. These stacks provide all the classic problems of 'coastaleering'; attempts on A'Chailleach were initially defeated by Atlantic waves breaking over its top! Even in calm weather the swell presents serious problems, such that it took seven attempts spread over two days before the party could leave Fowler's inflatable (Deflowerer 1) and step onto Stack Clo Kearvaig. After the ascent of Clo Mor Stack, the tiny outboard engine of the inflatable proved only just capable of beating the tide race which threatened to deposit the party on a small island which was due to be used for RAF Tornado bombing practice the following day.

The same year the small but sound gneiss rocks at Sheigra near Kinlochbervie began to receive attention from Rab Anderson and (separately) a party from Glenmore Lodge. These attractive cliffs had been climbed on since the mid 1970s by Paul Nunn, Bob Toogood and their friends, who had documented about 20 routes. A productive visit by Boysen and Carrington had added some harder climbs and then the Glenmore Lodge climbers added a further 15 or so climbs.

In 1990 Am Buachaille received another fine climb by Simon Richardson and Robin Clothier, although a slight error with the tides enforced probably the first ever bivouac on the stack. The thought of the ignominy of being named in the mountain accidents list in the SMC Journal encouraged the stranded party to abseil into the maelstrom the following day to brave the white water.

Intensive exploration of the East Caithness coastal cliffs at Mid Clyth, Latheronwheel and Noss Head also began that summer, and was pursued with even more dedication during the following years. The main protagonist has been Rob Christie, who with a small group of friends seems to have entered with gusto into the modern style of systematically working through the more obvious possibilities. He wrote his own mini-guide for private circulation, and this forms the basis of the East Caithness coast chapter in this book.

In 1991 Dave Turnbull with Andy Donson and C.Rees visited Hoy and found four routes in the modern idiom on the smaller cliffs within view of the Old Man of Hoy. The following year Crag Jones, Andy McNae and M.Carnall added four more. These explorations add flexibility to a visit to Hoy, and surely there are many more routes to be found on the excellent steep sandstone there.

Similarly in Shetland, Andy Long has enthusiastically been exploring the coastal crags. Some of the better areas were observed from local beauty spots, but others were found only during on-site inspection after detailed scrutiny of the geological map. The pleasant bouldering crag of Pundsar was discovered during a canoeing trip. However, some of the harder routes were produced during visits by raiding parties from the mainland. Wilson Moir and Colin Stewart found a number of excellent routes in 1988, and in 1991 Andy Donson and Dave Turnbull produced the most northerly E5 in the British Isles with New Squids on the Block. In 1992 Fowler's 'Deflowerer' came onto the scene to raid a few stacks, while others in the party added more lines to the more accessible coastal crags. These developments were recorded by Andy Long, whose personal mini-guide has been essentially reprinted as the final chapter of this book.

Notes on the use of The Guide

Classification of Routes

Summer

The normal British grading system of Easy, Moderate, Difficult, Very Difficult, Severe, Very Severe (VS), Hard Very Severe (HVS) and Extremely Severe has been used. The Extreme grade is sub-divided into E1, E2, E3, E4, E5, and so on.

Technical grades are given for routes of VS and above where known. Much effort has been made to elicit information from active climbers about routes, some of which will have all the relevant pitches graded, while others will have only the crux pitch so described. The normal range of technical grades expected on routes of the given overall grade are as follows: VS - 4b, 4c, 5a; HVS - 4c, 5a, 5b; E1 - 5a, 5b, 5c; E2 - 5b, 5c, 6a; E3 - 5c, 6a; E4 - 5c, 6a, 6b; E5 - 6a, 6b. Routes with a technical grade at the lower end of the range will be sustained or poorly protected, while those with grades at the upper end of the expected range will have a short and generally well protected crux section.

Although the British system is thought second to none by those who use it, it is known to confuse visitors from abroad. For their benefit, it can be assumed that 5a, 5b, 5c and 6a correspond approximately to the American grades of 5.9, 5.10a/b, 5.10c/d and 5.11a/b respectively. Eurocraggers should note that there is little or no fixed protection on most of the climbs here, and that if they are used to cruising bolted French 6c, they may suffer some distress while attempting the corresponding 6a pitches here, with their sometimes spaced and fiddly protection.

Grading information is in some cases scanty or even lacking, particularly in some of the older or more obscure routes; climbers should therefore be even more circumspect in their approach to such routes (which have been indicated by a dagger symbol). Information about these routes is always welcome.

Winter

Winter climbs have been graded from I to VI. Grade I indicates simple snow climbs, with perhaps a corniced exit. Grade II includes gullies with either individual or minor pitches, or high angled snow with difficult cornice exits, and the easier buttresses under winter conditions.

Grade III incorporates gullies which contain ice or mixed pitches. There will normally be at least one substantial pitch and possibly several lesser ones. Also sustained buttress climbs without great technical difficulty.

Grade IV gullies may include nearly vertical ice sections, while the buttresses will require a good repertoire of techniques.

Grade V climbs are difficult, sustained and/or serious. Some may be well protected but technically very hard.

Grade VI routes have exceptional overall difficulties.

Split grades indicate uncertainties due to the route being known to be variable in condition, or a borderline case. Routes are graded for average to good conditions. It should be borne in mind that winter grades are often an approximation, because conditions (particularly in this area) can vary rapidly.

The advent of extremely difficult buttress climbs, which differ so radically from the more traditional gullies and icefalls, has put the grading system under some strain. As an experiment, a two-tier grading system, which incorporates some of the principles of the summer technical grades, has been proposed. An explanation of this system is given at the back of the book, together with the proposed two-tier grades for the harder climbs in the area. If this system becomes accepted by the majority of active climbers then it will be used in the main body of future guide books. If you don't like it, it will go the same way as all other failed experiments.

Equipment and Style

It is assumed that a good range of modern nuts and camming devices will be carried for the harder climbs, both summer and winter. Most of the summer climbs described in this guide do not require the use of pegs, but they should be carried on some of the more extreme sea-cliff and sea-stack adventures. The use of pegs on new climbs should be extremely sparing; please keep to the Scottish tradition of bold climbs with leader-placed protection. On occasion it might be necessary to use pegs on winter climbs for belays or runners; please make all efforts to find a safe alternative before resorting to pegs, especially on winter ascents of summer climbs (on which pegs would be most unwelcome).

Most of the modern harder rock climbs that are described in this book will have been cleaned or otherwise inspected prior to an ascent. Although every attempt is usually made to grade them for an on-sight lead, it should be borne in mind that many of them may not yet have been done in this style.

Bolts

After extensive consultation with all interested parties, the Mountaineering Council of Scotland has issued a policy statement on the use of bolts in Scotland. This policy is endorsed by the Publications Sub-Committee of the Scottish Mountaineering Club.

"The MCofS acknowledge that there is a place for bolts in the future development of Scottish climbing. However, to ensure that the highly regarded ethos of, and future development of, traditional climbing (involving the use of leader-placed and second-removed protection) is not threatened, it is felt that the use of bolts should be limited to the production of sport climbs. There should be no retrospective bolting of established climbs for protection or belays, and there should be no minimalist bolting.

The production of sport climbs with bolts is acceptable on natural rock only when all the following conditions have been satisfied:

(1) On low-lying cliffs, provided that such development is not against the wishes of the landowner. Bolts are inappropriate on mountain cliffs and sea-cliffs.

(2) On routes where natural protection is absent or is inadequate for the repeated falls that such routes necessitate.

(3) Where the rock is steep and provides climbs of a high order of difficulty, at the forefront of developments of the day.

(4) Where there is no historical or local anti-bolt ethic.

Concerning quarried rock, it is felt that any future development should be constrained only by points (2) and (4) above.

Finally, it is felt that bolts should be located to ensure minimum visual impact and should be placed according to current best practices. It is intended that these principles are not seen as simply restrictive rules, but as a guide to promote the positive development of Scottish climbing, where sports climbing, rather than becoming a substitute for traditional climbing, grows alongside it."

In practice, these guidelines indicate that the use of bolts would be inappropriate on all of the cliffs and crags described in this guidebook. It goes without saying that the use of bolts on winter climbs would be entirely unacceptable.

Terminology

Left and right refer to a climber facing the cliff or facing downhill in descent. In cases of potential ambiguity a compass direction is also given. Pegs and other fixed gear are for protection only, except where specifically stated that they are for direct aid. Do not assume that they will either be in place or in a safe state of repair.

Pitch Lengths
Pitch lengths are given in metres, to the nearest 5m (except for very short distances). Ropes of 45m should be adequate for the vast majority or routes, though 50m ropes are useful in winter.

Diagrams
The climbs on some of the cliffs have been numbered. This indicates that there is a diagram depicting the cliff, which will be found close to the relevant text. The numbers in the text correspond to the numbers on the diagrams. If a numbered climb is not shown on the diagram it will be located in relation to the numerical order of those that are. For each diagrammed crag the numbering begins again at 1, so make sure you're looking at the correct diagram.

Recommended Routes
No list of recommended climbs is given, instead a star grading system for quality has been used. Three stars indicates a route of the highest quality. If a route has no star this does not necessarily mean that it is poor, it may also indicate that insufficient is known about that route properly to assess its quality. This is particularly true of some of the remote areas, where the star ratings may be found to be inconsistent. It is hoped that climbers using this guide will inform the authors of such inconsistencies so that future editions of the guide can be improved. Routes of poor quality are normally described as such or have a limited description.

   Dagger symbols printed next to a route name indicate that the route has not been checked, and that there are good reasons for believing that the description or grade may not be entirely accurate. Climbers attempting these routes should do so with caution, and should be prepared to exercise more personal initiative than normal. The dagger symbol is not a health warning; it does not necessarily indicate that the route is poor, badly under-graded or in any way worse than its neighbours. Information about these routes is always welcome.

First Ascensionists
The year of first ascent, where known, is given in the text. The full date and pioneers are listed in chronological order, area by area, at the back of the guide. Further relevant details of the first and subsequent

ascents where known are also listed in this section. Whether the route was climbed in summer or winter conditions is indicated by an S or W at the left end of each line. The abbreviations used in this list are standard and self-explanatory.

Maps and other sources of information.

Place names and map references have in general been taken from the OS 1:50000 Landranger Series maps. Occasionally information in the 1:25000 series has been used, but these maps are not necessary to navigate to and from the climbs. The 1:250000 OS Routemaster Series Sheet 2 map of Northern Scotland is very useful to put into context the whole of the areas described in both Volumes 1 and 2 of the *Northern Highlands* Climbers' Guide.

The meanings and pronunciations of local place names can be found in *Scottish Hill and Mountain Names* by Peter Drummond, published by the Scottish Mountaineering Trust (1991).

Due to the very large area covered in this guidebook, it is impractical to include detailed information on huts, bothies, campsites and other amenities. Much useful information can be found in the Scottish Mountaineering Club District Guide *The Northwest Highlands*, published by the Scottish Mountaineering Trust (1990).

Mountain Rescue

In case of an accident requiring rescue or medical attention, contact the Police. If a victim has to be left, be sure that the exact location is known before leaving the site of the accident, and that if possible the nature of any injuries can be reported. Try to leave someone with the victim, who should in any case be made as comfortable and as sheltered as the injuries allow. Some knowledge of rudimentary first aid is a desirable thing for a climber to have, so it is wise to consult one of the large number of suitable books on mountaineering first aid, rescue techniques and rescue helicopters.

Avalanches

Avalanche conditions are less common in the area covered by this guide than in the Cairngorms, or even Glen Coe, but they do occur, and climbers have been caught in them. To minimise the risk of exposure to avalanche it is sensible to avoid icefalls and gullies during periods of thaw and immediately following a heavy snowfall. The buttress climbs can provide alternatives in these conditions.

Avalanches occur most often following heavy snowfall or during thaw. All gullies and most slopes between 22 and 60 degrees should then be suspect. The greater the amount of fresh snow, the higher the risk. Fresh snow can include wind-blown deposits, so that stormy weather can maintain an avalanche risk for prolonged spells. Past and present weather conditions are very important. Climbers preparing for winter climbing should familiarise themselves with basic avalanche theory, using one or more of several useful books available on the subject. In the field, much can be learned by digging a hole and examing the snow profile, looking especially for different layers of snow with different degrees of bonding. Slab avalanches, for example, will be caused when a weakly cohesive layer of snow collapses underfoot. Such a weak layer is usually hidden under a firmer layer, hence its great potential as a killer. The top layer will often break into slabby fragments, the first warning.

If avalanched, try and either jump free, or anchor yourself for as long as possible, depending on circumstances. If swept down protect your access to oxygen by 'swimming' to stay on the surface, by keeping your mouth closed, and by preserving a space in front of your face if buried. Wet snow avalanches harden rapidly on settling, so try and break free if possible at this point. If trapped try to stay calm, which will reduce oxygen demand.

If a witness to an avalanche, it is vital to start a search immediately, given it is safe to do so. Victims will often be alive at first, but their chances of survival lessen rapidly if buried. Unless severely injured, some 80% may live if found immediately, but only 10% after a three-hour delay. Mark the burial sight if known, listen for any sound, look for any visual clue, search until help arrives if possible. Again, a working knowledge of first aid may save a life, as many victims may have stopped breathing.

Strathfarrar and Strathconon

This chapter describes climbs on a number of outcrops, most quite recently developed. Also included are some remote mountain winter routes, where solitude can be guaranteed.

STRATHFARRAR

The long glen of Strathfarrar is north of Glen Cannich in the area south of the road linking Garve to Achnasheen. The entrance road starts at Struy Bridge where the A831 between Beauly and Cannich crosses the River Farrar. This road is private and a gate near its junction with the main road at Struy is kept locked. An arrangement between the landowners concerned and Scottish Natural Heritage (who administer a small Nature Reserve in the glen) allows access by car up this road, the key of the gate being kept by the local representative of SNH who lives in the cottage beside the gate. The hours when permission is normally granted to drive up the glen are at present: Weekdays (except Tuesdays), 9.00am to 6.00pm; Sundays, 1.30pm to 6.00pm; Tuesdays, no access. (Please do not call at the cottage between 1.00pm and 1.30pm.)

The above information applies between Easter and the end of October. In winter the SNH representative may not always be at home and it is therefore advisable to telephone beforehand (046 376 260).

SGURR NA LAPAICH
1150m   (Map Ref 161 351)

Although this mountain can be approached from the dam at the head of Loch Mullardoch to the south, the shortest approach is from Glen Strathfarrar, especially if it is possible to drive to the little power station in Gleann Innis an Loichel. On the north-east side of the mountain is the following route.

Deer-Grass Gully   120m   III   (1978)
This climbs a central line on the cliffs below the east ridge. It has a 45m ice pitch.

The next climb is on the buttress which tops out on the slope leading down from Sgurr nan Clachan Geala towards the col before Sgurr na Lapaich. Since this is high above Loch Tuill Bhearnach, it is best approached from Loch Mullardoch.

Lapland Buttress 200m IV (1989)
1. 30m Start at the lowest rocks. Climb a V-recess then move out left.
2. 40m A series of slabby cracks lead right back to the crest below a steep wall.
3. 30m Climb the wall by a vertical right-facing corner (crux), which leads to a wide left-slanting crack. Regain the crest on the right.
4. etc., 100m. Follow the much easier crest to the plateau.

AN RIABHACHAN
1129m   (Map Ref 134 345)

This bulky flat-topped mountain lies to the west of Sgurr na Lapaich. Again, the easiest approach is from Glen Strathfarrar on the north side. The crags on the north-east of the mountain, some distance to the east of the main summit, provide the following climb.

Spindrift Gully 200m II (1969)
This gully cuts straight through the right half of a prominent rock face which lies just to the west of the Sgurr na Lapaich col. It is steep in its upper half and provides one ice pitch.

COIRE TOLL A' MHUIC *(Map Ref 232 420)*

The north Strathfarrar ridge is a fine hillwalk which links four Munros. Coire Toll a' Mhuic is the large corrie south of Sgurr Fhuar-thuill, the most westerly Munro of the group. The approach from the private road in Glen Strathfarrar is an easy stroll along a good path running up the west bank of the Allt Toll a' Mhuic. The climbing stretches from the south-east face of Sgurr na Muice to the south top of Sgurr na Fearstaig (880m). The south-east face of Sgurr na Muice has two parallel icefalls, visible from the approach. These provide the following routes:

1 Best Back 150m III/IV * (1979)
The left-hand icefall provides a fine route.

SGURR NA MUICE

SOUTH-EAST FACE

1. Best Back
2. Streaky

NORTH-EAST FACE

3. Trotter's Gully
4. Pigsty Gully

2 Streaky 150m III/IV   (1978)
Climb the right-hand and thinner of the two icefalls.

Continuing north past the nose of Sgurr na Muice, the backwall of
the corrie between Sgurr na Muice and the bealach to its north has
the following routes.

3 Trotter's Gully 240m III   (1978)
This is the obvious long curved gully within shallow walls. Climb easy
snow to a blockage, then follow the left fork. This gives a 35m ice pitch
up a narrow chimney which is the only difficulty. The exit can be
corniced. The (direct) right fork is Grade II.

4 Pigsty Gully 300m II   (1978)
Left of Trotter's Gully is a more shallow gully with a prominent cleft
top. Minor pitches run up to the cleft, which is often blocked by a large
cornice.

To the north of the col, the east face of Sgurr na Fearstaig's south
top has a series of short corners providing short Grade II/III routes.
This face also provides the following climbs:

5 Slanting Gully 300m I
This is the long ramp that wanders beneath the cliffs, exiting at the
far right. In normal conditions a 20m icefall develops just right of the
start and can give a pitch of grade III. The gully gives a steep descent
route often with a small cornice.

6 Red Campion 150m II   (1978)
The obvious wide corner ramp bordering the east face on the left.
Straightforward ground leads to a blockage, split by twin grooves. The
right one is easier and another short pitch leads to a fan exit.

7 Sea Pink Gully 120m II   (1978)
Right of Red Campion is a steep mass of rock which has a steep corner
on the right with narrow gully lines to the left. Gain the base by
following Slanting Gully for half its length. A traverse left then leads to
a narrow gully entrance. Follow this over an ice pitch and continue up
a hidden ramp to the top.

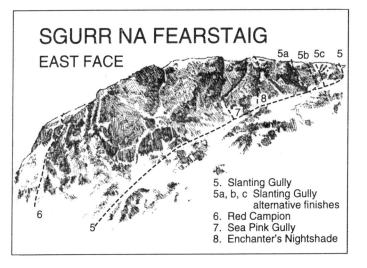

SGURR NA FEARSTAIG
EAST FACE

5. Slanting Gully
5a, b, c Slanting Gully
        alternative finishes
6. Red Campion
7. Sea Pink Gully
8. Enchanter's Nightshade

8 Enchanter's Nightshade 100m III *   (1978)
By far the best of the climbs on this face. To the right of Sea Pink Gully
is a clearly defined steep groove, slabby on the right. Thin ice leads
for 35m to a small recess and a vertical chimney groove. Exit right
over this to a steepening scoop blocked by a (normally) huge cornice,
often double. This can be outflanked on the left.

STRATHCONON

The road into Strathconon starts at a right-angled bend at Marybank
on the A832 road between Muir of Ord and Contin. This is the approach
for the more distant crags at the head of the glen as well as Creag
a' Ghlastail which actually lies in Glen Orrin. The lower outcrop crags
near the foot of the glen are mainly approached on the B road which
branches off just north of Contin and passes by Loch Achilty up to the
Loch Luichart dam at Glenmarksie.

GLENMARKSIE CRAG *(Map Ref 384 582)*

Once cleaned, the rock on this schist crag is impeccable. It sports pleasant middle grade wall and slab climbs and some harder routes. There is no seasonal restriction and, since it faces south-east, it gets plenty of sun, dries quickly, and is often climbable in winter. The landowner does not object to climbing but does not want 'heavy gardening' to take place. Please be thoughtful when cleaning routes. Many of the steeper climbs in the central and right-hand sections are sustained and technical, an analogy being that if the crag was turned upside-down, it would be full of incuts! The routes are generally well protected by wires and friends.

Access

Turn west off the A832 beyond Contin (marked Loch Achilty) and park just before the dam at Loch Luichart. The crag is reached in 15 minutes by a pleasant walk over the dam and up the hillside, keeping to the right, through birches, arriving below a scrambling groove leading to a rock glacis. The crag includes a central slab steepening to a wall, bounded on the right by a slab and headwall. Two small crags lie above and to the right. On the left of the Main Crag there is a gully with a small buttress above a rowan tree and left again a low wall that stretches up the hillside. The climbs are described from right to left.

1 Little Teaser 15m E2   (1990)
Just left of the small corner at the right end of the crag is a rust-coloured corner above a clean slab. Climb the slab, then leap up the overhanging corner (peg runner and RP3) to finish by memorable moves.

2 Hiroshima Grooves 30m HVS 5b *   (1980)
Right of the recessed glacis is an overhanging headwall with a V-groove above a slab. Start beneath a big roof and follow the slab to the right beneath the overlap to a shallow groove. Climb the groove which curves left to the headwall, then climb the nicely positioned crux up the V-groove.

3 Powder Monkey 25m E2 6b   (1990)
The large roof on the left front face of the lower slab, below the headwall. Start just left of Hiroshima Grooves and climb a short slab to the roof. Pull up and climb a thin crack to a shelf. Easy climbing either up the crack on the right or on the arete above leads to a fitting conclusion up the crux of Hiroshima Grooves.

4 Six Trees 30m   Mild VS 4b   (1979)
Scramble to the rock glacis via a little groove, left of Powder Monkey.
Climb the corner on the right of the bay to a slab and belays. Traverse
right across the slab to finish past trees; a good pitch.

5 Greased Lightning 35m   HVS 5a *   (pre 1977)
Takes the fine hanging chimney-groove on the left of the bay. Start in
a hollow and climb the right of two flake cracks to the glacis and
belays. Take the crux wall into the chimney and past a constriction to
the top. A fine climb of its type.
Direct Start: HVS 5a   (1980)
Climb a pinnacle left of the normal start to gain a bald slab and the
glacis.

6 Strategic Arms Limitation 35m   E4 ***   (1989)
The severely overhanging groove right of Greased Lightning at the
back of the glacis.
1. 10m 4c Start in the hollow and climb the crack left of Greased
Lightning to the glacis. (This pitch can be avoided by scrambling up
to the glacis on the right.)
2. 25m 6a Climb the strenuous and very sustained corner (which
overhangs one in four) to a flake at the top on the left, mantel onto
this and continue up the pleasant slab nose to the top. A very fine
route with adequate protection.

7 A Bit on the Side 20m   E1 5b   (1990)
Climbs the area between the chimney of Greased Lightning and the
curving crack of Callisto. Start at the little neck of rock at the left edge
of the glacis and step onto the wall. Climb up then step right onto the
slab bordering Greased Lightning. Climb this briefly before stepping
left below an overlap, then make a thin rising traverse left along an
undercut flake before a step left below the top overlap allows a finish
as for Deimos.

8 Callisto/Polish Peacemaker 20m   VS 5a **   (1982/1989)
A fine sustained route. Scramble to the left edge of the glacis below
the top pitch of Greased Lightning. Step onto the wall and foot traverse
left to a prominent crack. Follow the crack over a small overhang, and
where it bends back right, climb the left arete of Greased Lightning to
a tree belay.

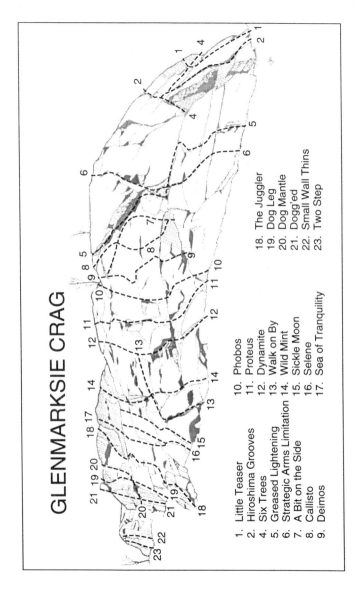

GLENMARKSIE CRAG

1. Little Teaser
2. Hiroshima Grooves
3. Six Trees
4. Greased Lightening
5. Strategic Arms Limitation
6. A Bit on the Side
7. Callisto
8. Deimos
9. Phobos
10. Proteus
11. Dynamite
12. Walk on By
13. Wild Mint
14. Sickle Moon
15. Selene
16. Sea of Tranquility
18. The Juggler
19. Dog Leg
20. Dog Mantle
21. Dogg'ed
22. Small Wall Thins
23. Two Step

9 Deimos 25m E2 5c ** (1989/1990)
A direct line taking the seemingly blank wall above the niche. Climb the short slanting crack left of Callisto to a triangular niche midway between the groove of Proteus and the slanting chimney of Greased Lightning. Climb the blank wall above, moving left to a little flake and then directly up to a hanging flake. Move to the right end of a hidden ledge, traverse left along this, then climb under the overlaps rightwards to a niche. Pull over, then climb straight to the tree.

10 Phobos 25m E2 5c ** (1989)
Excellent sustained climbing, low in the grade. Start right of a central groove (Proteus) at a thin crack which is climbed to an overhung ramp. Traverse left to a small ledge and then awkwardly into the big niche. Step out right onto the wall where hidden holds lead to another small ledge. Surmount the overlap above and climb the delicate slab which leads to the same tree belay as for Callisto.

11 Proteus 35m HVS 5a ** (1980)
This is a fine climb with much variety. Left of Phobos the wall is split by a steep groove.
1. 25m 5a Gain a ramp and step right under a roof, surmount this and climb the left rib to step right into a niche. Go up the groove and over small roofs, step up right to a shelf, then go up left past a flake to a small ledge and belays.
2. 10m 4c Climb the flake on the left, then the smooth slab to the top.

12 Dynamite 35m E2 5c ** (1990)
Left of Proteus is a black recess topped by overhangs. Climb the slab corner on the right over the overlap. Step left under the overhang, then pull over centrally via thin cracks and climb the pleasant slab direct to the top. An easier variation traverses under the roof to belay at the tree (E1 5b).

13 Walk on By 35m Hard Severe (1979)
Left of Dynamite is a wedge with a tree on top.
1. 10m 4b Climb the awkward pod on the left side of the wedge to the birch tree and belays.
2. 25m Traverse right across ledges to step up at their end, then climb the slab direct to ledges. Either walk off right or continue up Wild Mint.

14   Wild Mint   45m   Severe 4b   (1979)
A wandering route that takes the easiest line up the cliff. Climb the
right-hand corner of the block to a tree. Step left to a niche in a corner
and climb a slab rightwards to a break and broken slabs and belays.
Gain the slab groove on the left to ledges, go left to a steep corner
and finish up this by a large loose slab resting on top.
Variation: **Bear's Choice**   12m   Severe
Above the corner of the parent route, traverse right 3m then go straight
up to a ledge.

   Immediately left of the block containing Wild Mint and Walk On By
is a slab with two very pleasant routes which are less sustained than
those further right.

15   Sickle Moon/An Feur Ghorta   25m   HVS 5a *   (1982/1989)
Climb the slanting crack left of the block then up the curving crack in
the slab direct to the overhang. Pull over, step right then up the
left-trending ramp to the overlap. Step right and finish up the crack. A
good varied route.

16   Selene/An Fear Feusagach   25m   HVS 5b **   (1982/1989)
Start a metre left of Sickle Moon and climb the wall and left-curving
ramp. Step over the small overlap and climb direct up the shelves to
a crack. Climb the steep crux slab and finish up the crack left of the
top crack of Sickle Moon.

17   Sea of Tranquillity   50m   HVS **   (1990)
Probably the most enjoyable climb here, on excellent rock which is
similar to gritstone on the top pitch. Start as for Selene.
1. 35m 5a Climb the left-slanting ramp to step left below a fine crack
in a groove (or climb the groove past a bush direct). Climb the crack,
stepping left above the roof to reach a horizontal break. Step right to
the bush and climb the scoop to easier ledges. Climb the corner and
belay immediately above.
2. 15m 5a The desperate-looking headwall above is split by a thin
crack, just right of a shallow scoop. Climb to and up the crack, stepping
left to a small break at the top.

18   The Juggler   50m   HVS   (1979)
Very vegetated, but the top pitch is good. Start at the foot of a tongue
of rock, left of the corner which is left of Selene.

1. 4a Climb the right edge of slab, step left beneath overlaps, then go up to a pinnacle belay on the left.
2. 4c Step right, climb a wall past heather to a block belay.
3. 4c Climb the corner above past a mantelshelf, step right to heather, then go easily left to a wide crack and belays.
4. 5a Climb up to an inset right corner below a big roof. Step round the edge to a sloping shelf and finish up a steep slab.

19 Dog Leg 40m Difficult *   (1979)
The slabs on the left of the Main Crag are bordered by a gully. Climb the rust-coloured corner to the right of the gully, past a rose bush to belays in a wide crack. Climb the wall right of the crack, then go left on an horizontal break to a niche. A large head of rock (the Dog Head) has a V-corner on its right, climb this to finish. A good top pitch.

20 Dog Mantle 30m Severe 4a   (1979)
The route starts halfway up the gully left of the Main Crag. Traverse right to belays in the wide crack. Climb straight up the wall to the corner left of the large top overhang and finish up this.

21 Dogg'Edd 25m VS *   (1990)
A fine sustained line up the steep wall left of Dog Leg. Start in the gully, step onto the wall and climb this via thin cracks to the traverse of Dog Mantle. Climb the wall above via wider cracks to the base of the Dog Head and finish by the corner of Dog Leg.
Direct Finish: 7m E2 5b
Climb the unprotected and rather spectacular arete of the Dog Head pinnacle direct, the final move being the crux. Harder for the short.

22 Small Wall Thins 12m Severe 4a   (1979)
Left of the gully lies Small Wall, which has a rowan at its base. Climb the central groove, step left at the top and finish up a slab.

23 Two Step 12m Mild VS 4b   (1979)
Climb the slab above the tree, then the cracks on the left, and finish up Small Wall Thins.

Left of Small Wall is a cleaned area of cracks.

24 Staircase 10m Very Difficult   (1979)
Left of Small Wall is a cleaned area of cracks. Climb pleasant rock 3 metres left of the tree to the top.

25 Kojak 7m VS 5a   (1979)
A blank slab lies left of Staircase. Gain a ledge on the left, then either
go left up a thin gangway or right over bald crest at the same grade.
A splendid little problem with no protection.

Below Small Wall lies Lower Wall, a line of good bouldering rock
plus several short routes. Near the right end is a prominent overhang.

26 Sideline 7m Severe 4a
Climb the shallow corner right of the overhang.

27 Middle Wall 5m VS 5b
Take a central line up the wall left of Sideline.

28 Bitter Bother 10m Hard Severe 4b
Climb the short layback corner right of the overhang, then finish up
the top wall trending right.

29 Clutch and Thrutch 10m E1 5c *   (1979)
Start below the overhang and climb it. Once on the jutting ledge the
top wall is easier. A good safe problem in an alarming position.

Walking past further small walls and just right of a tree-filled corner
is a curved wall with four horizontal breaks.

30 A Touch of Class 10m E2 5b   (1979)
Climb the wall centrally using the breaks to a tenuous finish.

31 Victoriana 10m Difficult
Climb the old-fashioned corner to the left.

Above the Main Crag, to the right, lie two smaller crags: Middle
Crag and Top Crag. Middle Crag is immediately up right from the Main
Crag. Both Middle Crag and Top Crag can be reached by scrambling
up a little corner just right of the Main Crag and then swinging up right
over a flake; the crags are then above. This also provides the best
descent.

MIDDLE CRAG

32 Trade Route 10m Very Difficult   (1980)
Climb the slab left of a central groove, exiting right at the top.

33 Central Groove 10m Severe 4a   (1980)
Climb the slab right of the groove, then the groove to the top.

TOP CRAG

This is most easily reached by walking up right from the corner and
flake approach as for Middle Crag and then traversing a mossy slab
up right. Or scramble up the wide corner left of the slabby arete to the
left of Trade Route and walk right. The crag is quite impressive for its
height. It provides a good strenuous counterpart to the more delicate
climbs lower down.

34 Gritstone Corner 12m HVS 5a *   (1989)
This is the right-angled corner crack at the right end of the crag. It
provides a strenuous problem, often wet, using a variety of jamming
techniques. A sense of humour is required for success.

35 Right Unprintable 10m E2 6a *   (1991)
The rightmost of the shallow overhanging corners near the left edge
of the crag. A fine, athletic, well protected test piece.

36 Pom 5m VS 5b   (1990)
Climb the leftmost of four undercut cracked corners, just right of the
left edge of the crag.

37 Tiddly 4m 5b
The boulder problem on the wall just left of the left edge of the crag.

SCATWELL RIVER SLABS *(Map Ref 383 563)*

These impressive sunny south-facing slabs are situated 1km from
Loch Luichart Power Station along the minor private road from Loch
Achilty to Strathconon. Convenient lay-bys exist nearby. The slabs
are hidden from view but can be reached via a vegetated 'crevasse',
the outer crest of which forms the top of the slabs. Being one wall of
a gorge, with turbulent white water below, the slabs can only be
reached either by abseil or by a steep scramble down the left side
(looking down). The River Conon is well known for its spates; some
of the long traverses into the centre of the slabs could be very serious,
especially after heavy rain.

Despite their formidable appearance, the natural lines of weakness are climbed at quite low grades, though scope undoubtedly exists for harder routes up the unprotected blank but very vegetated spaces in between. The mica-schist is exposed on the bedding plane which gives poor friction. From the central tree above, three main lines are visible. A big corner on the right, the shallow groove below the tree, a long diagonal leading to the tree from the left, and some shorter cracked corners on the left boundary. The routes are described from the apparent left when looking down.

Piccadilly Line   12m   Difficult
The first of the cracked corners.

Northern Line   20m   VS 4c *
The next corner to the left. Follow a layback crack with a strenuous crux at a steepening. Finish up the corner of Circle Line.

Circle Line   20m   Severe 4a
Start from the tree belay at the foot of Northern Line and descend a few metres. Traverse the slab leftwards to the edge, then climb the pleasant crack through the overlap and up a steep little corner to the top. A harder direct start is possible, starting at the water's edge and initially following the next corner until a difficult move is made onto the slab, to join the parent route (5a).

Metropolitan and District   50m   Very Difficult
The long diagonal line that starts at the water's edge and slants up left to the big tree. Climb up to a tree, then continue up an impressive slab with minimum difficulty to the big tree. Loose.

Grand Central   60m   Very Severe 4c **
1. 20m Take the concave central groove that lies below the big tree. Start at the water's edge and make a delightful left traverse about 6m above the pool to a group of trees.
2. 40m 4c Step down to little edges and traverse up then left to a fixed peg. Climb the groove, (crux just above another peg), then go up the easier but impressive groove to the big tree.

SCATWELL UPPER SLABS *(Map Ref 381 564)*

This pleasant outcrop lies just over 1km from Loch Luichart Power Station along the road from Loch Achilty to Strathconon. There is a lay-by just below the crag, which can be reached in five minutes by skirting either side of a bog. The cliff is rough granulitic schist, with perfect friction on the slabs, but more blocky lower down. There is a long overhang at the bottom of the slabs. Shorter but steeper slabs extend right from the main crag. Due to the extraordinary friction it is possible to climb here in the rain if lichenous areas are avoided. Some of the climbs require RPs for protection. The routes are described leftwards from the centre of the crag, then from right to left.

1 Stranger than Friction 30m VS *   (1990)
An enjoyable climb with a strenuous but safe start and straightforward unprotected padding above. The centre of the crag has two overhanging grooves with a more broken corner just to the right.
1. 5m 5a Climb the right-hand groove to a drooping tree.
2. 25m 4a Climb the initially steep slab directly behind the tree, then go up and left to a heather ledge. Climb the short headwall via a niche.

2 Friction with Strangers 30m HVS 5b   (1992)
This takes the left-hand overhanging groove. Climb the groove to the slab above, then go steeply up this to easier ground.

3 Stretch 25m HVS 5b   (1992)
Start just left of Friction with Strangers. Climb the reachy break (Friend 1 up right) to the easier slabs above.

4 Bushwacker's Slab 25m VS 5a   (1990)
Start a little left of Stretch at a V-nick in the overhang and right of a similar break. Climb the overhang and little overlap above, then climb the slab between two heather bushes to finish more easily.

5 Early Learning Centre 25m Very Difficult   (1992)
Just left is another break. Climb this via the obvious line of weakness.

6 Strawberry Ripple 30m Severe   (1992)
Further left is a crack which trends left over several little overlaps. Follow this to the top.

SCATWELL UPPER SLABS

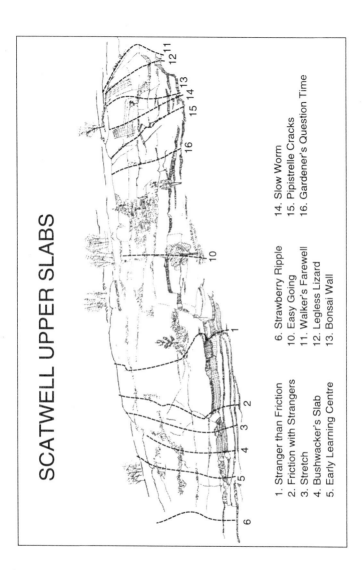

1. Stranger than Friction
2. Friction with Strangers
3. Stretch
4. Bushwacker's Slab
5. Early Learning Centre

6. Strawberry Ripple
10. Easy Going
11. Walker's Farewell
12. Legless Lizard
13. Bonsai Wall

14. Slow Worm
15. Pipistrelle Cracks
16. Gardener's Question Time

7 Coffin Slab 10m 4c (1992)
At the extreme left of the slab is is an overlap with a big rectangular block at its foot. This, and the following problems, start near the block.
Climb over the block, then surmount the overlap above to reach the slab. Descend down to the left.

8 Ready and Waiting 10m 5a (1992)
Right of the block are a couple of boulders. Step off the upper one onto the slab, then move up and over the overhang on finger holds. Unprotected.

9 Alive and Kicking 10m 5b (1992)
This is to the right of Ready and Waiting.

10 Easy Going 30m Mild Severe (1992)
Returning now to the centre of the crag, right of Stranger than Friction, there is a broken corner with a square inset section of slab with an overlap above. Start right of the broken corner at a birch tree. Climb to a section of quite bold slab at the top via a cleaned line.

Moving now some way to the right, above and right of the lower slab is a short steep slabby wall bordered on the right by a pale arete.

11 Walker's Farewell 10m VS 5a (1990)
Start in a recess below the pale arete, step over an overlap and climb the arete directly by friction; easier than it looks.

12 Legless Lizard 15m E1 5c (1992)
Climb easily up the right side of the buttress to a pine tree, then follow the thin crack between Bonsai Wall and Walker's Farewell.

13 Bonsai Wall 15m E1 5c * (1990)
Even the protection is miniature. Left of the pale arete is a small stunted pine. Start beneath this.
1. 10m Climb slabs direct to the tree belay.
2. 5m Climb the delectably tenuous wall via hairline cracks.

14 Slow Worm 15m E2 5b/c * (1992)
Start as for Bonsai Wall, then climb the left edge to a ledge. Climb the bold brown streak on small holds to the top.

15 Pipestrelle Cracks 15m Severe 4b   (1992)
Follow the quartz dyke just left of Slow Worm to an obvious crack left
of its brown streak.

16 Gardener's Question Time 20m E1 5c *   (1992)
Start at a yew tree.
1. 15m Climb over the overlap to belay on a small pine below the top
wall left of Pipestrelle Cracks.
2. 5m 5c Climb the wall just left of the crack behind the tree.

MEIG CRAG *(Map Ref 366 557)*
This provides a handy roadside crag about 1km west of the Loch Meig
dam on the road up Strathconon; please park with consideration to
other road users. It can be easily combined with Glenmarksie for a
spot of contrast. The short but sharp walk to the crag is beset by
man-eating potholes between the boulders. The crag faces due north
and has vegetated areas. It has a remarkable slab of brown rock at
its left end and some very good crack and wall climbs at its right end.
The biggest of the buttresses has a prominent corner, Meig Corner,
which lies well to the right of the crag. Descent can be made down
either side of the crag. Some routes finish on a ledge at three-quarter
height, which can be traversed onto or descended by the slab below
Shy Bride's Crack. Abseil descents are also possible where there are
trees. The routes are described from left to right.

1 Sidestep 20m VS 4c   (1992)
At the left end of the crag is a brown slab which is often wet. The slab
is split horizontally by a break that gradually rises to meet the corner
of The Promenade. Follow the break to a harder section near the
corner, then finish up this.

2 Nicked In Time 20m E2 5b *   (1991)
Climb the left-hand crack in the brown slab to the break. Continue up
the slab above then trend right up a groove to finish. A fine route on
excellent rock.

3 Gabbro Slab 25m VS 5a **   (1992)
This is probably the best of the easier lines, on excellent rock with
more than ample protection. Climb the centre crack of the slab to a
fault, then step right to the continuation crack and pull up by a small
tree.

MEIG CRAG - LEFT

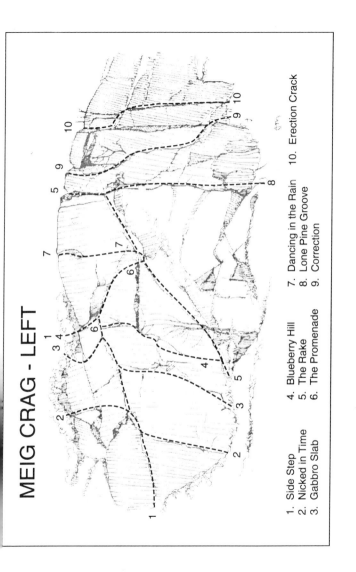

1. Side Step
2. Nicked in Time
3. Gabbro Slab
4. Blueberry Hill
5. The Rake
6. The Promenade
7. Dancing in the Rain
8. Lone Pine Groove
9. Correction
10. Erection Crack

4 Blueberry Hill 25m   VS 4c **   (1992)
Another good climb, with continuously interesting climbing in a good
position. Climb the crack right of Gabbro Slab, and follow it all the way
to an exit up the final ramp of Promenade.

5 The Rake 20m   Very Difficult   (1991)
The obvious slabby rake at the right end of Gabbro Slab.

6 The Promenade 20m   VS 4c   (1992)
Climb The Rake to a stance below the a steep headwall. Climb a crack,
then traverse left into a slanting groove which leads to the top.

7 Dancing in the Rain 20m   E3 5c *   (1992)
A bold and poorly protected route which takes the prominent hanging
flake in the headwall. Climb The Rake to the stance below the
headwall, then climb the crack to an undercling. The flake is obvious,
but a long way away!

Right of Gabbro Slab lies a group of tall birch trees that hides a bay
with a vertical corner, which is normally very wet. To its left lies a
two-stepped corner and to its right a prominent jam crack.

✓ *17/4/05 Neville Short.   Green + a little damp.*

8 Lone Pine Groove 25m   VS 5a *   (1992)
Between the brown slab and the bay is a prominent corner with a
solitary pine at two-thirds height. Climb the corner to the pine, then
continue up the corner (crux) to the top. A pleasant and well protected
route with good jamming.

9 Correction 20m   Mild VS 4b   (1991)
The two-stepped corner left of the wet corner. Scramble up to a ledge
with small trees. Climb the slabby corner past a small tree to a leaning
tree. Climb a crack to the overhang, move left to another crack and
then go up to a tree and the top.

Angst Arete, Meig Crag (Climber, John Mackenzie)

10 Erection Crack 20m HVS   (1991)
1. 15m 5b Climb the dusty wall to the crack, then the overhanging crack to an awkward landing onto a large flake. Climb the corner to tree belays.
2. 5m Finish up the short corner. Belay well back.

11 Sidewinder 20m VS 4b *   (1992)
This takes the buttress left of Limited Liability. Start below the corner and scramble left over blocks. Climb up, then trend right towards the edge before traversing left below the final wall. Finish on the grass ledge below the short top rocks. Either abseil off or traverse off right.

12 The Wee Nibble 10m HVS 5b   (1992)
Start from the ledge above the blocks of Sidewinder, then climb the wall direct, via a crack, to the finish of Sidewinder.

13 Limited Liability 25m E3 5c *   (1991)
About 15 metres left of Meig Corner is a steep right-facing corner which has a vertical crack leading to its base. Climb the overhung corner to the left of the vertical crack and traverse delicately right to the corner (often wet). Alternatively climb the crack, which is easier and better protected. Climb the corner, making use of the rib on the left at intervals. Belay in a fine cave. Abseil off or finish up the corner above.

14 Yellow Streak 20m E3 5b ***   (1992)
Between the corners of Limited Liability and Meig Corner are a central groove and a yellow-streaked one to the right, both overhanging considerably. Climb the yellow-streaked groove by serious but reasonable climbing (vital rock 3 runner) to a strenuous pull over the bulge to a rest. Continue straight up the bulging top wall, which has better protection. A good climb, but it requires a positive attitude.

15 Meig Corner 30m Hard Severe 4b *   (1979)
The fine corner with a tree at its base. Climb the corner to belays below a bulge. The crux above is short and easy ground lies beyond.
Variation: Mild Severe
Trend left to the edge at 7m, then climb to the ledge.

Glass Slipper, Creag Ghlas (Climber, Rob Brown)

MEIG CRAG - RIGHT

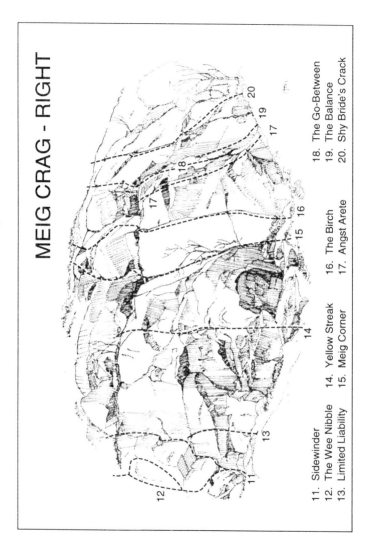

11. Sidewinder
12. The Wee Nibble
13. Limited Liability
14. Yellow Streak
15. Meig Corner
16. The Birch
17. Angst Arete
18. The Go-Between
19. The Balance
20. Shy Bride's Crack

16 The Birch 30m E2 5c ***   (1991)
Right of Meig Corner is a smooth gently overhanging wall split centrally
by a striking crack. This gives a superb sustained strenuous pitch with
excellent protection.
1. 20m 5c Climb the crack to a grass ledge and tree belays.
2. 10m 5a Climb the nose on the left and the heather above.

17 Angst Arete 15m E3 6a **   (1992)
An elegant and strenuous route requiring small wires. Right of The
Birch is an overhanging arete with a gash at three-quarters height.
Start left of the birch tree and climb flakes left and up to a big hold.
Climb the thin but well protected crack to below the overhang, then
climb this on positive holds to finish up a glacis.

18 The Go-Between 10m VS 5a   (1992)
The short wall just right of Angst Arete. Start at the birch and climb the
wall to a sapling. Continue straight up to finish.

19 The Balance 30m VS 4c   (1979)
Climb the rust-coloured corner right of Meig Corner to a tree belay,
4b. On the right is an arete which is followed over a huge balanced
block; finish up the crux slab above, 4c.

20 Shy Bride's Crack 15m E1 5b *   (1979)
Right of The Balance a crack splits the leaning wall. Climb easily up
a slab, then climb the off-width crack to the top. Sustained and
increasingly difficulty as height is gained.

ASPEN CRAG *(Map Ref 375 558)*
Take the minor road down Strathconon and park on the third layby on
the right west of the Loch Meig dam. The crag is almost obscured by
trees and is less than a rope length from the layby. Allow one minute.
   This crag is quite different from any of the other local crags in that
it is covered in generous incut holds, particularly in its top half. Despite
its steep bulging nature, the climbing is easier than first appearances
would suggest, giving spectacular, often strenuous moves with protection in the horizontal cracks that lie between bulges. Though it
faces north, the nature of the crag and the surround of trees ensures
much remains dry even in rain, with finishes that are juggy enough not
to be seriously affected by water.

Tantalus Groove 20m E2 5c   (1991)
This is the steep groove bounding the left of Icterus. Climb the groove
of Icterus to just below the flat hold, then traverse left and climb the
thin crack to an inset corner on the right, finishing by a tree. A bold
climb with some quite delicate moves.

Icterus 20m E2 5c *   (1991)
Takes the beetling buttress bordering the left of the crag which has a
steep left-bounding corner groove. An excellent climb, well sustained
up the lower groove which is both strenuous and technical. Start at
the foot of the groove which overhangs the base. Pull up to a tiny pine
then gain the groove with difficulty. Steep moves lead to a prominent
flat hold on the edge of the buttress, and the 'dragons teeth' underclings above. Step right to a flake crack in the corner, then pull over
the bulge on the left. Finish somewhat arboreally at a large birch
above.

The Dark Side of the Moon 20m E3 5c *   (1992)
The prominent roof left of Shadow Grasper is taken in a direct and
sustained manner. The finger-slicing roof is followed by long reaches
to easier ground. Climb direct to the top bulges, then climb these left
of a nose.

Shadow Grasper 20m E1 5b *   (1991)
A very good and somewhat intimidating route which climbs the bulges
just right of Icterus buttress. Start below a small tree and pull over the
juggy roof to reach it. Climb up left to a flat foothold beneath the crux
bulge and gain the slab above. Climb up pleasant rock to a short
corner which leads to a cramped left traverse and finish at the same
tree as Icterus.

Woolly Jumper 20m E2 5c   (1992)
Climb through the roof at a break just left of Sloshed in Action, then
finish in the same general line. The grade reduces to E1 if the peg in
Sloshed in Action is clipped.

Sloshed in Action 20m E2 5c   (1992)
An exciting excursion over the overhang right of Shadow Grasper.
Start at the tree belay at the start of Meridian and climb up to the roof,
peg runner. Surmount this on the left (strenuous), then continue more
easily up a groove and slab to finish up a short groove.

Gobstopper   20m   E3 6a **   (1992)
This takes the big roof between Sloshed in Action and Licking the Lip and gives the most exciting and serious climbing on the crag. Start as for Meridian and climb straight up to the roof, poor peg runner above. Gain the lip, cut loose, then swing right to jugs (Friend 1) and pull over. Continue straight up slabs to the big tree.

Meridian   20m   HVS 5a **   (1991)
An excellent introduction to the crag. Start at the base of the obvious ramp at a tree belay. Climb the crack behind the tree, then traverse up the ramp which gets gradually harder with height. Pull over the bulge in a fine position to gain a huge bucket hold on the right, then up the slab to finish.

Licking the Lip   15m   HVS 5a *   (1992)
An unlikely-looking climb at the lowest limit of its grade. Start right of Meridian, directly below a block beneath the roof. Climb delicately to reach the block, step right then swing through the overhang on the largest holds on the crag. Finish up the slab above.

Underneath the Arches   15m   E2 5b/c   (1991)
Start about 2 metres left of Mac The Knife and pull right over the roof just left of Mac The Knife. Continue straight up to finish.

Mac The Knife   15m   E2 6a *   (1991)
About 8 metres left of Burlesque Crack is a steep bulging wall with a small sapling high up. Start below a shallow corner and climb up to and over the bulge on the left-hand side with difficulty. Climb straight up to the sapling and overcome the top bulge, which is easier than it looks. A fine strenuous climb of character.

Jumping Jack Flash   15m   E2 5c   (1991)
Start right of Mac The Knife below the widest part of the roof. Pull staight over with long reaches and join the parent route to finish.

Creeping Stealth   15m   HVS 5a *   (1991)
About 5 metres left of Burlesque Crack the lower bulge is cut by a shallow quartz groove. Climb up to the bulge and pull over on the left. Climb straight up to a little overhanging corner at the right end of the top bulge and climb this on the left on hidden holds.

Chocks Away 15m HVS 5a   (1991)
The thinly protected and mossy wall left of Burlesque Crack is climbed
via a slight scoop, just right of Creeping Stealth. Step right and climb
the bold wall direct to the top.

Burlesque Crack 15m Severe   (1991)
Near the right end of the crag is a vertical crack, tree belay. Climb the
crack with surprising ease to the top.

The Aspen 15m HVS 5b   (1991)
Three metres right of The Aspen is a thin crack leading to an overhang
with a tiny Aspen beneath it. Climb the crack to the overhang, move
left and pull over the overhang strenuously. Climb up and right much
more easily. A fine lower half makes this well worthwhile.

Mid-Flight Crisis 12m VS 5a   (1991)
Five metres right of Burlesque Crack is a wall below the overhang.
Climb the wall and surmount the overhang centrally and continue
much more easily up the top slab, exiting as for The Aspen. Some
good strenuous moves on excellent rock.

Rock and Roll Suicide 10m HVS 5b   (1991)
Start well right of Mid-Flight Crisis below a bulge. Climb up to and
through the thin bulge and finish easily up the slab.

Uncertain Voyage 60m E2 **   (1991)
This is the left to right girdle traverse of the crag. By far the best route
here with some spectacular and exciting climbing, requiring a steady
team. Start left of the left edge of the Icterus buttress at a tree belay
a few metres up.
1. 10m 5b Climb the arete to flakes, then traverse right to the corner
and descend awkwardly to the flat hold on Icterus. Go up right to a
belay on Icterus.
2. 10m 5b Cross the slab, then descend the overhang of Shadow
Grasper to belay by the little tree below.
3. 20m 5b Traverse right and climb the ramp of Meridian to a cramped
position below the top overhang. Swing down right and take a hanging
belay by the sapling on Mac The Knife.
4. 20m 5b Traverse horizontally right towards Burlesque Crack, but
descend to handholds near the crack before gaining it and climbing it
to the top.

DAM CRAG   *(Map Ref 375 561)*

This crag is approached either from the Strathconon road to the dam at the east end of Loch Meig or along the road that leads from Loch Achilty and branches off on a private road near Little Scatwell. There is limited parking at the dam.

The crag lies below the north-east corner of the dam and is approached by traversing across scrub at the same level then descending to it. A curious roll of silky-smooth schist, punctuated by bore-holes and occasional protruding steels it gives limited but exciting friction climbing.

Due to its smoothness the slab dries almost immediately after rain. Other rather unsatisfactory climbs have been made either side of the existing routes.

Simple Delights   15m   Hard Severe 4b   (1991)
Easier than it looks. Start a little right of the railings and climb straight up the slab via the bore-holes and steels, pulling over the overlap right of the borehole thread. Very pleasant.

Battle of the Bulge   20m   6b (top rope)
The daunting and flawless slab left of Simple Delights which sports a curved arch-like overlap. Climb straight up to the overlap and pull through centrally. Cranking the tinies above gives an immediate manicure! An excellent problem.

The Gulf Crisis   20m   HVS 5b   (1991)
This climb, which is much easier than it looks, takes the slanting shallow corner left of the arched overlap. Traverse left from the railings to the foot of the groove. Climb the groove and pull onto the slab above via two drill-steels. More easily over the next overlap to finish. The best route here.

Thick as a Brick   20m   HVS 5b   (1992)
Start left of The Gulf Crisis. Climb the wall right of the brickwork to the top.

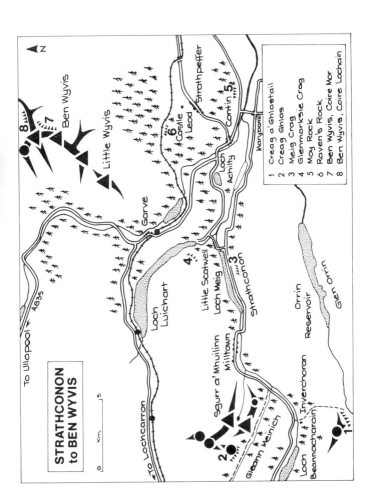

STRATHCONON to BEN WYVIS

0 Km 5

N

To Ullapool — A835

To Lochcarron

Loch Luichart

Garve

Little Scatwell
Loch Meig
Milltown
Strathconon
Loch Achilty
Loch Meig

Sgurr a'Mhuilinn
Gleann Meinich
Inverchoran
Loch Beannacharain
Orrin Reservoir
Glen Orrin

Little Wyvis
Ben Wyvis

Castle Leod
Strathpeffer
Contin
Marybank

1 Creag a'Ghlastail
2 Creag Ghlas
3 Meig Crag
4 Glenmarksie Crag
5 Moy Rock
6 Raven's Rock
7 Ben Wyvis, Coire Mor
8 Ben Wyvis, Coire Lochain

SGURR A' MHUILINN
879m   (Map Ref 265 557)

The climbing interest here is on Creag Ghlas (Map Ref 246 545), which has a huge craggy south-west face overlooking Gleann Meinich. It is easily approached by a pleasant wooded walk up the obvious land-rover track from Strathconon, then climbing steep ground from the forest break at the end of the road. There are two buttresses: the larger East Buttress is lower down on the right.

EAST BUTTRESS
The triangular East Buttress is less well-defined and more broken than the West Buttress. Descent is possible either on the extreme right of the crag or down the shallow gully that bounds the left edge (short abseil required). The routes are described from left to right.

Oh Dear   240m   Difficult to Mild VS   (1967)
This route follows the left-bounding edge more or less closely, and starts immediately right of the gully on the left. If the first slabby pitch is climbed directly the standard is just VS (4b). The rest of the climb is open to considerable variation.

Whoops   235m   HVS 5a   (1991)
This takes a central line up the buttress, aiming for a rounded buttress below the headwalls. The first and last pitches are good, but the whole is open to considerable variation.
1. 40m 5a Climb the crack in the middle of the slab tongue right of the edge of the cliff.
2. 35m Continue up right on short slabs and ledges to a ledge below a cracked slabby wall.
3. 45m Climb slabby walls, trending right to more walls.
4. 30m Ascend the wall left of the belay to a ledge and flake belay below the central rounded buttress.
5. 50m Climb the buttress above on good holds, then trend right and up to a wall. Belay on a wide ledge at a leaning flake.
6. 35m 5a Climb the steep crack immediately above the leaning flake to a slab. Climb this on the left to the top. Scrambling remains.

Boulder and Bolder   330m   VS   (1978)
This route lies on the right side of East Buttress. The lower section
follows the best rock, climbing avoidable difficulties. The upper section takes a natural line. Start at the base of the buttress where
terraces cross above smaller crags on the right, beneath a short wall.
Climb the wall and rib above to take an optional crack on the left, or
go right and take pleasant rocks leading to a ledge and cairn below a
steep slab. Climb the central crack up a triangular slab (4c); above
this go right to pale rock and up this to easier ground. Go right towards
the obvious arete. On the left is a fine shaped arete, bounded on its
left by a wide, deep chimney. Climb the crest of the arete and go right
to a stance below the steep right wall and corner above. Climb the first
crack right of the corner to the arete, go right across a slab to a deep
crack and up this to a fine stance and huge spike belay (4c). Take the
steep corner crack behind to gain easier rocks and so to the top (4b).

WEST BUTTRESS

The 150m high West Buttress, which lies straight above the road end,
is steeper and more compact than the East Buttress. It resembles very
high angled Etive-like slabs, and is just as smooth. A good selection
of Friends and large nuts is required for protection. A prominent rib
divides the West Buttress into smooth slabs on the left and a steep
pale sidewall bottomed by a heather chimney on the right. Descent is
possible down the steep heather gully behind Spare Rib (tricky in the
wet) or by a long ramble on the extreme left of the crag. The routes
are described from right to left.

1   Spare Rib   65m   VS   (1979)
The right edge of West Buttress is bordered by a shallow gully and
consists of slabs and grooves with a conspicuous overhang near the
top. The right wall overhangs. This route climbs the right edge of the
buttress.
1. 45m 4c From the foot of the buttress, climb slabs on the left to
heather. Cross to steeper rock on the right, past a spike, to a bulge-
topped groove on the right edge. Climb this to a thin groove left of a
heathery corner. Step right to a tree with various belays and a sliding
stance.
2. 20m 5a Gain a steep slab and go up left to a corner. Traverse right
under the overhang to the edge and continue up the groove to the
top.

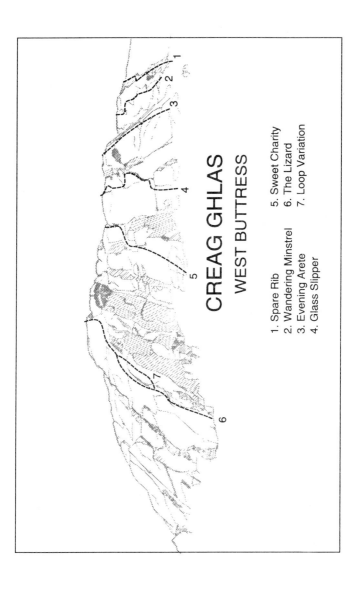

CREAG GHLAS
WEST BUTTRESS

1. Spare Rib
2. Wandering Minstrel
3. Evening Arete
4. Glass Slipper
5. Sweet Charity
6. The Lizard
7. Loop Variation

2 Wandering Minstrel 70m VS   (1992)
This takes a pleasantly indirect line to give the easiest climbing on the face. There is little protection.
1. 35m Start as for Spare Rib, then climb the broken slabs up and left to a terrace.
2. 35m 4b Above is a pale slab. Climb cracks slanting up right, then traverse up and left across the right-hand of two shallow corners. Continue traversing above the second corner to reach a square-cut sentry-box on the left of the buttress. Finish up this.

3 Evening Arete 90m VS *   (1992)
Left of Spare Rib is a fine-looking clean-cut edge that appears, when approaching from below, to form the right-hand boundary of the cliff. Start by scrambling up broken slabs to its base.
1. 30m 4b Climb the edge awkwardly to a heathery groove, then move up this to below a prominent bollard on the arete. Climb the slab direct to the bollard.
2. 40m 4c Climb the imposing edge up a crack, then by twin cracks just right, and then boldly directly up the arete until level with the leaning overhang on the left. Follow shallow grooves that cut up left above the overhang to a belay back in the corner (Friend 4).
3. 20m Scramble up the easy gully above.

4 Glass Slipper 65m HVS 5a **   (1992)
A fine route which takes an implausible line. Left of Evening Arete is a steep slab with a prominent curving overlap running up its right side. Start below the central crack of the slab.
1. 10m 4c Climb the crack up the slab to a flake below the curved overlap.
2. 20m 5a Gain the overlapped corner above, then follow this tenuously to an easing. Traverse left along the hand-rail to a narrow stance.
3. 35m 4c Climb the steepening cracks above to a stepped ledge. Climb the spike on the right, then traverse left below the top slab to a wide crack. Finish easily up this. Scrambling remains.

5 Sweet Charity 120m HVS   (1980)
Right of the central rib of the buttress is a long slab.
1. 35m 5a Climb the slab to a small ledge, step right to a steep edge then go up this and the crack round the edge (crux) to a heather niche and belay.

2. 15m 4b Climb the corner.

3. 35m Surmount a heather rake in the corner above and at the top descend into a grim chimney.

4. 35m Gain the raked slab right of the chimney, go past a flake then climb corners to the top.

6 The Lizard 150m HVS *   (1967)
Start at a cairned ledge beneath the central rib (which has a steep pale side wall with a heather chimney at its foot).

1. 25m 4c Climb the crest of the rib to a ledge. Climb the fine curved crack which lies between two mossy corners to a ledge.

2. 30m 5a Continue up the mossy corner above to a ledge.

3. 25m 4c Step right and gain the right edge of the slab above, climbing shallow grooves to a heather exit left of a little tree; block belays on the terrace.

4. 25m 5a An excellent pitch. Cross the terrace and climb up the slab above on the right, which has an initially delicate section up a right diagonal fault. Trend back up left, step up right then up left following the fault.

5. 45m 4b Cross heather and climb a cracked wall, cross more heather and gain a left-slanting groove. Climb this via a crack, then climb a prominent jam crack to the top.

7 *Variation:* **The Loop Pitch** 35m E3 5b/c **   (1990)
On the second pitch, leave the mossy corner after a few metres and make a delicate traverse right to the base of the right edge (Friend 0 runner; the last one!). Climb this and make difficult moves up to a little pink 'ledge'. Step left into a blind crack and layback up the improving edge to the ledge and belay at the top of pitch 2.

8 The Big Trundle 30m E1 5b   (1992)
A bold route which is not well protected. The last pitch of The Lizard is situated above a rocky gangway. Follow the gangway left to reach an obvious monolithic flake at the top of the wall. Start below this, then climb a right-slanting crack over a bulge. Climb easier rock right of the flake and finish strenuously. Belay up left.

SGURR A' GHLAS LEATHAID
844m   (Map Ref 244 564)

Climbing on this mountain requires the dedication to walk across acres of peat-hagged heather; it may be easier to combine it with a more pleasant hillwalk over the five tops of Sgurr a' Mhuilinn.

Lady's Gully   180m II/III   (1971)
The gully can be seen from Achanalt on the main A832 road between Garve and Achnasheen. The lower section is narrow and gives some steep ice over several pitches. Near the top the gully forks. Both forks have been climbed.
   The buttress left of Lady's Gully has also been climbed. It gives indistinct climbing with optional difficulties at about Grade II.

CREAG A' GHLASTAIL
(Map Ref 265 470)

This crag in Glen Orrin faces south-east and has a base at around 400m. It rises above a stand of Scots pine and forms a steep face of rather poor rock and vegetation, about 120m high. It is bisected by a deep and wide Central Gully. The left of the face is bounded by the prominent Waterfall Gully, the right wall of which forms the most continuously steep area of clean rock, which can only be reached by climbing the initial waterfall pitch. Climbing is only allowed on the crag between the end of August and the end of March.
   To get to the crag, from near the head of Strathconon leave cars before the bridge crossing the Conon and walk past the keeper's house at Inverchoran. Continue over the pass between Beinn Mhead-hoin and Carn na Cre on a landrover track which curves round below the foot of the crag.

The Curate's Egg   120m   VS   (1989)
Takes the most feasible line on the crag, the right-bounding edge of Waterfall Gully. It is steeper than it looks and has areas of vertiginous heather.
1. 15m Climb the flakey slab immediately right of the gully and left of the steeper but more broken skyline to a heather shelf.

2. 20m Traverse right under a tottering heather shelf, then stand on it from the right. Traverse back left on better rock, then climb up and back right via a slab and corner to reach a rectangular heather ledge.

3. 35m Climb the bounding corner of the shelf, then straight up to the central fault line above. Climb this steep section on flake holds to easier ground. Scramble up and right on steep heather to a bay with small trees and an excellent belay.

4. 20m 4c Climb the steep central break, initially by a crack on the right, to a loose chockstone. Step left into a parallel corner and go up to a steep exit to an easy groove.

5. 30m Step onto the rib on the right and climb this pleasantly to heather slopes above.

Descend by a long traverse left across the top of Waterfall Gully, below the top tier of crags, then take heather rakes back down to the gully bottom.

Ghlastail GTX   210m   V **   (1990)
A winter ascent of the Allt a' Ghlastail. A fine climb whose interest increases with height. If the top pitch is avoided it is only Grade III. As the base is at only 500m it needs about a week's frost to bring it into optimum condition. Follow the burn through the trees to the first pitch, a slabby waterfall. Climb this to easy ground, then climb a couple of short icefalls to the base of the mid-height slabs. Climb these in two pitches to a bay below a narrow ice hose which forms a distinctive gully when seen from below. Climb this to an amphitheatre below the top pitch. Take the superb ice pitch direct, just right of hanging icicles. This pitch can be avoided on the left by a steep ice funnel leading to a possibly large cornice, or a tamer right traverse out of the amphitheatre.

Three Stroke Gully   120m   II   (1991)
To the right of the trees and near the right side of the face is a shallow gully which is half ice, with pleasant bulges, and half snow.

Ben Wyvis and the Fannich Forest

This chapter covers the rock climbing on the crags of Strathpeffer (south of Ben Wyvis), the climbs on Ben Wyvis itself and the excellent climbing in the hills of the Fannich Forest. For convenience, the outcrop at Struie Hill is also included in this section.

RAVEN'S ROCK *(Map Ref 463 606)*

This impressive north-facing schist crag lies about 2km west of Achterneed along the Dingwall to Kyle line, 9km from Dingwall. It is either approached by walking along the railway line from the former Achterneed station, or by walking along a private road south of this and then joining the track for the last 500 metres. Cars should be left at Achterneed. For reasons of conservation there is no climbing on this crag from April to July.

The crag is extensive and stretches for 600 metres. There is a great deal of vegetation and all the lines needed cleaning. The cliff is in two parts. The top overhanging section of blackish rock is separated from a shorter overhanging lower wall by a grass slope. Proceeding west, roofs and cracks border a steep buttress which is in turn bordered by a corner. A black wall beyond is cut by a ramp. Further left are steep walls, then a roof topped corner. Next come a white wall and a black wall, separated by a tree-crowned ledge, which diminish in height westwards. The descent for most of the climbs lies behind the white wall and takes a shallow gully which is easy but vegetated.

The climbing is on very steep but generally sound rock, but neglect has allowed re-growth of some vegetation. Most of the better climbing lies on the more accessible right side, but to get to the first climb gain the grass slope from the right to reach a minor jutting buttress beneath the great top wall. This minor buttress has a central chimney.

1 Bone Idle 15m HVS 5b   (1980)
Climb the thin crack right of the chimney, step right to a ledge, crux, then go left and finish up a chimney.

2 Scorpion 50m Mild VS 4b   (1971)
A rather poor climb which takes the large slabby corner left of the prominent steep buttress which is the first major feature of the lower right section of the crag. Climb either the slab or the crack to reach a

fine cave formed by blocks. Step onto a yard-arm and climb a groove to mossy slabs and tree belays.

3   Tombstone Buttress   70m   E1 **   (1978)
This varied climb takes the fine steep buttress right of Scorpion.
1. 5b   Start in the gloomy pit at the bottom right and climb the black crack and roof to a slab. Go left across the slab to a chockstone and ledge above. A short wall leads to a thin grass terrace which is traversed left to the 'tombstone' belay.
2. 5b   Climb the fine steep crack to a large block. Follow the diagonal right-slanting crack; near the end, hand-traverse into a corner and spike, climb the corner to ledge and belays.
3. 4b   From the ledge step left to a crack splitting blocks and belay in Scorpion's cave. Finish up Scorpion.

4   Obituary   70m   E2 ***   (1980)
Start in the recessed right corner of Tombstone Buttress.
1. 5c   Climb cracks on left to a large roof. Traverse left to the front of the buttress and continue to a thin crack. Up this (crux), to follow holds leading to a cracked bulge on the right of the buttress. Climb the exposed crack and bulge to the second belay of Tombstone Buttress.
2. 4b   Finish up Tombstone Buttress.

5   The Sting   100m   E1 **   (1978)
This climb takes the obvious right-slanting hanging ramp that cuts the black wall right of Tombstone Buttress.
1. 5b   Climb a slab to below the ramp and take the crux bulge above on spikes to gain the ramp. Follow the easiest line on the ramp to a tree belay.
2. 4b   Follow the easier slab to an overhung niche and the tree above. Climb a bulge and corner behind the tree, step right, then go up wall of cracked blocks to a tree belay.
3. 5a   Climb the steep awkward crack to a large birch tree.

6   Roots   65m   Severe   (1978)
1. To the right of Sting is a broken parallel groove. Climb it and traverse onto a good ledge and belays.
2. 4a   Step up right (crux) onto a prominent block, then traverse right over a good slab. Near its end climb a wall to belay below Sting's third pitch. Escape right.

7 Shorty 15m HVS 5a   (1979)
Right of Roots is an overhanging wall. Start below trees and gain the
right-slanting line, surmounting the crux bulge beyond a small tree and
finishing rightwards.

8 Raspberry Traverse 70m Hard Severe   (1978)
1. 4b Right of Shorty is an inset corner. Climb this, step left and up an
awkward little wall to belay below trees.
2. 4b Traverse right around the corner and continue to small gnarled
tree. Go up left past a niche to tree belays.
True Finish: VS 4c
On the second pitch continue in the same line past the tree to the large
corner (The Croak).
Direct Start: E1 5b *   (1980)
Climb the centre of the steep wall to the right to a flake, step left onto
a thin ledge and traverse into the top of the inset corner.

9 Jacobite Wall 50m E1 *   (1979)
Right of Raspberry Traverse is the steep wall of the Direct Start and
right again a grass mound which hides a fine cave. Jacobites are
reputed to have hidden here after the '45.
1. 5b Start left of the cave and go up to a ledge and flake. Step right
to a long ledge and traverse right to a break. Go up left to a crack and
climb past a small bent tree to belay in a crack.
2. 4b Continue up the cracked corner and finish as for Raspberry
Traverse.

10 Kingfisher 50m HVS ***   (1978)
Takes the attractive wall left of the big corner.
1. 5a Start at the raised grass mound and climb a short wall to follow
the crack to a small tree. Go back up left and mantelshelf onto a slab
(crux). Step up right and then climb directly up the wall to belay well
left of the big roof.
2. 4c Follow a diagonal line up the overhanging headwall, starting by
some blocks to reach a jutting ledge. Step up left to climb a short wall.

11 The Croak 50m HVS **   (1978)
This climbs the steep corner right of Kingfisher.
1. 5a The lower corner is awkward and sustained but well protected.
Belay on the sloping grass ledge.
2. 4b Climb the slab above and swing round the corner to tree belay.

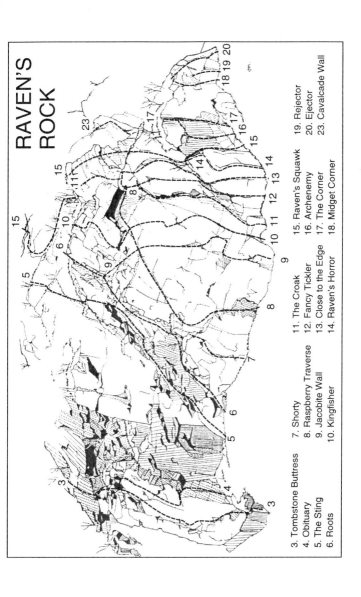

RAVEN'S ROCK

3. Tombstone Buttress
4. Obituary
5. The Sting
6. Roots
7. Shorty
8. Raspberry Traverse
9. Jacobite Wall
10. Kingfisher
11. The Croak
12. Fancy Tickler
13. Close to the Edge
14. Raven's Horror
15. Raven's Squawk
16. Archenemy
17. The Corner
18. Midget Corner
19. Rejector
20. Ejector
23. Cavalcade Wall

3. 4b From the flake ledge, either climb the loose wall above on the left, or walk along ledge to finish.

12 Fancy Tickler 30m   VS   (1980)
To the right of The Croak is a steep wall split by three cracks.
1. 4c Climb the short left crack to a grass ledge and tree.
2. 4c Climb the thin crack right of the arete, crux, to trend left to the tree belay on The Croak.

13 Close to the Edge 35m   HVS *   (1980)
1. 5a Climb the central crack in the wall, just right of Fancy Tickler, to the tree belay above.
2. 4c Gain a ledge, climb up right to a niche, step right and up the crack to belay as for The Croak. Traverse off right.

14 Raven's Horror 15m   HVS 5a   (1978)
This climbs the third (central) crack in the wall to a jutting hold. Traverse out right to the edge and finish up this. A bold, sustained little climb.

15 Raven's Squawk 90m   Mild VS   (1970)
The first and still the loosest climb on the cliff, but with some good moments. The length excludes easy ground.
1. Climb the slab and corner right of Raven's Horror to the ledge and tree belay.
2. 4a Gain the ledge and climb the wall just right of the niche of Close to the Edge to reach the flake ledge and belays.
3. 4b Climb the crack in the roof above, crux, then the loose wall to the descent gully.
4. 4b Scramble across the gully to the back tier of cliffs. Climb either the corner or the slab to its right to step left to a tree.
5. 4b Scramble easily up the gully to a shallow groove, climb this to a ledge and traverse right to a V-crack and exit up this.

16 Archenemy 20m   HVS 5b *   (1978)
Right of Ravens Squawk is a slab with a crack splitting a steep wall. Climb the crack to a small tree and niche and move right, crux, to a ledge. Traverse right to a corner to finish.

17 The Corner 15m   Very Difficult   (1978)
Climb the lower slab and then move into and up the pleasant corner on the right to the top.

18 Midgit Corner 5m Severe 4c   (1978)
The boulder problem corner left of Rejector.

19 Rejector 20m Severe 4c   (1971)
An amusing short problem right of The Corner where a slabby V-groove lies right of a short steep wall. Go up the wall to enter the groove, not easy, then finish easily up the groove.

20 Ejector 7m VS 5b   (1981)
The steep rib right of Rejector. Gain the spike, then step left to finish. A good problem, not so easy on first aquaintance.

21 Acceptor 10m Very Difficult   (1978)
The pleasant groove and slab to the right of Ejector.

22 The Chimney 10m Hard Severe 4b   (1978)
This climbs the good chimney-groove which lies around a corner right of the last routes. Climb it to exit left, swing back right to ledge and up a corner to finish.

    The descent gully is bordered on its true left by mossy crags. A short way up is a prominent white wall near a fallen tree.

23 Cavalcade Wall 20m Severe   (1978)
Climb the white wall to a central niche and exit left to a tree.

24 Zigzag 15m Difficult   (1978)
Below the white wall in the descent gully, at the gully mouth, is a curious double flake. Follow it rightwards, turn a corner then follow the flake crest back left again. Curious indeed.

    There are several outcroppings of rock right of the main area. On the far right of the crag, past a white wall, is a seemingly well-defined arete, Dismal Edge.

25 Black Crack 10m Mild Severe   (1978)
Right of Dismal Edge is a slanting wall with a chimney-crack to the right. Start left of this then step into it to exit via the flakes.

26 Black Wall 10m Mild Severe   (1978)
To the right of Black Crack is a wall. Climb it and step right to flakes to exit back left.

RAVEN'S ROCK QUARRY

This lies 500 metres west of Raven's Rock. It is very loose except on its right side where there is a smooth slab. Many variations are possible on this slab, some considerably harder and often loose low down. The corners to the left have all been climbed at about Very Difficult standard. The short but steep wall to the right of the slab has several climbs plus a technical girdle.

Pad Slab   30m   Severe   (1970)
Towards the right end of the slab is a tree-crowned ledge. Gain this and climb the slab and groove above, trending left.

Centre Fall   40m   IV   (1978)
In the centre of the quarry is a thin waterfall which freezes in most winters to give a fine problem, vertical low down but thin higher up.

RED ROCK   *(Map Ref 470 601)*

This small but imposing schist crag lies 800 metres east of Raven's Rock. The approach through the forest below is tedious, so the best way is to follow the private road to near a wooden bridge and then head up and left to the crag via a fire-break. There are no restrictions on access. The crag, which appears much larger than it is, has plenty of overhangs but since it is triangular, route possibilities are limited. The best line is the one below.

Red Wall Grooves   35m   VS 4c **   (1978)
The centre of the face has a prominent curving groove. Start from the ledge below where a mass of ivy festoons the left side of roofs. Climb up to the roof and tarzan across the ivy to a break, then climb up and step left to a ledge, belays on the right. From the left end of the ledge climb to hidden holds and reach the groove at a niche. Continue to the top in a fine position.
Direct Start: HVS 5a
The steep wall right of the normal start leads to the same ledge and avoids the ivy.

LITTLE RED ROCK

This is a small but technical crag a few hundred metres west of Red Rock. It is most easily reached by following the fire break from Red Rock then heading up through the trees. It has a maximum height of

12m and is about 30 metres long. Two large flakes form tight chimneys with walls in between. There are some interesting crack climbs as well as entertaining walls. Top roping is feasible as not all the routes are protectable and some of the landings are decidedly bad.

Elementary Flake   10m   Mild Severe
At the left of the crag is a flake; climb the short groove to gain the crest of the flake, then take the groove on the left to finish.

The Wee Nasty   10m   E2 6a *
Climb the thin groove in the centre of the flake to the crest. Finish up the middle of the wall. One of the better climbs but hard to protect.

Calorie Chimney   10m   Very Difficult
Climb the tight chimney at the right end of the flake to the crest. Climb the wall and slab to finish.

Medusa Crack   10m   VS 5a *
Right of Calorie Chimney is a recess with a cracked roof. Climb up to and over the roof to the top. The best climb here.

Razor Crack   10m   VS 5b
Right of Medusa Crack is a straight crack with a roof at the bottom. Climb the roof strenuously, then the crack more easily to tree belays above. The bottom roof can be taken on the right at the same grade.

Fat Ladies' Chimney   10m   Severe
The tight chimney above a block right of Razor Crack.

Any Way But This   10m   E2 5c
The steep corner-groove right of the chimney, entered and followed with difficulty from the chimney. A sustained problem.

MOY ROCK   *(Map Ref 496 550)*

Moy rock is a south-facing conglomerate cliff above the A9 just east of Contin. It is now becoming rather hidden by forestry development. The conglomerate is quite sound but the climbing is usually bold with runners often placed around the protruding 'pudding stones'. This requires long tapes and heavy karabiners. The crag also provides some low-level traverses which, being sheltered, might provide some sport on a rainy retreat from the north. Cars can be left in the lay-by opposite the rock and a little further to the east. Walk back to a side road and gate and turn almost immediately left up a track, all this within 100 metres of the main road. Take the first fire break on the right and plug steeply up to the crag, about ten minutes in all. For reasons of conservation there is no climbing between April and July.

The climbs are described from left to right. In the centre of the face is a bird-limed wall, bounded by chimney lines and walls. Further left a long slabby ramp forms an open corner.

Harderthanitlookscrack 40m Severe   (1972)
The long ramp gives slab and corner climbing, vegetated at the top.

Bird Lime Buttress is the lime-splashed wall between the two chimney faults. The next climb takes the deep chimney on the left.

Slanting Crack 40m Difficult   (1972)
Follow the deep chimney left of the slab over chockstones to a bay. Straddle the chimney to a ledge. Climb the short wall above on the left to the top. A harmless introduction to conglomerate climbing.

Boggle 50m Mild VS 4b *   (1978)
To the right of Slanting Crack is a slab.
1. 4b Climb the curving groove and crack to the slab and take this centrally to belays on the left below the top wall.
2. 4b Climb the steep plinth right of centre in an exposed position to reach an easy arete. Finish up Slanting Crack.

Speleological Nightmare 30m Hard Difficult   (1978)
To the right of Bird Lime buttress is a left-slanting chimney, bordered to the right by a tree-filled gully. Start in the left chimney, climb a groove and thread a tunnel to a cave and belays. Struggle through a tight hole to reach a saddle. Finish up a wide crack and exit up Slanting Crack.

Magnificrack 50m E2 **   (1978)
Right of the tree-filled gully is a curving flake crack leading to a vertical wall, which gives a magnificent but serious route.
1. 5b Climb the bulging flake to its apex (long sling runner). Follow the small ragged crack up the wall to a horizontal break, crux, climb the overlap on the left and then up a slab to a small tree. Belay on a larger tree to the left.
2. Continue up the short wall above the small tree to the top.

Perigrination   40m   VS 4c   (1978)
Climb the bulging wall at the right end of the cliff to a vegetated bay.
Exit on the wall right of the crack.

BEN WYVIS
1046m   (Map Ref 463 684)

The climbing on Ben Wyvis can be found in three different and remote
locations: Coire Lochain, Coire Mor and Coire na Feola.

COIRE LOCHAIN   *(Map Ref 487 707)*

This concave corrie, which is often in condition, faces due north and
has large cornices on its western half. The crags are about 120m high
and rather slabby and featureless, with a thin icefall on the left, slabby
walls in the centre, and an inverted triangular buttress on the upper
right. Beneath the triangular buttress are two broken sections cut by
snow rakes. Broken ground lies right of these, tapering off into a steep
snow wall. The cornices are greatest above the triangular buttress.

Access
Request permission from the keeper at the gate house to drive up
the rough road past Loch Glass to Wyvis Lodge, where there is
limited parking. Follow a track by the Allt Corravachie to reach the
corrie by striking across the hillside.

Caberfeidh   150m   III   (1982)
Start below the broken sections and climb the triangular buttress direct
to rock belays on the left. Continue up to the cornice and surmount it.
On the first ascent the cornice was of ice and double. A pleasant climb
with a good outlook.

COIRE MOR   *(Map Ref 470 690)*

This is by far the biggest and best of the mountain's features. The
approach walk is depressingly peat hagged; it is probably quicker to
traverse over the summit via the Garbat approach and drop down to
Coire Mor at its eastern end, rather than face the endless eastern and
southern approaches. In summer the only seemingly clean and stable
rock is the huge slab that lies to the right of the third big buttress, above

and left of the waterfall. It is clearly visible from below. The approach is via a wet corner which gives interesting scrambling. The following two routes are probably the only worthwhile summer lines. Both routes end on an arete which overlooks a big drop.

Klettershoe   90m   Very Difficult   (1970)
Start on the clean right tongue of slab and follow this direct to the arete. A shallow scoop at half-height is a landmark and the whole route is very clean. Though variation is possible, the direct line gives the best climbing.

Rubbers   90m   Severe   (1984)
Takes the line of the central corner which arcs round right at the top. There are optional starts, but the climbing improves at a red slab on the right of the corner. The bald and steeper slab right of the arched overlap gives some thin (4b) moves directly up the middle to finish just right of the overlap at the arete.

Wyvis Waterfall   50m   III   (1986)
In winter the waterfall freezes. Climb the right side of the cascade by a big ice pillar.

Slab Smear Left Hand   100m   IV/V   (1986)
Climb the left-hand of the two obvious ice smears.

COIRE NA FEOLA   *(Map Ref 470 688)*

This remote corrie, on the south-east side of the mountain, sports a 200m north-east facing crag rising from an altitude of 650m. From Newhouse (Map Ref 501 602), which is just off the Achterneed road, follow the Forestry Commission track (permission required) through the plantations for 4km to a small car park. Cross straight across the moor to the second fire-break, and follow this through trees, then diagonally across another moor to join a track, exiting at a gate which is diagonally north-east from the car park. Contour up the slopes of Point 890m to the east, and go round the shoulder into the corrie; there are small lochans directly beneath the main crag (allow 2 hours). The forest track can be very hard to find if returning in the dark (the gate is directly below the shallow gully that splits the southern slopes of Points 810m and 890m). In some conditions it may be best to approach from Garbat and go over the summit.

Descent can be a problem due to the avalanche-prone slopes on both sides of the crag, especially south of the summit. It may be best to descend the slopes of An Socach opposite the crag.

Discovery Buttress   255m   III/IV **   (1992)
This is a good mixed mountaineering route with some interesting route-finding. Start left of the toe of the buttress at the apex of a bay.
1. 30m Climb a right-trending groove to a snow patch and peg belay.
2. 30m Move right and climb a steepening groove to below an icefall, then move left to a balcony stance and peg belay.
3. 30m Either climb the icefall, or traverse right and climb iced rocks to a stance and peg belay.
4. 45m Climb the narrow icefall above to a steep exit to mixed ground. Traverse left round a rock nose to easier ground above a short corner.
5. 60m Continue up a snowfield to belay below a rock tower.
6. 60m Climb the left-hand runnel through the tower, then follow a fine snow arete which steepens to a cornice exit.

Gael Force Grooves   225m   III *   (1993)
In full conditions, the broad icefall left of Discovery Buttress presents a fine central plume.
1. 35m Climb the plume to traverse left to peg belays.
2. 50m Climb the icefall above on its right side to a shallow gully. Belay beneath a fine ice pitch.
3. 50m Ascend the ice pitch up left, then continue up more open ground to a central rock bay and nut belays.
4. 50m Continue up open slopes to a snow bay.
5. 40m Climb steepening snow to the cornice, which can be massive. On the first ascent, the cornice was double and it was negotiated by breaking down a snow wall to enter a deep crevasse by an ice tunnel. Fragile snow bridges led to the top.

STRUIE HILL CRAG   *(Map Ref 660 860)*

This small conglomerate crag lies 500 metres east of and 100m above the summit of the A836 at Struie Hill. It has been climbed on for many years by local climbers and first ascents are not known. It gives a few pleasant climbs.

Grey Slab Gully   25m   Difficult
Climb the narrow gully on the left of the face.

Alcove Slab   20m   VS 4c *
Right of the gully is a corner and wall topped by a small roof. Climb
the corner, surmount the roof and climb a slab to exit up a steep corner.
This is the best climb here.

Pink Slab   20m   Very Difficult
To the right of the last climb is a pinkish slab. Climb up to an overlap,
surmount it and finish up the grey slab. A good climb.

Jungle Jim   25m   Difficult
Right again is a chimney, often wet. Climb this and the open corner to
the top. A more pleasant variation is to climb the slab on the left.

THE FANNICH FOREST

The Fannaichs are the relatively remote group of mountains lying in
the wedge-shaped area between the Garve to Achnasheen and the
Garve to Braemore Junction roads. The line from Loch a' Bhraoin to
Kinlochewe may be considered the western boundary of the group,
separating it from An Teallach and the Fisherfield Forest further west.
The best winter climbing is on An Coileachan and Sgurr nan Clach
Geala, but there are also routes of interest on the north slopes of Sgurr
Mor.

AN COILEACHAN
923m   (Map Ref 241 680)

The climbing on this mountain is in Garbh Coire Mor, easily accessible
if you have the right connections!

GARBH COIRE MOR   *(Map Ref 250 674)*

Although relatively low-lying, this corrie comes into condition quite
frequently. However, being east-facing it is often prone to avalanche,
particularly on the slabby right-hand face. Optimum conditions occur
when a cold wind blows from the east. Access is from the south along
the private estate road from Grudie (on the Garve to Achnasheen

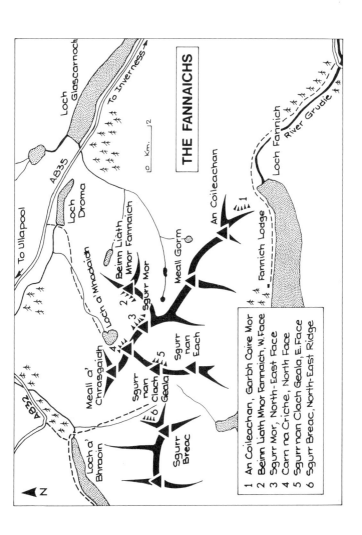

THE FANNAICHS

0   Km.   2

1 An Coileachan, Garbh Coire Mor
2 Beinn Liath Mhor Fannaich, W.Face
3 Sgurr Mor, North-East Face
4 Carn na Criche, North Face
5 Sgurr nan Clach Geala, E.Face
6 Sgurr Breac, North-East Ridge

road). There is a locked gate at the start of this road, but unfortunately in 1991 permission to drive up the road was very hard to obtain. From the parking place at Map Ref 264 666 the corrie can be reached in under an hour.

1   Short Shrift   180m   II/III   (1979)
This is the obvious narrow gully on the extreme left of the corrie. It remains hidden throughout the approach. Climb the gully over two ice pitches to its conclusion at 80m. From here trend up right on mixed ground for a further 100m.

2   The Ramp Tramp   200m   IV   (1985)
The left side of the corrie is a long and somewhat featureless slabby wall. This climb takes two ramps going diagonally right across a shallow depression towards the right edge of the wall and just left of and above a very steep section. Scramble up slabs and vegetation to start under the depression. Go diagonally left to reach the first ramp and follow it to its end (60m). Above this ramp the depression is barred by a smooth barrier wall, but at the very end of the ramp there is just enough vegetation to reach the ramp above. Follow this to broken ground, then go straight up to the top.

3   Primrose   240m   III *   (1976/1979)
This is the gully in the back left corner of the corrie. Climb a long ice pitch to reach the gully proper at 45m. Follow the gully until it forks at a large boulder. Either fork may be taken, but the right fork is considered to be more interesting and less heavily corniced.

4   Venus Fly Trap   250m   V   (1986)
This is the left-hand of two icefalls running up the steep buttress right of Primrose. After two pitches up the icefall go diagonally right on mixed ground and break through to a broad and prominent snow ramp. This leads easily up right to the top.

5   Burdock   210m   III *   (1976)
The next gully right of Primrose. Two long ice pitches lead to easier ground. The cornice is avoidable on the right.

6   The Turf Accountant   200m   IV *   (1987)
This follows a corner line in the steep buttress left of Dandelion, starting just to its left and aiming for a protruding block on the skyline.

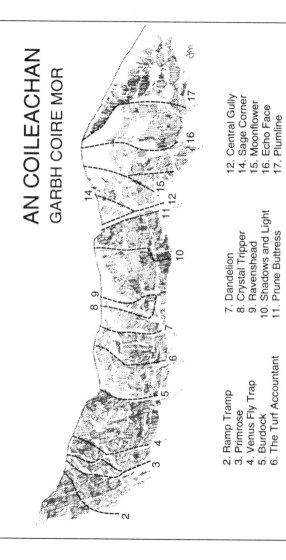

AN COILEACHAN
GARBH COIRE MOR

2. Ramp Tramp
3. Primrose
4. Venus Fly Trap
5. Burdock
6. The Turf Accountant

7. Dandelion
8. Crystal Tripper
9. Ravenshead
10. Shadows and Light
11. Prune Buttress

12. Central Gully
14. Sage Corner
15. Moonflower
16. Echo Face
17. Plumline

1. 30m Climb a left-trending ramp to a terrace beneath a rock band.
2. 20m Take the band direct via a sentry-box (hard) to gain the bottom left-hand side of the corner line.
3, 4. and 5. 150m Move slightly right then follow the turfy corner with increasing interest, passing just left of the square block to gain easy ground.

7 Dandelion 210m III/IV *   (1976)
The steep narrow gully right of Burdock. It has several ice pitches.

   To the right of Dandelion a steep icefall often forms. More rarely twin icefalls form, in which case the left one gives the next route, Crystal Tripper. If there is only one icefall it is likely to be Ravenshead.

8 Crystal Tripper 210m V **   (1979)
Start 30 metres right of Dandelion at an inset corner. Climb a short ice pitch to gain a snow band. Climb the left of twin icefalls for 30m to a belay on the left. Climb steep ice to reach rock, then traverse right to gain and climb a groove which leads to a second snow band. Climb the icefall above, with a bulge at 25m, then continue up ice runnels above to a snow fan exit, which is sometimes corniced.

9 Ravenshead 210m V **   (1981)
Start as for Crystal Tripper, 30 metres right of Dandelion. Climb up the short ice pitch to the snow band. Move right to the obvious icefall and climb this on its left side on mixed ground for 25m. Step right and gain the centre of the icefall which is followed to an obvious ice pillar. Climb this until it is possible to step left into a groove (crux) and go over a bulge to gain a belay (60m). Climb mixed ground moving right to follow an ice rake (45m). The upper bowl is gained and easier snow leads to the top.

10 Shadows and Light 210m V   (1984)
Start about 45 metres left of Prune Buttress, which goes up the right edge overlooking Central Gully.
1. 15m Climb a snow slope to an obvious steep shallow groove.
2. 45m Climb the groove over several overlaps to a large overlap.
3. 30m Pass the overlap on the right.

Beta Gully, Sgurr nan Clach Geala (Climber, Andy Cunningham)

4. 45m Climb delicate iced slabs to a steep snow ledge.
5. 30m Traverse right to gain a shallow weakness. Follow this for a further 45m to the top.

11 Prune Buttress   210m   III *   (1979)
This takes the edge of the buttress on the left of the large Central Gully. Various lines are possible, the best being on the extreme edge which has some impressive positions. There is a direct start just left of the edge which is harder (IV).

12 Central Gully   210m   I/II
The obvious wide gully in the back right of the corrie.

13 Sideshow   70m   IV *   (1991)
A strenuous, well protected climb on frozen turf. Follow Central Gully to a steep narrow corner in the left wall (at a point beyond where the icefalls of Sage Corner appear).
1. 15m Climb the corner over a bulge to a saddle on the right below a big spike.
2. 20m Gain the shelf above the belay, move left a few metres and attack the thin crack on the right. This leads to easier ground.
3. 35m Climb mixed ground, then traverse right below a short wall to a hanging ramp. Climb the intervening step and continue up the ramp to the top.

14 Sage Corner   165m   II/III   (1979)
About halfway up Central Gully, where it widens, break out right and climb iced slabs and snow to a prominent icefall bordered on its right by a large corner. Climb the icefall which consists of short vertical steps and finish up snow.

15 Moonflower   240m   III   (1984)
Start on the right of Central Gully opposite the foot of Prune Buttress. An obvious snow ledge leads out right. Follow this to beyond the skyline then climb shallow right-trending snow grooves with short awkward steps to the top.
Direct Start: 120m   IV   (1984)
Start about 45 metres left of Echo Face and climb iced slabs and grooves trending left to gain the original route.

Archway, Beinn Dearg (Climber, Roger Everett)

16   Echo Face   360m   III **   (1979)
Start in the centre of the large slabby face right of Central Gully. Climb
icefalls then snow aiming for a groove capped by a small bulge.
Surmount the bulge and climb thinly iced slabs for 90m. Above this
easier ground leads via a snow funnel up and right to the top.

17   Plumline   360m   III/IV **   (1979)
This takes the fine corner on the right of the corrie, right of Echo Face.
Climb up in three pitches to the obvious rock barrier. In some conditions this can be overcome on the left. Otherwise take an inset groove
on the right, hidden from below, to reach a deep cave with an excellent
pulpit stance. Step out left on steep ice and climb to another cave.
Continue up the corner over occasional ice pitches to a corniced exit.

BEINN LIATH MHOR FANNAICH
953m   (Map Ref 219 724)

This mountain, together with Sgurr Mor and Carn na Criche, forms the
northern ramparts of the Fannaichs. All have a number of routes on
their north flanks, which are easily reached from the path up to Loch
a' Mhadaidh which starts at Lochdrum.

Wot Gully   140m   II   (1967)
This route is on the west face, and takes the leftmost of three gullies
by an icy ramble followed by a cave pitch and steep snow.

Downward Bound   180m   III   (1980)
An icefall right of Wot Gully gives 60m of climbing in short steep
sections. Above is a snowfield that is prone to avalanche. Either
traverse into Wot Gully or climb the buttress above the snowfield.

SGURR MOR
1110m   (Map Ref 203 718)

The tremendous north-east face of Sgurr Mor gets the morning sun,
which can affect the climbs later in the season and cause avalanche
conditions.

Gelid Groove   240m   IV *   (1991)
Start by a cave left of the icefall just left of Easter Gully.
1. 50m Climb the steep initial bulge, then go up pleasant ice to a peg belay on the left.
2. 40m Continue up to the top bulge and climb this to snow.
3. 50m Move up and right to a minor snow rib with rock islands.
4. and 5. 100m Between the rib and the buttress on the right is an optional ice pitch. Above this snow leads to the top.

Easter Gully   240m   II   (1967)
A straightforward snow gully on the south corner of the east face.

The Resurrection   450m   III ***   (1980)
The face right of Easter Gully has a large icefall at the bottom, two long snowfields separated by a smaller icefall in the middle, and a steep upper wall overhung by huge cornices. This serious route of alpine character finds a devious way up the face, escaping right at the top. Follow a gully up to the bottom left of the lower icefall.
1. 35m From a niche traverse right and cross a bulge, then weave up to a blocky shelf. The initial section is Grade IV, but is avoidable.
2. 45m Climb ice above, then traverse left to a bulge and go up iced slabs to a peg belay on the right.
3. Climb snow to an icefall in the centre of the face.
4. 40m Climb the icefall.
5. Go up left to a steepening scoop and continue to below the vertical headwall, cave belay.
6. Traverse away right around a steep rib and where the headwall ends climb steep snow to a corniced finish.

East Face   300m   III *   (1967)
Climb a shallow runnel in the face right of The Resurrection. There are several ice pitches of which the first is the hardest.

CARN NA CRICHE
961m (Map Ref 197 725)

There is a large north-facing crag above Loch a' Mhadaidh. Although unimpressive from a distance, it is both large and steep with the lower 60m being an unbroken band of steep rock. The upper section has a central scoop bounded by ribs, and a flanking wall on the left. On the right a ramp leads up to broken ground.

The Boundary   275m   IV/V *   (1983)
About a third of the way from the left end of the lower band is a thin
icefall which may only form in a hard winter. Climb the icefall for 60m
to the top of the band. A short way above trend slightly right at a fork
and continue over an overhang and steep ground, following the
obvious line to the top.

Grand Illusion   310m   V **   (1991)
This route climbs a fairly central line, starting at a shallow chimney well
left of the right-slanting ramp and a short way left of a blunt projecting
rock boss.
1. 45m Climb the chimney to an overhang, then move right to a ledge
on the edge of a parallel groove. Climb the groove to the top of the
rock boss, then trend left up a turfy fault to a short narrow chimney.
Climb this to a poor belay on a small ledge.
2. 50m Climb the steep turfy groove above to an ice slot cutting
through overhanging rock. Climb this to a turf groove and the snowfield
above. Trend right to a thread belay below an obvious roof.
3, etc. 215m Climb a narrow ramp trending right, then move left and
zigzag up the centre of the face to the top. Distinctive features en route
are a left-slanting ice groove, a prominent dark rock and a steep
groove cutting through the headwall.

Brumous Buttress   280m   III   (1991)
This climbs the ground just right of the rib bounding the right side of
the central scoop.
1. and 2. 90m Climb the lower ramp until it begins to level off.
3. 45m Climb either of two breaks just right of a prominent block to
belays on the right.
4. 50m Traverse up and left, then take an ice pitch in some narrows
just right of a jutting buttress, to a belay on an isolated block.
5. and 6. 95m Climb up to the next rock band, then take the buttress
on the left or traverse off right to easier ground.

Into The Groove   95m   IV   (1992)
Lying on the lower right-hand wall (directly above the loch), this route
follows the groove left of centre, which separates steeper cleaner rock
on the right from more vegetated rock to the left. Climb the groove in
three pitches. Finish up the right-hand exit via a shallow blocky slot
(the left-hand deeper chimney is blocked by several roofs). Descend
to the left via the ramp between the upper and lower crags.

SGURR NAN CLACH GEALA
1093m   (Map Ref 184 715)

The fine crags on the east face of this mountain (at about Map Ref 191 717) are not marked on the OS map. There are several possible approaches, none easy. The best is from the east end of Loch a' Bhraoin, reached from a track starting at Map Ref 163 763 on the Braemore Junction to Dundonnell road. Follow the path south along an unnamed glen and after about 3km strike up east to the col between Carn na Criche and Sgurr nan Clach Geala. The descent from this col requires care as the slope may be corniced. Another approach is to leave the Garve to Ullapool road at the west end of Loch Droma. Cross the dam and follow the pipeline to the Allt a' Mhadaidh. Join the track on the north side of the burn and follow it towards Loch a' Mhadaidh. (The burn is most easily re-crossed about 1km further west than shown on the map.) From the loch climb up to the col between Sgurr Mor and Carn na Criche and make a diagonal descent into the corrie. (On returning from the top it is easier to go via the col between Carn na Criche and Meall a' Chrasgaidh which gives an easy descent to the north.) A third approach is from the south. From Grudie Bridge go to Fannich Lodge (private road) and a little further on branch north, following the Allt a' Choire Mhor over boggy ground to the corrie.

The main cliffs comprise a wedge-like cluster of six narrow but- tresses, numbered 1 to 6 from left to right, separated by five gullies, Alpha to Epsilon. From the top of these cliffs a graceful ridge leads south-west to the summit of the mountain, beneath which there is a more broken buttress. Access to the base of the cliffs is by a rock step and a steep apron of snow. The rock step is most easily passed at its right by a slanting rake running up to buttresses 5 and 6.

1 Alpha Gully 240m II   (1965)
The leftmost gully. It may contain two or three small ice pitches or it may be only steep snow. Take the left fork 15m below the top of the gully. The gully finishes after 120m on the crest of No.2 Buttress which gives a further 120m of good climbing.

2 Sunrise Buttress (No.2 Buttress) 150m IV   (1978)
This route follows a line in the centre of the buttress. Start at the foot of Beta Gully and climb ice bulges for three pitches, then an obvious gully system. Turn the overhang at the top on the left and continue up the arete to the top.

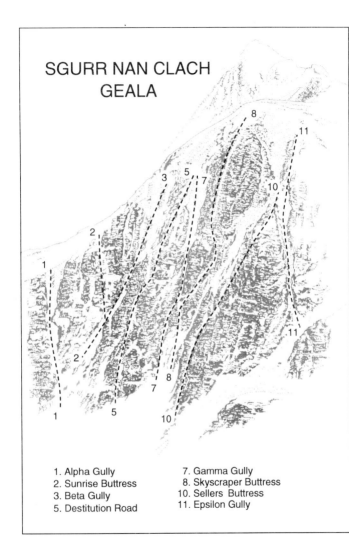

SGURR NAN CLACH GEALA

1. Alpha Gully
2. Sunrise Buttress
3. Beta Gully
5. Destitution Road
7. Gamma Gully
8. Skyscraper Buttress
10. Sellers Buttress
11. Epsilon Gully

3 Beta Gully 270m III   (1970)
An icefall gives access to the gully, which is straightforward up to a
trifurcation. Here a short left fork goes out to No.2 Buttress, a centre
fork contains a steep pitch, and a right fork avoids this pitch and rejoins
the Centre fork above.

4 Cuileag Buttress (No.3 Buttress) 250m IV   (1983)
This route takes a line of low resistance but still gives good climbing
in its upper half. The crux pitch is much harder than the rest. Start on
the left about 20 metres right of Beta Gully and climb vegetation for
60m. Go left and climb a short ramp which ends on a platform close
to Beta Gully. Traverse right to gain the buttress crest (40m). Climb a
steep groove just left of the crest (crux) (20m). Above this the angle
eases and the crest is followed to the top.

5 Destitution Road 200m V *   (1986)
This takes the central icefall of Cuileag Buttress. Climb directly up the
middle of the buttress using the general line of a shallow corner to gain
the icefall. Climb this direct past a jutting nose of rock, then traverse
right to gain a blocky corner cutting through the overhangs. Climb this
to the easier crest of the buttress.

6 Cuileag Corner 185m IV/V *   (1985)
This takes a line of discontinuous corners on the right side of Cuileag
Buttress. The precise line and difficulty depends on the amount of ice.
1. 45m Climb vegetated slabs to belay under the corner system.
2. 45m Enter the corner by a thin slab and short steep wall.
3. 45m Go up the corner to a big roof. Traverse right beneath the roof
and go up ice into a fault on the right edge of the buttress. Climb the
fault past two steep sections.
4. 50m Continue up the fault to reach the easy ground common to all
the routes on this buttress.

7 Gamma Gully 210m IV **   (1965)
This is probably the best of the gullies on the crag. Climb up for 30m
to enter and climb a deep narrow 30m slot. Some 20m higher is the
crux, a steep 10m ice pitch with smooth rock walls on either side.
Another 10m ice pitch follows, then climb steep snow and occasional
rock steps to gain the large scoop above Beta Gully.

8 Skyscraper Buttress 240m V ***   (1978/1986)
This provides one of the best winter routes in the area. On the original
ascent Gamma Gully was followed until after the slot, when a traverse
right was made onto the buttress. It will be necessary to go this way
if conditions are lean. Two better and harder starts are available. The
Direct Start takes the icefall at the base of the buttress, moving across
left at the top to belay under a roof, just left of a shallow undercut
groove. Climb the groove and move up left to join the traverse line of
the original route. The right-hand start climbs the right corner of the
icefall to belay in a snow bay. Move out right onto the rib overlooking
Delta Gully and climb an obvious groove, then go diagonally left above
the overhangs to join the ordinary route.
   From the traverse ledge out of Gamma Gully the ordinary route
climbs up and right for 40m (crux). After a brief easing, the buttress
rears up to give another excellent 30m pitch in cracks on the crest.
Continue by the line of least resistance to the top. A splendid climb.
Summer: Severe   (1961)
The lower part of the buttress is very vegetated. Take the Gamma
Gully start, thereafter follow the line of least desperation, more or less
as in winter.

9 Delta Gully 240m IV *   (1972)
After two pleasant steep pitches the gully widens and is followed more
easily with impressive rock scenery on the two enclosing buttresses.

10 Sellers Buttress (No.5 Buttress) 240m IV *   (1972)
Start at the lowest rocks and climb by grooves and shallow corners
always to the left of the crest. Near the top move up right to finish up
the crest. About 130m of easy snow common to Delta and Epsilon
Gullies leads to the plateau.
Summer: Very Difficult   (1961)
Start beneath a clean rock rib on the left of the buttress and follow the
crest of a prominent shoulder. Continue up a shattered rib to the top.

11 Epsilon Gully 140m III/IV   (1974)
This starts somewhat higher up the snowy ramp on the right of Sellers'
Buttress. After a hard start the gully is straightforward.

   On the south-east face of the mountain, starting a good deal lower
and to the south of the summit buttress, there is one route.

12 First Footing 400m III   (1982)
The ground below the bealach between Sgurr nan Each and Sgurr
nan Clach Geala is bounded on its right by slabs and ledges which
are often iced. Start beneath the right end of the slabs. Climb a short
ice pitch to a series of easy gullies and open snowfields. Trend right
for 225m, making for an obvious icefall in the headwall. Climb the
icefall (40m). Continue into a narrow blind gully then traverse out left
to a poor belay (30m). Move up left into a hidden chimney (30m) and
climb it. Easy ground above.

SGURR BREAC
999m   (Map Ref 158 711)

This hill is easily reached from the glen that runs south from the east
end of Loch a' Bhraoin. The lower end of its north-east ridge presents
a large broken crag (Map Ref 162 716). The crag is divided by a deep
snow gully with a short pitch low down (Grade I/II). Left of the gully is
a rather discontinuous buttress, whilst on the right is a wall split by a
corner and a short deep gully near its right end.

Neverending Story 300m II/III   (1991)
The buttress left of the central gully. Start under a roof just above the
toe of the buttress.
1. 45m Move left and climb a snow ramp leading onto the face.
2. 45m Climb a slabby wall and snow to a cave.
3. 35m Move right into a short turfy groove. Climb this and the broken
ground above to a sapling.
4. 40m Climb an obvious icy corner (well left of an icefall) and a
continuation groove to a belay on the left.
5, etc. 135m Wind up between small outcrops to the top.

Ptarmigan Corner 110m III/IV   (1991)
The obvious corner on the right of the crag.
1. 45m Climb the open corner and a steep chimney to a snow patch.
Belay under an overhang.
2. 40m Continue up the corner to a sapling. Move right into a slot with
a thin flake. Pull out right and continue up a turfy groove to belay under
broken rocks on the left.
3. 25m Steep snow leads to the top.

Beinn Dearg and the Freevater Forest

This chapter includes both summer and winter climbs, some readily accessible, some as remote as any in Scotland. Those in the western part of the group are best reached from the Ullapool side, while the climbs in the Freevater Forest are best approached from the east.

BEINN DEARG
1048m (Map Ref 259 812)

This massive mountain offers excellent winter climbing, though in summer it is mostly too vegetated to provide good rock routes. The majority of the climbs are approached from the west up Gleann na Sguaib, but the wild Coire Ghranda is well worth a visit.

GLEANN NA SGUAIB

From the Braemore to Ullapool road, at the head of Loch Broom, a forestry road runs up Gleann na Sguaib to the upper limit of the Inverlael Forest. A good path then leads up to the Bealach Coire Ghranda, passing first below the cliffs of Diollaid a' Mhill Bhric, the long sloping north-west shoulder of Beinn Dearg, and then below the large west buttress of the mountain. In heavy snow the path drifts badly, but in normal conditions it gives a relatively short and fast approach to the lower climbs. The climbs are described from right to left, as one approaches up the glen. Between Diollaid a' Mhill Bhric and the west buttress is a broad gully, the Cadha Amadan, or Fool's Pass, which provides a convenient descent from many of the climbs.

There are six well-defined gullies on the line of cliffs under Diollaid a' Mhill Bhric.

1 WhatawaytospendEaster 120m I   (1967)
The first gully provides a straightforward snow climb.

1a White Settlers Gully 180m III   (1989)
Climb the icefall 30 metres right of Bonus, and the gully above. The gully ends in a barrier icefall which is climbed on the right.

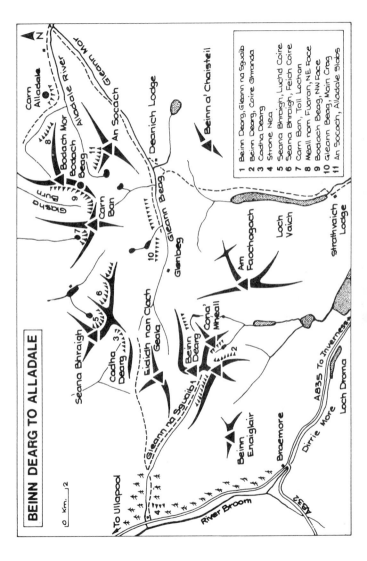

BEINN DEARG TO ALLADALE

0 Km. 2

N

To Ullapool

River Broom

Braemore

Dirrie More

Loch Droma

A835 To Inverness

A832

Beinn Enaiglair

Gleann na Sguaib

Eididh nan Clach Geala

Cadha Dearg 3

Seana Bhraigh

5

6

Cona' Mheall

Beinn Dearg

Am Faochagach

Loch Vaich

Strathvaich Lodge

Glenbeg

Gleann Beag

10

Carn Ban

7

9

Glasha Burn

Bodach Mor
Bodach Beag

8

An Socach

Alladale River

Carn Alladale

Gleann Mor

Deanich Lodge

Beinn a' Chaisteil

11

2

1. Beinn Dearg, Gleann na Sguaib
2. Beinn Dearg, Coire Ghranda
3. Cadha Dearg
4. Strone Nea
5. Seana Bhraigh, Luchd Coire
6. Seana Bhraigh, Feich Coire
7. Carn Ban, Toll Lochan
8. Meall nam Fuaran, NE Face
9. Bodach Beag, NW Face
10. Gleann Beag, Main Crag
11. An Socach, Alladale Slabs

2 Bonus 150m III   (1976)
Right of the second gully is a diagonal snow slope which joins the gully after 100m. Follow this for 60m then move diagonally right to gain and climb a narrow gully.

3 Rev. Ian Paisley Memorial Gully 150m I   (1967)
The second gully is also of straightforward snow.

4 Pickwick 180m II/III   (1976)
Right of the third gully is an obvious right-trending groove. Follow this and when the line becomes indefinite continue right and then swing back left into a large snow bay. There is a choice of finishing routes.

5 Orangeman's Gully 150m III/IV *   (1968)
The third gully is narrow, twisting and bow-shaped. The first pitch, which can be hard, starts up a chimney and goes left under an overhang on iced slabs. Continue up two more ice pitches to easy snow above the bend.

6 Emerald Edge 200m IV *   (1986)
This climbs a series of short ice walls and steep snow shelves on the buttress between the third and fourth gullies, finishing up the right edge of Emerald Gully. Not recommended in lean conditions. Start 50 metres right of Emerald Gully at an icefall forming the lowest point of the buttress.
1. 30m Climb the icefall for 15m to a snow basin, then follow this to a broad icefall forming a corner at its left edge.
2. 30m Climb the icefall, trending left for 20m, then climb a shallow groove leading to the first snow shelf.
3. 20m Climb the snow shelf direct to the base of an overhanging rock wall and belay.
4. 30m Take the steep groove to the left of the belay and continue over a rock wall to the second snow shelf.
5. 30m Follow the left-trending shelf to a belay 20m from the edge of Emerald Gully on the third rock step.
6. and 7. 60m Traverse 10m right to the base of an exposed ice pillar. Climb this and a steep turfed groove above, exiting onto another narrower snow shelf which is followed to a small cave. Climb the rocks above (the right shoulder of Emerald Gully) to the final snow slopes and summit cornice.

BEINN DEARG - GLEANN NA SGUAIB

5. Orangeman's Gully
7. Emerald Gully
8. Archway
9. Wee Freeze Gully
10. The Centre Party
11. Fenian Gully
12. Papist's Passage
13. The Wall of Retribution
14. The Tower of Babel

7   Emerald Gully   150m   IV ***   (1970)
The fourth gully. A highly recommended climb that can be hard in lean
conditions. It usually has at least two big ice pitches.

7a   Jewel in the Crown   160m   V   (1991)
This takes the impressive icy corner left of Emerald Gully. Unfortunately it is slow to come into condition. Start 20m below the first steep
pitch in Emerald Gully.
1. 25m Move left across mixed ground, then climb a steep icy corner
for 10m. Exit onto a snow terrace below the corner.
2. 20m The corner overhangs at first. A strenuous pull from the right
gains a frieze of icicles and entry into the corner. Climb this to a good
stance on the left.
3. 45m Move right and climb a steep ice wall, then continue up mixed
ground to a small cave in a terrace.
4. and 5. 70m Two pitches up ice, snow and mixed ground lead to the
cornice.

8   Archway   250m   III/IV **   (1988)
Start at the lowest point of the buttress left of Emerald Gully.
1. 2. and 3. 150m Follow open grooves just left of the steepest rocks
to reach a prominent cave-like depression beneath huge roofs.
4. 40m Climb up right through the roof of the cave.
5. and 6. 60m Follow an interesting gully and groove system up right
to finish.

9   Wee Freeze Gully   220m   IV   (1976)
In the middle of the buttress left of Emerald Gully is a right-slanting
line that appears to fade out at half height. In fact it continues further,
and a direct line can be taken from its termination to the top.

10   The Centre Party   200m   III   (1981)
Just right of the next gully (Fenian Gully) is a large shallow recess
which is climbed from bottom right to top left. Above this a shallow
gully trends right for a pitch to easier ground. Go straight up to a large
roof which is by-passed on the left.

11   Fenian Gully   170m   III/IV **   (1968)
The fifth of the main gullies provides quite a sustained climb but with
no particular crux. It is recommended as it is often well-iced.

12 Papist's Passage 180m III   (1968)
The sixth gully, just left of Fenian Gully. The main obstacle is a huge chockstone above a cave at 75m, climbed by the right-hand corner.

13 The Wall of Retribution 250m III/IV   (1981)
The buttress left of Papist's Passage is crossed by a broad snow terrace. Below this are two icefalls which start just right of where the base of the buttress begins to slant up left. Climb either icefall to the terrace. Above, a vegetated scoop leads to an upper icefall which proves unexpectedly steep, but leads to easier ground.

14 The Tower of Babel 130m Very Difficult   (1962)
This is the imposing corner-tower right of the Cadha Amadan, the wide gully separating the climbs described above from the West Buttress. It is reported to have the best rock on Beinn Dearg and offers an airy and pleasantly varied climb. It is possible to include a lower 30m tier by starting below the entrance to the gully, but this has an awkward earth pull-up (Mild Severe) to the top where an easy shelf leads in from the foot of the gully. Climb the crest of the tower more or less directly on excellent holds for 60m. Then climb a cracked rusty slab just left of the true crest for 20m. By a mossy recess on the left climb the steep wall ahead to a level promontory. Beyond are two steps; climb the first direct, then the second by a crack in the slab which forms the left wall of the ridge. Step up left into a square-cut recess and finish easily.
Winter: IV   (1989)
Follow the summer line. The two final walls are the hardest pitches.

THE WEST BUTTRESS
Beyond the Cadha Amadan the cliffs rise up to their greatest height in the so-called West Buttress. In fact the cliffs have a north-west facet (well seen as one approaches up the glen) then bend round to face north and finally face north-north-east above a small lochan below the col between Beinn Dearg and Meall nan Ceapraichean. The cliffs are highly vegetated in summer. In winter there are a few well-defined classic lines and large areas of buttress with rather ill-defined but enjoyable routes with many variations.

15 Inverlael Gully 240m II   (1963)
This is the obvious deep gully left of the Cadha Amadan. In summer there is a large chockstone at mid-height, but in an average winter this is mainly covered.

16 Gastronomes' Gully 350m I   (1967)
The shallow gully left of Inverlael Gully. It is reached by traversing left along a snow terrace from the Cadha Amadan above the lower tiers.

Left of Gastronomes' Gully the cliff is rather ill-defined but has some short icefalls high up that have been climbed. Coming round below the north face a prominent feature is a steep ice ribbon in the lower half of the cliff, The Ice Hose. Above this is a snowy bay from which one line goes diagonally right to a narrow icy cascade and another slants left. In between is a somewhat vague spur in the upper part of the face with a toe pointing down towards the Ice Hose, but much of this is foreshortened when viewed from below. The next climb takes a line right of the Ice Hose and eventually gains a rib on the right of the narrow icy cascade .

17 The Silken Ladder 350m III   (1969)
Start opposite the middle of the lochan, at least 50 metres right of The Ice Hose. Climb mixed turf, snow and slabby rocks then trend slightly left up a short icy section parallel to The Ice Hose. Continue up towards the narrow ice cascade and climb steeply onto the rib on its right. Follow this, then regain the ice trough above the cascade by a delicate step. Follow the trough and the easier rocks above to the top.

18 The Ice Hose 350m IV **   (1979)
Climb the prominent ice ribbon directly for 140m. From its top either follow the shallow gully leftwards or gain the buttress on the right (with the downward-pointing toe), get on to the crest and follow this to the top. A long sought after and recommended route.

The obvious long gully on the left of the buttress is Penguin Gully. The next two climbs are on the buttress to its right.

19 Eigerwanderer 350m III   (1969)
Start about 15 metres right of Penguin Gully at a minor V-shaped gully. Climb up, passing two side branches (that lead to Penguin Gully) and past a broad snow ledge which leads right towards The Ice Hose. The shallow gully continues as a steep shelf slanting right which is awkward to start. Follow this for 90m until the wide shallow gully leading up left from The Ice Hose is reached. This peters out after 60m, and 30m further go right to a broad shelf leading to a little col on West Buttress, immediately below the cornice.

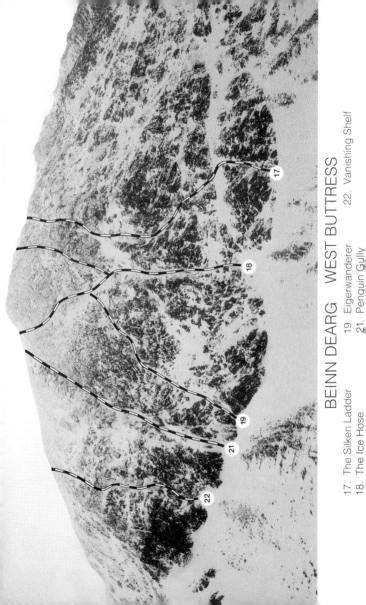

BEINN DEARG   WEST BUTTRESS

17. The Silken Ladder   19. Eigerwanderer   22. Vanishing Shelf
18. The Ice Hose   21. Penquin Gully

20 West Buttress 350m Difficult   (1962)
This takes the poorly-defined columnar rib on the right of Penguin
Gully. Although vegetated in its lower reaches the rock improves with
height and it offers a logical and sporting route of the traditional type.
Climb the rib for 75m, then traverse right and continue up a secondary
rib, turning two successive walls on the right as may be expedient.
After 90m of indeterminate climbing the choice narrows and the rib
becomes fluted. From a small cairn, go up left to climb a hidden crack
behind a giant detached finger. Climb the nose above on the right on
good rock, and continue straight up on good holds. The angle eases
and pleasant easy climbing and scrambling leads to the top.

21 Penguin Gully 350m III ***   (1964)
This classic climb, concealed during the approach, provides one of the
longest climbs on the mountain. It is probably one of the few ice routes
where consistent conditions prevail from January to April. A steep
icefall gives a direct start at grade III/IV. This can be avoided by a
dog-leg gully trending right then left (the start of Eigerwanderer) to join
the main gully about 75m above the start. The main gully contains
several ice pitches and may occasionally have a through route behind
a chockstone.

22 Vanishing Shelf 300m IV *   (1969)
This is the steep twisting gully left of Penguin Gully. It gives sustained
and interesting route-finding in the lower section. Thereafter the gully
proper terminates in a chimney *cul-de-sac* and the natural line continues by a spiralling shelf on the left.

COIRE GHRANDA   *(Map Ref 268 800)*

Coire Ghranda can be approached by either of two paths which leave
the roadside from the west and east ends of Loch Droma, 5km from
Braemore Junction. The west path leaves from Lochdrum and climbs
up the long sloping south-east tail of Beinn Enaiglair. On reaching the
ridge follow a branch track down to the Allt a' Gharbhrain, which must
be forded. Now climb up north-east to Loch nan Eilean and continue
northwards, contouring and climbing gently to reach the corrie. The
alternative approach leaves from the east end of Loch Droma and
follows a path which climbs around the end of the ridge to reach the
Allt a' Gharbhrain at a ruined sheiling near its mouth. The burn can be
difficult to cross in spate. Climb up north and left of Leac an Tuadh to
join the previous route at Loch nan Eilean.

For climbs on the upper cliff of Coire Ghranda it is also possible to go straight up from the higher reaches of the Allt a' Gharbhrain towards the top of the cliff (at about Map Ref 265 810) and then descend to the routes. Another possibility is to take the Gleann na Sguaib approach and cross the col between Beinn Dearg and Meall nan Ceapraichean.

The corrie has a wonderful wild atmosphere. On the north-west side are the broken cliffs of Cona'Mheall which get more sunshine and offer pleasant scrambling. Only one winter route and one summer route are recorded here. On the south-east side the cliffs are divided into a lower and an upper crag. The lower crag is long and slabby, starting near the loch, and sports only one summer route, by the ubiquitous Dr Bell. The upper crag, above and well right of the lower crag, is steep and forbidding. It is likely to be wet in summer but in winter has some excellent routes. There are several scenic gullies to the south of the lower crag.

Yon Spoot 250m III   (1969)
At the left (south) end of the lower crag is a deep gully cutting in rightwards, and blocked by a great chockstone. Yon Spoot is the gully immediately left of this. Further left are two more gullies, from one of which an attractive icefall rises out left near the top. On the first ascent of Yon Spoot three pitches near the top provided the main difficulty.

Grotto Gully 250m IV   (1987)
The deep gully with the great chockstone on the left of the lower crag. On the first attempt several small bergschrunds were crossed and a short rocky step climbed on the left to reach a formidable ice pitch falling from a deep grotto of icicles below the chockstone. After climbing 10m up the ice an escape right was made on to the heathery buttress and the gully rejoined above the ice pitch. The rest is straightforward snow. A true direct ascent would be very worthwhile.

Bell's Route 150m Severe †   (1946)
Start up the rocks close to their lowest point, above a tiny peninsula (the larger and northern of two) on the west side of the loch. The line keeps directly above the peninsula all the way. Go straight up slabs for 90m to the third of three terraces. Climb a difficult corner to the left, then scramble to the last terrace. Climb a steep, smooth slab on small holds, and at a critical point move left to gain a thin ledge (wedging

stance about 3m above). After another 5m make an exposed delicate move left into a steep, open overhanging corner with a stance in a recess 3m up it. Direct exit is impossible, so move out right on rounded rock, then zigzag up a niche beneath the plateau to a huge belay (very exposed and vegetated). The final exit is easy.

Snort Trail   185m   IV **   (1987)
On the left-hand side of the upper crag is a prominent smooth groove or shallow gully running the full height of the crag. Several short ice pitches lead to the base of the upper corner which contains a long thin ice ribbon (110m). Climb the corner (40m). Continue more easily to the cornice (35m).

Traumatic Interference   160m   IV   (1987)
This route takes the first line of weakness left of the steep central section of the upper cliff, about 30 metres right of Snort Trail.
1. 40m Trend diagonally left into the gully line.
2. 40m Climb a right-trending ramp in the gully over a couple of bulges and belay below the obvious icefall.
3. 40m Climb the icefall.
4. 40m Finish up grooves and icy corners.

Ice Bomb   115m   V/VI ***   (1988)
An excellent route up the very impressive fault in the centre of the cliff, passing just right of the prominent ice boss. Start beneath the ice boss at the highest point of the snow.
1. 30m Traverse 5m left on tufts and move up to gain a right-trending groove. Follow this, ignoring an easier-looking variant on slabs to the right at 15m, and belay 20m below and left of the prominent ice boss.
2. 20m Ascend diagonally right on mixed ground and cross the left end of a slanting barrier wall to gain snow beneath the ice boss.
3. 30m Climb the ice-choked groove just right of the boss to gain a constricted chimney leading to snow beneath the final sharply over-hanging corner.
4. 35m Move up the corner for 6m to an icicle formation. Tension left across the overhanging wall from an *in situ* Friend and pull onto slabs. Move up to the exposed arete on the left and across to a groove. Ascend this for 3m, move back right to the arete and continue easily up the slope on the right to the top.

Body Freeze   150m   IV *   (1986)
Towards the right side of the upper crag is a prominent ice-choked
groove in the upper section. This is the substance of the route. Start
at the obvious line leading up to the ice.
1. and 2. 60m Trend right to a stance below a steep step.
3. 30m Surmount the step and continue to below the ice groove.
4. and 5. 60m Follow the excellent ice groove to the top.

Spaghetti Gully   240m   I   (1967)
This is the twisting gully on the Cona'Mheall side of the corrie (well
seen from the summit of Beinn Dearg).

Tower of Enchantment   80m   Very Difficult   (1990)
From the outlet of Loch a' Choire Ghranda, the left skyline of the Cona'
Mheall face appears as a fine tower. Scramble up to the base of the
final tower and traverse to its right side which forms a continuous
slabby wall. There is a choice of lines, with a nice finish up a steep
crack.

CADHA DEARG   *(Map Ref 276 865)*

There is a steep north-facing crag at the head of Gleann a' Chadha
Dheirg which, in the right conditions, can provide good winter climbing.
The most straightforward approach is from Inverlael. Follow the
forestry road up Gleann na Sguaib but take a left branch and get onto
the stalkers' path that heads up the Allt Gleann a' Mhadaidh. This
continues east for about 6km, whence a descent can be made to reach
the crag. The crag can also be reached from the Loch a' Choire Mhoir
bothy below Seana Bhraigh, and from the Glenbeg bothy.

Geddes's Gully   250m   V   (1986)
A good climb, though some of it may be lost in very heavy snow
conditions. The gully splits the highest part of the crag and slants
slightly right. On the first ascent there were two steep sections. The
big icicle in the final amphitheatre was not reachable and steep thin
ice was followed just to its right.

Captain Patience   280m   V   (1986)
Climb the first pitch of Geddes's Gully, then trend left heading for a
short chimney at mid-height. Climb this, then trend back right to finish

10m left of Geddes's Gully. On the first ascent this route gave five long ice pitches, initially on ice smears and frozen turf and higher up on thickly plated ice.

STRONE NEA   *(Map Ref 188 847)*

This gneiss outcrop overlooks the Braemore to Ullapool road about 1km south of the head of Loch Broom. A steep twenty-minute climb through a plantation leads to the foot of the rocks. Although seeming shattered and vegetatious, the rock is not as bad as it looks.

The Shaft   90m   Very Difficult   (1962)
Climb the crest of a slender pillar on the left of the main rock mass, with a choice of two parallel ribs at the start.

The Shaft, West Face   120m   Difficult
Follow an obvious scoop direct through lush vegetation. The upper part is arboreal.

Glen Lael Buttress   120m   Very Difficult
The next buttress up the glen.

Summit Slabs   60m   Very Difficult
These lie on the main crag right of The Shaft. They are reached by the intervening gully and give a pleasant climb.

Nick-Nack Wall   90m   Severe   (1962)
On the main crag opposite The Shaft there is a 'blank' wall corrugated with small incuts. Climb this to an eyrie above the obvious overhanging crack in the centre of the crag. Above the eyrie step right, surmount a short bulge and follow discontinuous rocky ribs to finish.

Ivy Chimney   90m   Severe
On the steep right wall of the main crag is a vertical chimney with several trees. Climb this in four pitches.

ROYAL HOTEL BUTTRESS   *(Map Ref 134 944)*

This compact quartzite crag lies about 500 metres east of Ullapool above the town. Approach via a minor road going east from the A835 and take a path through the gate marked 'Hillwalk this way'. A fifteen minute walk leads to the crag which lies at the crest of a shallow gully on its left side. The crag faces south and is sheltered and has few pronounced features. A short wall on the extreme left, a grassy ramp and to its right a corner border the main wall which is very steep, clean and sound and has a few thin crack lines. The routes are described from left to right.

Yellow Edge   20m   Very Difficult   (1988)
The pleasant corner that forms the left edge of the main wall is much easier than it looks.

Telegraph Road   25m   VS 4b   (1988)
Start right of Yellow Edge in the centre of the south wall. Climb straight up to a prominent jutting flake and then take the wall above. A fine climb and well worth doing.

Telstar   25m   HVS 5a   (1988)
Where the crags swings south-east is a little hanging rib, a few metres beyond Telegraph Road. Climb the bold rib, then up to shelves to finish by a crack.

Beached Whale   25m   E1 5b **   (1991)
Between Telstar and Morse Crack is a little square-cut overhang low down. Climb over this and then straight up the very steep wall to a crack and shelf. Gain the cracked rib above and step right into a corner. Climb this to an awkward landing to finish up the top wall of Morse Crack. A very fine sustained route, well protected.

Morse Crack   25m   VS 4c   (1988)
The crack just right of Beached Whale. Either enter it direct or from the right. Climb the crack, which is sustained and well protected, to a shelf. Finish by a tricky little wall.

The Linesmen   25m   VS 5a   (1991)
Start right of Morse Crack at some boulders. Take a line of foot-ledges left, crossing Morse Crack. Make strenuous moves across the horizontal crack of Beached Whale then, keeping at this level, swing round the corner in a fine position. Move easily up and left, climb the crux of Telegraph Road, then step left to finish up the arete bordering Yellow Edge.

CREAG NAM BROC   *(Map Ref 147 958)*

This unusual metamorphosed sandstone crag, which stands on a plinth of limestone, lies to the north of the Ullapool River opposite a deep limestone quarry. It faces south-west and the clean and solid rock has superb friction. The main feature is a huge central roof. The easiest access is from a bridge on the private road at Map Ref 154 953, whence a pleasant walk of a few hundred metres leads to the crag. All the routes were climbed by G.E.Little and J.M.G.Findlay.

Very Gneiss Wall   25m   Severe *   (1991)
This climbs a wedge of clean red rock between a sapling-filled groove and a tree-sprouting crack. Start on a limestone plinth by a briar and climb the centre of the red wall on good holds.

One Armed Bandit   35m   HVS *   (1991)
A largely amiable route with a sensational and strenuous crux.
1. 20m From the foot of Very Gneiss Wall climb up and left to a cracked slab which leads to a detached block on an exposed edge (at the left end of the huge roof).
2. 15m 5b Round the corner, above a small roof, a horizontal horn of rock is just out of reach. Gain the horn then move left to a small ledge. Finish direct on superb rock.

Primitive Dance   20m   E3 5c ***   (1991)
On the left flank of the crag two obvious lines of weakness break a steep, multi-coloured wall. The left comprises a diagonal fault running up to a slim corner. This route starts up the right-hand weakness, an open, deceptively overhanging glassy groove. This gives a series of strenuous moves (good protection). The thin crack above is easier.

Head to Head   25m   E2 5b **   (1991)
Start just right of the left end of the diagonal fault left of Primitive Dance. Climb the wall to the fault, move right on side-pulls to gain the slim corner, then climb the corner to the dubious capping block. Pull left onto the edge to finish.

Short and Sweet   12m   VS 5a *   (1991)
Start at the rounded flake on the left flank of the crag, just left of the right-trending fault. Climb bulging red rock to better holds on the wall above, continue to a shallow groove and follow this through overhanging rock (strenuous) to belay on a ledge right of a sapling.

SEANA BHRAIGH

926m   (Map Ref 281 878)

Seana Bhraigh offers a variety of winter climbs in a remote setting. Although the mountain is quite low, it often retains snow until late in the season. Most of the climbs are in the north-facing Luchd Coire directly under the summit plateau, but there are a few other climbs in outlying corries. A good base is the MBA-maintained bothy at Loch a' Choire Mhoir.

Access

The easiest approach is from the north. Leave the Bonar Bridge to Ledmore Junction road (A837) at Oykel Bridge and follow the unmade estate road up Strath Mulzie for about 10km to Corriemulzie Lodge. From here it is an easy walk of about 8km to Loch a' Choire Mhoir, followed by a straightforward climb of 200m to reach Luchd Coire. There are longer approaches from the west and south. From just north of Ullapool an estate road leads east for about 13km to Rhidorroch Old Lodge, whence a walk of about 12km via the Allt nan Caorach leads to Loch a' Choire Mhoir. Alternatively there is a rough approach from Gleann Beag to the south. Follow a path up to Lochs Sruban Mora and Sruban Beaga and cross the plateau to descend into Coire Mor. Or, if staying at the Glenbeg bothy, a direct approach to the summit of Seana Bhraigh may be preferred, followed by a descent into Luchd Coire.

LUCHD COIRE

This is the large north-facing corrie directly beneath the summit plateau. On the left is An Sgurr, which presents a steep face corrugated into six scoops and ribs bounded on the south by a gentle slanting gully. Moving right, the wall then falls back in a face containing Bealach Gully. The Chute is the obvious broad gully running down from the plateau at the back of the small inner corrie. The right face of this inner corrie has cliffs, only 90m high, containing Query Cleft. Below them lies easy ground which slants up right to meet the plateau; an easy descent route. Next right is the Central Massif with two parallel 'posts', slightly reminiscent of Coire Ardair; Press-On Gully slants up to their right from a shared start. The right boundary of the Massif is the deep-cut Pomegranate Gully, with Flowerpot Buttress up the edge on its left. Beyond this lie the steep Diamond Buttress, Pelican Rib, Summit Buttress and Far West Buttress, separated respectively by Diamond Diedre, Pelican Gully and Sham Gully. The cliffs accumulate a respectable quantity of snow. Some pitches on most of the easy gullies will bank out under a heavy build-up.

1 Bealach Gully 90m II   (1963)
Start up The Chute and break left about 90m below the plateau. The last 60m may contain two pitches.

2 The Chute 300m I   (1963)
The broad gully in the south-east corner of the corrie provides a convenient descent route.

3 Query Cleft 100m III   (1963)
The next gully right of The Chute is a deep twisting slit, sometimes hard to pick out. For the first 25m keep on ice left of overhanging rocks to a long snow shelf. Steep snow for 30m leads to the deepest part of the slit, where an ice-bridge sometimes forms overhead. A 15m pitch in the slit and 30m of steep snow lead to the cornice.

4 Y Gully Buttress 300m II   (1983)
The big sprawling buttress left of Sunday Post. A Y-shaped gully splits the frontal face. The lower 200m follows the stem and right branch of the Y. The latter becomes a ramp, which peters out on the right of the buttress, whence pleasant mixed ground leads to the crest. This leads easily, with an optional tower, to the plateau.

5 Sunday Post 300m III   (1963)
The left of two conspicuous gullies either side of a central rib on the Central Massif. A good climb with sustained interest.

6 Monday Post 300m II   (1963)
The right-hand gully. Escape is possible to the right.

7 Press-On Gully 300m I   (1963)
From the bottom of the central rib a gully slopes up right. This gives a long steepening snow climb, but without pitches. The cornice may give difficulty.

SEANA BHRAIGH, LUCHD COIRE

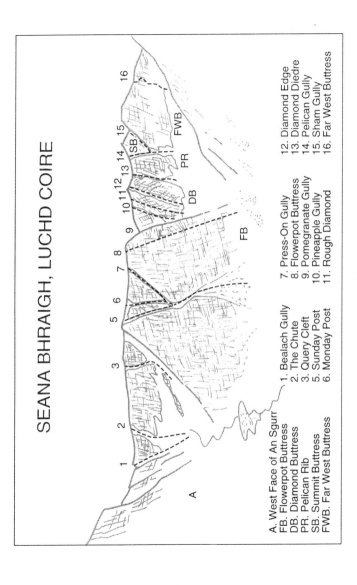

A. West Face of An Sgurr
FB. Flowerpot Buttress
DB. Diamond Buttress
PR. Pelican Rib
SB. Summit Buttress
FWB. Far West Buttress

1. Bealach Gully
2. The Chute
3. Query Cleft
5. Sunday Post
6. Monday Post

7. Press-On Gully
8. Flowerpot Buttress
9. Pomegranate Gully
10. Pineapple Gully
11. Rough Diamond

12. Diamond Edge
13. Diamond Diedre
14. Pelican Gully
15. Sham Gully
16. Far West Buttress

8 Flowerpot Buttress 270m III   (1978)
This takes a natural line near the well-defined right edge of the Central Massif. The route crosses a big raking terrace at three-quarters height and continues directly to the top.

9 Pomegranate Gully 300m II   (1963)
The long deep gully between the Central Massif and Diamond Buttress. It may contain several ice pitches, the first just under halfway up and another about 100m higher.

10 Pineapple Gully 200m III   (1978)
The gully on the left flank of Diamond Buttress. It is entered by climbing the right wall of Pomegranate Gully, starting a short way below its first pitch.

11 The Rough Diamond 270m IV   (1971)
Start at the left side of the steep frontal face of Diamond Buttress, in a small recess at the foot of Pomegranate Gully. Go straight up the flank of the buttress, following a line of weakness with a steep chimney near the top. Finish close to the top of Pineapple Gully.

12 Diamond Edge 250m III/IV   (1978)
This climbs the frontal crest of Diamond Buttress, right of The Rough Diamond. Start left of the crest, up the higher of two obvious right-slanting ramps. Finish up a big diedre cleaving the upper nose. An elegant line with fine situations.

13 Diamond Diedre 240m II   (1965)
The prominent diedre right of Diamond Buttress has several pitches.

14 Pelican Gully 240m II   (1964)
The next gully to the right holds snow better than most others in the corrie. It shares a start with Sham Gully, but goes left underneath Summit Buttress while Sham Gully forks right. There may be an easy pitch before the fork, another just after the fork and a broken mixed pitch higher up.

15 Sham Gully 180m I   (1963)
The gully slanting right between Summit Buttress and Far West Buttress. There are no difficulties after the fork.

16 Far West Buttress 180m II   (1965)
Climb well to the right of the buttress, starting from a big 'Fairy Cave'
at the foot. Finish on the north ridge of Seana Bhraigh well west of the
summit. A more direct line would be harder.

FEICH COIRE

Feich Coire lies east of Luchd Coire, separated from it by the fine ridge
of An Sgurr (called Creag an Duine on the OS map), which is less
forbidding to climb than it appears. The corrie is easily reached from
the bothy at Loch a'Choire Mhoir.

Eagle Gully 240m II/III   (1978)
This is the gully in the back right-hand corner of the corrie. There
should be one or two ice pitches at the start and a short easy pitch
near the top.

Sagittarius 400m II   (1983)
This is the thin gully line, very clearly seen from the bothy, situated at
the east end of the broken south wall of Feich Coire. Climb initial
overlapping slabs, or heather on the right, to the upper part of the gully.
This gives good snow climbing with one or two short pitches.

CARN BAN; COIRE TOLL LOCHAN
(Map Ref 330 880)

This lovely secluded corrie of Carn Ban (842m, Map Ref 338 876) lies
about 3km east of Loch a' Choire Mhoir. It has one obvious climb, **Toll
Gate** (210m, III), starting almost immediately above the lochan.

MEALL NAM FUARAN
670m   (Map Ref 387 897)

There is a little climbing here, on the crag at Map Ref 391 897.
Campsite Cleft (210m, II/III) takes the longest gully which slants
diagonally leftwards up the highest part of the north-east face.

BODACH BEAG
837m   (Map Ref 355 878)

The following climb is on the north-west face.

Freevater Gully   220m   III   (1986)
From the approach up the Glasha Burn two buttresses can be seen
below the summit of Bodach Beag. They are separated by a broad
couloir. From the foot of this couloir a hidden gully cuts diagonally left
up the left-hand buttress. This provides good sport for the first 100m,
with a number of short ice pitches.

GLENBEG

Gleann Beag lies at the head of the longest of the Strathcarron glens,
Gleann Mor. The large outcrops near the head of the glen are still
undeveloped, but much of the rock is vegetated or lichenous and may
not give worthwhile summer routes. However, for the lover of remote
winter climbs it is a good centre as Seana Bhraigh, Coire Ghranda of
Beinn Dearg and several other remote corries are within reach.

Access
The MBA-maintained bothy at Map Ref 314 835 is the obvious place
to stay. The easiest approach is from the south, leaving the A835
Garve to Ullapool road at Black Bridge, about 3km east of Aultguish
Inn. Drive up Strath Vaich on a good private road (if the gate is
unlocked); 1km before Strathvaich Lodge, just before a bridge, a
locked gate bars access to a road which continues up the east side of
Loch Vaich, crosses the watershed and enters Gleann Beag about
3km below the bothy. Permission to use the road may be obtainable
from the Strathvaich Estate; a vehicle with high clearance is advisable.
Another approach is from Strathcarron, up the unmetalled road in
Gleann Mor to Deanich Lodge. There is a locked gate near Alladale
Lodge and permission to use the road may be sought from the
Glencalvie Estate. Again a high clearance vehicle is advised.

Niagra Slab   170m   Very Difficult   (1966)
These slabs face south-west and are at Map Ref 345 846, about 150m
above and 1km short of the road-head from Strathvaich. They are on
the north side of the glen and are well seen as one approaches along
the road from the Strathvaich watershed. Start at the foot of the slab

where it is very narrow and go straight up the centre. The crux is at about 25m. Higher one is forced to the right side of the slab (belay), then across left to a watery shelf at 105m. For the next 30m follow the watercourse. Turn the main overlap just right of the waterfall and finish up 30m of pleasant slabs.

THE MAIN CRAG   (Map Ref 320 838)

This is on the north side of the glen, about 1km west of the roadhead, on the south flank of Carn Loch Sruban Mora. The crag has two tiers; additionally there are short steep exposures of rock below the tiers and west up the glen for 1km. The top tier is much the most formidable, consisting of a tower-like bastion, separated by a deep chimney from a clean wall on its right. Both the bastion and the wall are vertical or overhanging throughout and are about 75m high. The adverse lie of the strata makes approach difficult from the west, but if approaching from this direction keep to the floor of the glen until below the rocks.

Deanaich Slabs   180m   Moderate   (1962)
The right flank of the Main Crag, which faces the road, is a sea of waterworn slabs. They are at an easy angle and may be climbed almost anywhere.

Rowan Chimney   60m   Mild Severe   (1962)
The deep-cut chimney between the bastion and the wall on its right gives a bizarre and grimy route. There is a rowan at 20m, a short deep chimney above and a culminating pitch round the outside of two large chockstones.

Unnamed Wall   40m   E3 6a †   (1975)
This route may be either left or right of Rowan Chimney. It takes a line of weakness in a clean, steep wall (two peg runners) which is more difficult than it appears. Climb steeply to a slabby shelf, step left and climb the steep wall to the top.

The Madonna   Very Difficult   (1962)
Invisible from the roadhead, but well seen from about 1km further up the glen, is a twin-headed pinnacle lying a few hundred metres west of the Main Crag. The short side might be awkward but on the first ascent the pinnacle was climbed direct from the valley side. A difficult stride across a 20m deep crevasse was the only obstacle.

Campiglio   105m   Very Difficult   (1975)
This is the ridge to the right of the gully below The Madonna, reached
by going right about 80m below The Madonna. Follow the ill-defined
crest close to the steep left side.

COTTAGE SLABS
These are on the south side of the glen, standing about 1km west of
Glenbeg bothy. The slabs are too easy to be of more than passing
interest. Both branches of an obvious Y-crack towards the right have
been climbed (Moderate).

AN SOCACH (ALLADALE)
745m   (Map Ref 375 873)

The 240m high Alladale Wall is on the north-east face of An Socach
at the head of Glen Alladale, about 8km from Alladale Lodge. Leave
the main road at Ardgay, just south of Bonar Bridge, and take the road
up either side of Strathcarron. Turn south over the river at the telephone kiosk at The Craigs and continue past Amat Lodge to Alladale
Lodge, about 18km from the main road. There is a gate which is
sometimes locked a little short of the Lodge, but permission to pass
this can usually be obtained from the Factor, Benmore Estate Office,
Ardgay. Just before Alladale Lodge a rough track goes down to the
left. About 2km along this, beyond the woods, is an excellent bothy. A
good path continues from here, eventually turning right up a glen
towards Bodach Mor, but a branch path descends to the river whence
good going on the south side leads to the crag past the gnarled
remnants of the Alladale Forest.
     When first seen from the bothy the cliff seems tiny, and does not
reveal its full height until one is directly below it. The rock is an
extraordinary form of glaciated quartzite, polished so smooth as to
lose all the normal quartzite characteristics. There is no scree and less
loose rock than on any comparable Scottish cliff. The climbing is mainly
delicate balance work on small wrinkles. Protection is poor, belays
difficult and even pegs are often impossible to place. To obtain any
protection a climber is forced to use cunning, perhaps an added
recommendation. Being clean polished, the rock is disproportionately
affected by rain, but dries out almost immediately.

Neart nan Gaidheal, Ardmair (Climber, Martin Burrows-Smith)

The cliff consists of an East Wing, unimpressive and ugly but fairly clean. A vague grassy Rake divides it from the Central Buttress. Rather broken in the lower part, it is absolutely clean for over 150m. It is separated from the West Face by the only notable feature on the cliff, The Gully, which is deeply cut in its lower half but higher turns into a shallow scoop. The West Face is again clean rock for the upper 120m. Many lines are seen across all the faces slanting up to the right, but these are not continuous and can seldom be used for escape. Owing to the monolithic nature of the rock there are no obvious lines of weakness to provide definite routes.

The climbs are described from left to right.

1 Narcissus 180m HVS   (1975)
This climbs through the obvious diamond-shaped depression in the lower part of the East Wing. Start in the centre of the depression. Climb up to a weakness in an overlap, then move right on the lip and continue to a ledge. Move left and climb slabs to steepening rock and overlaps. Move left to the foot of a corner and climb this to a grass ledge. Traverse right along the fault-line then go up to a broken corner. Climb the left wall to a grass ledge, move right into a depression then scramble to the top.

2 Snowdrop 180m VS †   (1967)
Start near the wet recess at the centre of the East Wing and scramble to a small corner and belay. Climb to near the right-hand corner of a diamond-shaped depression. Follow a line parallel to the edge past a grassy groove on the left to a corner above the top of the depression. Climb the corner and exit left to a stance. Follow a narrow quartz band to below an overhang and traverse left to a large grass ledge. Move down the ledge to a small overhang and some quartz and continue to the top by short walls, corners, grooves and traverses to finish by some trees. Peg belays were used throughout.

The next few climbs are on the Central Buttresses. There are two stepped ledges on the lower buttress leading up left, across the main lines of the crag. The rock below Upper Ledge is somewhat discontinuous. Another notable feature is the group of central overhangs,

Skeletons, Ardmair (Climber, Graham Dudley)

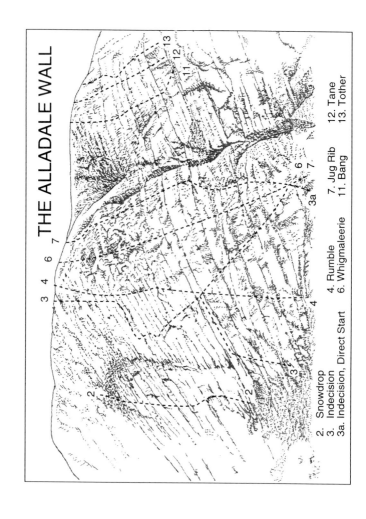

THE ALLADALE WALL

2. Snowdrop
3. Indecision
3a. Indecision, Direct Start

4. Rumble
6. Whigmaleerie

7. Jug Rib
11. Bang

12. Tane
13. Tother

above mid-height and slightly left of centre. The exposure of clean rock is enormous.

3 Indecision 240m Hard Severe (1963)
The route keeps to the left side of the buttress; it has some unsound rock. Start at the foot of the Rake and climb broken rocks to a platform with blocks. Now climb ledges and short faces to gain a prominent ledge which appears to girdle the face (but which actually peters out halfway). Traverse right and climb the ledge to its junction with the Upper (stepped) Ledge, which is followed left to its end with a good belay above. Traverse right up a crack, then hard left to a seam of white rock and a ledge. Go up the ledge to the right and a small crack (crux) onto a clean face. By a short left traverse gain a ledge which leads away right above the Central Overhangs (35m, sustained). Two pleasant easier pitches lead to the top.

Direct Start: 120m Severe (1963)
This follows the Upper Ledge to its junction with the Original Route. Start at the big overhang at the bottom right of the Central Buttress, and go up and slightly right for 20m to loose blocks beside a grass ledge. A 6m traverse then leads to the bottom of the Upper Ledge, whence the line is obvious. A good natural line, but rather spoilt by frequent escapes to the left.

4 Rumble 255m VS (1968)
A direct line up the Central Buttress, passing the Central Overhangs at the obvious break. Start directly beneath the break and climb directly and with increasing difficulty towards it. Above Upper Ledge, climb a delicate slab leading to a narrow shelf (slanting down left to a small rowan on Indecision). Move right along the shelf and climb a steep slab into a leaning diedre in a direct line beneath the main overhang. Go up the diedre a short distance and then cross the slab on the left (wet), to surmount the bulge above by its left edge. Belay on grass ledge. Climb the next slabs to twin cracks, which are followed through the overhangs to easier ground. Peg belays throughout.

5 Guano Slabs 240m Very Difficult (1977)
This takes a direct line between Rumble and Whigmaleerie. Climb straight up to the left end of a slanting overhanging crack about 100m up. Climb in two pitches to a prominent nose on the skyline and continue to the top.

6 Whigmaleerie 240m Severe   (1962)
A central line on Central Buttress, starting at the same point as
Indecision, Direct Start, and by-passing the Central Overhangs on
their right. The overhanging crack about 100m up (as in Guano Slabs)
helps to locate the climb. Take a fairly direct line, trending slightly left.
After 90m there are no further escapes and the angle steepens; climb
to the right of a slanting overhang crack (12m, crux). Continue on steep
but rougher rock to easy ground.

7 Jug Rib 210m Severe   (1963)
Start as for Indecision Direct Start, keep to the right side of the buttress,
and follow the line of least resistance. Climb slabs for three pitches to
a big grassy ledge encroaching from The Gully (peg belays). Climb
the steep curved ridge above on good holds to a ledge (20m). Climb
to a ledge and thread belay (30m). A prominent mark halfway up is a
break between two 'scrolls' of rock. Climb through the break. From
here two good easier pitches lead to easy ground.

8 Gully Buttress 35m Severe   (1963)
At its steep pitch, The Gully twists right of a clean rock tier. The tier
gives a fine pitch surmounting a small overhang at 10m, followed by
a groove trending right. The rock is perfect.

9 The Gully 150m Very Difficult   (1963)
This gully separates Central Buttress from the West Face. Stay in the
gully until it widens to a grassy scoop halfway up, where difficulties
end. The final pitch is the only one of any merit. Pleasant scrambling
on good rock to the left of the scoop leads to the top.

The climbing on the West Wing is very good, on slightly more helpful
rock, but again without many natural belays. The lower half of the face
(below a big grassy ledge encroaching from the right) is very vegetated
and best avoided. Above, the rock is clean for 120m with excellent
climbing (except on the east flank). There are three prominent features
in the upper half; a large triangle on the left, a double overhang on the
lower right and a single overhang above it.

10 East Route 240m Very Difficult   (1963)
This rather indeterminate route keeps to the left of the face. It starts
at the lowest rocks and then climbs the left side of the triangle. The
rock is loose in places (not recommended).

11 Bang 150m Severe **   (1966)
Climbs straight up the middle of the face. Start at the foot of Tane.
Traverse left to a large central pocket of grass at a slightly higher level.
Now climb straight up the central slabs to a grass ledge (45m, peg
belay; the first 10m are the crux). Climb the black cracked diedre on
the left, to the right of the triangle, to a very steep exit right to a ledge
(25m, peg belay). Continue straight up more slabs, with a delicate
section at 6m. Now the angle eases, allowing variation. Move left to a
grassy diedre with a crack (30m) and finish by an enjoyable pitch to
the right (40m).

12 Tane 135m Very Difficult **   (1963)
Start at the large grass ledge projecting into the West Face from the
right halfway up. Above is the twin overhang and above that the upper
overhang. Climb the incipient rib towards the twin overhang; pass this
through the gap in the middle to a ledge (peg belay shared with Tother).
Continue direct (crux) to the right of the upper overhang, and so to the
top.

13 Tother 135m Very Difficult **   (1963)
This starts about 12 metres right of Tane and goes right of the twin
overhangs by a crack (crux) to the ledge and peg belay. Now traverse
up right across steep walls to a broken depression with a steep rib on
its right. Climb the rib to the top.

Coigach and Assynt

This chapter includes some readily accessible excellent sandstone crags, as well as the more remote cliffs of Suilven and Quinag. Because of the relatively low altitude the winter climbing potential here is not high, but there is at least one route which must rate as one of the best winter expeditions of its standard in Scotland: The Fiddler's Nose. Also in Assynt is one of the finest sea-stacks off the mainland coast, The Old Man of Stoer.

RHUE SEA-CLIFFS

These cliffs, in the region of Map Ref 093 976, lie on the north-west side of the Rubha Cadail peninsula and are reached by turning off the A835 about 3km north of Ullapool and driving down a dead-end road to Rhue itself; limited parking. From there, walk west (crossing the fence at a stile) to the shore about 200 metres right of the lighthouse, and follow it round under the cliffs. This can be done at most states of the tide if the sea is not too high or rough. The more easterly crags can be reached by cutting north over the hill and using one of the scrambling descents to sea-level. These approaches take about 10 minutes.

Generally the rock is sea-washed Torridonian sandstone but in places it is affected by seepage, particularly the Main Cliff. The cliffs face north-west and get the sun in the evening. Protection is generally good; big Friends are useful in some of the big horizontal breaks. Although variable, the rock runs to surprising holds in places. Stakes are in place at the top of the Main Cliff, but these should be used in pairs and checked well before use.

The western section is the largest and most extensive area. It is dominated by the huge central buttress of The Main Cliff with its jutting roofs. The whole area can be traversed at sea-level at most states of the tide if the sea is not too rough. The exception is on the right of The First Prow which has a short, interesting hand traverse at high tide. When approaching from the west, the first feature is The Embankment Wall; a short wall which gives good easy bouldering and easy micro routes. This abuts a jagged buttress, The First Prow, with a slab corner on its right.

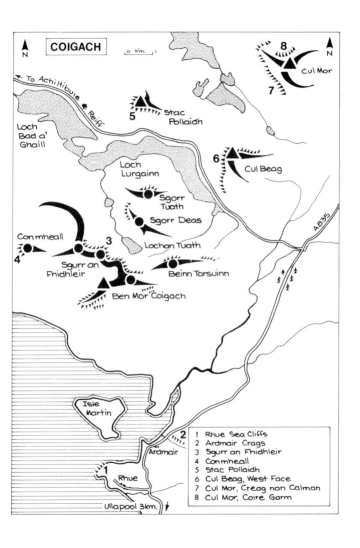

COIGACH

0 Km. 1

To Achiltibuie

Reiff

Loch Bad a' Ghaill

Loch Lurgainn

Stac Pollaidh

Cul Mor

Cul Beag

Sgorr Tuath

Sgorr Deas

Lochan Tuath

Conmheall

Sgurr an Fhidhleir

Ben Mor Coigach

Beinn Tarsuinn

A835

Isle Martin

Ardmair

Rhue

Ullapool 3km.

1 Rhue Sea Cliffs
2 Ardmair Crags
3 Sgurr an Fhidhleir
4 Conmheall
5 Stac Pollaidh
6 Cul Beag, West Face
7 Cul Mor, Creag nan Calman
8 Cul Mor, Coire Gorm

THE FIRST PROW

This is defined on the right by a slabby corner (a possible descent), and on the left by the deep corner of Black Rain.

Halcyon Days   15m   HVS 5b
Start just right of the jutting prow left of the slab corner. Climb overhangs past a thread and into a short hanging corner. Go up and left to finish.

Food for Thought   12m   E2 5c
Climbs just left of the nose. Take a short corner to below the roof and undercling right to gain the crack above. Exit right below the top roof.

The Bee's Knees   12m   E1 5b
The short deep right-facing corner in the middle of the wall. Climb directly to, then up the corner. Step right and climb up using holds by a thin crack to the top.

Rhumorours   12m   VS 4c
The clean-cut left-facing corners about 2 metres right of Black Rain are climbed direct.

Black Rain   12m   VS 4c
The deep corner gives a good, well protected route, but is slow to dry.

THE UNDERCUT WALL

The next section of cliff has a distinctive horizontal slot just above high tide mark and a band of big roofs guarding access to the wall above.

Ruder Games   15m   HVS 5b
Start about 3 metres left of Black Rain at a short overhanging flake crack running up into a large hanging flake. Climb the crack to the flake, step right and continue more easily to the top.

Beechgrove   18m   Severe
Start near the left end of the slot at an obvious slabby break through the roofs. Pull up the corner onto the slab and go left below the roofs to a slab corner leading to the top.

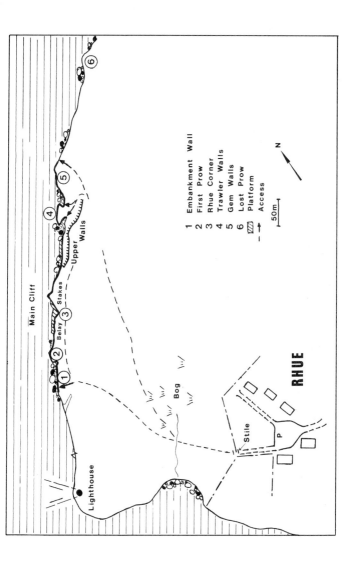

THE MAIN CLIFF

This is the highest and most imposing section of the cliff, dominated by the huge roofed prow; a line for the future! Before this, however, is the obvious Rhue Corner with its big smooth side walls cut by a horizontal slot.

Rhue Corner   20m   E1 5b
The big corner with smooth side walls gives a fine climb.

Perestroika   25m   E4 6a
The obvious open bottomless groove in the big wall left of Rhue Corner. Start right of the groove and climb up to a horizontal break. Traverse left to a crack in a block and climb the groove to the top.

Cat's Whiskers   25m   E2 5c
The obvious corner crack with twin roofs left of the giant prow. Start below the right end of the lower roof and climb the wall up to it, then follow the crack round the next roof to the upper slab. Go up and left to climb the crack in the leaning headwall.

The Barchan   20m   HVS 5a
On the left of the Main Cliff, before it becomes vegetated and the platform becomes more broken, is a buttress with a pot-holed roof high up. Start in the centre of the buttress right of two easy ramps going left. Climb up by short walls and cracks to a higher slab going left to the buttress edge. Return diagonally right to gain a big dirty groove and finish up the crack in its right wall.

THE UPPER WALLS

Moving left, the cliff becomes more broken, consisting of several walls and buttresses with a good deal of vegetation, and is set further back from the sea. At the left side is an inland bay with a gully and huge chokestone descent down broken rock. Left of this is the obvious prow of the Trawler Walls with an inland and seaward face.

Torridonian Sandman   30m   E1 5b
The central line on the lower and cleanest wall near the left end. Scramble up grassy rock to a block and climb the wall via a thin crack and corner. Move right and climb the bulging crack and groove. Finish precariously right and back left, or abseil off.

THE TRAWLER WALLS

These are the walls on either side of the prow, the sea face being the more extensive and stretching to an easy slabby area on the right which gives access up and down.

Fawlty Towers 15m HVS 5a
The tower at the back of the sheltered bay and left of the huge chockstone. Start at the lowest point beneath the central of three cracks. Climb up into the crack and use it to gain a large ledge. Move up and right to the continuation crack, pull over and climb straight up the wall above, or continue rightwards.

Back Stroke 10m E2 5c
The thin crack on the landward face of the prow, climbed direct.

Front Crawl 10m VS 4b
The nose of the prow. Start at the lowest rocks and climb to the break which is followed left onto the nose itself. Finish direct on huge holds.

Scuttlebum 12m E1 5b
Start just left of the prow at a large scalloped recess. Climb a series of walls and breaks to under the top roof, then traverse right to finish round the edge.

Madame Butterfly 12m E1 5b
Takes the left-slanting flake crack left of Scuttlebum. Start off a block and climb a short shallow corner to the break, then follow the crack.

Red Admiral 12m HVS 5a
The open right-facing corner in the upper wall is reached as for Madame Butterfly.

Swimming with Sharks 10m VS 5a
The wide crack with a roof low down, left again.

The Jester 8m E1 5a
The blunt arete left of Swimming with Sharks. Gain the jutting block from the left.

Looney Tunes 8m VS 4c
The crack in the left side of the wall where it meets the easy slab.

Picnic Crack   10m   Very Difficult
Left of the area of easy slabs is a crack running up the steeper slab.
Start at a huge flat boulder and after a short steep start, follow the
crack.

After the slabby area, there is another section of short cliff which is
bounded on its left by a deep gully cutting diagonally back inland. The
rib on its right and the bottom of the gully gives a descent.

GEM WALLS
This is the area left of the diagonal gully which, although generally
shorter, is of excellent rock with good lines. It starts with a higher
recessed area and further left is characterised by some large blocky
roofs. This area dries fairly quickly and there is a descent at its left
end.

The Ostrich   20m   E1 5b
Start just right of the deep corner in the centre of the wall and gain a
strange scooped flange from the right. Move up and left to a thin crack
which leads to the horizontal break. Move right along this, then finish
by the fault and cracks right of the end of the roof.

Rack or Ruin   20m   E1 5b
A fine route up the highest part of the face. Gain and climb the deep
left-facing corner and continue up to the top roof. Cross this by the
right-hand of twin cracks, then step left into the corner and so to the
top.

Bow Street   12m   VS 4c
The crack system left of the corner of Rack or Ruin. Pull over a bulge
into a scoop and climb via cracks to the break. Climb the corner to the
roof and finish leftwards.

The next section of cliff, although shorter, is of good rock and is
characterised by a large sentry-box on its right.

High Diver   12m   Severe
A line just right of the sentry-box. Start below its right corner and go
up and right onto the front face. Climb up the open corner by the jutting
block. Protection is in the crack on the right.

Box of Delights   12m   E1 5b
Climb the crack up the left corner of the sentry-box to the roof, then move out left to finish up the steep crack above.

Midget Gems   12m   Hard Severe 4b
The right-facing corner left of the sentry-box gives an excellent little climb.

Buoys in Blue   12m   Severe
The crack a few metres left of Midget Gems.

Watch this Space   12m   HVS 5a
The crack and corner on the right of the central roof section, going left on a short wall under the top roof in a spectacular position.

Fearless Fly   12m   HVS 5a
Climb the crack and corner on the left of the lower roof and move right under the top roof to finish.

Rhued Buoys   12m   E1 5b
The crack left of Fearless Fly, moving left round the corner at the top roof.

Rude Awakening   12m   E1 5b
The last feature on this section of cliff is a large sloping roof with a black right wall. Climb up and right underneath the roof to finish up the corner.

The rock peters out from here eastwards, then reappears for a short section at the Lost Prow, but there are no recorded routes. There are 'rumours' (forgive the pun) of good bouldering and short problems on the outcrops of the mast hill behind the sea cliffs.

ARDMAIR CRAGS   *(Map Ref 117 987)*

These south-west facing buttresses, about 25m high, are very close to the A835 about 5km north of Ullapool. They lie above the stream which drains north-west from Lochan Sgeireach into Loch Kanaird just beyond Ardmair. There is limited private parking at the entrance to the fish farm opposite the crags, but it is better to park on the roadside verges nearer to Ardmair. Approach by a path which winds up left of the stream.

The rock is Torridonian sandstone of generally good quality, improving going uphill from the road. Most of the climbs follow cracks with good jamming and protection. However, the rock between the cracks tends to be very inhospitable. The crags are described in order proceeding away from the road.

FISH FARM WALLS
This first set of walls are somewhat broken but still steep. In the central section there is a wall with three closely grouped cracks leading to a heathery break overhung by a steep headwall.

1   The Fish Business   35m   E2 5b   (1989)
The central and widest of the cracks. Climb a groove in the lowest rocks and scramble to the foot of the wall. Move up left to a slabby ramp, step right onto a nose and pull onto a ledge below the crack. Climb the crack to an awkward exit onto the heathery break, then move up and right to climb a short corner.

2   Loan Shark   35m   E1 5b   (1989)
The left-hand crack. As for The Fish Business to the ramp, then take the left-hand crack to the ledge and up to the heathery break. Traverse right under bulges to climb an open groove up rightwards to the top.

2a   Hammerhead   30m   HVS 5a   (1991)
This route lies on the upper wall, which is steep and characterised by a big roof on its right side. A bulging rib leads to the left-hand side of the big roof. Start below the orange scooped wall and make a difficult swing to reach the rib. Follow this awkwardly to the top.

MONSTER BUTTRESS
This substantial buttress can be seen in profile from the road and is characterised by a big diagonal fault on the left of a steep bay of red, convoluted and weathered rock. Although the highest of the cliffs, the rock is not always of such good quality as elsewhere. On the right of the main bay is a greenish pillar, then a broken diagonal fault which separates the main section from the right-hand sector, which consists of several shorter walls of good rock. The first two routes lie on a small buttress which lies directly below Le Pontif, next to the path. It has a small capped groove at the foot of the change in angle. These two routes may be used as approaches for the routes above.

3a Laggavoulin 10m   VS 4c   (1991)
Climb the cracks just left of the nose, then trend right round the crest and go up to finish.

3b Little Red Rooster 10m   HVS 5a   (1991)
Start up the short capped groove, then trend right up the brown rock. Short, but good climbing.

3 Le Pontif 25m   HVS 5a   (1989)
The steep groove at the left-hand side of the main buttress, left of the steep bay. Climb rightwards and back left to finish.

4 Les Rosbif 30m   E2 5c   (1989)
The central of the three obvious ramp-lines right of the big bay gives good climbing after a flakey start. From the big diagonal fault make steep moves out right into the start of the ramp. Climb it and the crack above to the top.

5 Shaker Loops 30m   E1 5b   (1989)
About 10 metres right of Les Rosbif a steep crackline splits the green wall. Climb the crack, some shakey holds to start, to the horizontal break. Continue above, then move left to better holds and a hard move to belay on the third (right-hand) ramp. Heather terraces lead to the top.

6 Gravity's Rainbow 25m   E1 5b   (1989)
A good, exposed route up the right side of the narrow green pillar. Climb the right-facing corner. Go up then move left under the roof, up twin cracks then go right up a ramp. Return left onto the crest of the pillar and finish up a crack.

7 The Brahan Seer 25m   E2 5c   (1989)
Takes the obvious left-facing, slanting open corner. Climb up to, then up the corner. Return left up the steep diagonal crack.

The right-hand section is separated from the main section by a left-slanting diagonal fault at a point were the base of the cliff is at a higher level. About the middle of this section at the top of the cliff is a block overhang shaped like an enormous foot which is a handy landmark.

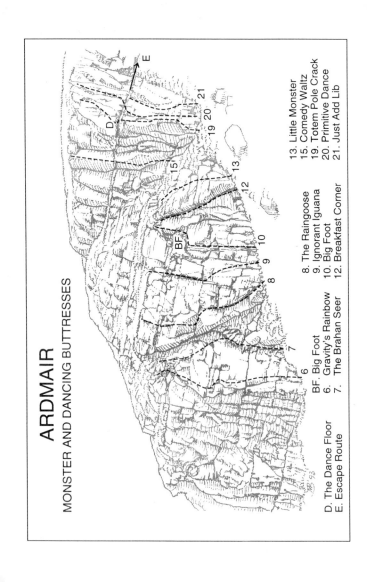

ARDMAIR

MONSTER AND DANCING BUTTRESSES

D. The Dance Floor
E. Escape Route

BF. Big Foot
6. Gravity's Rainbow
7. The Brahan Seer

8. The Raingoose
9. Ignorant Iguana
10. Big Foot
12. Breakfast Corner

13. Little Monster
15. Comedy Waltz
19. Totem Pole Crack
20. Primitive Dance
21. Just Add Lib

8 The Raingoose 20m   E3 5c/6a   (1989)
Start just right of the broken diagonal fault and climb a wide diagonal
crack left onto a prow. Make awkward moves over a bulge into a corner
and climb to its top. Traverse left under an overhanging prow onto a
big ledge and climb a diagonal crack which goes right onto the front
face again. Finish easily up cracked walls.

9 Ignorant Iguana 25m   E1 5b   (1989)
The corner system at the left end of the sloping ledge system below
the big foot. Climb a vague groove about 3 metres left of the upper
corner onto the sloping ledge. Climb the corner, move right above the
roof and continue up to ledges occupied by a big 'ready to roll' boulder.
Finish by the short crack above.

10 Big Foot 20m   E4 6a   (1989)
Climb the crack leading directly to the big foot and finish right of the
overhang; steep, strenuous and sustained on the upper wall. Finish
up the right-slanting corner at the top.

11 Summer Isles City 20m   E1 5b   (1988)
Takes the crack in the right wall of the corner right of Big Foot. Start
at a set of shallow cracks right of that route. Climb up and left onto the
glacis then right into the corner. Climb the crack in the right wall, narrow
at first then awkwardly wide. Finish by the obvious crack.

12 Breakfast Corner 20m   HVS 5b   (1989)
The obvious left-facing, left-slanting corner near the right end of the
cliff is climbed direct.

13 Little Monster 20m   E1 5b   (1989)
Just right of Breakfast Corner is a bulging wall. The route takes the
thin crack up this. Climb the thin crack and the bulge at its top to a
ledge. Finish up cracks in the wall above.

DANCING BUTTRESS
The next buttress up has a very obvious flat ledge, the Dance Floor,
at about three-quarters height and is separated from Monster Buttress
by a slanting fault, above which is a fine cracked wall. This is on the
left of the steep narrow prow which is cut by two obvious cracks and
is characterised by a blocky pillar on the crest. Right of the prow the
lower tier of the buttress decreases in size but the upper tier becomes

larger. Some of the routes have two pitches separated by the Dance Floor; it is easy to interchange pitches or walk off right. The first routes lie on the cracked gully wall and offer pleasant well protected climbing.

14 Spider Jive 30m HVS 5a   (1989)
High up the gully on the left is an obvious arete with a crack in its left side; the line of the route. Start at the initial rocks a short way up the gully. Climb easy rocks to where they steepen and go up the wall below the arete to gain a vegetated ledge. Move right on this then back left onto a ledge below the crack (this can be gained directly as well). Climb the fine crack then the arete to finish.

15 Comedy Waltz 30m E2 5b   (1989)
This takes the arete direct. Start as for Spider Jive and climb easily up to the dead holly. Move right to gain a flake crack and climb this to a large ledge (runners up to the right). Move left onto the arete and climb this (poorly protected) to the top.

16 Carved from Stone 35m HVS 5a   (1989)
Start 6m up the gully below twin cracks just right of a dark brown streak on the wall. Climb up to a ledge and use cracks to surmount the bulge. Follow the left-hand crack, keeping left of the small tree, to gain an easy slab (just left of the Dance Floor). Walk up the slab to the obvious scooped roof and climb this acrobatically on large holds.

17 Moondance 20m VS 4c   (1989)
This is the deep, dog-leg crack in the centre of the wall. Start at the fault about 2 metres left of the prow. Climb the fault and the crack which springs directly from its top. When it finishes continue up the thin crack (right of the tree in the corner) to the Dance Floor.

18 Sculptress 20m VS 4c   (1989)
The thin parallel cracks in the wall just left of the nose. Start up the fault as for Moondance. Climb the fault, move right and follow the twin cracks, staying just left of the nose all the way to the Dance Floor.

19 Totem Pole Crack 30m VS 4c   (1986)
The left-hand crack up the nose, starting left of the prow.
1. 20m Climb just left of the edge until the large corner in the nose can be gained and climbed to the top of the pinnacle. Follow the left-hand crack above to the ledge.
2. 10m Cross the overhang on its left and climb right to the top.

20   Primitive Dance   30m   E2   (1989)
The right-hand crack. Start in the open corner in the prow.
1. 20m 5b   Climb the crack and follow the line up and right into the
next fault. Traverse back left and then up onto the blocks. Climb the
crack onto the Dance Floor.
2. 10m 5c   Move slightly right to below an open corner with an undercut
start. Climb bulges and a small roof with difficulty. Continue up the
corner crack until it runs out, make an awkward step right onto a
sloping ledge and finish more easily.

21   Just Add Lib   20m   HVS 5a   (1989)
The obvious flakes and ramp on the wall right of the nose. Start below
shallow scoop at 2m. Climb gradually steepening cracks to an obvious
perched block, pull onto this and continue trending right along sloping
ramps to the final shallow V-scoop. Climb this to the Dance Floor and
walk off right or finish up the top pitch of Totem Pole Crack.

22   Dawn Patrol   20m   HVS 5a   (1989)
The central of three ramp lines on the upper tier. Start just left of the
obvious narrowing in the ledge leading to the Dance Floor. Climb the
deep groove and the continuation corner-ramp which trends left.

23   Mandolin Rain   25m   HVS 5a   (1989)
The rightmost of the three ramp lines. Start just right of Dawn Patrol
and climb a short crack with a jammed block to a ledge with aspen
trees. Move over juniper ledges on the left to a fine corner-crack. Step
left at the top of the corner and finish by a bridging crack in the final
short corner (crux). Surprisingly good climbing in the top half. A VS
variation continues from above the top of the fine corner-crack.

ARAPILES WALL
The next buttress consists of an impending wall of reddish orange rock
with a terrace slanting across it from near its right side.

24   Antipodean Cruise   20m   E2 5c   (1990)
Climb the corner line through the right end of the terrace, with an
obvious horn of rock drooping down from the second ledge.

25   Biological Warfare   15m   E1 5b   (1989)
The left-facing corner at the right end of the cliff, right of the end of the
terrace.

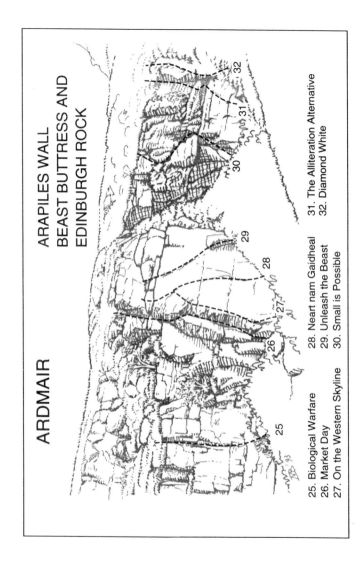

ARDMAIR

ARAPILES WALL
BEAST BUTTRESS AND
EDINBURGH ROCK

25. Biological Warfare
26. Market Day
27. On the Western Skyline

28. Neart nam Gaidheal
29. Unleash the Beast
30. Small is Possible

31. The Alliteration Alternative
32. Diamond White

BEAST BUTTRESS

This buttress has a steep front face and a slabbier left wall. It is separated from Arapiles Wall by a steep fault full of trees. The front face has a distinctive left-slanting diagonal crack which starts by a small pillar, the line of Unleash the Beast.

26 Market Day   25m   E1 5b   (1988)
Takes the pronounced scooped corner on the slabbier left wall of the buttress. Climb onto a ledge then up the large scooped corner to a small roof. Pull over this and continue more easily up the two short walls above.

27 On the Western Skyline   20m   E4 6a   (1989)
The blunt left arete. Start on the left of the wall and climb a short awkward corner onto the edge leading to a ledge. Move right on this to a flake leading to a thread. Move up and left, then back right to finish up the top crack of Neart nan Gaidheal.

28 Neart nan Gaidheal   20m   E5 6a   (1989)
The left-trending thin crack left of Unleash the Beast. Start at the short overhanging niche and climb direct through the final bulges onto the ledge. Walk off left or finish by one of the other routes.

29 Unleash the Beast   25m   E4 6a   (1989)
The obvious diagonal crack line on the front face is strenuous, technical but very well protected. Bridge up between the pillar and the crack until a hold on the wall allows entry into the crack. Follow the crack on jams to the large ledge. Either finish up the continuation crack or walk off to the right.

EDINBURGH ROCK

This is the next buttress uphill and is characterised by a big deep groove system on its left side.

30 Small is Possible   12m   Very Difficult   (1989)
The obvious ramp lines on the left of the buttress. Climb diagonally right to a ledge, follow the left-slanting ramp, then climb the clean crack in the wall above.

31 The Alliteration Alternative   15m   E1 5c   (1989)
A crack and groove line near the right edge of the buttress. Start at the obvious diagonal crack in the initial brown wall. Climb the crack to

gain the ledge with difficulty. Go up the short corner, step right onto a platform and finish up the fine open corner.

32 Diamond White 10m E1 5c   (1989)
The cracked roof and nose on the right of the buttress. Climb a short wall and a short deep groove to an awkward exit onto the big ledge on the left. Move right and finish up the crack.

AIRS ROCK

This is the second of the two small buttresses that are reached before Big Roof Buttress and is recognised by the cracks on the left wall which are separated by a heather ledge.

33 Small is Beautiful 12m Hard Severe   (1989)
Climb the obvious corner on the left of the side wall, then a continuation crack in the wall above. Finish up a slab.

34 Microlight 10m Hard Severe 4b   (1989)
The fine jamming cracks on the left wall, which are separated by a heather ledge.

35 The Parapente 20m E1 5b   (1989)
Climb the thin flake crack just left of the corner of the buttress to reach a large ledge. Go right into and climb the obvious corner.

36 The Way It Is 15m Difficult   (1989)
Takes the right-slanting ramp on the right of the buttress, passing a small tree.

BIG ROOF BUTTRESS

The most extensive and best buttress with the unmistakable jutting nose, which gives one of the finest lines in the area. The first climbs are on The Side Wall, the left side of the buttress running uphill at right angles to the main crag.

37 A Bit on the Side 10m HVS 5a   (1989)
Near the top end of the wall is a crack in a shallow left-facing corner just above some large boulders. Climb the crack, a bulge and the wider crack to finish. A good exercise in jamming.

38 A Spot of Deception 10m   E1 5b   (1989)
Takes the crack and short corner just right of the previous route. Climb
the obvious crack to its top, move right and go up the short corner and
the crack above to the top.

39 Acrimonious Acrobat 20m   HVS 5a   (1989)
The steep crack and groove right of the last route. Climb the obvious
corner to the roof, then move left into the main crack.

40 Twitching Twister 20m   E3 6a   (1989)
Right of Acrimonious Acrobat. Climb a thin crack to the right of a large
block beneath the roof. Step left and up to the break, cross the roof
and continue up the groove above.

41 Muscle Hustle 20m   E4 6b   (1989)
Climb Twitching Twister to below the roof. Hand traverse back right to
the edge of the block and surmount the roof using the crack on the
right. Continue to a standing position on a small pillar on the headwall,
and finish with a pull up and left.

42 Convoluted Contortionist 20m   E3/4 6b   (1989)
The obvious wide crack through the roof near the right of the wall,
finishing up the crack above, gives a thought-provoking roof and
jamming problem.

43 Bolshie Ballerina 20m   E2 5b/c   (1989)
The right-hand crack in the wall above the roof of the previous route.
Climb easier rock and a short corner-crack above the tree to a traverse
left to gain and climb the crack.

44 First Fruits 40m   HVS 5b   (1989)
The first line up the slab right of the previous route. Start from a boulder
right of a small corner and beneath a crack higher up. Step off the
boulder and climb to the crack which is taken on the right to gain slabby
ground leading to heathery scrambling.

45 Grumpy Groper 45m   E1 5b   (1989)
Good climbing up the wall and slab just left of the right edge of the
Side Wall. Climb a vague groove, pull over the bulge and continue to
a heathery ledge via the obvious crack. Ascend the wide crack above,
then its continuation to reach easier ground.

ARDMAIR   BIG ROOF BUTTRESS, LEFT-HAND SIDE

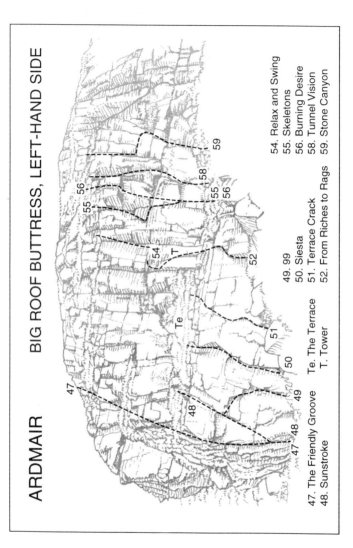

47. The Friendly Groove
48. Sunstroke

Te. The Terrace
T. Tower

49. 99
50. Siesta
51. Terrace Crack
52. From Riches to Rags

54. Relax and Swing
55. Skeletons
56. Burning Desire
58. Tunnel Vision
59. Stone Canyon

The main part of the buttress starts with the distinctive brown Terrace Wall. This lies below a heathery platform with small trees which extends right to a detached tower. There is a scrambling descent from this terrace on the uphill side. Beyond the tower is the roof section with its collection of fine crack, corner and groove lines which form the finest features of the cliff, pride of place going to the stunning roof crack. Beyond, the crag develops into a bay bounded on the right by a cracked pillar after which is another shallow bay with more fine crack and corner lines. These extend to a big right-facing corner, after which the cliff rapidly diminishes in height.

46 Blanka 40m E2/3 5c   (1990)
This climbs the left rib of the face starting just left of The Friendly Groove. Climb the crack to a sloping ledge, then move up and slightly right to an overhang. Undercut left and pull round the bulge to a ledge and belay. Continue up a small wall and the overhanging nose above.

47 The Friendly Groove 40m HVS 5b   (1989)
The obvious groove up the left edge of the Terrace Wall. Climb the groove and cracks to a horizontal break, cross the roof at the crack and continue up leftwards to the top. Alternatively finish the route on the terrace by moving right above the roof.

48 Sunstroke 20m E1 5b   (1989)
Takes a diagonal line right of the previous route. Climb The Friendly Groove for a short way until moves right lead onto the wall, then move up to below a big roof. Move right onto the ramp and climb this to the top.

49 99 20m E2 5c   (1989)
Start about 5 metres from the left edge of the wall. Gain the obvious hollow flake and climb this with caution, exiting left to a short ramp (common with Sunstroke).

50 Siesta 15m VS 4c   (1989)
The obvious ramp in the middle of the brown wall gives a pleasant climb with a steep finish onto the terrace.

51 Terrace Crack 15m VS 4c   (1989)
Near the right end of the wall is a fine flake crack running rightwards. Climb this then move right to finish on the terrace.

52 From Riches to Rags 15m   E4 6a   (1989)
A sustained and strenuous route up the front face of the tower. Climb the obvious left-facing corner to the break, then the thin crack in the tower (with some difficult moves) to the ramp section and the top.

53 Rock-a-Bye-Bye 10m   HVS 5b   (1990)
Climb the line of a stepped crack on the east face of the tower above the descent from the terrace. Start down at the left edge.

54 Relax and Swing 10m   E2 5c   (1989)
At the right end of the terrace above the tower and above some large blocks is a prominent short slanting corner with a leaning left wall. This provides some good climbing.

55 Skeletons 20m   E3 5c   (1989)
The obvious right-angled corner at the top of the cliff just left of the big roof. Start below the corner. Climb the crack and corners up to below the main corner then make hard moves to gain the top of the block. Climb the excellent corner above.

56 Burning Desire 25m   E5 6b   (1989)
The superb roof crack is well protected, stenuous and extremely spectacular. Start at a crack below and left of the roof (as for Skeletons). Climb the cracks leading right to a ledge below an overhanging crack. Climb the crack (crux) to a horizontal rest of sorts under the roof. Climb the roof crack on underclings, jams and hidden holds in a mind-boggling position to a jug on the lip. Pull over and finish easily. Originally done with some aid at the crux (E3 5c); well worth doing at that standard for the roof.

57 Space Monkey 20m   E2 5c   (1989)
A very good route up the deep narrow groove immediately right of the big roof. Start just right of the lower roofs, climb the wide groove and move left into a crack which leads to a short diagonal crack, then the groove itself. Climb this via some exciting positions to the top.

58 Tunnel Vision 25m   E1 5b   (1989)
The big deep V-groove right of Space Monkey. Climb a thin crack just right of a wide crack to gain the groove which is followed to an exit through the obvious slot.

59 Stone Canyon 25m E2 5c   (1989)
The groove right of Tunnel Vision starts some way up the cliff and is
gained at mid-height from the right. Climb up easily to the left end of
a vegetated ledge and move up to the big ledge on the left; belay
recommended. Move left into the groove, move up and over the
overhang at its top and finish up the right-angled corner above (crux).

60 Furious Fiddler 25m E3 5c   (1989)
The second groove-corner right of Tunnel Vision. Climb easily up to
the left end of a vegetated ledge, step up left to the base of the corner
(as for Stone Canyon). Climb the corner to a slabby ledge then pull
over the roof directly above the corner.

61 Town without Pity 25m E2 5c   (1989)
The groove and crack in the nose about 15 metres right of the big roof.
Climb the groove and crack, past an awkward bulge, to prominent twin
cracks at half-height. Climb mainly the left-hand crack and continue
up the left-slanting crack line to the top.

62 Thorn in my Side 25m E3 5c   (1989)
To the right of the previous route a wide crack splits the top half of the
cliff just left of a rowan tree on a heather ledge. Start below the wide
crack at another short groove with wild roses. Climb the left-hand crack
until hard moves right give access to a flake crack and continuation
onto the big ledge. Finish up the wide crack in the wall above.

63 Still Waters 25m E1 5c   (1989)
Varied and interesting climbing up the twin cracks left of Buried
Treasure. Start at a crack in an overhung bay below the cracks and
use it to gain the ledge. Continue using the corner crack and the crack
on its left to a vegetated ledge, move left and climb the narrow chimney
(just right of a rowan tree on the big ledge). Finish up a heather ramp.

64 Common Ground 25m E2 5c   (1989)
This takes a left-slanting line to finish up the crack right of the top crack
of Town without Pity. Climb Still Waters for about 6m to a small pod in
the left crack, move left into Thorn in my Side at its flake crack and
follow this to the ledge. Gain the top of the block on the left of the ledge
and finish up the crack and corner above.

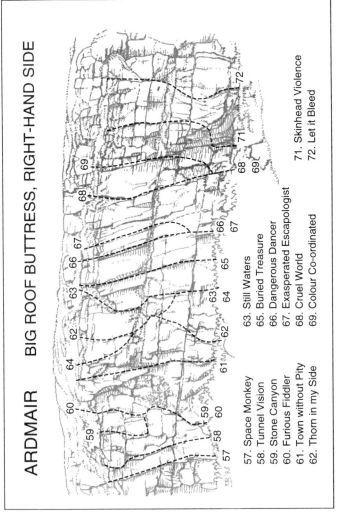

ARDMAIR   BIG ROOF BUTTRESS, RIGHT-HAND SIDE

57. Space Monkey
58. Tunnel Vision
59. Stone Canyon
60. Furious Fiddler
61. Town without Pity
62. Thorn in my Side

63. Still Waters
65. Buried Treasure
66. Dangerous Dancer
67. Exasperated Escapologist
68. Cruel World
69. Colour Co-ordinated

71. Skinhead Violence
72. Let it Bleed

65 Buried Treasure 25m E1 5b   (1989)
Interesting climbing up the left-facing corner-groove which runs the
full height of the cliff about 40 metres right of the big roof. Surmount a
short wall then climb the corner to the top, crossing a heather patch
and small holly tree at about mid-height.

66 Dangerous Dancer 25m E3 6a   (1989)
The obvious corner in the upper section of the cliff right of Buried
Treasure, gained by the crack line directly beneath it. Move up to a
big handhold, then step left using the sapling to a large but dubious
foothold, then go up to gain the crack.

67 Exasperated Escapologist 25m E4 6a   (1989)
Excellent varied climbing up the thin leaning crack line and wider
continuation crack. From the big handhold of Dangerous Dancer,
move right to the base of the crack which is followed to the roof. Step
right into the corner then transfer left to the wide crack which is followed
to the top, either directly or via a pull left to a well-positioned resting
place on the arete.

68 Cruel World 25m E2 5c   (1989)
The flake crack then the groove on the left side of the large bay. Start
at a large boulder right of an overgrown corner. Step off the boulder,
and move up to the obvious left traverse to a thin crack. Climb this
then a groove with hard moves onto the halfway ledge. Finish up the
dirty groove above.

69 Colour Co-ordinated 25m E1 5b   (1989)
Start as for Cruel World. Step off the boulder and continue direct to a
large ledge beneath a bulging corner. Take cracks in the right wall to
the top of a block, move right, then back left to finish direct.

70 Turn Turtle 25m E2 5c   (1989)
Start 4 metres right of Colour Co-ordinated and climb a shallow groove
capped by a jutting triangular block. Finish by the short corner.

71 Skinhead Violence 25m E1 5b   (1989)
This climbs the left side of the bulging wall. Start up the open corner
of Turn Turtle until short corners and ledges leading up and right can
be gained. Climb these and a crack to the heather ledge. Climb the
continuation crack to finish.

72 Let it Bleed   20m   E1 5b   (1989)
The cracks in the wall just before the big corner of Friends Retrieval.
Climb cracks first left then back right to a heather ledge just below a
holly tree. Continue up the corner and crack system to the top.

73 Friends Retrieval   20m   E1 5b   (1986)
The large right-facing corner at the right end of the cliff. Start in the
corner which leads up left and follow it to its top. Move left and climb
the flake crack, exiting left. Return right and climb grooves to finish by
a jutting nose. Steep and spectacular, but still slightly dirty.

SGURR AN FHIDHLEIR
703m   (Map Ref 094 055)

A prominent landmark, this superb pointed peak lies just north-west
of Ben Mor Coigach and is clearly seen from the minor road from
Drumrunie to Achiltibuie. It is easily approached from the south-east
end of Loch Lurgainn, a few kilometres from Drumrunie junction. The
Nose was the scene of many attempts before it was finally climbed.
There is a good deal of vegetation, particularly in the lower sections
of the climbs, and some loose rock, but in dry conditions the exposed
sandstone slabs give very rewarding climbs. On the rare occasions
when it is in winter condition it is well worth visiting. The East Face left
of the Nose is a formidable sweep of high-angled slabs. The most
obvious feature, clearly seen on the approach from Loch Lurgainn, is
the right-facing corner of Magic Bow. The Phantom Fiddler follows the
rib on the left of the corner. On the right between Magic Bow and the
Nose are G-String and Fidelio.

1 South Gully   III   (1979)
The narrow gully high on the left flank of the East Face.

2 The Phantom Fiddler   215m   HVS   (1968)
This route climbs the slabs and walls left of Magic Bow. Start below
the corner of Magic Bow and scramble up walls and slabs to reach a
short corner and a huge jutting block belay below the main corner line
(100m). Technical grades are not available for pitches 2 to 5; pitches
6 to 8 are based on The Magic Line.

SGURR AN FHIDHLEIR

2. The Phantom Fiddler 4. G-String
3. The Magic Bow 5. Fidelio N. The Fiddler's Nose

1. 30m 4c Climb the 5m corner, then a wall via a detatched flake to beneath an overhang. Step right and climb the groove above to belay at the foot of the main corner.

2. 15m Traverse left by a 10m slab to reach a higher heather terrace with a prominent spike.

3. 25m Climb straight up a slabbed wall above the spike, veering left near the top, and continue to a large terrace.

4. 25m Move right and climb the next wall by a strenuous layback to reach a jutting block at 6m. Traverse 3m right and climb exposed slabs overlooking the bow-shaped groove.

5. 20m Continue more easily to a stance below a prominent inverted V-chimney.

6. 20m 4c Climb the chimney and follow the slab right to belay.

7. 30m 5a The fine layback crack, inset in a groove in an arete with an undercut start, is climbed to pass an overhang on the left. Gain the foot of a groove with a crack on the left wall. Climb the groove to easier ground.

8. 50m Scramble to the top.

3 The Magic Bow 195m E1 *   (1967)

The main feature of the face is steeper than it looks. When dry it gives good, if indirect, climbing. Start as for Phantom Fiddler to the huge jutting block belay (100m).

1. 30m 4c Climb the 5m corner, then a wall via a large detached flake to beneath an overhang. Step right and climb the groove above to belay at the foot of the main corner.

2. 25m 4c Layback and bridge to a ledge and block belay.

3. 15m 5a Move right on ledges for 6m, then up through a bulge and straight up thin slabs to reach a right-slanting traverse line. This point can also be reached direct via the corner.

4. 30m 4a Traverse right for 15 metres, then climb straight through a bulge and easy slabs to a grass ledge.

5. 35m 5a The awkward bulge leads to steep slabs. Go up and right to a short black groove, move right and climb a short groove to the top of a large square block.

6. 15m 5b The middle of three short cracks is hard, but well protected.

7. 45m Easier rock leads to the top.

Nose Direct, Sgurr an Fhidhleir (Climber, Roger Everett)

Variation: **The Magic Line**   HVS **   (1989)
This combination of Magic Bow and Phantom Fiddler takes in some of the best rock on each and gives good, direct climbing. Follow Magic Bow to the belay above pitch 3.
4. 30m 4c Step back into the corner via a small overlap and continue, with a diversion onto the left wall, to another grass terrace. Traverse the wall left to the arete and climb a short groove to a ledge and belay.
5. 20m Climb up to the stance below the prominent V-chimney of Phantom Fiddler.
6. 7. and 8. 80m The last three pitches of Phantom Fiddler.

4   G-String   210m   E1   (1977)
This route starts from a good rock ledge about 75 metres right of and level with the start of the groove of The Magic Bow. Above the ledge is steep rock bounded on the right by a series of right-slanting overhangs. Gain the ledge by terraced walls. Go up and over a bulge at about 12m, then right to a slab. Go right, up for 5m, then left to a good ledge and belay. Above, a groove goes up to the left of a block overhang. Above and left is another block overhang, the two separated by a groove. Enter the groove using a flake on the lower overhang and move right onto steep slabs. Move up and right to a small, but long ledge. Enter the groove above from the right and climb to a good stance and peg belay. Climb straight up to a big ledge, move right and round into a grassy corner. Climb a thin slab on the right to belay. Climb up and right over a bulge, enter a corner and finish by a wide crack on the left wall.

5   Fidelio   210m   HVS *   (1979)
This follows a prominent line of weakness between the Direct Nose Route and the slabs of The Magic Bow. Climb preliminary tiers to lesser overhangs, then traverse left into a large open corner on the right of a rock beak, about a third of the way up the face. Above the corner follow the left-trending grooves to break through the main rightwards slanting overhangs at their mid-point. Continue by grooves up the obvious slabby corner in three excellent pitches. On the final pitch climb the slab direct by a thin crack.

Expecting to Fly, Stac Pollaidh (Climber, Andy Tibbs)

6 Nose Route   250m   V   (1979)
This takes a line left of the Direct Nose Route and quite close to Fidelio.
Two staggered icy corners, approximately level with the Pale Slabs
and about 30 metres to the left, are the main features. Take as straight
a line as possible, up icy grooves, to the corners, climbing the left one
then the right. The right-slanting overhangs are breached by a difficult
pitch up a left-leaning jam crack, followed by a short traverse left.

7 Direct Nose Route   245m   HVS **   (1962)
This fine route, one of the classics of the area, has a long history. It
was the scene of a remarkable early attempt by Ling and Sang, and
it later repulsed such redoubtable names as Baird, Parker and Young.
The line follows an obvious grassy groove twisting up the centre of the
buttress to the Pale Slabs and then finishes directly up the spur in a
magnificent position. Start at the base of the buttress, a little right of
the crest, aiming for grooves in the slabs above.
1. 50m 4b A fine pitch up a slab, left of the grassy groove, leads to
broken ground.
2. 50m 4b Follow the grassy groove to a fine cave below a roof.
3. 30m 4a Step right and follow the groove to easy ground below the
First Pale Slab.
4. 20m Follow steep grass rightwards to the grassy groove on the
right. Climb this to a little bay.
5. 15m Traverse the grass ledge left to the Hansom Cab stance.
6. 15m Climb the Second Pale Slab via the grassy groove on the left
(or the finer crack to the right) to a good ledge.
7. 15m 5a From just right of the edge, step onto the slab with difficulty,
then go up left to a groove and good ledge above.
8. 25m 4c Step right and surmount the overlap by an old peg runner.
Climb the slabs above just right of the arete to a ledge.
9. 25m 5a Take the steep corner above to the final thin crack up a
little wall (old peg runner, crux). Easier climbing leads to the top.
Winter: VI ***   (1987)
A superb climb of Alpine stature, giving good strenuous climbing using
both frozen turf and torqued picks. Follow the summer line. A harder
alternative to pitches 5 and 6 (more in keeping with the rest of the
route) takes the corner above the little bay and then traverses a
narrower grass ledge to the arete. Pitch 7 is most easily climbed by
an overhanging corner just left of the arete. Pitch 8 tip-toes up the
slabs to the right of the arete between havens of turf. Pitch 9 has good
torques. Protection is mostly excellent.

Alternative Finish: **The Tower Finish** 90m E1   (1979)
Start from the good ledge above pitch 7 of the Nose Direct Route.
8. 20m Climb up and right via thin grass steps to an exposed nook
below an impressive vertical wall.
9. 45m 5b/c Climb up and slightly right to an overhang. Overcome this
on the right and continue up the wall to a groove with a steep slab on
the right. Climb a crack in the slab, step right and mantelshelf into a
groove. Step right into an exposed nook.
10. 15m Climb the crack above to a ledge, traverse left into a groove
and follow this to a chimney, then a groove. Easier ground leads to
the final ridge.

8 North-West Face 300m III   (1979)
This is the ramp-gully to the right of the nose, easily seen from directly
below. The diagonal gully leads right with one pitch of climbing into the
long final gully. This could be dangerous in bad snow conditions.

9 West Face 300m III   (1979)
According to the latest O S map this face has rotated to the north.
Follow a depression left of centre to grooves and more open climbing.
Join North-West Face above the shoulder and finish up that route.

CONMHEALL
544m   (Map Ref 064 055)
This hill lies about 3km west of Sgurr an Fhidhleir, overlooking the
coast south of Achiltibuie and the Summer Isles. A prominent pinnacle
flanks the hill on its left (north).

Acheninver Pinnacle 150m Very Difficult   (1955)
From the lowest rocks climb a large right-angled block and follow the
right edge of the pinnacle to its top. A wide crack about halfway up is
turned on the left (or may be climbed direct, Severe).

Levitation Towers 120m E1 5b   (1978)
An unusual route up the triple-towered, knife-edged arete which juts
out right of the Acheninver Pinnacle. Climb cracks and a tight chimney
to flake belays. Continue up an awkward corner crack to a level
section. Go easily up and along the arete to the second tower and
belay on the right below a crack. Climb up to a perch then move up
and right to a sloping ledge. Gain the rib above, follow this to an alcove
and climb a corner to belays. Continue along the crest to the next tower
which is climbed direct. Finish by interesting scrambling.

Middle Crag   75m   Severe   (1962)
The second rocky buttress right of the Acheninver Pinnacle is a slabby
face between the arms of a Y-gully. Start from the lowest rocks and
take a more-or-less direct line, finishing up a wide shallow chimney.

   Other 30m routes have been made on the rightmost buttress. The
rock is sound and rough, but scant of holds.

STAC POLLAIDH

613m   (Map Ref 107 106)

Rough, red, pebbly sandstone characterises this famous and easily
accessible mountain. An aptitude for jamming and bridging is bene-
ficial as many lines follow cracks and corners. Friction and protection
are usually good, but the rock can be alarmingly blank. The cliffs have
a stupendous outlook, face the sun and dry quickly after rain. A wide
selection of camming devices will be useful on all routes and because
of the blocky nature of the sandstone some care should be taken with
the rock. The ridge to the west summit bristles with pinnacles and it is
a popular excursion with as much scrambling as desired.

WEST (No.1) BUTTRESS

Routes with many variations between Moderate and Difficult can be
climbed on the left profile of the West Buttress. The original route
(Walker and Inglis Clark, 1906) started some 15 metres left of the
prominent pinnacle known as The Forefinger, or Baird's Pinnacle.
Solly and Collie also recorded routes in this area. All parties mentioned
an awkward crack in the upper reaches, variously dealt with by
'combined tactics, artificial chockstones and jammed handholds.' It is
expected that such methods will be spurned by the modern purist.

1   North-West Corner   90m   Difficult   (1962)
The northerly corner of the West Buttress can be climbed more or less
directly by a narrow rib of no great difficulty.

2   West Buttress   90m   Difficult   (1906)
The buttress is split at one-third height by a large grass ledge which
can be gained by a number of lines. One of the easiest is an obvious
left-slanting gangway about 15 metres right of Baird's Pinnacle. Continue up the groove directly above the pinnacle in two pitches.

3 Baird's Pinnacle 20m VS 4c *   (1957)
The obvious finger crack on the inner face gives strenuous jamming.

The face to the right of the pinnacle is split by a variety of ribs, corners, cracks and chimneys, before the two long corner lines of Enigma Grooves and November Groove.

4 South Face Route 60m Very Difficult   (1959)
This starts up rocks left of a chimney in the centre of the face. From easy ground traverse right (round the foot of the central column) into a grassy groove. After 10m, climb a chimney on the left and follow easier rocks to a ledge. From its right end go direct to the top.

5 South Rib 60m Severe   (1959)
Three vertical ribs characterise the face. This route climbs the left-hand one, bounded on the left by easier rocks stretching towards Baird's Pinnacle. Good climbing. Easy rocks lead to the sharp nose-like overhangs which are gained by a small pinnacle and steep rocks. Turn them by the chimney on the right. From a large ledge 6m above the chimney, climb a wall by two thin cracks and finish over awkward undercut rocks.

6 Anyways 60m Very Difficult   (1959)
Start at the obvious left-slanting gangway splitting the lower part of the wall some 40 metres right of Baird's Pinnacle. Gradually work to the left up various cracks and corners until a short stomach traverse beneath a jammed block leads to the final pitch of the Original Route.

7 Party on the Patio 85m Severe   (1985)
This climbs cracks and corners in the left rib of Enigma Grooves. Start below the gangway of Anyways.
1. 30m Climb up and right to gain the rib overlooking Enigma Grooves. Follow this until it is possible to traverse up and left to belay beneath a steep corner.
2. 10m Traverse right, round the corner and belay in a hidden chimney above Enigma Grooves.
3. 15m Climb the chimney on the left, then continue directly, moving back right near the top to a large terrace.
4. 10m 4b Immediately to the right, climb the steep corner with a crack in its left wall, then an awkward bulge above (nut for aid).
5. 20m Move left and climb a chimney with a through route.

8 Enigma Grooves 70m HVS *   (1965/1979)
The left-hand diedre gives a traditional mountain route requiring
stamina, care and some chimneying technique. More enjoyable in dry
conditions. Start in a bay right of the toe of the buttress and directly
below the corner line.
1. 25m Climb the easy wall left of the wide crack to belay beneath the
start of the main corner.
2. 25m 5a Climb the poorly protected crack, (often wet and greasy),
then the wide chimney above to a platform.
3. 20m 5b Continue to a ledge on the left, then the strenuous chimney
above, past a chockstone, finishing up the crack.

9 November Groove 70m VS   (1953)
Some scrappy climbing in the right-hand diedre, but a pleasant crux.
Start in the same bay as Enigma Grooves.
1. 25m 4b Climb the clean wall on the right to a layback crack and
follow this past a wide crack on the right. Continue left up easier,
broken ground to a ledge at the start of the groove.
2. 20m 4b Climb the groove, grassy at first, and surmount the
overhang on the right to reach a belay.
3. 25m 4b Continue up the groove line to an obvious right traverse
leading to a crack. Follow this to the top.
Winter: IV   (1989)
Follow the summer line, except pass the overhang on pitch 2 on the
left, then follow the ridge of Jack The Ripper a little way before
regaining the main line.

10 Jack the Ripper 75m E1 ***   (1964)
Good climbing on the airy rib right of November Groove, followed by
a superbly sustained final pitch (at the upper limit of its grade) on
excellent rock. Start as for November Groove.
1. 25m 4b Pitch 1, November Groove.
2. 20m 5a Traverse right and climb cracks in the slabby rib until a
difficult step up is made on the arete. Blocks and cracks lead to a belay.
3. 30m 5b A left-leaning crack leads to a ledge. From its right end
climb the steep corner line above with difficulty until an awkward move
leads left onto a ledge. Finish up the crack.

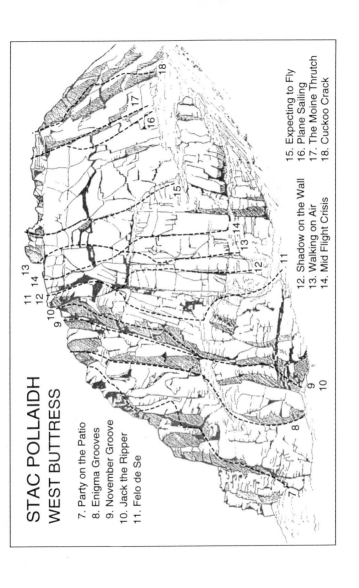

STAC POLLAIDH
WEST BUTTRESS

7. Party on the Patio
8. Enigma Grooves
9. November Groove
10. Jack the Ripper
11. Felo de Se

12. Shadow on the Wall
13. Walking on Air
14. Mid Flight Crisis

15. Expecting to Fly
16. Plane Sailing
17. The Moine Thruth
18. Cuckoo Crack

11 Felo de Se 75m E2   (1969/1989)
The crack line right of Jack the Ripper leads to an excellent jamming
pitch up the hanging corner on the prow.
1. 45m Broken walls right of Jack the Ripper lead to the crack which
is followed to a large ledge.
2. 30m 5c The awkward chimney on the right leads to easier ground
below a block overhang. The prominent corner on the left gives
sustained, well protected jamming to the top.

Right of this route is a vegetated groove line, then an impressive
east-facing wall of compact sandstone. The left side of the wall dries
fast after rain, the right seeps from above. The first three routes start
from the ledge system on the lower wall, reached by a scramble left
from the gully.

12 Shadow on the Wall 60m E4 **   (1989)
Steep climbing up the prominent groove and crack on the left side of
the wall. A full set of Friends is useful.
1. 30m 6a From the left end of the ledge climb the groove until difficult
moves lead to an *in situ* thread runner. Continue up the crack and the
wide flake crack above, then traverse the horizontal break left with
care, to a good belay.
2. 30m 5c Pitch 2, Felo de Se.

13 Walking on Air 60m E4 ***   (1989)
A tremendous route giving technical climbing up the crack line and
stepped corner splitting the main overhang. A large Friend is necessary for the belay. Start just right of a block on the ledge, below twin
cracks on a very red section of the wall.
1. 30m 6a Climb the cracks with difficulty to better holds and continue
until it is possible to traverse left into a crack and corner. Below the
break a scoop and rib on the right lead to a belay in the horizontal
break.
2. 30m 6b Step onto the large block and climb to a triangular niche.
Climb the crack, passing a poor peg runner with difficulty and move
up awkwardly into a niche. Follow the stepped corner until it is possible
to step left to finish up the wide crack.

14 Mid Flight Crisis 65m E4 ***   (1989)
Another excellent route crossing Walking on Air from right to left. The
second pitch takes the superbly situated crack on the prow, right of
Felo de Se. Again, large Friends are required. Start at the crack line
right of Walking on Air.
1. 30m 6a Climb the right-hand of two cracks for 4m, then move left
to the other crack. Continue up and right, then back left to follow the
crack to belay at the horizontal break, left of the large block.
2. 35m 6a Step up left, climb a thin crack over the roof to a small niche.
Step left to a large hold and traverse left into the diagonal fault. Move
up the fault to a niche, old peg, pull directly up to a wedged block and
climb the crack to the top.

15 Expecting to Fly 40m E4 6a ***   (1988)
A fine route with a strenuous and delicate crux in an exposed central
position. It follows the grey groove and diagonal crack breaking
through the band of overhangs right of the mossy recess. Start at the
upper terrace above the short rock step. Up easy rock to an old peg.
Climb flakes on the right before moving back left into the main crack
line which leads to the hanging groove below the roof. Use a flake
crack to gain a bridge in the groove. Steep moves bring good
layaways, which lead with difficulty to a niche. Continue up the crack.

16 Plane Sailing 25m E3 5c *   (1989)
Good climbing on the wall just left of the corner system of The Moine
Thrutch. Start at an easy corner, below the roof at the right end of the
wall. Climb the corner until a crack line leads to below the roof. Move
through the roof at the weakness on the left and make some hard
moves to get established in the thin crack line above. Follow this
rightwards until forced into the wide chimney-crack on the right.

17 The Moine Thrutch 35m VS   (1988)
This is the corner flanking the right side of the main wall. Start as for
Plane Sailing.
1. 25m 5a Climb the corner and move right over grassy rock to a short
corner below a wide crack. Follow the corner to a spacious ledge on
the right, then another corner to belay on a ledge.
2. 10m 5a Move left from the belay and thrutch the left-slanting crack
to the terrace. Climb the short wall above.

18 Cuckoo Crack 35m   VS   (1977)
A distinctive chimney-groove flanked on the right by a bow-shaped
wall gives the line. Start about 10m up and right of The Moine Thrutch,
below the groove.
1. 15m 4a Climb the line of least resistance to a large ledge below
and right of the chimney-groove.
2. 20m 5a Climb the chimney-groove, then step right and climb a
steep groove to the terrace. A short wall leads to the top.

No.2 BUTTRESS
Down and right of West Buttress, this crag presents a series of steep
groove and crack lines finishing on the right with the prominent corner
and cracked slab of Vlad the Impaler. The original route on this face
climbed the far left side of the buttress via a monumental thread and
then followed the crest.

19 Release the Bats 155m   VS   (1985)
Start at the left end of the buttress, to the right of broken rocks and
below a left-slanting gangway.
1. 25m 4b A steep 5m crack leads to a gangway, which is followed up
left to a ledge. Traverse right and belay in a corner.
2. 20m Climb the corner to a ledge, then go up a right-slanting
chimney to another ledge.
3. 20m 4b Take the groove above, stepping left where it divides, then
go back right round an awkward corner to a belay.
4. 15m An easy slab and ledges on the left lead to a belay beneath
the upper tower.
5. 40m 4b The first crack on the left of the tower is short and strenuous,
leading to the upper arete and an awkward descent to the final
headwall.
6. 35m 4a Climb a crack in the headwall, immediately left of the
continuation of the arete. Finish up slabs.

20 Bloodsucker 45m   E2 5c   (1988)
A traditional struggle up the first deep chimney slot right of Release
the Bats. Finish up that route.

21 Wingless Warlock 55m   E1 **   (1989)
Good climbing in the obvious crack line in the right wall of the groove
about 5 metres left of Stakeout. Start below the crack.

1. 25m 5b An awkward steep groove and bulge leads to ledges in the main groove line. Move up to a very steep crack, then step right to a crack in the arete. Climb this and its flake crack continuation to exit right onto the belay of Stakeout.
2. 30m 5b As for Stakeout.

22 Stakeout 55m E3   (1988)
A difficult and bold first pitch leads to corners and cracks up the prominent tower on the skyline. Start at the right end of a raised terrace directly below the tower, where a crack line slants from right to left below a white blocky roof.
1. 25m 5c Climb the crack past vegetation, until a hard move can be made left round the roof into a sentry box. Continue up and right onto a slab, then return to the groove on the left and follow it to a ledge.
2. 30m 5b Climb the corner above and continue by delightful cracks and corners to the very summit of the pinnacle.

23 Vlad the Impaler 75m HVS **   (1985)
Enjoyable crack climbing up the prominent cracked slab and corner at the toe of No.2 Buttress.
1. 40m 5a Climb wide cracks up the centre, then the right side of the slab to a surprising exit to a detached summit.
2. 35m 4b At the back of the large ledge above is a twisting crack. Climb this and finish up an easy arete.

24 Nosferatu 40m HVS 5a   (1987)
This route climbs the buttress immediately right of Vlad the Impaler. Start at the foot of the chimney crack, the easternmost feature of the buttress. Climb the chimney for 7m, then move left into the centre of the face. Continue with increasing difficulty up twin cracks in the centre of the buttress to an excellent finish. (The chimney has been climbed at Very Difficult.)

24a Calum the Clansman 45m HVS   (1992)
This takes a line to the right of Nosferatu, but starting on the right side of a rocky ridge next to the big scree-filled gully.
1. 15m 5b Climb a curving layback crack up a slab, then a narrow ridge to a belay in a small gully just above the Nosferatu chimney.
2. 30m 4c Follow a right-slanting crack until moves left gain another crack at an overlap. Follow this and a slab to a large ledge. Traverse right into the gully to descend, or finish up Vlad the Impaler.

UPPER No.2 BUTTRESS
This is the small overhanging buttress on the right at the top of the wide gully below the main wall.

25 Bats in the Belfry 50m VS   (1991)
Climb easily onto the concave slab at the right end of the buttress.
1. 35m 4c Climb a thin crack up the slab and continue to a cave.
2. 15m 4a Move right to a slab on the right, and so to the top.

PINNACLE BASIN
The large gully to the right of No.2 Buttress splits near the top. The left branch leads to the pinnacles, three of which have a fancied resemblance to the Sphinx, Tam O'Shanter and the Virgin and Child (the tall, claw-like pinnacle).

26 Virgin and Child Pinnacle 20m VS 5a   (1957)
This fine slender pinnacle is climbed on its shortest side (facing the mountain) via a crack.

27 The Irascible Porcupine 90m HVS   (1987)
Two contrasting pitches up towers in the buttress in the centre of the basin, down and right of Virgin and Child Pinnacle.
1. 35m 5a Climb the crack up the front of the first tower, exiting left near the top.
2. 25m Scramble down the back of the tower to the col.
3. 40m 5b Climb the wide crack directly in front with difficulty, first leftwards (overlooking the pinnacle) then directly.

28 Pretty Bourgeois Crack 45m E2 5c *   (1988)
A well-protected exercise in hand jamming. This route takes the obvious steep corner-crack line overlooking the right branch of the gully. Scramble up to a belay left of the base of the crack which is followed with pain to the top.

No.3 BUTTRESS
This broken buttress forms the right flank of Pinnacle Basin.

29 Summer Isles Arete 120m Very Difficult   (1974)
The obvious ridge in the buttress gives an entertaining expedition, including a stomach traverse.

THE KEEP

This is the small buttress on the ridge, right of the tourist scree and separated from the East Buttress by a narrow gully. Ascend the gully direct, or, from the ridge climb over The Keep and down into the bealach dividing it from the East Buttress. Descend the gully southwards for a few metres until a grass terrace leads round to the right (facing out).

30 Angus The Arsonist 45m HVS   (1988)
About 10 metres along the ledge a column leans against the face forming a chimney with jammed blocks.
1. 30m 5a Climb the chimney to a ledge. Move right up a steep corner, then go up a wall on the left to a belay.
2. 15m 4c Climb the obvious corner above to the top.

31 The Cheshire Cat 40m Severe   (1991)
This climbs the hidden triangular central buttress of The Keep, starting from its lowest point. Climb a chimney-crack system on the left of the buttress. On reaching the buttress edge traverse right under a prominent tunnel and finish up a crack to the right.

32 Coigach's Burning 20m E1 5c   (1988)
Start at the fine crack line at the very end of the terrace. Climb the crack to a heather bay, continue to an overhanging finger crack and pull into a recess with difficulty. Finish up the gully on the left.

CUL BEAG

769m (Map Ref 141 088)

Cul Beag has a line of steep gullied cliffs on its north side overlooking Gleann Laoigh, but no climbs have been recorded there. On its west face, overlooking Loch Lurgainn, there are extensive areas of rock. A number of climbs have been done and there is potential for more. Unfortunately identification of some of the earlier climbs is difficult.

Seen from Linneraineach there are the following features: (a) On the first tier of crags there is a monolithic pear-shaped slab. (b) Right under the summit there is a Y-shaped gully which extends down to a chimney on the right of the pear-shaped slab. (c) From a little way right of the pear-shaped slab a gully slants up right to a small col on the summit ridge. (d) Well over to the right, below a flattening in the right skyline, is a clear chimney-crack line in a slabby wall.

Quelle Delicatesse   50m   VS   (1959)
Start below the pear-shaped slab. Climb a grassy break rightwards to the right edge of the slab and follow the edge to the top.

Tant Pis   40m   VS   (1990)
Start at the foot of the rib 5 metres left of Quelle Delicatesse. Climb straight up for 12m to a vegetated niche. Traverse easily right for 10m then climb steeper cracks to the slabs above. Follow a crack system up the middle of the slabs to easy ground.

Kveldro Ridge   200m   Very Difficult   (1979)
This seems to take the skyline ridge left of the Y-shaped gully. As one approaches the pear-shaped slab from below the left skyline appears as a three-tiered ridge. Start about 90 metres left of the pear-shaped slab, and climb up avoiding the initial tier.
1. 45m Scramble up to a cracked wall.
2. 25m Climb the wall by a crack.
3. 25m Climb the next wall by a groove on the right.
4. and 5. Scramble 75m to the final tier.
6. 30m Climb a left-slanting chimney to finish just below the summit.

Lurgainn Edge   75m   Difficult   (1958)
This appears to take the crest right of the gully referred to in (c) above. Above the pear-shaped slab, Dr Bell mentions a difficult chimney at 30m and another at 60m, followed by roof-tile slabs to the top.

Curving Chimney   65m   Very Difficult   (1959)
This is the line mentioned in (d) above. A slabby wall on the right of the lower tier is split by a curving chimney. Climb steep grass at the base, then climb the chimney until forced out to the right. Cross to a pulpit. Traverse back left to the chimney line and continue to the top.

Lickerish Quarter   90m   Severe   (1979)
Start at the foot of Curving Chimney. Climb the rib on the right for a few moves then traverse up and across to a corner (15m). Climb the corner or slabs on the left to the pulpit and continue directly to the top.

CUL MOR
849m   (Map Ref 162 119)

This mountain has several sandstone cliffs, some of which could provide some excellent climbing. So far, development has been sporadic.

CREAG NAN CALMAN
There is a line of sandstone cliffs overlooking Loch Dearg a'Chuil Mhor at Map Ref 158 110. They are best approached from Knockanrock via the beautiful Gleann Laoigh. The cliffs offer numerous possibilities for steep and probably loose climbs. Only one has been recorded.

Buffalo Ballet   130m   VS   (1979)
To the left of the cliffs overlooking the loch is a gully sloping up left (East Gully) with a series of chimney cracks rising from its foot. Start to the right of the foot of the gully. Climb a groove then a chimney and go right to easy ground. Follow a gully to beneath a chimney-crack. Climb a rib on the left of the gully (25m) to below a narrow chimney, climb this and the following chimney. Traverse left below an overhang to a narrow rib, climb to the top of the rib and move right across a steep slab to gain the top of the overhang. Follow the chimney to the top.

COIRE GORM
A well-hidden and impressive corrie with a lot of steep rock. Approach from the A835 via a good track starting 800 metres north of Knockanrock. Continue to a shoulder on the north-east ridge (below the final rise to the summit) and descend with care into the corrie bowl. The north-facing back wall of the corrie is bounded on the left by a deep-set easy gully and on the right by an expanse of steep walls. Up and left of the steep walls is a depression of easier ground; left of this is a large crag liberally endowed with grooves and corners. The following route takes a chimney-gully line rising slightly left from the right side of the groove-lined face. It is best seen from below the steep walls.

The Cul   165m   V **   (1991)
An enjoyable route with a great outlook which provides much more than meets the eye (at the lowest limit of its grade). Start at the foot of the first steep chimney.
1. 30m Climb up the back of the chimney with interest. Exit right of the capping overhang.

2. 50m Continue up the easy gully above.
3. 35m A couple of steep steps lead to a tunnel under a huge fallen block. Belay at the foot of another deep chimney.
4. 50m Climb the chimney with difficulty. Exit right and climb the runnel on steep thin ice to easy ground. Either scramble to the top of the mountain or traverse left to the north-east ridge.

SUILVEN
731m   (Map Ref 154 184)

This beautiful and impressive peak is one of the most famous in the North-West. From Lochinver and the coast it completely dominates the view inland, appearing much larger than its true height. Seen from the mountains to the north and south the long whaleback of its ridge extends for 3km from Caisteal Liath in the west to Meall Beag in the east. Being such an isolated mountain, surrounded on all sides by lochan-strewn moorland, adds greatly to its grandeur, and gives to the climbs a splendid feeling of openness. It also means that strong winds can be a problem. The rock is sandstone, and the climber must be prepared for vegetation and greasy rock in the wet. There are easy ways up and down the mountain on either side of the obvious col, Bealach Mor, between Caisteal Liath and the middle peak.

Access
All the routes are on the north-west end of the mountain. There are two possible approaches. One is from Inverkirkaig: follow a good path up the River Kirkaig, as far as Fionn Loch, which is skirted to the west, then climb gradually over the moor to the north-west base of the peak. A longer but equally attractive way is to start from Little Assynt at the west end of Loch Assynt. Take a stalkers' track to the bothy at Suileag. If possible ford the Amhainn na Clach Airigh and continue south as directly as possible. Otherwise, keep on the path on the north side of the river to a bridge, cross over and follow the path to a point about 500 metres short of the outflow of Loch na Gainimh (Map Ref 167 198), where a cairn marks the start of a rather boggy and ill-defined path leading south-south-west across the moor to the foot of the mountain. Either way the combination of the long approach and a climb will give a good 10 to 12 hour day.

   At the right end of the north-west face is a vegetated gully (Pilkington and Walker, 1892).

Western Approach Route 140m II (1992)
This is a winter ascent of the Pilkington and Walker route; it makes a fine prelude to the traverse of the main ridge. The start of the gully can be reached by a long traverse from the right, but a direct entry can be made up a 20m ice pitch (Grade III).

Left of this is the cleanest and most continuous piece of cliff on the mountain, where three routes have been recorded.

Rose Route 140m Mild Severe (1957)
Start just left of the conspicuous black waterslides on the lowest tier of rock under Pilkington's Gully. Climb a steep little wall and turn a steeper one on the right to reach a fine red slab. Climb this obliquely to the right for 6m to the ledge above, with a dubious flake belay, (12m). Go up 2m from the ledge and traverse left round a nose to the foot of two narrow slabs, the right set back from the left. Climb 6m up between them to a large ledge at the edge of the nearest waterslide, with a jammed stone belay, (12m). Make an exposed traverse left round a corner to the broken ledges of the Terrace, directly below the south edge of the main buttress (9m). The rest of the climb follows this edge. Start at the obvious corner of the buttress about 15m left of the gully (there is a lesser corner further right). Go up 4m and over or round a large block; at 8m a small slab leads to a mantelshelf onto a flat block on the right. Traverse right to the edge of the buttress and climb 6m to a stalactite belay at the foot of a small chimney, (20m). Climb the chimney and bypass a small wall on the right leading back to a dark corner on the left at 11m. Traverse right round a projecting block to a good ledge near the edge and climb up to a broad ledge, (25m). Climb more easily to the top (60m).

Portcullis Route 180m Severe (1947)
Start a little left of Rose Route at the bottom of the lower wall. Climb trending first left then right to the Terrace. A short way above the Terrace make a long delicate traverse left. A mantelshelf and a short traverse left leads to a short corner. Exit out right strenuously and reach a ledge by a delicate move. Continue with slight deviations to the top.

Heatwave 140m Severe (1968)
Start as for Portcullis and take a slightly more direct line to the Terrace. From here the route takes an almost parallel line to Rose Route and eventually joins it, after many short traverses and some loose rock. The easiest line on the wall ahead is taken to the top.

Gray's Route (Very Difficult) starts in a bay about 40 metres left of Portcullis Route. It climbs up to the left side of the Terrace, goes right, then up the wall above and eventually joins Portcullis about two thirds of the way up the buttress. (See The Rucksack Club Journal, 1935).

QUINAG
808m   (Map Ref 209 292)

Quinag is a large and complicated mountain which presents several cliffs with worthwhile climbing.

THE BARREL BUTTRESS of SAIL GHARBH (Map Ref 214 302)

The steep north face of Sail Gharbh is clearly visible when driving south from Kylesku. Like so many of the steep sandstone cliffs of the area it is rather vegetated. The distinctive Barrel Buttress is easily reached in about one hour from the road to the east. Viewed from below the barrel-shape is very obvious. A fault on the left of a broken lower tier leads into a line of corners on the steep upper tier. This is approximately the line of Raeburn, Mackay and Ling's original excursion in 1907 (Very Difficult and vegetated). The frontal face of the upper tier is bounded by a chimney on the right, and the only two rock climbs recorded lie on this frontal face. The lower tier can be avoided by climbing the gully on the right and traversing left. The gullies on either side of the buttress provide winter climbs.

Y Gully   300m   II   (1979)
The deep gully on the left of the buttress. The two forks are about the same standard; the right fork is particularly scenic.

Y Buttress   360m   II   (1979)
The buttress in between the two forks of Y Gully. The steep summit tier is turned on the right.

Cave Gully   300m   III   (1979)
This narrow gully lies on the left side of the buttress, overlooking the right branch of Y Gully. The steep section of Barrel Buttress is passed by a cave pitch.

Mild 100m VS (1962)

Start below the upper tier, a little to the right of the chimney at the left side of the frontal face. Climb steeply on good rock to a 45m crux pitch up twin cracks in a slabby wall.

Bitter 105m VS (1963)

To the left of the chimney on the right side of the frontal face are a number of grooves. Start up the V-shaped depression just left of these grooves.

1. 20m Climb to a small protruding nose with an ancient peg.
2. 35m 4c Either climb the crack and wall on the right to a grass ledge, then move 3m left to belay; or traverse left below the nose and climb a slabby wall to reach the same point.
3. 20m 4c Climb the crack above to a block on a grass ledge and traverse right to belay.
4. 30m Continue directly to the top.

Cooper's Gully 300m I (1979)

The gully right of Barrel Buttress. The prominent chimney right of and facing Cooper's Gully has also been climbed (III).

THE WESTERN CLIFFS

From Tumore at the north-west corner of Loch Assynt a path leads for about 2km to the Bealach Leireag from where the long western scarp of Quinag is clearly seen. The cliffs are on the whole rather broken and vegetated, but steep sections exist that may reward those prepared to make the effort to reach them. The following features, from right to left, are useful in locating the climbs. (a) Bealach a' Chornaidh, which is the col between Spidean Coinich (764m) and the unnamed Junction Top of Quinag (745m). (b) The Junction Top (745m). (c) A small col. (d) A square-topped tower. (e) A second col. (f) A third col. (g) A broad mass of cliff under Spot Height 776m (Sail Gorm). The first climb lies on the buttress below and left of the Bealach a' Chornaidh.

The Family Way 55m Hard Severe (1973/1982)

The buttress has three 'obvious' ribs, and is split in the middle by a shallow gully. Start below the central rib.

1. 25m Climb to a small overhang. Move round the left edge to a crack which is followed to a rock platform on the crest. An easier alternative

is to climb a mossy groove that starts in the central shallow gully, then traverse right to a steep crack which leads to the crest.
2. 30m Continue up the crest, finishing by a steep chimney.

Tenement Ridge 150m   Very Difficult   (1961)
This is the prominent rib that rises from right to left on a lower crag below the square-topped tower. It is bounded on the right by a deep gully and rises in a series of rock steps separated by spacious ledges. Start from a heather ledge by climbing a sloping corner with a slab on its left. Variations are possible on most pitches, but there is an unavoidable 5m wall on the final section of the ridge, just before it joins the main mountain.

The Pillar of Assynt 120m   VS   (1968)
This is the very narrow clean-cut column directly below the second col. Climb 60m of steep heather and rock to the base of the pillar. Climb up the centre then right to a sentry-box on the right edge, immediately below the first overlap (30m). Traverse the right wall for 3m to enter a strenuous crack which is climbed for 8m, then traverse back horizontally left across a smooth wall to regain the right edge of the pillar. Alternatively, the overlap can be passed by traversing to the left edge of the pillar and pulling round on good layaway holds. From above the first overlap climb a crack in the front of the pillar and move to the right edge to pass the next overlap. Continue up to the top of the pillar. A narrow gangway and col lead to an easy shattered rib, then grass slopes to the col.

Ricketty Ridge 150m   VS   (1968)
This is the most continuous of the rocky ribs in the centre of the wide crag between the second and third cols. The rock is loose. Climb the first pitch by a delicate upward traverse left. Continue straight up the spine of the ridge to the first steep section. Climb this on the recessed right side to finish up a corner crack which leads to the foot of the final 45m column. Make a hard hand traverse right, then climb straight up the column and turn the top fringe on the left edge. After a narrow neck and a short step the ridge merges into the hillside.

Below the third col is deep gully that is useful for descent. The next route takes the gully that rises from a bay at the top of the slope just left of this.

The Gully of Nedd   200m   IV   (1986)
The only details are that the steep top pitch was bare and was avoided by a tricky right traverse to gain and climb a parallel snowed-up turf runnel.

Noggin The Nog   80m   IV   (1991)
This climbs a chimney in the right wall of the bay, just left of the gully that descends from the third col. There is a shallower groove to the right and the two features define a small tower on the ridge bounding the gully. Climb the chimney in two long pitches, with much back and foot, to easier ground.

The Waste Pipe   150m   II   (1965)
This is the next deep gully, towards the far end of the buttress. Good rock scenery.

The Wind Pipe   150m   VS   (1969)
The second deep gully at the north end of the cliffs. It contains a 35m Great Chimney pitch that overhangs some 5m. This presented great difficulties on the first ascent despite ideal conditions.

Toby   150m   VS   (1977)
This follows the third buttress left of The Waste Pipe. Start at the lowest rocks and climb to a grassy ledge and belay. Climb the edge, turn a nose at 15m on the right and continue up the edge to a small stance. Step left and climb a cracked wall to a roof. Move left, climb a bulge and continue to a belay. Scramble to the top.

BEINN AN FHURAIN
860m   (Map Ref 303 215)

There is a cliff formed round the nose east of spot height 860m. Traversing round under the cliff from the col between Beinn an Fhurain and Conival, one soon comes to a short gully with an icefall just to its left. This provided a rather scrappy climb with three steep icefall pitches, technically grade V but of a non-serious disposition. Climb the initial icefall (40m), then traverse easily right into the gully. This leads to a steeper icefall (40m) which continues as a thinner version leading into an icy chimney (45m). Either escape off left or scramble up to a choice of steep mixed pitches leading to the top.

EAS A' CHUAL ALUINN
(Map Ref 282 278)

This is often claimed as the highest waterfall in Britain. The shortest approach is to leave the A894 road about 5km north of Skiag Bridge and follow the path which skirts the south end of Loch na Gainmhich and climbs over the Bealach a' Bhuirich. Descent to the foot of the waterfall could be tricky. The fall is only likely to freeze completely in exceptional winters. The top is at an altitude of about 200m.

Eas Coulin   200m   IV/V   (1986)
The waterfall is concave and rises in three steps, each steeper than the last. On the only known ascent water was still flowing in the centre and the first two steps were climbed on the right side. The second step was steep and 60m in length, but a series of large ice mushrooms and short ramps eased the difficulty. A long traverse below the final step led through the spray and up to a good rock belay beside the crux, a 6m vertical pillar.

THE OLD MAN OF STOER
(Map Ref 018 353)

Probably the most impressive sea-stack on the north-west coast, this also has a reasonably easy route of ascent. However it is advisable to establish the times of the tides and to take extra ropes in case a Tyrolean is necessary. Drive to the lighthouse at the end of the road on the west side of the Stoer peninsula, from where a walk of about 3km leads to the Old Man. Scramble steeply down the 90m face opposite the Old Man to a broad shelf. There is usually a channel about 8m wide at its narrowest point, which may be waded or swum. A Tyrolean may be used to bring across the rest of the party and protect the retreat. From its slender base the pinnacle bulges at mid-height before it begins to taper. Large rough-grained sandstone holds make the climbing easier than it appears, at least on the Original Route.

Jon Yeamsley - 2/6/02

✓ **Original Route**   65m   VS ***   (1966)
1. 20m 5a From 4m up the landward face follow twin horizontal cracks left onto the south-west face, then climb straight up on good holds to a big ledge on the arete. (This pitch is avoidable in calm seas by a longer swim).

2. 20m 4b Climb a steep slab above the ledge to a fringe of overhangs, pass these by a crack and step left to reach ledges; continue for 10m to a cave belay above a large chockstone.

3. 10m 4c Traverse round the edge on the right to the landward face and trend up right, avoiding the first upward break, to reach a small ledge and belay.

4. 15m Climb the V-chimney above to easy ground and finish up a corner crack.

Descent: Abseil directly down the arete to the first belay ledge (45m). Traverse a thin ledge on the landward face to another abseil point and abseil again to the base.

North-West Corner   60m   E2 **   (1987)
This takes the right arete of the landward face, as seen from the cliff top. Friends are essential, preferably take a double rack.

1. 15m 5c Climb the poorly protected arete on its left side, with difficulty at 6m, to a ledge and Friend 3 belay.

2. 20m 5b A flake just left of the arete allows holds to be gained leading up right to a resting place on the arete. Move up right round to the right-hand side and follow a left-slanting crack to regain the crest. Move left to a fine belay ledge.

3. 25m 6a Climb the obvious left-trending ramp past two old peg runners (very hard) to a ledge at its top (junction with Original Route). Move out right to a large ledge just left of the arete and follow the arete to the top.

Ring of Bright Water   80m   E1   (1987)
Start at the right end of the seaward face. Climb a short wall to a slab under a roof. Traverse left round the roof and round the arete to gain a steep flared crack on the north face. Climb this to its top, then traverse left along a ledge to peg belays on the east face (5b). Climb a bulge above the belay to gain a hanging slab. Follow this up left to gain the deep groove of the Original Route. Follow this to the top.

The Reiff Sea-Cliffs

The village of Reiff (Map Ref 965 144) is a collection of crofts, new and old, at the road-end north-west of Achiltibuie. The Reiff sea-cliffs on the Rubha Mor Penninsula include all the climbing areas from the Pinnacle crags of Roinn a' Mhill (just five minutes walk from the village) to the Golden Walls of Rubha Coigeach, and then almost 2km further to Rubha Ploytach. Their locations are shown on the general map. There is a plan map of each of the climbing areas, and detailed plans of each crag; careful scrutiny of these maps is important to locate the individual climbs in this quite complex area. The furthest cliffs are about an hour's walk from Reiff.

ROINN A' MHILL

This is the headland nearest the village, which has four climbing areas; The Pinnacle Area, The Point, The Bouldering Cliff and Black Rocks. See the map of Area 1 on page 173.

PINNACLE AREA

FIRST GEO
This is a narrow boulder-filled inlet with a number of corners and steep walls on its east side and an easy slab on the west. It has a unique through cave emerging at an old blow hole some 25 metres inland. The inlet is tidal, so most of the routes are best climbed at half to low tides. Access is down the easy slab via the boulder-filled crack above the cave entrance. See Map 1A on page 177.

1 Amorous Prawn 5m Severe
The short rightmost corner at the seaward end of the east wall. Choose from a couple of corner starts.

2 Lanky 12m Very Difficult
Climb the blocky rib left of Amorous Prawn.

3 Sandbag 15m Mild VS 4b *
The obvious deep corner; finish leftwards.

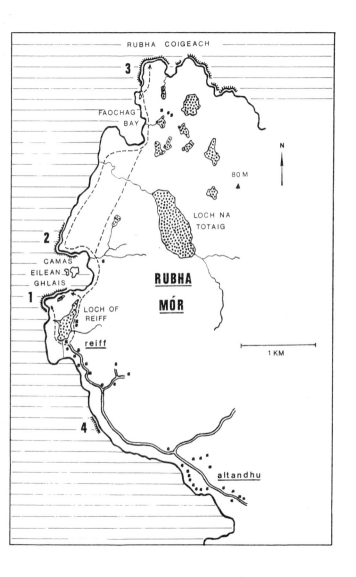

The next corner has an undercut ledge at its base and although it has not been climbed direct, it gives the start to the next two routes.

4 Kurgan 15m E4 6a ***
From the ledge, traverse the first horizontal break right to climb a short hanging groove. Finish direct from the large break via a bulging crack. Fine powerful climbing.

Scuttlefish 15m HVS 5a *
From halfway up the corner, follow the flake out left onto the slab and trend right, passing a large ledge, to the top.

Reunion 10m Very Difficult
From the bottom of the next corner on the left, climb rightwards up the slab to the top of Scuttlefish.

5 Octopus' Garden 10m Very Difficult
Climb the corner direct from the start of Reunion.

The slab on the west side of the inlet may be climbed almost anywhere at Very Difficult. **Nice Touch** (10m, Moderate) takes the crack at the landward end next to the descent. **Bedbug** (10m, Difficult) climbs up to the right end of an overlap then finishes direct. **Sponge** (10m, Difficult) moves left round the overlap and follows a line diagonally leftwards to the top. **Scurvey** (15m Very Difficult) climbs boldly close to the left edge, then traverse left along the base of the slab to start.

SECOND GEO
This is a larger inlet with an impressive undercut headwall and a long wall on the east side, which terminates at a sea-washed promontory. The west side of the inlet comprises a fine exposed slab and the pinnacle itself. The back of the geo is non-tidal. There are a number of approaches, including descending Slab and Corner (route 12), or a ramp on the east side, tucked under the headwall. Alternatively, right of the corner of Tangle of the Isles, descend a broken fault onto a narrow slab shelf, or descend off the end of the east side promontory onto a platform, then down a short chimney on the right to step onto a rock fin under a large rock nose. The rock fin is sea-washed at high tides. Belay on the 'fin', or at the base of Tongue 'n' Groove for the following five routes:

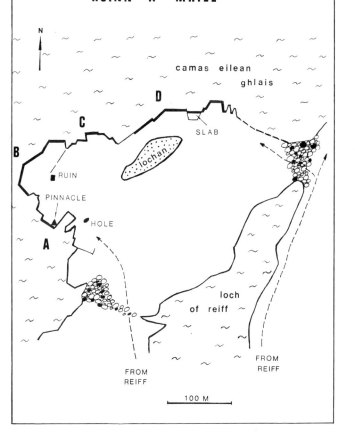

AREA 1
ROINN A' MHILL

camas eilean
ghlais

D

SLAB

C

B

lochan

RUIN

PINNACLE

HOLE

A

loch
of reiff

FROM
REIFF

FROM
REIFF

100 M

6 Tongue 'n' Groove 10m Very Difficult
Climb the groove immediately left of the rock nose, starting up the slab under the nose itself.

Aerial Display 10m HVS 5a *
The next groove line left, with spectacular moves through the bulge.

Gulf Air 15m Difficult
Start up a corner chimney left again, then finish up the open groove above.

7 The Toothed Comb 15m Mild Severe
Traverse left under Gulf Air to climb a short steep corner to easier ground.

Atlantic Swell 20m Very Difficult *
Continue the left traverse round a rib to finish up a groove overlooking the corner of Tangle of the Isles.

8 Tangle of the Isles 10m Hard Severe **
Good sustained climbing up the prominent black corner in the middle of the east wall.

Abacus 10m Mild VS 4b *
Climb the crack in the left wall of Tangle.

Garbagio 6m HVS 5a
Take the first direct line through the overhangs a few metres left of the broken descent fault.

Dunlin 8m E2 5b
Climb bulging broken rock 3m left of Garbagio to a horizontal fault above a block. Move left to finish up a short groove.

Power Seizure 8m E3 5c/6a *
A few metres left of Dunlin, climb a vague scoop up to the roof and protection. Surmount the roof and climb the wall above to finish just left of Dunlin.

   The next five routes are on the impressive headwall.

9 Scrunch 6m HVS 5b
Above the ramp descent are two thin crack lines in the short undercut slab. Climb into the thinner right-hand crack.

Stechie 8m HVS 5b *
The left-hand crack line, finishing leftwards.

10 A Walk Across the Rooftops 20m E3 5c ***
Fine strenuous climbing out along the traverse across the overhanging headwall. Start as for Stechie and finish up vague cracks at the end of the hand traverse. Big Friends are helpful.

Strangeways 10m E4 6b **
Strenuous technical climbing up the overhanging crack above the start of the traverse of A Walk Across The Rooftops. Where the crack bends left, finish out right.

11 Immaculate Deception 12m E1 5b **
Start at the bottom of the slab on the west side under the headwall by a protruding block. Steep positive climbing over the small roof leads into the left-trending crack.

Immaculate Escape 8m VS 4c
Wimps traverse right into the crack above the roof of Immaculate Deception.

12 Slab and Corner 20m Difficult *
Follow the corner throughout. The finish up the wide crack on the right is Severe.

13 Jellyfish Slab 20m Difficult *
Pleasant climbing up the middle of the slab.

14 Edge of The Sea 20m Very Difficult
Exposed climbing up the left edge of the slab. Take a diagonal line out to the edge from near the middle of the slab.

THE PINNACLE
The best approach is to follow the easy descent to the north and walk round under the Pinnacle Walls. The pinnacle platforms are above the high tide level, but a rough sea combined with high tide may cut off the platform at the block, so descend by the Difficult corner.

15 Moonjelly 10m Very Difficult ***
Excellent bold padding up the vague central scoop on the pinnacle slab.

Both the left and right edges of the slab yield at Severe and Very Difficult respectively; good climbing. On the landward face of the pinnacle are **Special K** (Difficult), which steps up the the righthand edge, and **K Squared** (Very Difficult), which takes the 'Y' crack in the middle of the face. On the seaward (west) side is **Corkscrew** (10m Difficult), which starts under the prow then moves up and traverses right onto the edge, which is followed right under the final bulge. The pinnacle also offers a frightening hand traverse across the 'beak' on the seaward (south) side. Descend by downclimbing or abseil.

PINNACLE WALLS

16 Barrier Reiff 10m HVS 5b *
Starting 2 metres left of the platform edge overlooking the second geo, climb a thin corner crack and pull left round a small roof to finish direct.

Sip from the Wine of Youth Again 10m HVS 5a *
Start as for Barrier Reiff and follow the obvious right-slanting diagonal crack over a bulge out to the edge. Finish up the slab.

Totally Tropical 10m E4 6b
Left of Barrier Reiff is a large roof halfway up, bounded by a thin left-slanting diagonal crack. Climb the crack to underclings at the left end of the roof then move up right to a shelf. Finish up the short wall.

17 Channering Worm 10m E3 5c ***
Superb varied climbing. Start at the middle of the undercut buttress left of Totally Tropical. Pull over the roof and snatch for the 'crazy spike'. Leave this reluctantly and make hard moves up and right to finish via the easier left-slanting diagonal crack.

Yellow Dogs 10m E3/4 5c **
The grossly leaning groove tucked into the left side of the Worm Buttress. An excellent workout! Climb the groove direct and hand traverse the break out to the right edge. Fight to stand on the ledge and reach for the top.

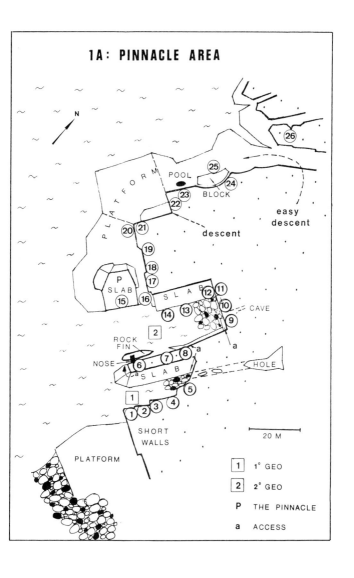

1A: PINNACLE AREA

N

PLATFORM

POOL

BLOCK

㉕ ㉖ ㉔ ㉓ ㉒ ㉑ ⑳ ⑲ ⑱ ⑰ ⑯ ⑮

easy descent

descent

SLAB

P SLAB

SLAB

⑪ ⑫ ⑩ ⑬ ⑭ ⑨

CAVE

ROCK FIN

NOSE

a ⑥ ⑦ ⑧ a

SLAB a

HOLE

⑤

1

① ② ③ ④

SHORT WALLS

PLATFORM

20 M

1	1° GEO
2	2° GEO
P	THE PINNACLE
a	ACCESS

18 Slanting Corner   10m   Mild Severe *
Climb the corner below Yellow Dogs.

The obvious parallel diagonal crack just left of the corner is taken by **Skel** (Severe) and the shallow groove and diagonal crack just left again is **Xyles** (Severe).

19 The Krill   10m   Mild VS 4b
Climb the recessed overhanging crack left again. Finish direct.

Puckered Wall   10m   VS 4b *
Steep jug pulling up the wall left of The Krill.

20 Pop-out   10m   HVS 5a *
Start right of the arete. Climb into and struggle out of a short closed groove. Move left and finish up the right side of the arete.

Hy Brasil   10m   VS 4c **
Start left of the fine arete and follow the first obvious line out right onto it. Finish direct.

21 Westering Home   10m   E1 5b ***
Climb the crack just left of the arete. Good stuff, delicate at the top.

Fly by Wire   10m   E2 5c
Thin climbing up the twin parallel cracks left of Westering Home.

The Left-hand side of the wall is bounded by **Descent Corner** (10m, Difficult). Left again is another wall.

22 Midreiff   10m   Severe *
Climb the shallow corner in the middle of the left wall. Move diagonally in from the edge.

Sandstone Shuffle   10m   Very Difficult
Bold climbing up and left round the left arete. Finish direct above the ledge.

Enigma Grooves, Stac Pollaidh (Climber, Rab Anderson)

23 Earth Shaker   10m   E2 6a **
Directly above a little pool is a short corner on the leaning wall. Boulder up to it from either the left or right, move slightly left above and finish direct.

More of the Same   10m   VS 4c *
Just left of Earth Shaker is a small hidden right-trending corner. Climb the corner then go left over the roof to finish.

Cave Wall   5m   Severe
This wall lies above a huge block separated from the main face by a deep fissure. Climb the centre of the wall from the top of the block.

24 Diagonal Crack   8m   Difficult *
From the top of the block climb the left-trending crack.

25 Le Mer   5m   VS 5a *
Good moves up the crack and pockets on the front face of the block.

26 Juniors' Groove   8m   Very Difficult *
The deep groove hidden in the right wall of the gully between the first two promontories beyond the descent fault.

Rockette's Climb   10m   VS 4c
Right of Junior's Groove, take a right-slanting crack line to a small ledge. Move left onto the face and finish up a crack.

Kiddies Korner (Moderate) gives nice climbing up the left edge of the steep slab opposite Junior's Groove and **Toddler's Crack** (Moderate) takes the crack line a few metres right of Kiddies Korner.

A few routes have been recorded on the The Wedding Wall, which lies left of Kiddies Korner on the front of the promontory, starting from a tidal platform. From right to left, these are: **Something Old** (Very Difficult), the narrow left-slanting crack just left of the edge; **Something New** (Very Difficult), which takes the right-trending diagonal crack, passing a triangular niche, and starting from the left end of a big ledge; **Something Borrowed** (Very Difficult) climbs the thin left-slanting parallel cracks just left; **Something Blue** (VS 4c) follows the left-trending diagonal crack line near the left end of the wall. Finally, **Something Else** (HVS 5a) starts at the left end of the wall. Climb directly to a small flake and layback to the top.

The Old Man of Stoer

THE POINT

A handful of short routes have been recorded on the broken walls between the Pinnacle Area and the Bouldering Cliff. The tide affects most of the routes in this area, but as usual, the bouldering here is first-class, on short walls and slabs at and above tide level. The routes are short, and the first, the obvious short corner crack (Severe), is tucked round the corner of the last promontory of the Pinnacle Area, on the west side. The bulging wall to the left is VS 5b. Next left (facing the routes), is a short upper wall with twin parallel cracks (Severe). Left again, above a tidal platform and left of a wide deep crack (descent), is a narrow steep black wall. A line up the right edge is Very Difficult. The cracks and horizontal breaks up the middle of the wall are HVS 5a. Lastly, the chimney-cleft on the left of the wall is Difficult.

The cliff sets back, presenting a long north-facing black wall and further along the front face is a very obvious square-cut slot in a steep slab. A route through the 'sentry box' is Very Difficult (tidal). At the right end of the sentry box slab is a black overhanging crack (VS 4c, tidal).

Further left again there is a north-facing short black wall with a tidal platform at its base. The corner ramp at the right end is Difficult, the crack in the middle of the wall is Severe, and the bulging wall to the left of the crack is HVS 5b.

Left again, the crags become more broken and turn east towards the Bouldering Cliff.

BOULDERING CLIFF

On the left of the grotty gully descent is a low angled slab. The slab may be climbed almost anywhere at Moderate; the right edge (facing the slab) can be used as a descent. The first route, which is affected by high tide, is Sneaky Slab (Difficult); round the edge of the right end of the easy slab is a hidden tapering slab. Start from the lowest platform. See Map 1C on page 182.

1 Graphite Grease 10m Hard Severe
Start at the base of the descent gully. Climb the corner and steep crack tucked into the left side of the easy slab.

2 Hors D'Oeuvre 5m VS 4c
Climb the first corner left of the descent gully (facing the crag), starting from the short ramp.

3 In the Land of Dreamy Dreamers 5m HVS 5a
The next corner left.

4 Eliminator 6m E1 5c
Left again, climb to an obvious rounded ledge and finish out right.
Poorly protected but short.

5 The Corner 10m VS 4c *
Obvious.

6 White Horses 10m E2 6a *
The arete direct! Dynamic moves off the ground lead to a bold finish.

7 Scallog 10m E1 5c
Start just left of the arete and climb the wall up and left to join the top
of Black Zone.

8 Black Zone 10m HVS 5b *
Awkward moves up a diagonal ramp lead right to a high ledge. Either
finish by Golden Eyes or step out right.

9 Golden Eyes 10m E1 5b **
Climb the corner left of Black Zone to finish direct.

10 Romancing the Stone 10m E3 6b ***
Very hard moves up the thin crack just left of the next arete. Either
finish direct (Friend placements in the break), or finish up The Hand
Traverse.

11 The Hand Traverse 15m HVS 5a ***
Start at the obvious ramp-fault. Gain and traverse the break rightwards
across Romancing the Stone to finish up the arete.

12 The Ramp 15m Severe **
Good climbing up the right-slanting fault-line.

13 Hole in the Wall 10m E2 6a **
Climb the middle of the wall left of The Ramp to the 'hole', move left
and layback the shallow flake to its top. A long reach gains the break.
Traverse right to finish.

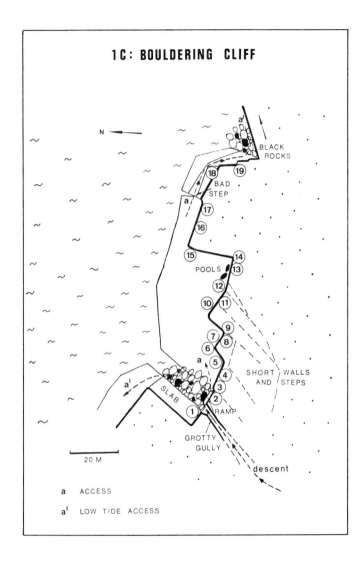

1C: BOULDERING CLIFF

N

BLACK ROCKS

a'

⑲

⑱

BAD STEP

a

⑰

⑯

⑮ ⑭

POOLS ⑬

⑫

⑩ ⑪

⑨

⑦ ⑧

⑥

a ⑤

④

③

②

SHORT WALLS AND STEPS

a'

SLAB

①

RAMP

GROTTY GULLY

descent

20 M

a   ACCESS

a¹   LOW TIDE ACCESS

Toad in the Hole 20m E5 6a ***
Climb Hole in the Wall to the first break, then continue straight up the middle of the narrow wall.

Next left is an amazing grossly-leaning wall which not surprisingly still awaits an ascent. The unclimbed line of the area!

14 Wyatt Earp 20m E3 6a ***
This route takes the big right-hand corner of the unclimbed wall.

15 Leaning Meanie 20m E2 6a **
A face climbers nightmare! This is the short overhanging jam crack near the left edge of the wall. Finish easily via the upper chimney.

16 Crack of Desire, *Variation Start* 10m E3 6a
Take the shallow ramp line leading left to the big break and halfway point of The Crack of Desire.

17 The Crack of Desire 20m E3 5c/6a ***
The right-slanting diagonal crack line. Climb to the large break via the lower corner crack. After the bulge above, break out onto the left wall to finish direct.

Desire Direct 20m E4 6a ***
Follow the diagonal crack of The Crack of Desire all the way.

Shootin' the Tube 20m HVS 5a *
Start just left of Crack of Desire. Climb into and up the short corner to a big ledge. Move right and climb the wall to the finish of Monster Breaker. A bit artificial in the top half but good climbing none-the-less.

18 Monster Breaker 25m VS 4c
Starting at the right-hand side of the rockfall bay, follow the rightwards slanting pale tapering slab.

No Picnic at Hanging Rock 40m E4 5b,5c **
A girdle of the main Bouldering Cliff. Start up the right edge of Monster Breaker and follow the break round to finish up The Ramp. Belay above the crack of Leaning Meanie.

Left of Monster Breaker the landslip has left a smooth steep groove, Excellence by Design. The cracks in the upper wall on the right is **An Dobhran Mara** (20m E3 6a *). Start up the corner directly under the cracks and at the roof step left to a ledge on the arete. Pull into the thin crack; at its top, hand traverse right and go up to gain the top system of cracks.

19 Excellence by Design   20m   E2 6a
The 'new' smooth groove yields to all sorts of contortions.

One Scoop or Two?   25m   VS 4c
The hanging slab just left. Climb into and follow the wide corner crack until a right traverse leads to a light-scarred scoop. Move right and up into the second scoop; finish direct.

BLACK ROCKS

Basically an extension of the Bouldering Cliff past the landslip inlet, Black Rocks first trends north-east through various slabby buttresses and steep walls, then, rising in height, turns east to form a number of leaning aretes and wide grooves. It ends abruptly at a huge low-angled slab. For a short distance thereafter the cliff once more gains height (Orange Wall) eventually petering out into scrappy zawns before reaching the boulder beach of Camas Eilean Ghlais. Access to most of the routes here is relatively complicated and affected by high tide. At very low tide it is possible to continue round from the Bouldering Cliff by slithering over seaweed covered boulders and a pull up on barnacled rock. Alternatively descend the huge low angled slab easily near the right edge.

For the Orange Wall Area from the base of the slab cut back right onto platforms under the cliffs proper. This is possible at all tide levels. For Black Rocks Main Cliffs, the following access is only possible at low tides. From the base of the slab, cross the head of a small inlet and follow a traverse line to the right at the same height, out to a ledge on the promontory (Difficult). Climb right and up over two short walls to the top of a small slab. Descend this to sea level at the base of a blunt arete and climb, awkwardly at first, up and right over blocky ground to ledges at the base of a wide groove (Hourglass Groove, Very Difficult). The aim now is to gain platforms on the far side of a narrow inlet further right. Either downclimb a curving flake crack starting round the corner on the right (4c) or, using a spike anchor at the start of the flake, abseil or lower into the inlet and swing onto the platform. The simplest approach, and the best at high tide, is to abseil down the line of The Grooves using a large block anchor. This leads directly onto the platform which rounds the arete to Tystie and Black Gold slabs.

The routes are described from the easy descent slab firstly westwards (The Main Cliffs Area), then eastwards to the Orange Wall area. See Map 1D on page 186.

BLACK ROCKS MAIN CLIFFS

Black Rocks Sea Traverse (40m VS 4c *) is a fine expedition, climbed in three short pitches, as described above. It is possible only at low tides.

7 Chilli Puds 25m   Mild Severe
Start at the base of the descent slab at the head of the inlet. From the start of the right traverse as above, climb the steep cracked black slab onto a flat arete. Thruch up the awkward short crack on the left onto the top of a second slab and finish up the groove above.

Barrel of Laughs 25m VS 4c *
Climb the slab corner left of Chilli Puds to the flat arete, possible belay. Continue right along the ramp line to finish.

Hourglass Groove 15m HVS 5a **
The first wide groove encountered on the sea-level traverse, rising above black blocky ground. Low tide access, or abseil in. Climb the steep crack on the right to the narrows and follow the crack leftwards up a series of ramps.

Shifting Sands 15m HVS 5a *
A counter route to Hourglass Groove. Climb the series of big steps on the left to the narrows (slightly easier but less well protected than the crack on the right). Continue straight up the crack on the right to the roof and undercling right to finish.

6 The Grooves 20m Severe *
The left side of the wide groove above the platform at the end of Black Rocks Sea Traverse.

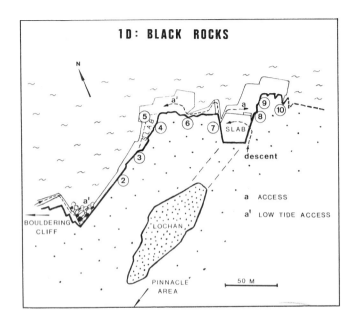

Glaikit Flake   25m   VS 4c
Climb up the right side of The Grooves and follow a left-trending flake
line, crossing The Grooves, out to the arete. Swing round and up to a
large ledge. Either finish left up an easy slab, or more in keeping with
the climb, step right and up the wall to the top.

Dark Truths   20m   HVS 5a
The broken right wall of The Grooves, finishing by two short steep
corners.

Auld Nick   10m   Mild Severe *
Climb a right-trending deep crack, starting at the base of a flat faced
arete right of The Grooves. Finish up Tystie Slab.

By traversing the lower platform round the corner a large area of
slab is reached.

Black Donald 25m Severe *
A good route up the corner tucked into the left side of the slab. Finish by Tystie Slab. Watch out for jammed ropes.

5 Tystie Slab 30m Very Difficult ***
Excellent climbing. Start near the left edge of the slab and take the easiest line using pockets and horizontal breaks. Finish up left where the slab narrows considerably.

Tystie Left Edge 30m Severe *
Try keeping to the slab edge overlooking Black Donald.

4 Batman 25m HVS 5a *
Wild climbing up the hanging groove in the headwall above Tystie Slab. Climb the next slab right of Tystie to a ledge belay (Difficult). Move left over awkward steps to gain and climb the hanging groove.

Moving right, the slab finishes at a short black corner running up to a huge break in the headwall. This is **Poll Dubh** (VS 4c/5a), which yields to strenuous laybacking and bridging. The best finish through the break is by climbing left and up a short corner crack, then back right along a rampline.

At the base of Poll Dubh, yet another black corner cuts into the left edge of the slabby buttress further right. This is **Black Pig** (VS 4c ***) which gives superb steep climbing on good holds. Move in rightwards and surmount the first overlap to gain the corner. Finish left under the final overlap.

Lower ledges lead right under the black slabby buttress and steeper walls towards the rockfall area of the Bouldering Cliff. These ledges are awash at higher tides or during heavy seas. However, it is possible to abseil onto a platform at the base of the large unstable-looking break in the headwall around Black Guillemot (abseil down the left side of the break, facing out). This platform gives access to the remaining routes.

3 Black Gold 25m VS 4c ***
Climb the centre of the black slabby buttress starting by a short groove at the lowest point. It is also possible to move onto the slab rightwards from the start of Black Pig if the sea threatens (Mild VS 4b).

Starting further right, under the left end of the unstable break, is **Route With No Name** (VS 4c *) which follows a left-curving crack to finish via the upper wall just right of Black Gold. **Glomach** (Hard Severe) climbs the slabby corner under the middle of the break, then pulls right where it steepens and finishes rightwards along the blocky ledge. **Black Guillemot** (VS 4c *) takes the thin right-curving crack in the black right wall of Glomach. Gain the crack by swinging right from under the small roof low down.

Great Black Back   20m   E3 6a **
An attempt to climb the right arete of the bay under the break. Start up the leaning black corner on the left and hand-traverse right onto the arete along the horizontal break. Climb the arete to where it bulges and move left across to the final move of the corner. Easily up to the next horizontal break, move right and finish on good holds left of the arete.

2   Rick's Route   20m   E1 5b
Further right round the arete the crag steepens. Climb a leaning crack just left of a huge perched block.

   Atlantic Trough (Very Difficult) follows the fault line beneath Rick's Route to gain the top of the huge perched block. Finish by the short wall above.
   The following two routes lie on the final slabby part of Black Rocks before it deteriorates into the rockfall zawn. Approach by traversing right from the start of Atlantic Trough along various horizontal breaks (Severe), or at low tides climb direct into the routes up barnicled rock; a bit masochistic! **Sore Loser** (VS 5a *) climbs a short steep black corner, then moves left above to the top of the perched block and finishes as for atlantic trough. **fiddler On The Rocks** (Very Difficult) starts further along the right traverse and climbs out of a black crevice onto the slab above. Trend left to finish through a break in the short headwall.

ORANGE WALL AREA
This is the area to the right of the descent. The climbs are described in relation to Meikle Neuk, firstly leftwards as far as Gallus Corner, then rightwards.

8   Meikle Neuk   10m   Severe **
The fine corner at the right-hand side of the west-facing leaning wall.

Flying Pig   10m   E2 6a *
Your chance to try a 'first generation dyno'! Climb the wall immediately left of Meikle Neuk past a large ledge at one-third height. Take large Friends for the horizontal breaks.

9   Orange Wall   10m   E1 5b **
Climb up to the ledge and finish by the flake above. Good stuff!

Huffin Puffin   10m   E1 5c **
Good climbing; hard to start and well protected above. Start at the left end of a triangular niche at the foot of the wall. Up to the first break by a large pocket, move slightly right and finish direct.

   Slap 'n' Tickle (VS 5a) is the short boulder problem crack at the left-hand end of the Orange Wall. Round the corner the crag is even shorter but gives good easier lines. **Vee Slab** (Moderate *) is the short hanging slab immediately left of the edge; finish left. **Wee Step** (Difficult) is up the front of the face left again. **Chimney Sweep** (Difficult) gives good back and footing up the recessed chimney-groove further left. **Wee Wall** (Difficult) starts by ducking down under the nose of rock, continues round the corner then climbs the centre of the wall on the right. **The Leap** (5a) starts from the right (east) side of the nose: jump for the top and struggle up.

10   Gallus Corner   5m   Difficult *
The fine corner-crack.

   The following routes are described proceeding rightwards from Meikle Neuk. **Hanging Groove** (Severe) leads into the short groove right of Meikle Neuk, after an awkward start. The next corner right is **Slanting Corner** (Hard Severe *). **Mossy Slab** (Difficult) is the slab on the right of the deep damp recess.
   The final routes here lie on the broken short black walls to the right. They are split by a large left-trending ramp with a right-slanting diagonal crack above the lower end; a possible descent. The crack at the left end of the lower wall, finishing up the left side of the upper wall, is **Deep Crack** (Very Difficult). **Mean Streak** (HVS 5b) starts near the bottom of the ramp and climbs the orange streaks on the upper wall. **Jen's Fault** (Difficult) is the obvious right-slanting fault, starting from the bottom of the ramp. **Lunch Break** (Severe) climbs the left diagonal crack at the right end of the upper wall, and finishes up before Jen's Fault.

SEA-CLIFF AREA

This is a complicated coastline of promontories, inlets, caves and platforms on the north side of Camas Eilean Ghlais. Most of the rock, although sound, is either broken or low-angle and may be climbed almost anywhere. Since the coastline faces south it can feel almost equatorial on a sunny day!

Seen from the approach path along the bay or from the top of the Bouldering Cliff or Black Rocks, the coastline has a large conspicuous cave near its right end. Immediately left of this is a square-cut promontory; the Sea-Cliff. Further left is another conspicuous rectangular cave above which Route Cavity climbs. Left of the rectangular cave are two rounded slabby promontories; the one to the left sports a deep wide crack on its right side. This is Sea Stud.

The approach to the various promontories, except the Sea-Cliff, is easy scrambling down ramps and slabs beneath the climbs. High tides affect access to routes on the Sea-Cliff, Overhanging Chimney, and routes on the west side of the Weathered Tower. See the map to Area 2, An Stiuir, on page 195

THE SEA-CLIFF

Approach from the cave entrance on the east side of the promontory, where fallen blocks lead to a large rock fin. At half to low tides a descent gully (Moderate) in the east corner leads to the rock fin. At high tide, abseil to small platforms at the base of the climbs. At low tides, the narrow gully bounding the west side of the promontory leads to routes on that side. Route lengths range from 10m to 15m. On the right wall at the bottom of the descent corner are **Sea Pink** (Very Difficult), the deep curving crack line from the bottom of the descent corner, and **Nipper** (VS 4c), the cracks immediately left of the right arete.

Starting just left of the descent gully, **Sea Sic** (Hard Severe) climbs a bottomless groove and finishes out right. **Sea Quim** (Very Difficult) starts 5 metres left of the descent gully and takes a left-facing slab corner. **Sea Stytis** (Severe **) is 5 metres left again, a short slab and deep left-facing corner cracks. **Sea Weed** (Very Difficult *) is the groove in the right wall above the start of Sea Stytis. Left is a short inset slab higher up is **Sea Phylis** (Very Difficult **), which gains the hanging slab and follows a right-curving crack to the top. The numbers of the following routes refer to Map 2A on page 193.

1 Sea Men   HVS 4c **
Climb a dark corner-crack below the left end of the hanging slab and finish direct via the steep crack above.

Immediately left of Sea Men is a steep smooth unclimbed corner. The next corner left is gained by abseil or a 5a sea-level traverse. **Sea Ping** (Very Difficult *) climbs the corner direct, and **Sea Parrot** (VS 4c *) takes the right-trending crack from the base of the corner. **Sea Squared** (Severe *) starts 2 metres left of Sea Ping and climbs an obvious left-slanting crack, then moves right at half-height to finish up a wrinkled slab.

2 Sea Squid   Severe *
The next open corner left again.

Sea Moon   Mild VS 4b **
On the front face left of Sea Squid climb a steep crack, turn the roof on the left and finish right up the slab and arete.

3 Sea Scorpion   Mild Severe
Around the nose of the promontory (4c traverse), on the west face, climb a large steepening right-facing corner crack. At low tides approach down the gully on the west side.

Sea Traverse (VS 5a *) is a fine sea-level traverse around the promontory from Sea Stytis, finishing up Sea Scorpion.

Sea Spurt   Severe
A few metres left of Sea Scorpion in the mouth of the narrow gully, climb a line of shattered cracks, easing at half-height.

West of the Sea Cliff is a long narrow promontory with deep narrow inlets either side. **The Cramp** (VS 4c *) climbs the crack up the front of the promontory, starting virtually opposite Sea Spurt. On the front face of the next short promontory west is a wide gash:

4 Overhanging Chimney   10m   Very Difficult
Back and foot work up the back of the wide gash. Access is gained at low tides from across the boulder inlet to the west.

West again is the Weathered Tower, featuring curious sculptured rock on its front face. On its left side is a steep crack.

5 Seascape 8m   E2 5c
Step off the ramp and struggle up the crack to a ledge on the left edge.
Move right and climb cracks to finish.

On the west side above the narrow inlet are two obvious crack lines.
Fair Whappit (VS 4c *) and **Gie Stappit** (VS 5a) are the right-hand
and left-hand cracks respectively. The following routes are on the wall
above the ramp leading to sea level at the rectangular cave entrance:

6 Baby Face 6m   Difficult
Climb the wall at the start of the ramp.

Coast to Coast 8m   VS 4c
Further down the ramp is a square-cut recess. Climb the right corner
of the recess over a small roof.

Le Bugie Hanno Le Gambe Corte 8m   HVS 5a
The wall immediately right of Coast to Coast. It takes longer to
pronounce the route name than it takes to climb it!

7 Aslan 8m   Mild Severe
Start at the left-hand corner of the recess and take a diagonal line to
finish up vague cracks further left.

8 Route Cavity 10m   HVS 5a *
Atmospheric climbing. From sea-level at the lowest point of the ramp,
climb leftwards up to the roof. Move right over the roof, step back left
on the lip and finish leftwards up cracks in the steep slab.

The next promontory is ringed with slabs, but on the west side the
slab is topped by steeper walls particularly around the cave entrance.

9 Pimps Corner 6m   Difficult
Climb the first corner on the right wall on descending the west slab.

10 Tutti Frutti 8m   HVS 5b *
The next undercut corner on the left.

11 Narnian Crack 10m   Very Difficult
The obvious crack in the wall further down the slab.

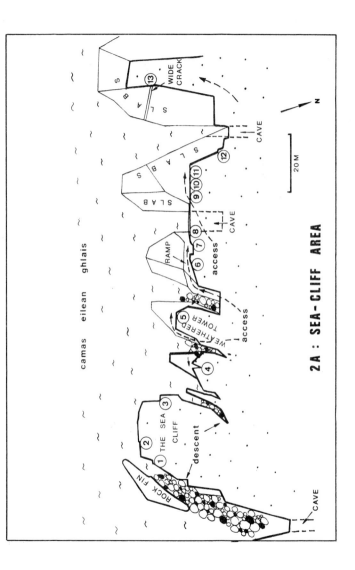

2A : SEA-CLIFF AREA

12 Carmine Corner 15m Moderate
Climb the first wide corner encountered on the slab above the inlet.

13 Sea Stud 10m Difficult
The obvious wide crack in the east slab of the next promontory.
Downclimb or abseil to the start.

AN STIUIR PROMONTORY
This is the final promontory of the Sea-Cliff coastline, separated from
it by a boulder-strewn non-tidal inlet. The inlet runs past some stagnant
pools north-east to the Seal Song area. The routes are on two short
tiers divided by a platform, merging at the north-east corner of the
promontory into a ridged shelf running west of the dry inlet, to finish
at Seal Song itself. The climbs are short, offering fine bouldering or
protectable leads and have not been individually named. Only the
technical grade is given above Severe.

Approach the Upper Tier either along the ridged shelf onto the
dividing platform, or cross the dry boulder inlet and scramble up the
east side onto the platform. This tier is characterised by a cluster of
corners and aretes at its west end. The routes are described from right
to left when facing the crag. The first feature is a very short bulging
sculptured wall, climbed near its left end (4c). Just to the left is a corner
with a mantleshelf start (Difficult). The wall immediately left of the
corner is also Difficult. The wall to the left has a large protruding
triangular block above it. Climb the wall directly under the block (4b).
The crack near the left end of the wall is Mild Severe.

Moving left again, the first arete climbed direct is 5a, as is the first
clean cut corner. The fine arete left of the corner is 5b, and the thin
crack in the right wall of the second corner is 5a, move right to finish.
The second clean cut corner is 4c, as is the arete to its left. Finally, the
the crack in the wall left of the arete is Very Difficult.

The Lower Tier is approached via a narrow platform which traverses
from the dry inlet to finish under the corners of the upper tier. The
routes are described from right to left using this approach. At high tides
with a big swell, the ledge will be awash! The first obvious feature is
a wide slab above a narrow ledge. The cracks at the right-hand end
and in the middle are Moderate, and the left end of the slab is Difficult.
Further along the inlet, immediately left of a dark vertical dyke, the
immpressive horizontally faulted wall is 5b. The small corner tucked
into the left edge of the above wall can be climbed at Very Difficult,
after stepping off a large boulder to start.

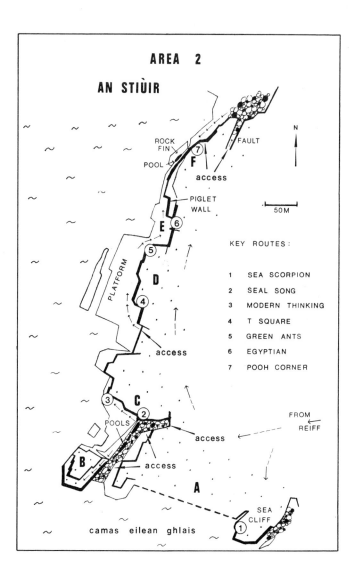

AREA 2

AN STIÙIR

ROCK FIN
POOL
FAULT
F
access

N

50M

PIGLET WALL
E
6

KEY ROUTES:

5
PLATFORM
D
4

1 SEA SCORPION
2 SEAL SONG
3 MODERN THINKING
4 T SQUARE
5 GREEN ANTS
6 EGYPTIAN
7 POOH CORNER

access

3 C
2
POOLS

FROM REIFF

access

B

access

A

SEA CLIFF
1

camas eilean ghlais

The stepped corner at the back of the recess on the left is Moderate. This may be used an access to the upper tier, and as a descent. The short black slab left again, with an awkward start, is Difficult. The next corner 2 metres left is Severe, and the the deep corner left again (moving right to finish) is Very Difficult. The left wall of this corner gives nice moves at Very Difficult, and the next corner, past an awkward step on the ledge, is Difficult (as is the short corner to its left).

The next feature on the lower tier is an overhanging wall, which can be climbed starting at a flake where the wall bends round to the west (5a). Just left of the bend in the wall is a small roof. A groove between the roof and a jutting flake can be climbed at Mild Severe. The wall just left of the flake is also Mild Severe. The steep prominent deep crack left again is Very Difficult. The wall just left of the crack, bulging but extremely juggy, is Severe. On the long wall further left, the right-slanting crack line is Very Difficult. Left again, the wall with sloping holds is 4c.

By traversing round on the north side of the promontory at low tide under a black concave wall, there is a good short north-west facing wall with a series of cracks. Described from right to left, the shattered corner crack is Severe. The wide zigzag shattered crack on the left is 4b, and the awkward jam crack next left is 4c. The thin crack left again is 4b, and the diagonal cracks at the left end of the wall are Severe.

SEAL SONG AREA

The Seal Song area comprises a line of fine cliffs running west from the head of the dry boulder inlet between An Stiuir and the Sea-Cliff area to an impressive leaning wall above a large sloping tidal platform. The crag faces south, is very sheltered, particularly above the boulder inlet and is easily accessible; altogether a good choice on a doubtful day.

The best approach on a first visit is to follow the northern coastline of Camas Eilean Ghlais (Sea-Cliff area) until the dry boulder inlet is reached. Drop down into this and head inland to the cliffs. With more familiarity locate the head of the inlet and descend broken ground to the boulders.

The section of cliff above the boulders is dominated at the west end by superb twin parallel crack lines; Seal Song and Elastic Collision. The climbs are described in relation to these two routes, first rightwards as far as Molehill, then leftwards.

Seal Song   15m   E3 5c ***
Good strenuous and sustained climbing up the left-hand crack.

Elastic Collision   15m   E3 5c ***
Equally fine climbing following the right-hand crack. Technically a bit easier but more sustained than Seal Song.

Razor's Edge   15m   E1 5b *
Right of Elastic Collision there is a chimney-slot high up. Start right of this below a small sharp-edged undercut flake. Climb up to and pull left round the flake to gain a crack leading into the chimney.

Gussetbuster   20m   E1 5b/c *
Start as for Razor's Edge and follow the obvious diagonal crack line rightwards through an awkward bulge at mid-height.

Atlantic Crossing   20m   E1 5b
Follow a left-slanting diagonal line from Seal Song to the finish of Gussetbuster.

Plaything   20m   Mild VS 4b
Right of Gussetbuster is an apex formed by two corners leading to a roof. Climb up to the roof, move right and finish up the wall above.

Every Which Way but Loose   20m   HVS 5c
Right again is a large undercut slab corner. Hard moves to start, either direct or moving in from the left, lead into the easier corner. An alternative start may be made up the undercut edge to the right, pleasant VS 4c.

Street Surfer   15m   E1 5b *
Climb the undercut corner right of Every Which Way and finish up the wall above past a prominent thin horizontal flake at 12m. Spooky!

Postbox Wall   12m   HVS 5a
Right of Street Surfer, climb a short wall with a 'letterbox' hold low down, into a right-curving crack. Finish back left.

Molehill   12m   Very Difficult
At the right-hand end of the cliff, gain and climb cracks in the 'flowery' slab leftwards to the top.

The first climb left of Seal Song is:

Diamond Back 20m   HVS 5a *
Start immediately left of Seal Song and climb the short wall to the ledge. Follow the ramp line of Moody Blues for a short distance until it is possible to step right into the hanging diamond-shaped groove.

Moody Blues 15m   VS 4b
Climb the obvious slanting ramp under Diamond Back. The initial steep wall is avoidable on the left.

Overhanging Crack 15m   Severe
Left of Moody Blues is a lower parallel crack line. Climb this with an interesting crack to start.

Deep Chimney 12m   Hard Severe
The obvious chimney further left.

Next is a rather broken area of rock leading to the impressive leaning wall. **Reiffer** (10m Difficult) climbs the middle of the broken buttress on the left of Deep Chimney. **Guttersnipe** (10m Difficult) starts in the recess to the right of Reiffer, and climbs the corner-crack to the headwall. Move right and up to finish.

Wendy's Flying Circus 15m   HVS 5a
Start beneath a nose of rock low down, a few metres left of Guttersnipe. Climb up to and over the roof and continue direct to finish up a right-trending crack in the final headwall.

The Grateful Dead 15m   Severe
Start near Guttersnipe and traverse under the nose of rock to climb a light-coloured concave slab. Finish up and right.

Trout Mask Replica 12m   HVS 5a
Start 4 metres right of The Executioner. Climb the short grossly-leaning wall to the pale slab on The Grateful Dead. Traverse left into an easy slabby groove and finish up the short overhanging corner.

The Executioner 12m   E2 5b **
Good sustained strenuous climbing following the left-slanting crack tucked into the right end of the leaning wall.

Modern Thinking   15m   E4 6a **
Tremendous climbing up the obvious stepped corner line at the left end of the leaning wall. Start 4 metres right of the arete and climb up to the first horizontal break. Move left and up to the hand traverse, which leads back right into the base of the corners.

The next routes are round the arete on the west wall. Access is subject to the tide level.

Skullsmasher   12m   VS 4c *
Ascends the steeper area of rock at the right end of the west wall. The crux is moving off the high ledge for the top.

Brainbiter   12m   VS 4b *
The steep vague crack left of Skullsmasher leads into an easier groove to finish.

Heidbutter   12m   MVS 4b
Left of Brainbiter, a steep start to gain a flake crack leads into the easier slab corner.

Lobotomy   12m   Severe
Near the left end of the sloping platform is a curious flake on the steep lower wall. A strenuous start past the flake eases onto the slab. Finish rightwards to the top of Heidbutter.

Alpine Escape   12m   Difficult
The climbs the broken area of rock at the left end of the face. Move leftwards across the wall to finish up the corner.

Opposite Seal Song itself, amongst a complicated area of broken rock, is a prominent curving crack. A number of short problems have been recorded here. The curving crack, climbed from the lowest point, is Difficult. The steps on the slab both left and right of the crack are Moderate. Further right the short black 'spiky' groove is Severe. The wall just right of the groove, starting at a small alcove, is 5b.

Further right again, above the pools and opposite the start of An Stiuir promontory, is a steep black slab with a huge bay cut in at the base. The left-hand corner of the bay, swinging left through the roof, is 5a. The cracks running out of the right corner of the bay are Severe.

MINCH WALL

Approximately 80 metres north of the Seal Song area, this is an area of short west-facing walls above an extensive non-tidal platform. The routes are described from the descent, north to the corners of Where the Green Ants Dream, right to left when facing the cliff. Approach the climbs down a large easy-angled broken area at the south end of the walls. There is very good sheltered bouldering on the short wall above a big platform left (facing out) of the descent. See the general map of An Stiuir on page 195.

Everybody's Fault   Severe
The left-trending fault immediately left of the descent. Hard to start.

Faultless   VS 4c
Take a left diagonal line just left of Everybody's Fault, finishing up the big flake on the top leaning section.

T Square   Very Difficult
Climb the deep corner-crack 20 metres left of the descent, beyond a loose blocky area.

Social Democrat   E1 5b *
A few metres left of T Square on the west face, climb the short undercut corner.

Scavenger   E1 5b/c
Start right of Social Democrat. Gain an undercut ledge and climb the wall above left of the arete.

Parabolic Head   E1 5c *
The next hanging groove left of a cracked nose.

Judicial Hanging   HVS 5b **
The obvious deep undercut crack 3 metres left again.

Dunskiing   VS 4c **
Start just left of the previous route and climb into and up a shallow corner. Move left round the final short prow. The direct finish up the arete is **Telemark** (HVS 5a *).

Athlete's Foot   Mild Severe
Hard moves lead into the triangular niche left of Dunskiing; finish rightwards.

Friends for Life   HVS 5a/b **
Climb the wide bulging right-curving corner crack to the finish of
Athlete's Foot.

Bank of Scotland   E3 5c **
From the top of the bulging crack of Friends for Life, take a rising left
traverse across the overhanging wall.

Jim Nastic   VS 4c ***
Start at the left end of the overhanging wall left of Friends for Life.
Climb over ledges trending right to a platform at mid-height. From its
right end, finish via a thin crack in the slab. A direct finish can be made
at the same grade up a crack at the left end of the platform.

Domino   HVS 5a **
Start as for Jim Nastic, then trend left to climb a short hanging corner.
Finish rightwards.

Slip Jig   Hard Severe *
Climb the obvious left-trending stepped corner line 2 metres left of
Domino.

Polka   Mild VS 4b *
Take a line up the scooped rock between Slip Jig and Clam Jam.

Clam Jam   E1 5b *
Start 8 metres left of Slip Jig. Climb up to break through the right end
of a scalloped-shaped roof to finish up a finger crack.

Eddy Current   E3 5c
Bold climbing up the pocketed wall through the left end of the roof of
Clam Jam. Start down in the 'crevasse'.

Where the Green Ants Dream   20m E1 5c/6a ***
Set into the left arete of the Minch Wall is a line of corners. After a hard
boulder problem start, follow the easier corners to the top.

Making Bacon   20m E4/5 6a ***
Start as for Green Ants and hand traverse left along the first break.
Climb up into a scoop, peg runner, and up the wall to the top break. It

is possible to move right here into Green Ants for a rest. Hand traverse left to finish back right up the obvious slab and groove.

BAY OF PIGS

This area is really a continuation of the Minch Wall, set back on the platform forming a bay of fine steep walls. Access as for the Minch Wall, descending broken rock at its south end, or abseil.

Reiff Encounter   20m   E3 6b ***
About 5 metres left of Green Ants is a thin crack splitting the huge undercut base. Hard moves through the undercut lead to a peg runner. Combined tactics will reach the peg! Move up on good holds to a ledge and finish rightwards to the top of Making Bacon.

Sexcrementalism   15m   E1 5b *
Start 10 metres left of the arete of Green Ants and climb strenuously up the obvious Y-crack to a ledge. Finish more easily up the corner-crack.

Blackadder   15m   HVS 5a **
Climb the deep overhanging black crack in the right corner of the bay and finish back right up the slabby fault.

Free Base   8m   E5 6a/b
The fierce right-slanting crack line in the leaning wall above Black-adder.

Chicken Run   25m   Difficult *
Traverse right along the shelf above the initial overhanging crack of Blackadder to finish up the same slabby fault.

The Thistle   12m   E5 6b ***
The impressive and deceptively steep crack springing from the recess in the wall left of Blackadder. Well protected, but very powerful moves at the top thin crack.

Walk Like an Egyptian   18m   E4 6a ***
The obvious line of corners at the back of the bay. Climb the corners until it is possible to graunch up the bomb-bay groove to finish easily leftwards.

Awesome   12m   E5 6b **
The right-slanting line starting from the upper platform left of Egyptian.
An awkward start leads slightly right of the crack, returning left to follow
it to an easier finish up the less steep wall.

Cleopatra's Asp   14m   E5 6a **
Belay at the foot of Awesome. Hand traverse the break rightwards to
a resting ledge on the edge. Move back left to climb the right side of
the wall to horizontal breaks (good Friends). Make a hard move up to
gain a jug below the next horizontal break. Move up and right to a
fighting finish!

The obvious corner 5 metres left of Awesome is HVS 5a. Climb the
left edge of the slab to the horizontal break, then move right into the
corner.
From the base of Egyptian a short wall extends left for 25 metres.
This is Piglet Wall, which has some fine mini-routes to be led or
bouldered.

Curving Crack   HVS 5a **
Climb the left-curving shallow corner crack 10 metres left of the right
end.

Dreams of Utah   HVS 5a/b *
Starting 4 metres left of Curving Crack, climb a thin crack leading into
a triangular niche at the top. The climb may be continued above the
ledge at the same standard.

Sandstone Cowboy   HVS 5a
Start just right of Dreams of Utah. Climb rightwards to a good hold and
finish as for Curving Crack.

Chokestone Crack   Very Difficult
Follow a deep left-slanting crack to a bay.

Vision of Blue   E1 5b *
The cracked wrinkled wall just left of Chokestone Crack.

The Kraken   E2 6a *
Sustained climbing up the shallow groove in the wall left again, with
the hardest moves at the start.

On the final short south-facing wall there are three obvious corners. From right to left these are **Creeping Jenny** (VS 4c *), **Jackie in the Box** (Difficult), and **Dulcie Bridge** (Very Difficult).

POOH CLIFF

The climbs here lie approximately 100 metres north of the Bay of Pigs, where the rock heightens and steepens above a series of narrow platforms, to eventually run out onto a storm boulder beach at the north end. The routes are on an 80 metre section of excellent rock ranging in height from 6m at either end, to 12m in the middle; they include some fine wee classics!

Approach either by walking north along the clifftop from the Bay of Pigs, and descend a fault line onto the boulder beach, or from the Bay of Pigs, scramble above the final routes of the Piglet Wall and walk under a narrow steep buttress onto the platform at the south end of Pooh Cliff.

Firstly there are a number of climbs on the narrow leaning wall between Piglet Wall and Pooh Cliff. From right to left these are **The Shield** (Severe), the flakey groove line bounding the right end of the leaning wall; **storm in a Teacup** (E2 5c *), strenuous climbing up left-trending cracks near the right end of the wall; and **Sea Shanty** (E2 5c *); the diagonal crack line on the left of the wall.

The routes of Pooh Cliff proper are described from the boulder beach end southwards, left to right when facing the cliff.

Owl   Difficult
From the extreme left end of the narrow platform tucked under the cliff, climb a short left-slanting stepped corner.

Short Sighted   Severe **
Climb the shelfy groove near the left end of the narrow platform, with an awkward mantleshelf start.

Big Ears   VS 4c
From the start of Short Sighted, climb diagonally rightwards up the bulging wall.

Big Nose   VS 4c
Jug pulling up the short overhanging prow to the right. Finish right of the capping block.

Descent   Moderate
The steps right of a damp black corner.

Rose Root   Very Difficult
Climb the short crack in the steep ledgy wall right of the descent.

Further right the cliff heightens above a raised platform.

Tigger   Mild VS 4b *
From the left end of the platform take a steep thin crack in the left wall.

Bear Necessities   Mild VS 4b
Climb the steep wall left of Tigger.

Pooh Corner   VS 4c ***
The excellent black corner above the middle of the raised platform.

The Ramp   Severe *
An obvious left-slanting rampline at the right end of the platform.

Live Entertainment   E1 5b/c *
Strenuous climbing up the bottomless groove to the right.

Honey Pot   Hard Severe
The steep wide crack in the next corner to the right.

Sticky Fingers   VS 4c **
On the wall right of Honey Pot, climb a shallow scoop direct over a
bulge and finish leftwards.

The Alcove   HVS 5a
Climb a short leaning groove at the right end of the platform to a large
ledge. Finish either left towards Honey Pot, or traverse easily off right
and up, or jump for the pool!

On the right, the platform narrows above the pool into an awkward
raised triangular step. The next two routes start from the step.

Kanga   HVS 5b *
Climb the short corner above the step to the large ledge.

Roo   VS 5a/b *
Climb the shallow corner in the wall at the right end of the step, with a long reach from the horizontal break, and pull onto the ledge.

Eeyore   HVS 5a ***
Past the triangular step the platform widens once more, with a fine concave wall on the right. Steep unobvious climbing up the middle of the concave wall.

Body Swerve   HVS 5b
Climb the innocuous groove at the right end of the concave wall, finishing right under the roof.

Jelly Wobbler   E1 5b **
Follow the awkward finger crack in the left-curving black corner right of Body Swerve.

Winning Edge   VS 4c
Climb a right-trending crack from the start of Jelly Wobbler and finish up the flake edge.

Scoop   Difficult
Right again take a short groove above large blocks.

The crag deteriorates rightwards from here to pass the narrow leaning wall and back to the Bay of Pigs.

RUBHA COIGEACH

Rubha Coigeach is the most northerly point of the Rubha Mor peninsula with some of the best climbing on the coastline, offering a varied selection of routes of all grades and of up to 25m; well worth the effort for a visit. The walk from Reiff takes about 1 hour. Either follow the coast north from An Stiuir area, with fine views out to sea and into the many little inlets on the way, or cut inland from the croft at Camas Eilean Ghlais (aim for cairns on the slab left of a boggy slot draining from Lochan an Rathaid and follow it above the lochan to drop down crossing the Allt nan Clar-Lochan), to join the coast path at Faochag Bay. This is slightly quicker. The first tantalising glimpse of the cliffs is seen in profile as an impressive square-cut leaning wall above a small offshore island. The crag stretches continuously round the headland for over one kilometre. Rounding Faochag Bay, cross the burn draining from Loch na Faochaig and contour round over a shoulder on the northern side of the bay to descend steeply into a boulder-strewn fault on the left. Follow this north to the cliffs proper.

There are numerous good camping spots in the area, particularly around Loch na Faochaig, with usually plenty of driftwood for fires to be found along the rocky shoreline of the bay. See the map of Area 3, Rubha Coigeach on page 208.

GOLDEN WALLS

These comprise Area A on the Rubha Coigeach map. Where the cliff begins, a curious small 'phallic block' protrudes above a flat platform. On the bigger main west face, the platform narrows into a ledge which conveniently leads under the cliff for much of its length. Where it peters out, it is necessary to scramble along the walls and boulders of a tidal channel between the cliff and the offshore island to reach the start of routes left of the Golden Wall proper. The island provides a good viewpoint for the climbs opposite, although access is difficult at high tide levels. Watch out for the Great Black Back Gulls on the island during nesting season; they are even bigger and fiercer than they look!

From the 'phallic block' the first routes lie round the corner just to the left: **The Slab** (6m Mild Severe) is just right of **The Chimney** (6m Severe; route 1 on the diagram on page 215).

Funky Disco Pops   8m   HVS 5b
Just left of The Chimney, climb to a horizontal break by way of two pockets. Finish straight up.

Andrews Clark   8m   HVS 5b *
The thin crack a metre left of Funky Disco Pops.

Thunderhead   8m   E1 5c
Just left again, climb directly via small pockets, horizontal breaks and long reaches.

Strange Crack   8m   HVS 5b
Climb the short strenuous corner crack just left of Thunderhead.

Break Off   10m   E3 5c *
Left of Strange Crack is a big rounded flake. From the top of the flake, move right and strenuously over the bulge. Finish slightly left.

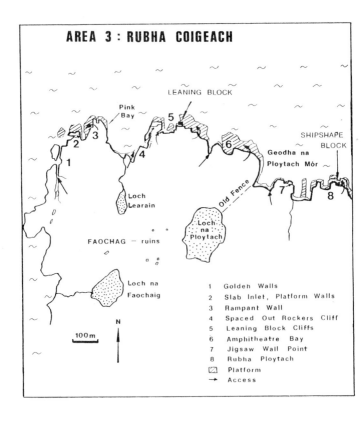

AREA 3 : RUBHA COIGEACH

LEANING BLOCK

Pink Bay

SHIPSHAPE BLOCK

Geodha na Ploytach Mór

Old Fence

Loch Learain

Loch na Ploytach

FAOCHAG – ruins

Loch na Faochaig

100m

N

1   Golden Walls
2   Slab Inlet, Platform Walls
3   Rampant Wall
4   Spaced Out Rockers Cliff
5   Leaning Block Cliffs
6   Amphitheatre Bay
7   Jigsaw Wall Point
8   Rubha Ploytach
▨   Platform
→   Access

Walk left under a beak of bulging rock to a peculiar puckered wall for **Spasticus Autisticus** (10m E1 5b), which trends right up the wall to finish up the left side of the nose.

Next is a wide chimney which fans out at the top. The right-trending ramp line has been climbed at Very Difficult.

Klondyke 20m VS 4c
The shattered fault line in the left side of the chimney.

Andrew the Milkman 20m HVS 5a
A few metres left of Klondyke, climb the wide crack through bulges.

Safe as Milk 20m Mild VS 4b
Climb the obvious corner a few metres left again.

Milkshake 20m Severe
From halfway up Safe as Milk, traverse left above the triangular roof to finish easily up a groove in the edge.

Walk on to a bulging section which partially blocks the ledgeway under the cliff. The wall above and immediately left is broken by two ledges with short leaning bits between and gives surprisingly good climbing.

Goldie Horn 20m E2 5b
Move onto the first ledge from the right of the nose obstructing the 'path' and steeply up to the next ledge. Finish via the even steeper wide cracks.

To the left of the obstruction, the ledgeway opens out again beneath two crack lines. **49'ers** (15m HVS 5b) starts right of the right-hand crack line, and climbs direct through the ledges and bulging walls. **Ruben Tadpole** (15m E1 5b) is the right-hand crack line, and **Bubblyjock** (15m E2 5c) the left. **Murphy's Law** (15m HVS 5a *) is the prominent corner left of Bubblyjock, strenuous at the top.

Halcyon Daze 15m HVS 5b *
The wall to the left of Murphy's Law, finishing by an obvious hole-like feature at the top. Technical to start.

Verushka   15m   E3 5c **
The rounded pillar left of Halcyon Daze. Climb to the undercut and move steeply up to a horizontal break. Move slightly left and back right to finish straight up.

Carnival of Folly   15m   E1/2 5b **
The bulging wall left of Verushka. Climb up and right to finish left of Verushka.

Sniffing the Frog   15m   E2 5c *
Start between Carnival of Folly and Moronic Inferno of the Golden Wall. Climb the scooped wall to a horizontal break 2m below the roof; large Friend runners. Move up to the right end of the roof (crux) and pull through this on good holds. Continue up and slightly left to the top.

Next is the fine Golden Wall, with four obvious crack lines.

Moronic Inferno   15m   E3 5c **
The rightmost crack, low in the grade. The lower section is straightforward. Hurry past the upper bulge on good holds.

Split Personality   15m   E4 5c ***
The thin crack just left is technical to start, hard in the middle and steep at the top. Well protected but sustained.

Crann Tara   15m   E3 5c ***
This is route 2 on the diagram on page 215. Take the right-hand finish.

The Rite of Spring   15m   E3 5c ***
Gain a round hole 3m up, traverse left into the line and finish via a wee corner. Quite bold at the start, but the diligent will find a few runners.

The ledge peters out past here, but continues narrowly at a lower level for a bit. Up the very edge of the Golden Wall, but starting just to the left and lower down is **Sweet Chastity** (15m E1 5b *), which starts up an easy wall, then continues with more difficulty up the edge to the top.

Westering Home, Reiff (Climber, Julian Fincham)

The next section of cliff forms a large recess. Scramble up some 5m to some higher ledges.

Sammy Seal   8m   E1 5c
The short finger crack in the black wall just left of Sweet Chastity.

Skid Row   10m   E2 5c
Climb the leftmost of two obvious overhanging curving cracks. Route 3 on the diagram on page 215.

Past the large recess the system of ledges peters out completely into the tidal channel. The first obvious feature left of the recess is a corner.

Ordinary Route   15m   Severe
Climb the corner with some loose rock. Short Severe access walls have to be climbed to belays if tides threaten.

The Road to Nowhere   15m   E4 6a ***
A fine climb following a shallow groove right of Ordinary Route. Belay as for Ordinary Route, or just right of it. Climb a strenuous crack on the right to a horizontal break and make a difficult move over the overlap into the groove above. Leave the groove with difficulty and climb boldly via a flange to a horizontal break (Friend runner). More awkward moves lead to the top.

The buttress left of Ordinary Route is bounded on its left by the big corner of Seannachie. The fine-looking slim buttress cut by horizontal breaks between the big corners of Ordinary Route and Seannachie is E4 6a, with one *in situ* peg.

Seannachie   20m   VS 4c *
Gain the corner by a traverse in from Ordinary Route.

Routes beyond this point will only be reached by abseil at high tide levels. At low tides approach along the tidal channel.

Horripilation   20m   E2 5c
Starting approximately 10 metres left of Ordinary Route, climb a vertical crack system running up the wall to finish up a 4m scary semi-detached flake right of the crack.

Split Personality, Reiff (Climbers, Roger Everett and Guy Muhlemann)

Dragons of Eden   20m   E2 5c **
Start 5 metres left of Horripilation and climb a thin crack straight up the face to a ledge. Finish by a nice solid flake crack.

Saint Vitus Gets on Down   20m   E2 5c *
Follow the shattered crack line just left of Dragons of Eden to the same ledge. Finish steeply up the groove on the left, crux, artificial.

Shades of Night   20m   E2 5c *
Start 10 metres left of Saint Vitus. Climb out of a large alcove topped by an overhanging crack to gain an easier chimney crack. Follow this to a roof near the top then traverse out right onto the face to finish.

Necronomican   25m   E1 5b ***
The large corner near the left end of the cliff. Very enjoyable and well protected, but watch out for turbulent tidal water near this end of the cliff. Route 4 on the diagram on page 215.

The Presence   25m   VS 4c **
Follow an obvious right-slanting ramp to finish via an exciting sustained 3m wall. Start as for Necronomican.

   The cliff now cuts back inland above a high platform to a steep chimney in the corner before running back north to the Slab Inlet area. To avoid the long traverse along the tidal channel, the climbs here can be reached by abseil onto the platform. The first two routes are on the fine black north-facing wall above the high platform. The wall is split by a chimney-fault line.

Nothing Special   15m   Difficult *
Start up the chimney and follow a line of steps leading right.

Black Magic   15m   VS 4c ***
Smart climbing up the centre of the wall left of the chimney. Route 5 on the diagram on page 215.

The Black Chimney   20m   Very Difficult
The chimney in the corner left of Black Magic. It requires a favourable breeze to dry!

The next two routes lie on the slabby wall left of the chimney. Access is only at low tide levels.

The Comeback   20m   VS 4c **
Take the right side of the slabby wall. Start by trending right up a very shallow scoop.

Snookered   20m   VS 5a
Left of The Comeback is an undercut shelf at head-height. Hard strenuous moves to gain the shelf lead to easier climbing straight up the wall above. Finish just left of the big recess. Slightly loose.

SLAB INLET
North of the west-facing steep slabby wall of Black Magic bay, the next main feature is a narrow inlet with a distinctive low-angled slab forming its seaward (north) side. The landward side is a 12m black wall with three shallow corners. The inlet is tidal with the base of the routes awash at high tide. Access is at low tide either by scrambling down the outside edge of the slab (Moderate), or from the east side of the Platform Walls sneak through a tunnel to emerge at the back of the inlet. This is Area B of the Rubha Coigeach map on page 215.

The Ali Shuffle   12m   VS 5a **
The right-hand and most prominent corner on the landward side. Very well protected. This corner must always be approached by abseiling down the line. Route 6 on the diagram on page 215.

Break Dance   12m   E2 5b *
Climb the wall to the left of The Ali Shuffle and just right of the arete. Friend runners in every break!

Fingerbowl   12m   Severe
The left-hand corner with the crux at the bottom.

The Slab; Landward End   12m   Difficult
The back of the slab forms a prominent V-groove and gives an interesting exercise in horizontal bridging before turning into a more conventional corner.

The Slab; Seaward End   12m   Moderate
The outside edge of the slab may be used as a descent.

On the west-facing seaward wall, north of the inlet itself, is a corner with a deep fissure and a crack in the right wall. Approach by abseil at low tides only.

Atlantic Crack   12m   E3 5c ***
A magnificent overhanging crack, mostly finger width, with the most technical move at the top. Route 7 on the diagram opposite.

Eag Dubh   12m   HVS 5a *
The chimney-crack left of Atlantic Crack.

PLATFORM WALLS
North of Slab Inlet is a huge flat platform which dips west into the sea. East of the platform a geo cuts back inland. The Platform Walls consist of a long black north-facing wall above the huge platform, and an east-facing wall overlooking the tidal inlet. They are marked as Area C on the Rubha Coigeach map opposite. A tunnel cuts through the headland connecting the back of the Slab Inlet with the Platform east wall. Access is by scrambling down a black slabby area (sometimes slimy) at the back of the geo onto the platform under the east wall, or more fun, at low tide use the tunnel from the Slab Inlet. Firstly, there is a superbly-positioned route on the overhanging backwall of the geo, a right to left traverse above the big roofs.

Mad Dogs and Englishmen   25m   E3 5c ***
Pull easily onto the obvious traverse line with an awkward step down at 3m. Go back to the break and hand traverse to the first groove. (It is possible to climb down here to a very exposed ledge and a hands off rest). Continue round the arete and into the next groove, where a left exit gains a good ledge and an easy finish up the slab above.

The Platform routes are described from left to right along the east- then the north-facing walls. The first feature of note is a buttress with a big roof 3m up, left of the tunnel entrance.

Autumn Sonata   10m   E4 6a **
Climb up to below the roof. Move right and up to a horizontal break. Gain a good hold high up on the left and climb up to a small overlap. Finish via an obvious little corner above.

Next is the tunnel and right of this is an undercut and overhung slab.

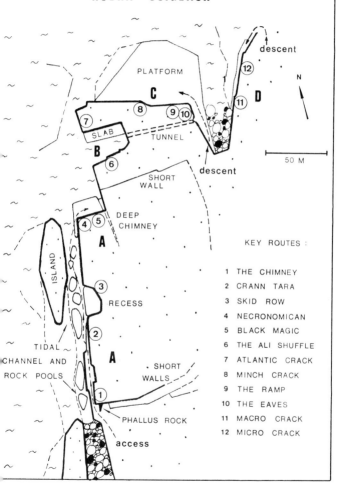

RUBHA COIGEACH

PLATFORM

C

D

descent

N

⑫

⑦ ⑧ ⑨⑩ ⑪

SLAB

TUNNEL

B

⑥

descent

50 M

SHORT
WALL

DEEP
CHIMNEY

④⑤

A

ISLAND

③

RECESS

②

TIDAL
CHANNEL AND
ROCK POOLS

A

SHORT
WALLS

①

PHALLUS ROCK

access

KEY ROUTES :

1   THE CHIMNEY
2   CRANN TARA
3   SKID ROW
4   NECRONOMICAN
5   BLACK MAGIC
6   THE ALI SHUFFLE
7   ATLANTIC CRACK
8   MINCH CRACK
9   THE RAMP
10 THE EAVES
11 MACRO CRACK
12 MICRO CRACK

The Eaves   12m   Very Difficult *
Chimney up the outside edge of the tunnel until an exit can be made onto the slab. Traverse twin horizontal cracks rightwards and climb a right-slanting crack up to the capping roof. Avoid this on the right. Route 10 on the diagram on page 215.

Eaves Direct   10m   Mild VS 4c
A direct start through the undercut base to the end of the traverse.

Submarine Badlands   12m   VS 4b *
Tucked in between the slab and the vertical wall round the corner is a shallow groove. Climb the groove leading round the corner to a sensational finish above the wall.

The vertical wall on the right is split by a fierce crack rising out of the roof of a small recess and bounded on the right by two corners.

The Ramp   12m   Mild Severe
Starting right of the recess, take a line up to the left-hand corner. Route 9 on the diagram on page 215.

Corner Wall   12m   Very Difficult *
The left-hand corner. A flake on the left leads to a ledge and the overhanging corner above.

Reap the Wild Wind   12m   VS 4b *
The shallow right-hand corner is deceptively steep.

On the wall right again is a thin right-slanting crack line rounding an edge at half-height onto a long juggy wall.

Minch Crack   12m   Mild VS 4b *
Start up the edge to join and follow the crack. The crack line climbed throughout is 4c. Route 8 on the diagram on page 215.

Mars Crack   12m   Severe *
Climb the fine crack cutting the long juggy wall near its left end. The finish of this and the next route has been affected by a recent rockfall.

Mickey Mouse   15m   Mild Severe *
Access only at low tide. Near the right end of the long juggy wall of Mars Crack there is a shallow groove-crack line. Make a long traverse out to the line from the left end of the undercut base. Sometimes there is a worrying swell running up the sloping platform.

RAMPANT WALL

This is the west-facing wall of the tidal inlet; Area D of the Rubha Coigeach map on page 215. Low tide leaves weedy pools under the headwall but it is possible to slither across on boulders to platforms on the far side, using the same descent as for the Platform Walls. The headwall above the pools is damp and overhanging, but further left (looking across from above the Platform Walls) is a steep slab with four prominent right-slanting crack lines which appear as ramps from a distance.

Access is by scrambling down well left of the slab. Only the right-hand crack is inaccessible at high tide. The left-hand crack is the shorter since it starts higher on a small platform.

Mini Crack 8m Mild Severe
Some 3 metres left of the left-hand crack is another right-slanting crack, not obvious from a distance.

Minor Crack 8m HVS 4c
This is a shallow right-facing corner immediately left of the left-hand crack. Unprotected.

Micro Crack 10m Hard Severe 4b
The left-hand of the main cracks is pleasant and quite technical. Route 12 on the diagram on page 215.

Seepsville 12m Hard Severe
The next main crack. As the name sugests, a bit unpleasant.

Between Seepsville and Micro Crack is a very thin right-slanting crack which only becomes definite above a small overhang at half-height. This is the line of **The Receding Hairline** (12m HVS 5b), which climbs straight up the wall to a horizontal break, then moves right then up to and over the small overhang before following the crack to the top.

Macro Crack 15m E1 5b *
The next main crack on the right. Route 11 on the diagram.

The Gods   20m   Hard Severe 4b **
The right-hand crack starting at sea level, which is approachable only at low tide. Start easily up a deep flared overhanging chimney, and climb up to roofs. Traverse right under the roofs and up onto a nose in a sensational position. Friend belay (avoiding rope drag). A delicate step up into the thin crack above leads to better holds and a finish out left.

East of the Rampant Wall, on the right of the descent, is a small bay surrounded by short walls. This offers some good bouldering.

PINK BAY

Pink Bay extends from the small bouldering bay mentioned above, round to the back of the large inlet where the crags deteriorate into grassy slopes. The rock tends to be vegetatious and fulmar-ridden on the bigger walls, but there are some fine steep prows and short clean areas. The best place to picnic and most convenient access is by two short square-cut promontories divided by a narrow zawn, 'Wee Geo'.

Chimney Crack   8m   Very Difficult
The obvious wide crack in the left wall (facing out) at the head of the Wee Geo.

Eye Catcher   8m   Severe *
The thinner crack right of Chimney Crack.

Sgarbh an Sgumain   8m   Mild Severe *
Step across the gap and launch up the wall right of Eye Catcher. Follow the breaks trending right and up.

Critical Mass   10m   E1 5c *
This lies round the corner from Sgarbh an Sgumain on the front face of the promontory. Descend to this face from the other (north) side and onto a sloping platform, accessible at lowish tide. Climb a shallow corner near the right edge and traverse left under a low roof into a steep central crack line. Follow this to the top.

Running Flush   10m   HVS 5a **
The front face of the right-hand (south) promontory. Belay in the geo and swing round onto the face and follow a left-slanting line to finish up a crack.

For access to the crags inland (south), down-climb the corner at the back of the promontory onto a high platform. With a bit of scrambling, this leads round under the remaining climbs.

B.F.B.   12m   Severe *
Climb the middle of the slab at the base of the descent off the promontory. Head for the crack at mid-height.

Gabhagan   18m   E2 5c *
Scramble along about 100 metres to the second obvious prow, which forms a sharp arete. Climb the line of corners on the right side of the arete which lead rightwards to under a huge roof. Undercling left to finish (crux).

SPACED OUT ROCKERS CLIFF
Another 10 minute walk round the coast from the Rampant Walls leads to a large bay biting back inland. Access to the sensational route which follows is down the steep grassy slopes at the back of this bay. It is best however, to continue round the top of the cliff to have a close look at the route. The line is stunningly obvious; a crack line traversing 60 metres left across the vertical wall. It is possible at low tides to scramble down into a gully north of the cliff and return under the 'crevasse' wall to the base of the route. A bit of exposed soloing leads to the start of the route at a big niche just left of the edge.

Spaced Out Rockers on the road to Oblivion   60m   E2 ***
1. 20m 5c From the big niche, traverse horizontally until below the left end of a ledge system. After hard moves up to gain the ledge, belay at the right end.
2. 40m 5b Go to the left end of the ledge and up to an obvious handrail. Follow this (belay where convenient) until it is possible to gain an upper handrail which passes an obvious niche to finish in a corner. Good belays back from the cliff top. This was first done in four pitches, but it could be done in fewer if a good range of Friends (and lots of them!) are carried.

Further exploration of the coastline from the Spaced Out Rockers Cliff eastwards, has revealed some fine crags and produced the usual good quality sandstone climbing that is typical of Reiff. The diagram of Rubha Coigeach on page 208 is helpful to locate the climbing areas.

Spaced Out Rockers Cliff and Leaning Block Cliffs are best approached by following the inland route to Faochag Bay, then cut inland
to the loch and ruined crofts of Faochag and head north to pass above
Loch Learain on its east side. For a direct approach to Amphitheatre
Bay from Faochag, skirt past Loch na Ploytach on its west side. For
Jigsaw Wall Point and Rubha Ploytach, pass Loch na Ploytach on its
east side and head north to the coastline. This is a touch boggy north
of Loch na Ploytach. On the first visit however, follow the coastline
round from the Spaced Out Rockers Cliff to become more familiar with
the area.

LEANING BLOCK CLIFFS

This area lies about 100 metres from Spaced Out Rockers cliff. It has
a general northerly aspect with fine views across to Suilven, Canisp
and Quinag.

The majority of climbs are around a tidal bay with a black backwall,
an undercut east-facing wall lying above a sloping platform and a huge
detached block on the east side. Despite the aspect, the majority of
walls dry very quickly after rain, and, during the summer months, most
routes catch some sun.

The climbing is excellent, with solid crystaline sandstone running to
steep walls split by fine cracks, corners and breaks. The routes are
from 15m to 20m long, and they are easily approached down a
boulder-filled gully on the west side, or down the huge sloping platform
on the east.

At low tide, it is possible to walk under all the routes. High tide will
affect access to routes on the undercut east-facing wall and from
Harold, near the gully descent, to Cyclops on the leaning block itself,
although it is possible to squeeze through the block chimney to climb
the routes around Wall of Silence. The first routes lie on the undercut
east-facing wall right of the descent gully; all finish easily up the final
slab. The route numbers refer to Map 3G.

1   Route with no Name   E1 5b *
The obvious diagonal crack line near the left edge, gained by a hand
traverse from the right.

P.T.S.D.   E2 6a
Climb the thin crack line just right of the previous route, with a long
reach for the slab.

Further right, a long roof lies below the final slab. The roof is crossed at its widest point by **Short 'n' Sweet** (E2 5c *): Climb easily up to a notch in the roof (runners) and reach over using a good undercling.

2 Aroofoeryerheid HVS 5a *
Just right of centre on the wall, there is a break in the roof, but it is capped by a higher one. Climb to beneath the two roofs and escape awkwardly left.
Variation: **Hoodwinked** HVS 5b
Take the right-hand finish to Aroofoeryerheid. Painfully awkward!

Slimer Difficult *
The short crack at the right end where the wall drops in height.

The black backwall left of the descent gully sports some fine cracks and corners. Unfortunately, this wall suffers from some seepage and can be slow to dry.

Pirates of Coigach Hard Severe ***
This fine route starts in the jaws of the descent gully from an overhung ledge on the landward side. Swing round onto the front face and climb up to join and follow a ramp leftwards across the black wall.

3 Harold Very Difficult
The first obvious corner left of the descent gully.

On the wall to the left of Harold are two crack lines. The right-hand crack gives good climbing, hard to start (E2 5c ***). **Maud** (HVS 5a) takes the next crack to the left, and is dirty at the top.

4 Reiffer Madness VS 4c *
The brown corner set in the angle of the black north- and west-facing walls of the bay.

Memphis Belle E1 5a
The obvious diagonal black fault running left from a shallow corner near the centre of the west-facing wall.

The next two lines are obvious on the wall close to the left edge of the west-facing wall. **Waigwa** (HVS 5a **) climbs the black pocketed cracked wall.

5   Golden Fleece   HVS 5b ***
The next obvious crack line a few metres left of Waigwa.

Sunshine on Reiff   E1 5a/b **
Follow a scooped line up the left edge of the wall.

Round the edge of Sunshine on Reiff is a superb steep black slab running to surprising 'grips' and giving the next three routes. Small camming devices are useful.

Van Hoover's awa'   E1 5b ***
Start 3 metres left of an obvious crack near the right edge. Trend left on good holds up to half-height and finish direct.

6   The Good, the Bad and the Ugly   E2 5c **
Climb the middle of the steep slab, starting up a short corner crack and finishing easily by a short left-facing corner.

The Africaan Problem   E1 5b ***
Start at the extreme left end of the slab by the entrance to the chimney. Trend right to a big ledge and climb up via a shallow gnarly flake to finish left under a stepped roof.

Next is the leaning block itself, a fine lump of rock partially detatched at one side (and standing on a bunch of small boulders) presenting a remarkable chimney which may be traversed and used as access from the sloping platform at mid to high tides. The routes here are arguably the best in the area.

Block Chimney   Very Difficult **
Interesting and fun climbing up the west end of the chimney.

The next routes lie on the overhanging west-facing wall of the block and are all extremely photogenic.

Wall of Silence   E3 5c ***
Fine sustained climbing following an obvious crack line right of centre.

7   The Gift   E5 6a ***
Excellent powerful climbing up the left arete of the west wall. Start at the edge of the raised platform, step left onto the seaward face and

3G : LEANING BLOCK CLIFFS

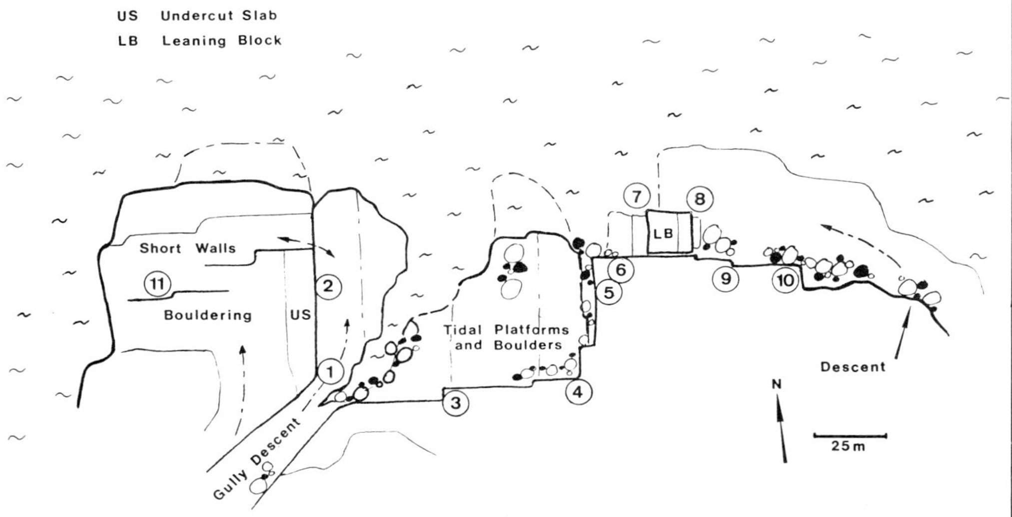

US   Undercut Slab
LB   Leaning Block

Descent

25 m

N

Tidal Platforms and Boulders

Short Walls

Bouldering

US

LB

Gully Descent

up into a cave. Move back right and make hard committing moves up the arete to a jutting block and a well-earned hands-off rest, if you can find it! Another hard move leads to jugs and the top.

The Screamer   E4 6a ***
The wall between Wall of Silence and The Gift. Start midway between the two and climb bulges to the big break. Move diagonally left past a semi-rest at a hand ledge to a short wide break. Trend right and up to the final wide break to finish up left. Steep, strenuous exciting climbing protected with small and large Friends.

Another good (unnamed) line, sustained and very strenuous, heads for a groove in the centre of the north-facing wall of the block (E3 5c ***).

8   Cyclops   E2 5c ***
The other (east) arete of the block. Start at the lowest point of the arete and climb via a series of breaks to a huge thread. Finish up a short groove on the left. If the tide threatens, a start may be made off the block to the left.

Cross-Eyed   E2 5b ***
Starting off the block under the east-facing wall, this route follows an obvious line curling right, crossing Cyclops at the huge thread on the arete and finishing via the diagonal crack on the seaward face. Very strenuous, but well protected.

Blind Bandit   HVS 5a **
Start on the block as for Cross-Eyed and climb straight up by a flake and horizontal breaks to the roof. Pull through the left end of the roof and trend rightwards up the bulging wall to finish.

Play it Again Stevie Wonder   E3 6a/b *
Start 2 metres left of Blind Bandit under the widest part of the roof. Pull over the roof using a good pocket, followed by powerful moves with long reaches to the good breaks. Finish straight up.

Crossover   Very Difficult
Start up the ramp on the left of the chimney, step across onto the slab at twin horizontal breaks and trend right to a 'Thrifty' crack. Finish leftwards.

The north-facing wall east of the block is characterised by a right-slanting ramp and two corners at the right end.

Bow Wave VS 4c *
Right of the start of the ramp, take a crack on the front face to join the ramp where it narrows. Follow this to its top, and climb straight up to finish.

9 Coigach Corner VS 4c ***
Start up the ramp and follow the fine corner above.

Olympus E2 5b/c **
The deep widening crack straight up from the start of the ramp.

The wall to the left has two fine routes on sound hidden holds.

Brave Heart E3 5c **
Climb the middle of the wall to a short roof at half-height. Pull over and finish straight up the hard wall on improving holds.

10 Empty on Endorphins E1 5b ***
Start under the left arete of the wall on top of a large boulder. Strenuous initial moves over the undercut base lead to the huge break. Take a left-slanting diagonal line to the top, keeping a couple of metres right of the arete. Nice and steady!

Finally, there is good bouldering and a few routes on the short black walls west down sloping platforms from the top of the gully descent, on a level with the top of Slimer. The obvious corner halfway along the upper black wall is Very Difficult, and the crack and steps to the left can be climbed at Severe. **Une Petite Rock Star** (Hard Severe) takes the crack right of the corner, and **Petit Homme** (4c) climbs the wall right again.

AMPHITHEATRE BAY
This is the next area of climbable rock some 150 metres east of the Leaning Block Cliffs, past a narrow boulder filled inlet. Visible from the platform descent to the Leaning Block, is an obvious crack splitting the western prow of the bay. This is An Sulaire. Hidden round the corner is the amphitheatre itself, an amazing bowl of undercut rock rising above an enormous sloping platform dipping into the sea at the west

end of the bay. Contemplate the result of a slide under wet conditions down this platform! There are no climbs recorded to date in the bay, but the scope is obvious. Only on close inspection does the true angle of dangle reveal itself as you stand at the bottom craning the neck back into an ache! Then check out the size of the boulders dislodged from the undercut washed up into the back of the amphitheatre and awe at the strength of the seas needed to do this and start rounding them off.

There are weaknesses however and after a bit of cleaning at the top this area will produce some fine lines. Access is straightforward; either at low tides down the narrow boulder-filled inlet and turn right under the prow onto the huge platform, or, walk over the top of the bay and descend easily onto the top of the platform.

An Sulaire   30m   E1 5b **
Start at the lowest point directly under the crack in the front of the prow. Climb a shallow hidden black corner up to the big ledge. Finish up the crack. Tidal.

JIGSAW WALL POINT
This headland is named after the mosaic-patterned gold-coloured west-facing wall of the area, easily visible when approaching from the west. The cliffs run past this wall into a seaward face with a small square-cut bay, then continue round to the fine-looking east face. Unfortunately, convenient platforms and ledges peter out at the small bay, making access difficult from here round. However, descent to Jigsaw Wall itself and the west end of the seaward face is made easily down a wet grassy slope at the end of Jigsaw Wall.

Jigsaw Wall   15m   HVS 5a ***
The obvious vertical crack line near the left end of the wall. Move up an easy slab to pull leftwards through the roof into the crack. Climb this until the corner on the right can be gained. The corner leads round a huge block to finish.

Traditional Chimney   10m   Very Difficult
The chimney bounding the left end of the Jigsaw Wall.

The east-facing cliffs gain height to 25m and run to the back of Geodha na Ploytach Mor, firstly through a series of walls and corners, then a steep slab topped by a short leaning wall and eventually become more broken above the boulder beach. This end of the crag is affected by seepage draining through the vegetation at the top, but has some good-looking steep walls. Descent onto the boulder beach at the back of the bay is also difficult, with the gully of the Allt Loch Airidh Blair looking the most feasable way down without abseiling! (It is possible at low tide to traverse round from Rubha Ploytach.) Access to the seaward end of the east wall is by abseil down the wall to the right (facing out) of the corner of Kermit's Cave Route which is located by the massive jammed boulder near the top. This leads onto semi-tidal platforms which may be traversed in both directions depending on the state of the tide.

The cliffs on the point tend to be more broken than in other areas, particularly true of the east-facing walls, and scope for good quality lines is rather limited.

Kermit's Cave Route   20m   HVS 5a
The most prominent corner on the east-facing walls of the headland. Chimney up to the off-width narrows and take the left side of the jammed blocks to an easy finish.

Damburst   20m   Very Difficult
Climb the groove system trending left from the right-hand end of the wall to the right of Kermit's Cave. Start from the lowest platform. Tidal.

RUBHA PLOYTACH

Rubha Ploytach is a collection of small rocky headlands generously ringed by non-tidal raised platforms, hence access to most of the routes is very easy. The descent is at the east end, through some large boulders onto the Shipshape Block platform. Access to the lower east-facing walls under this platform is more difficult; either abseil, or downclimb one of the easier routes to ledges and sea-level platforms beneath the climbs.

The climbing at Rubha Ploytach is again superb, with the majority of the routes in the lower grades. The climbs on the east-facing walls being particularly good. The area also offers a few harder gems! Seepage affects the climbs at the back of the dividing bay around the Black Back Wall. The climbs are described from east to west, starting from the lower east-facing walls. The route numbers refer to Map 3J on page 229.

1   Making Waves   E1 5b
Past where the sea-level platform widens, the crag heightens before it leads into a section with an undercut base. This route climbs the left side of a narrow pillar on an orange wall, to pull through a bulge and finish up a wide crack.

Right of Making Waves is a fine, shorter khaki-coloured wall.

First and Ten   Very Difficult ***
Climb stepped right-facing corners at the left end of the khaki-coloured wall.

Mosaic   Severe **
A few metres right, climb cracks up the centre of the wall.

Fancy Free   Severe *
Using the same start as Mosaic, from a small recess, climb up and follow a right-curving line near the right edge of the wall.

Labrador Chimney   Difficult **
The chimney tucked into the right end of the khaki wall.

Groovey Mover   Mild Severe ***
Just right of the chimney is a defined rib. Follow the groove blocked by roofs in the rib.

The Slide   Difficult ***
Climb the wide corner just right of Groovey Mover, crossing a roof to start.

2   Touchdown Montana   Mild Severe **
The obvious main corner on this wall, starting from a smooth recess.

Up the Junction   Very Difficult
The groove line running up the right edge of the east-facing walls.

The next routes are on the seaward face of the promontory. **Second and Goal** (Severe **) takes a shallow scooped line rising from the left side of a roofed recess low down. **Ace of Diamonds** (Hard Severe) climbs into a diamond-shaped recess and follows the ramp line rightwards from the start of Second and Goal. Next right is a gently leaning black wall. **The Joker** (VS 5a **) starts from the end of the ledge, and takes a line up the middle of the wall.

RUBHA PLOYTACH : 3J

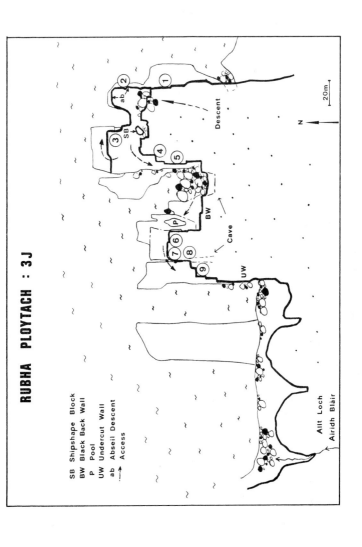

SB Shipshape Block
BW Black Back Wall
P   Pool
UW Undercut Wall
ab Abseil Descent
→   Access

20m

N

Descent

Cave

Allt Loch
Airidh Blàir

Next is a tidal square-cut bay with difficult access. Its east-facing wall is gained by descending easily west of Shipshape Block onto a lower platform and walking back under a smooth black seaward wall. **Marie Celeste** (HVS 5b **) climbs the thin vertical crack in the centre of this wall (Route 3). **Celtic Horizons** (VS 4c **) lies at the right end of the bay, and climbs steeply up via horizontal breaks to gain a short crack in the upper half.

The Shipshape Block itself provides the following climbs: **Shipwreck** (5b *) lies up the middle of the landward side of the block. **La Mouette** (4c) climbs just right of the right edge of Shipwreck. **Bow Draw** (4c *) is the undercut 'bow of the ship'

On the wall behind Shipshape Block, opposite Shipwreck, are (from left to right): **Hispanola** (Difficult), the deep wide right-slanting crack; **Titanic** (Severe *), the thinner diagonal crack just right; **Armada** (Severe *), the thin left-slanting crack just left of the corner; and **Sea Witch** (Severe), the corner.

The walls gain height west of the Shipshape Block, past an easy right-angled corner. The next routes are round the corner on the west face of the big dividing bay. **The Toaster** (E2 5c ***) gives weird, strenuous, reachy climbing up a series of widening breaks on the wall just round the edge. Climb via a crack at half-height. **Three Step** (Very Difficult * ; Route 3) is the stepped corner right of Toaster, and **Giant's Steps** (Mild Severe) takes the right edge of Three Step.

On the west-facing orange-coloured walls right of Giant's Steps are: **Pretty in Pink** (Severe **), the first thin crack line right of the edge; **Jug Abuse** (Difficult **), which hauls on handles via the thin crack up the wall just right of Pretty in Pink, to finish by prominent parallel cracks; and **Trefoil** (Very Difficult *; Route 4), the set of three slightly offset left-facing corners where the wall changes angle.

Right again, the platform narrows, the wall bulges at the base, becomes more compact and turns a rich gold colour. There are two obvious lines on the wall before it ends near a fine right-angled corner.

5   Ros Bhan   HVS 5a *
Start 3 metres right of Jug Abuse. Strenuous climbing gains a ledge at 3m via a wide horizontal break and a short corner. Take the crack to the next ledge and finish by a corner.

Lilidh   E2 6a **
The crack line 4 metres right of Ros Bhan. Jump for the first break and move right to stand on a short ledge. Trend slightly right and back left to finish up the top part of the crack.

On the Black Back Wall, right of the low cave, **Edge Trimmer** (VS 4c) climbs just right of the orange left edge of the wall, and finishes up a groove in the edge. Immediately right of the main corner in the middle of the wall is an undercut curving corner-crack topped by a roof. **Skingraft** (VS 4c) climbs the corner, moves right under the roof, then goes up the open corner on the right.

The next two routes are on the east-facing wall of the bay above the pool. **Billy the Fish** (Severe) takes the crack up the centre of the wall, and **Pinch an Inch** (Mild VS 4b *; Route 6) climbs the right end of the horizontally broken juggy wall, starting at the left end of a narrow ledge above the pool. **Flippertijibbit** (VS 4c) takes the right arete of the wall. From the top ledge, move right and finish up a crack in the final short wall.

The next two routes are on the seaward prow of the promontory.

The Clansman E2 5c **
Start left of centre and climb on small holds up the bulging wall to the big break. Move left, then a long reach gains the ledge. Return right and finish up the corner.

7   The Claymore E2 5c **
Start under twin diagonal cracks high up. Trend right up the bulging wall and back left to the break. Take the steep crack to the next break and finish by the left-hand of the twin cracks.

The platform under the prow is cut at the right end by a deep narrow channel leading under the west face of the promontory. It disappears into a long 'sounding' spooky cave. The following two routes are on the fine juggy black wall above the fissure.

Sundew Mild VS 4b **
Start at the left edge and climb to a short right-facing corner. Trend left and up to finish.

8   Nightshade Mild VS 4b ***
Further right, start off a jammed boulder and climb over a small roof using a long spike to finish via the crack line.

9   Millstone Corner Mild VS 4b **
The tunnel ends at a black shattered corner. This route climbs the clean open black corner in the right wall.

The next routes are round the edge from Millstone Corner on the west-facing wall. **Going Hypo** (E1 5b *) starts a few metres right of the edge, under a wide slot at the top. Climb up and trend right to under stepped roofs. Finish left through the slot. **Maid in a Box** (E1 5b *) takes the corner and flake crack on the right.

STONE PIG CLIFF

This lies beneath the road from Altandhu to Reiff and is hidden from view. The east end of the crag is short, squat and compact, sitting on a non-tidal platform, whereas the western side opens out into a tidal bay with bigger square cut walls and corners. The east-facing wall at the west end of the area is gently overhanging, but more broken, eventually turning the corner into easier angled rock and slabby corners.

Driving towards Reiff where the road rises high above the coast, a large boulder silhouetted on the horizon can be seen above the road looking like a pig gazing out to sea (use your imagination!). There is limited parking near the corner beneath the 'pig.' The crag is directly below, and is approached by descending to the east and walking back under the cliff. The first short walls range from 5m to 8m, before running into the larger walls of the tidal bay beyond a small cave and an area of more broken rock. At higher tide levels a shelf runs to the base of Wirly Girly from just past the cave. Access to routes west beyond Wirly Girly, including the leaning wall, is at low tide only, or where possible by abseil to small platforms at the base of the routes. Descent may be made at the west end, down a slabby corner crack left (facing out) of a narrow inlet.

The first routes are on the short south-facing walls at the east end of the cliff. From right to left (facing the cliff): **Quick Step** (Hard Severe), steps off the platform to climb a left trending line; **Route 1** (VS 5a *) takes the shallow scoop in the wall 4 metres right of the first arete; **Curve Gybe** (HVS 5b *) is the capped groove and wall just right of the first arete; **Duck Gybe** (E1 5c) climbs the arete, with the hardest moves off the ground. **Chalk Block** (Severe) takes the crack in the right side of the large recess left of the arete, and **Walk the Plank** (Mild VS 4c *) takes the curving crack in the left side of the recess.

The next routes are round the impressive prow left of the recess. **The Prowl** (HVS 5a) climbs the hanging groove set in the left side of the prow. **Sea-nick** (Very Difficult) takes the right side of the inset fault just left of the prow, and **Sea-sore** (Difficult) takes the left side of the fault, with hard moves to start. **Vitamen Sea** (Mild Severe *) follows the left-trending crack starting at the left end of the inset fault. **Broadside** (Hard Severe) climbs a small left-facing corner about 3 metres left of Vitamen Sea. **Limey** (VS 4c *) climbs the arete left of Broadside. **Seal Launch** (E2 5c **) takes the difficult corner in the right side of the next inset wall on the left. **Hard Tack** (E2 6a *) starts from a protruding block at the base of the wall left of the corner. Climb the crack to the break, and finish through the slot up the wall above. **Jolly Jack Tar** (Severe) climbs out of a bomb-bay groove 6 metres left of the corner to go up under and finish right through the roof.

The cliff now leads past a small cave into more broken ground at the right end of the tidal bay. Two poor routes have been recorded: **Jim Lad** (VS 5a) climbs up into the cave, and laybacks round the flake in the right side of the roof, finishing leftwards. **Crud** (Difficult) gives scrappy climbing up the broken rock left of the cave.

A step down and across a gap under a chimney line leads to a sloping platform-ramp finishing at a square-cut buttress. Two corner lines start above the ramp; **Swine Dyke** (12m VS 4c) is the 'concrete' filled chimney line. **Aquatic Jambouree** (12m E1 5c *) takes the left-hand corner; **Wirly Girly** (10m E1 5b *) takes the short overhanging corner at the end of the ramp - dodge the bottom bulge by moving in above from the left. At low tides, it is possible to climb a barnacled corner crack up to the end of the ramp.

Obelisk   20m   E1 5b
A low tide route up the front of the square-cut buttress at the end of the ramp. Climb the right edge of the lower tier, then long reaches on horizontal breaks lead to the next ledge. Finish by the steepening shallow groove line above.

Skinny Dipper   20m   Hard Severe
On the wall left of Obelisk, take a rising right-slanting line across the slabby black rock to a more difficult short corner finish.

Next is a loose vegetatious corner followed by a smooth black concave wall, usually wet; thank goodness! Left again is an obvious curving crack line.

Strongbow   20m   E2 5c ***
Follow the crack throughout, which forms a shallow corner in the lower half. A fine overhanging well protected pitch.

Left of Strongbow is an undercut arete, then a bulging wall leading to a deep dank chimney bounding the right side of the east-facing leaning wall. This wall has scope for fine strenuous routes. One route has been recorded on the extreme left end.

Tinsel Town   15m   E2 5c **
From under the left end of a huge recess, move up left to enter an obvious short groove with difficulty. Step right onto a ramp and from the top of this under the bulges, swing left onto Icarus to finish.

Round the corner on the south-west facing cliff, the crag becomes more friendly, easing into a series of slabby corners and aretes. Again the base of the routes is affected by high tides.

Icarus   15m   VS 4c **
Fine climbing up thin cracks and pockets near the right edge of the right-hand slab.

Naloxone   15m   VS 4b *
The right-hand stepped slab corner.

Long Hot Summer 89   20m   VS 4c
The left-hand stepped slab corner with a long right traverse under the big overlap. Climbing the slab edge direct to the end of the right traverse is Severe.

Automaton   20m   HVS 5a *
Climb Long Hot Summer to the overlap, pull straight over this and step left above to finish up the short hanging groove.

Daunt's Arete   15m   Difficult **
The slab arete left of Long Hot Summer, gained by a curving crack in the right side. Good climbing.

Slabby Corner Crack   10m   Moderate
Left of Daunts Arete the slab is undercut and bounded on the left side by a slabby corner crack. Useful as a descent.

Left again is a narrow inlet with a lot of easier angled rock. There is good bouldering on short walls to the east of Stone Pig Cliff, with a long traverse round a 'cirque' of 3m walls above a large platform.

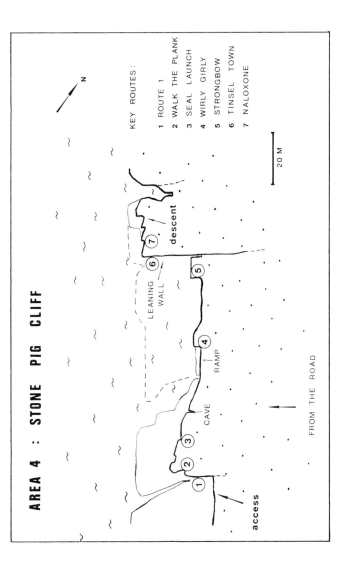

AREA 4 : STONE PIG CLIFF

KEY ROUTES:

1 ROUTE 1
2 WALK THE PLANK
3 SEAL LAUNCH
4 WIRLY GIRLY
5 STRONGBOW
6 TINSEL TOWN
7 NALOXONE

20 M

N

descent

LEANING WALL

RAMP

CAVE

FROM THE ROAD

access

The Sutherland Mountains

This chapter describes the climbing on the most northerly Munros and Corbetts. Here seclusion can be almost guaranteed, adding the ingredient of adventure to some excellent climbing on frequently good rock in magnificent surroundings.

FOINAVEN
911m   (Map Ref 317 507)

Foinaven is the nearest large mountain to Cape Wrath, and since its summit, Ganu Mor, is (probably!) just short of Munro status, the area has always been a backwater for the average hillgoer. This is a significant attraction, a remote and desolate area into which to retreat for a few days. However, a new road up Srath Dionard will, to the regret of many, make the crags much more accessible and they can now be contemplated for an ambitious weekend. It is hoped that, despite its inaccuracies, what follows will be a reference from which to improve its mysterious reputation.

While there are some rock routes here which would be classics anywhere, the majority have all the features of traditional mountain routes, with some loose rock and vegetation, potential wet seeps, difficult route-finding and sometimes poor protection. The rock is quartzite except for Cnoc a Mhadaidh and Creag Dubh, which are gneiss. The gneiss is slabbier, more vegetated and slower to dry than that at Carnmore. Nevertheless it is rough with very little loose rock. The quartzite is very different, cleaner and much steeper with plentiful holds, but the protection is often sparse and there are some loose blocks. On easier-angled climbs this can extend to block-covered ledges or even scree.

Foinaven main ridge runs nearly north-south with Srath Dionard to the east and the Laxford to Durness road to the west. The west side is mostly a straight slope of scree. The east side is more complex with three ridges projecting out from the backbone. At the south end, is the big rounded peak of Creag Dionard and its projecting plateau, Plat Reidh. Between these four features are three corries; from north to south these are Coire Duail, an unnamed corrie and Coire na Lice. The unnamed corrie has no climbing interest but there are cliffs at the

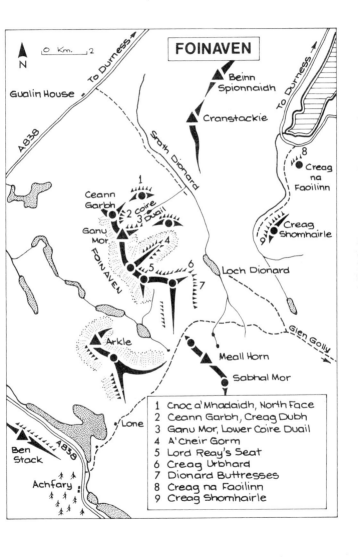

FOINAVEN

1 Cnoc a'Mhadaidh, North Face
2 Ceann Garbh, Creag Dubh
3 Ganu Mor, Lower Coire Duail
4 A'Cheir Gorm
5 Lord Reay's Seat
6 Creag Urbhard
7 Dionard Buttresses
8 Creag na Faoilinn
9 Creag Shomhairle

top of the other two, Creag Dubh at the head of Coire Duail and Lord Reay's Seat at the head of Coire na Lice. The remaining climbing, indeed the majority, lies on the east end of the four projecting features, where they face into Srath Dionard: Cnoc a' Mhadaidh on the north-most ridge running east from Ceann Garbh; three ridgelets on the southmost ridge (A' Cheir Gorm); and a line of big crags on the east edge of the plateau. These are Creag Urbhard, the five Dionard buttresses and Creag Alistair.

Access

It is possible to approach Loch Dionard, centrally positioned in the range, from four different directions, north-east, north-west, south-east and south-west, all equally long distances. The ugly new landrover track up Srath Dionard makes the north-west approach the easiest. The track leaves the A838 just north-east of Gualin House (Map Ref 310 570), cuts down to the River Dionard and goes fairly close to its true left bank. This makes Cnoc a' Mhadaidh very accessible, and this is also the quickest route to Creag Dubh and Lord Reay's Seat. It is probably still quickest for the remaining crags but a more scenic route may be preferred.

A much more attractive route is from the north-east via Srath Beag. From the south end of Loch Eriboll, a short track leaves the A838 under Creag na Faoilinn. It soon disappears and a boggy walk leads to Strabeg Cottage (bothy). From here Srath Coille na Fearna is followed (passing under Creag Shomhairle) and the river crossed to climb up to the Bealach na h-Imrich, which gives a superb view of Creag Urbhard and the First Dionard Buttress (7km to Loch Dionard).

An alternative, and arguably better approach to Creag Alistair, is from the south-west, leaving the road near Achfary (Map Ref 296 402) and proceeding to Lone, whence a good track goes north-east up the Allt Horn, over a col and into the head of Srath Dionard. Finally, the long south-east approach starts from the ruined bothy at Altnabad on the Altnaharra to Loch Hope road. Follow a private road to Gobernuis-gach Lodge (Map Ref 437 417) whence a path leads north-west up Glen Golly, over a low watershed, to the head of Loch Dionard.

CNOC A' MHADAIDH   *(Map Ref 326 525)*

The north face of Cnoc a' Mhadaidh is a curious crag, unimpressive from a distance despite the huge roof which dominates its right side.

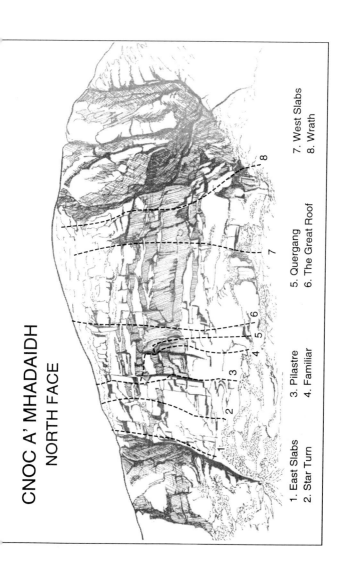

CNOC A' MHADAIDH
NORTH FACE

1. East Slabs
2. Star Turn
3. Pilastre
4. Familiar
5. Quergang
6. The Great Roof
7. West Slabs
8. Wrath

The crag is generally slabby except for the roof, which stretches across at mid-height from the right edge two-thirds of the way towards the left boundary, a deep slit gully. Three routes venture into the roof, but only by using aid. The left demarcation of the roof is a fine pillar taken by the best route, Pilastre. Left of the base of the pillar is a small roof, passed on the left by Star Turn. The routes are described left to right.

1 East Slabs 150m VS 4c   (1975)
Climb the slabs at the east edge of the crag, just right of the slit gully.

2 Star Turn 170m HVS   (1976)
The climb starts at a large block underneath the small roof.
1. 20m Climb an overlap a little to the left and go up a slab to a ledge below the small roof.
2. 35m 5a Go up a crack left of the roof and climb slabs to a stance below a black slab.
3. 35m 5b Go up the slab to an overhanging wall, gain a hanging ramp (nut for aid) and climb to a small stance on the upper slab.
4. 40m 5a Climb up left, then straight up, finishing up an awkward wall at a flat shelf.
5. 40m Finish up a groove and slabs, usually wet.

3 Pilastre 175m HVS **   (1973)
The best climb on the crag; direct and clean. Just left of the crag centre a prominent square-cut pillar stands out from the slabs and cuts through the overhangs. The climb takes a series of right-facing corners on the pillar. Start 10 metres right of Star Turn, at a thin crack directly beneath the corners, reached by scrambling across heather from the base of the slit gully.
1. 20m 4c Climb the crack and the bulge to the left to gain a grass terrace.
2. 30m 5a Climb up, then traverse left to below the corner. Gain the corner via a jammed flake and climb it. Move left at the top, then step right into the upper corner.
3. 30m 4c Climb the corner to an overhang, traverse left to the crest and go up cracked blocks, then shallow cracks in a red wall, and continue to a grass terrace.
4. 15m 5a Climb a big grassy corner to an overhang (junction with Quergang), traverse left and slightly down to its edge, then go up and left to a grass ledge with a tree.
5. and 6. 80m Climb a chimney and heather above.

4 Familiar 200m HVS   (1983)
Start on slabs about 15 metres right of Pilastre.
1. and 2. 90m Climb the slabs, the last section being a diagonal ascent
rightwards towards the main roof. Belay some 15m below the Fisheye
Corner of Quergang.
3. 30m 5b A steep wall bars entry to a groove on the left. Climb it and
the groove to the stance after the abseil on Quergang. Finish as for
Quergang.

5 Quergang 200m HVS (aid)   (1971)
Start in the middle of the crag below the large crack splitting the central
overhangs.
1. 30m Climb vegetated slabs to a large grass terrace.
2. 40m 4c Climb a red slab in the centre to a fault trending right. Follow
it to belay in a crack descending from the roof.
3. 40m 4c Follow the crack to a wet bay. Climb 5m above the bay then
strike out across slabs to the left, passing several overlaps and
heading for a junction of overhangs and the steep central area of cliff.
Belay at a very wet black ledge.
4. 30m 5b Climb a wet slab to the base of Fisheye Corner, a peculiar
overhanging crack. Climb the corner (3 or 4 aid pegs in the upper
reaches, which may be avoidable by a low exit) to a hanging block
ledge.
5. 15m Abseil to a grass ledge on the left (junction with Familiar) and
climb to an eyrie belay.
6. 10m Take the corner above to a good ledge.
7. 35m 5a Traverse a slab left below steep walls (to join Pilastre).
Continue leftwards and round the rib as for Pilastre to gain the ledge
and tree.

6 The Great Roof 200m HVS 5b and A3   (1975)
The route climbs the lower slabs right of Quergang, then follows the
20m roof crack using large pegs. Finish up the slabs above. No further
details are available.

7 West Slabs 200m HVS 5a and A3   (1976)
Climb the lower slabs towards the right of the crag, then the great roof
(on aid) where a pillar abuts against it.

8 Wrath 150m E1   (1978)
The climb is on the extreme right end of the cliff, starting under the
right extremity of the great roof.
1. 30m Climb easily up the right edge of the slabs from the gully, going
in a little to belay under an overhanging wall.
2. 35m 5c Climb a steep groove on the left to a break, move right and
climb a "flying ramp" (peg runner) on to slabs above.
3. and 4. 85m 4c Continue up slabs and grooves.

CREAG DUBH   *(Map Ref 314 512)*

This is a slabby gneiss cliff at the head of upper Coire Duail, on the
right (north-west) side of the corrie set against the top, Ceann Garbh.
The left side and very back corner of the corrie is a scree slope leading
up to a col on the main ridge. This provides the descent: traverse left,
descend to the col, and take a short scree run to grass. The cliff is
100m high next to the col and increases to about 300m at its right-hand
end.
  The cleanest rock is on two buttresses in the centre. Being slabby
and set into the hillside, the cliff attracts drainage and is best visited
when the hill is dry, although the odd wet streak can be tolerated
because the rock is rough and clean (in parts).

Access
Approach either via Srath Dionard and Coire Duail, or across the moor
starting near spot height 143m (the Rhiconich side of Loch Tarbhaidh)
and crossing the col between Cnoc a' Mhadaidh and Ceann Garbh to
traverse into upper Coire Duail (shorter but rougher walking).
  From right to left the main features are: a prominent gully beyond
which is steep broken ground (the north-east Buttress); the Central
Slabs with a big corner with a red left wall (Seers Corner) at the top of
the cleanest rock; a shallow gully line leading into a recessed area
high up; a sweep of steep overlapping slabs with red rock at their base
and separated from a clean rounded pillar by a twin groove system
either side of a narrow flat-topped rib.
  Left of the pillar the cliff continues steep but diminishes in height.
There are a number of recesses and scrappy buttresses rising from a
grass terrace above low-angled lower slabs. The routes are described
from right to left (lower to upper).

Foinaven, Creag Urbhard

North-East Buttress 350m III (1986)
Follow the crest of the buttress, which bounds the deep gully on its right side, starting at the lowest rocks. Progress was made by icy grooves and the occasional snowy traverse.

Overseer 200m V (1992)
Start at a bay immediately left of the central slabs. Climb icy grooves for two pitches (70m), then continue up a series of icefalls trending right for a further two pitches (90m). Easy ground then leads to the top.

Seer's Corner 200m VS † (1977)
A climb of uncertain grade on the Central Slabs, up the big corner with a red left wall at half height, at the top of the cleanest rock. Start at a light-coloured slab directly below the corner. Climb the slab to a white tongue of rock, continue up this and cross an overlap to enter a groove leading to a spike belay in a recess. Go up the big corner in two pitches, then more easily to the top.

Red Grooves 140m Very Difficult † (1968)
The climb follows the conspicuous line of pink cracks and grooves on the right of the sweep of steep overlapping slabs (slanting diagonally right under the sweep of slabs?). "Scramble to start and follow crack and groove for two pitches of 100ft each. A 30ft pitch leads to grass ledge and peg belay (110ft). Climb groove on right, exit right and follow short chimney to ledge and belay on left (100ft). Continue by cracks (60ft) and scramble to top".

Coire Duail Grooves 200m Severe † (1969)
The exact location of this route is uncertain. As a guess, it might start as for Red Grooves but finish more directly (further left). "Start left of the central slabs, follow a series of obvious grooves for 90m to a flake belay below a dark overhanging corner on the left. Climb this to stance and belay. Follow the corner on the right for 45m to a grass ledge. From the highest point on the ledge climb a chimney and a grooved slab on the right. 60m of scrambling leads to the summit".

The Fly, Foinaven (Climber, Bob MacGregor)

Gualin Wall   110m   Severe †   (1971)
Again, the exact location is uncertain; possibly the same as Sava. "This
climb lies on the left-hand part of the crag. The start is on the large
grass terrace above the broken lower rocks, and directly below an
obvious corner in the upper part of the cliff. Climb directly up slabs,
trending right at the top. Belay on upper grass ledge below a wet crack
(150ft). Avoid the crack by pleasant climbing up the wall on its left,
trending right at the top to a ledge at the foot of the corner (100ft).
Climb the corner, and exit on the right wall. Scramble to top (100ft)".

Sava   120m   Severe   (1975)
The route follows the obvious crack and groove system bounding the
sweep of overlapping slabs on the left (presumably one of the twin
grooves which lie either side of a narrow flat-topped rib). Scramble to
start, then follow cracks and grooves to large grass ledge. Step left
and climb corner and cracks above to a large prominent corner; climb
this to belay near the top. Continue by the groove above and go directly
up by flake cracks to the top.

Promised Land   110m   VS   (1989)
Climbs the clean rounded pillar left of the overlapping slabs.
1. 50m 4b Start up a thin tongue of clean rock below and left of the
pillar. Follow this to where it merges into steeper clean rock, then
traverse right into the centre of the pillar.
2. 35m 4b Follow the vague crest initially straight up, then trending
right to a point about 5m left of the bounding corner (the left-hand of
twin "Sava" corners) and finally trending back left to a ledge and big
spike below a prominent 3m wedged block well seen from below.
3. 25m Gain the top of the block from the right. From there, slabby
ground diminishes in angle to the top.

LOWER COIRE DUAIL   *(Map Ref 326 512)*

Windfall   250m   IV   (1986)
The most obvious icefall in the centre of the north-facing crag in lower
Coire Duail. Start at the lowest point and climb by steepening slabs to
finish directly via icicle terrain.

A' CHEIR GHORM   *(Map Ref 331 500)*

South-east of Ganu Mor, the main top of Foinaven, this long ridge branches east from an un-named top on the main ridge (spot height 867m). It has a band of cliff along its north side, but this is mainly scree. The only climbing appears to be at its north-east end, on the end buttresses visible from upper Srath Dionard below Loch Dionard. Seen from here, three ridges converge on the apparent summit. The spur has been described as 'conical and graceful', the rock as 'insecure'. Detailed descriptions are assumed unnecessary. From left to right are the **South Ridge** (200m, Very Difficult), **Cave Ridge** (100m, Moderate) and **North Ridge** (180m, Difficult). A small cave is visible from below on the central ridge, hence the name.

LORD REAY'S SEAT   *(Map Ref 322 492)*

Lord Reay's Seat is a small peak on the main Foinaven ridge just south of spot height 867m. It is immediately north of the col Cadha na Beucaich, at the head of Coire na Lice. The name is also used for the 230m steep and narrow quartzite crag which is the east face of the peak and forms the headwall of Coire na Lice. It is typical quartzite; clean rock but with occasional loose blocks. The crag is very remote and most easily approached from Srath Dionard, starting from the north end of Loch Dionard and following the stream valley up and left into Coire na Lice. The routes are described from right to left.

Original Route   250m   Difficult   (1964)
An easier and indirect version of Fishmonger. A start was made up the right edge of the buttress, joining Fishmonger after pitch 2. The final tower (pitches 5 and 6 of Fishmonger) was circumvented by following a rib on the left skyline before returning to the ridge for the finish.

Fishmonger   250m   Severe   (1964)
The obvious chimney to the right of the central nose is the general line. A fine natural line finishing at the summit. Start at the foot of the chimney.
1. 25m Climb the chimney to a small wet overhang. Belay on the left.
2. 25m   Go left and back right to regain the chimney above the overhang. Climb up right to an obvious large platform.
3. 25m The line of the chimney continues a little to the left as a steep broken wall. Instead, traverse a big ledge 20m right to the foot of another chimney. Climb this chimney to a scree shelf.

4. 35m Climb the obvious chimney ahead (easier but loose).

5. 10m The final tower lies ahead, with a prominent chimney up its centre. Climb up to gain the chimney.

6. 25m Traverse 3m right, then climb an 8m crack (crux) which lies between a detached pillar and the main cliff. Traverse left for 5m to regain the chimney left of the nose. Climb a right-angled corner with a crack to a belay. Now follow a narrow summit arete to a gap, cross it, then easy scrambling to the top.

Pobble 200m VS **   (1971)

A magnificent climb, especially with the direct finish. It follows a line of chimneys which bound the steep nose on its left but start above a grass ledge 25m up. Start left of a light-coloured patch of rock. Climb up, then right (exposed) to the foot of the first chimney. Climb the chimneys for 80m to a grey crinkly slab. (The direct finish takes a big left-facing corner above, seen in the centre near the top skyline from the approach to the crag). Climb the slab then trend left to an ill-defined arete. Climb the arete, traverse right above a steep wall, then return leftwards and climb a short corner. Easier ground leads to the summit.
Direct Finish: 45m HVS **   (1983)
Above the crinkly slab, trend right across a slab to reach the steep left-facing corner. Climb it direct with a short excursion rightwards at the very top.

Breakaway 180m VS †   (1976)

Another climb of uncertain grade, starting just left of Pobble.

1. 40m Climb 5m to a ledge right of a white rock scar, then continue up a left-slanting groove to large flake belays.

2. 45m Climb the wall above for 10m to a small ledge, continue up a smooth groove, then move rightwards to a terrace.

3. 35m Climb a groove immediately right of a rock scar.

4. 35m Take easier rock to an arete (Pobble touches here), belay below an obvious corner left of the arete.

5. 25m Climb the corner to the top, as for Pobble.

CREAG COIRE NA LICE

The south side of Coire na Lice is a continuous cliff about 1km long; it is also known as Creag Dionard North Face. It has an unusual appearance with distinctive folding of the rock and an almost Dolomitic nature. One can imagine the lower slabby rocks raked by stonefall from the steep walls above. Someone adventurous might care to explore the impressive central section of the cliff. In the meantime there is a route at either end. **Rhino Buttress** (120m, Difficult) is the most easterly buttress, following the large central rib and avoiding the separate steep wall on the top right. **Cantilever Climb** (150m, Difficult) starts near the small lochan in the upper corrie and climbs a shallow gully to the grassy terrace 60m up, which girdles the crag. Go to the Cantilever, a large block leaning against the cliff. From here go by a corner and ridge to the top.

CREAG URBHARD   *(Map Ref 350 488)*

This is the most extensive and best-known of the Foinaven cliffs. The climbing here characterises the area; a huge cliff (200m to 350m high and over 1km long) of complex structure, with difficult route-finding, poor protection and some loose blocks. The rewards are those of traditional mountaineering, with most routes in the middle grades and a superb remote backdrop. Creag Urbhard dominates the upper part of Srath Dionard and overlooks Loch Dionard. The rock is quartzite, somewhat smoother than on the higher crags and thus slippery on wet seeps, but with square-cut holds often sloping down to the left.

The main features of the face are four waterfalls and three tiers separated by two wide right-slanting ramp systems. The First Waterfall bounds the crag on the left (the big buttress further left being the First Dionard Buttress). The top tier slants up right from here and peters out not far beyond a gully, from which the Second Waterfall (only a trickle in dry weather) flows. The second tier starts at the base near the left end and stretches virtually the whole length of the cliff, containing the steep sections of the Second, Third and Fourth Waterfalls. The third tier starts at the base of the Second Waterfall.

The section of cliff between the First and Second Waterfalls is called the South Ridge (a misnomer), and consists of the top two tiers separated by The Terrace. The top tier has a number of diedres and fissures and the best rock on the crag. The face to the right of the Second Waterfall is Central Buttress, which has all three tiers. The dividing terraces are known as the Upper and Lower Pavements. The Upper Pavement is effectively a continuation of The Terrace. Part way along Central Buttress is the remarkable Third Waterfall which falls from the lip of an overhang to the Lower Pavement (it still flows in dry weather but is hard to pick out), then along the Lower Pavement and finally to the ground.

Right of the Third Waterfall, Central Buttress soon becomes less compact and ends somewhat arbitrarily in a recess containing the Fourth Waterfall, which has a small flow and finishes on a wide vegetated ramp below and right of the Lower Pavement. Right of the Fourth Waterfall is the broken North Face, then the North Ridge which overlooks the foot of Loch Dionard. Finally to the right is the triangular Far North Wall, containing 'the fifth waterfall'.

SOUTH RIDGE

1   The First Waterfall   130m   III   (1980)
This requires very cold weather to freeze, due to its large flow.

2   Fiscal's Rib   150m   Very Difficult †   (1986)
'It follows a grey rib high up and left of Pantagruel'. Precise line unknown, but it possibly coincides with Pantagruel.

3   Pantagruel   170m   Severe   (1959)
Start at a short stepped groove left of an obvious left-facing corner at the left end of the base of the cliff.
1. 35m Climb the groove for 20m, then traverse right to a heather platform.
2. 35m Go straight up towards twin overhangs.
3. 35m Avoid the overhangs on the left and climb to a big heather ledge.
4. 30m Traverse up and left, then right and straight on to a slabby gangway.
5. 35m Climb the gangway for 20m, then finish by a 15m wall.

4   Whitewash   170m   HVS   (1976)
This takes the centre of the wall but trends right to coincide in part with Gargantua but finishes more directly. Start at some low-angled slabs right of the basal left-facing corner and below an obvious overhang low down.
1. 35m Climb to the right end of the overhang; climb the bulge using a crack which is followed to a belay.
2. 35m Above is a vague groove. Climb this direct for 20m and traverse right to belay below an overhang.
3. 30m Climb the right end of the overhang using a rib to reach the foot of a small blank wall. Turn the wall on its left by an overhanging

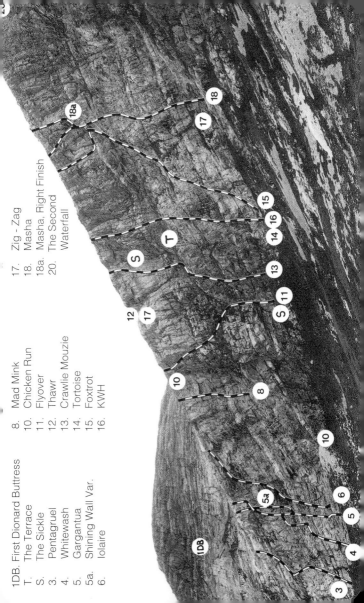

1DB. First Dionard Buttress
T. The Terrace
S. The Sickle
3. Pentagruel
4. Whitewash
5. Gargantua
5a. Shining Wall Var.
6. Iolaire

8. Mad Mink
10. Chicken Run
11. Flyover
12. Thawr
13. Crawlie Mouzie
14. Tortoise
15. Foxtrot
16. KWH

17. Zig - Zag
18. Masha
18a. Masha, Right Finish
20. The Second Waterfall

groove, then climb rightwards to belay at the foot of a prominent corner (probably joins Gargantua here).
4. 50m Climb the corner to the rock gangway.
5. 20m 5b Climb the corner (avoided by Gargantua) to finish.

5 Gargantua 170m   Hard Severe   (1959)
This good route follows an obvious long groove at mid-height on the wall for three pitches. Start at a corner below the groove and just left of the terrace of Iolaire.
1. 10m Climb the corner.
2. and 3. 60m Move left, then follow a crack. Move right and go up a vague corner to belay below and left of big overhangs.
4. 5. and 6. 70m Passing the overhangs on the left, go up the obvious groove to the rock gangway.
7. 35m Ignore the obvious direct finish above (Whitewash). Walk up the gangway to the right and climb a 20m crack in the wall.

5a Shining Wall Variations   HVS
Climb the arete right of the obvious long groove to reach the gangway (5a). Finish up the final corner of Whitewash (5b).

6 Iolaire 155m   HVS *   (1979)
A good route starting just right of Gargantua but passing the big roof system by a chimney on its right (the Gargantua groove is on its left). Start 40 metres left of the scree cone of Chicken Run, at the left end of a rocky terrace (Gargantua can start here too but trends left).
1. 40m 4b Climb a big crack direct.
2. 25m 4c Continue up 5m to the big roof system, then trend right under it to belay just before a prominent chimney-crack.
3. 25m 5b Gain the chimney-crack awkwardly and climb it to belay below a corner.
4. 25m 4c Climb the corner to the rocky gangway.
5. 40m Follow the gangway up right to finish without difficulty.

To locate the next set of routes to the right, find an obvious scree fan at the base of the cliff below a waterfall which drains The Terrace. High above this is a long band of overhangs slanting up left. The next feature on the upper wall to the right is the huge diedre of Chicken Run, the biggest on the upper tier.

7 The Terrace 600m III (1979)
The waterfall above the scree fan forms a steep ice pitch (tricky for the grade) which leads to The Terrace itself, which is much easier. Traverse to and finish up the snow gully above The Second Waterfall (icefall).

8 Mad Mink 90m HVS (1987)
This climbs the wall on the top tier left of the huge diedre of Chicken Run, with an airy and enjoyable second pitch on good rock. Follow the ramp of Chicken Run for one pitch before climbing three short walls to the foot of the buttress. Start below the crack line leading to the left end of the long overhang which cuts the wall at two-thirds height.
1. 35m 4a Follow the vague crack line on the left to a break.
2. 45m 5a Traverse 3m right and climb a steep blocky wall. Continue up and left to a clean-cut chimney which leads to the overhang. Climb this direct to a short corner on the right.
3. 10m Easily up the corner.

9 The Fly 200m IV (1979)
The distinctive feature is an icefall descending from the huge diedre of Chicken Run; it needs a long freeze to form. Climb the initial icefall to gain The Terrace (as before) and follow this for 60m. Climb diagonally left across heather and a short rock corner to reach the icefall. Follow ice to a ledge which escapes out leftwards from the main corner to finish up easier-angled ice.

10 Chicken Run 200m Hard Severe (1965)
A natural line, with plenty of nature involved. Start just right of the waterfall and follow a ramp rightwards underneath The Terrace. Gain The Terrace and ultimately the huge diedre. Follow its back; the final chimney is the crux.

SOUTH RIDGE, RIGHT SECTION

Most of the routes follow distinctive features on the top tier. There are also a number of features along the base of the cliff. Despite this, some descriptions are vague, particularly on the lower tier and the routes are open to variation. Repeat ascentionists (particularly of the "classic" line, Fingal) have usually followed their nose rather than the description. Despite the best efforts of the author, this is recommended. Working right along the top tier from the huge diedre of Chicken Run are the following features: (1) on the right wall of Chicken Run diedre is a vegetated ramp, Flyover; (2) a number of shallow corners on the front face lead across to a left-slanting chimney line, the finishes of Zigzag and Thawr; (3) beyond a smooth wall is a big vertical diedre, similar to Chicken Run. This is the handle of "The Sickle", while its blade curves to the left down the lower tier; (4) next right is a left-slanting chimney (the route KWH) which is almost a continuation of the start of Zigzag, a left-slanting turfy corner on the lower tier starting near the base of the Second Waterfall; (5) a number of diedres lead across to two deeper chimneys forming a V (Masha); (6) right again are a number of diedres becoming less prominent as one approaches the upper gully of the Second Waterfall and the end of the South Ridge.

11 Flyover 180m III/IV (1979)
The route starts up the Blade of The Sickle, from a long terrace just above the base of the cliff and covered with small trees, and goes left to finish up the vegetated ramp mentioned above.

12 Thawr 400m III (1980)
Start up The Terrace, then take the left-slanting chimney line which is the finish of Zigzag.

13 Crawlie Mouzie 260m Severe (1967)
Start at the right end of the tree-covered terrace. Climb by the line of least resistance (and most vegetation) to the Terrace. On the upper tier climb a shallow diedre in the centre of a smooth wall between Zigzag and the Sickle handle. Move right above the diedre to belay beside jammed blocks. Continue straight up, then go 30m right to avoid roofs to finish. (The finish looks good, if a little improbable. Conceivably it might finish up the handle of The Sickle.)

14 Tortoise 260m Hard Severe (1969)
Right of the tree-covered platform is a section of steep rock with overhangs. Tortoise is presumed to climb just right of these. One could start at a low mound resembling a tortoise at the base of the cliff, or not far right of it. (In fact the route is not named after the mound but after Clive Rowland.)
1. 40m Climb diagonally left on slabby rock to a terrace below imposing walls.

2. 35m From the right end of the terrace ascend to overhangs, move left and climb slabby ribs to a belay.

3. 35m Climb easily to a terrace, move slightly right and climb steep walls, moving right to a stance.

4. 5. and 6. 150m Climb directly up a series of corners on the front of the buttress (between the Sickle handle and KWH).

15 Foxtrot 320m HVS   (1983)
Takes a right-rising line following a conspicuous pale line of waterworn rock, starting near Tortoise and finishing just left of the V-chimney system of Masha. Start on top of the low tortoise-shaped mound. Follow the watershed line rightwards for four long pitches (crossing KWH and Zigzag) to belay at a small rowan at the foot of a gully leading into Masha corner. Climb up the shallow gully above to a platform, then up into the confines of the gully (45m). Continue up the gully, then break out left to belay on a ledge immediately above a flake (25m). A short wall and groove above leads up left to the bank of overhangs near the top of the cliff. Climb the wall and groove for about 10m, surmount an overlap on the left, then climb a groove until it is possible to escape right at 20m to a commodious platform and belay (25m, 5a). Continue up a slabby ramp to the top (60m).

16 KWH 280m Severe   (1966)
Another vague start but the finish is obvious, a big left-slanting chimney line right of the Sickle handle and beyond the final buttress of Tortoise. The best guess for the start is a grassy ramp approximately midway between the low tortoise mound and a short left-facing corner. There are harder but cleaner alternatives nearby. Find a way up to the Terrace, crossing Foxtrot. Climb the chimney-diedre, escaping from the vegetation leftwards near the top on to the clean arete (finishing near Tortoise).

17 Zigzag 300m Very Difficult   (1962)
Near the base of the Second Waterfall starts a left-slanting line of turf in a shallow corner. The route goes up right of this for 60m before descending left into a similar left-slanting fault, which leads to the Terrace. A long traverse left leads to an obvious left-slanting chimney line, left of the Sickle handle. Thawr takes this, but Zigzag climbs the cleaner rock on the left.

18 Masha 300m   HVS 5a *   (1972)
Start at the foot of the Second Waterfall, just right of Zigzag, and climb
up to the big V-chimney just below the top of the cliff. When closer, it
is a shallow chimney leading into a big diedre.

18a Right-hand Finish 110m   VS *   (1983)
The final diedre is often very wet; this gives a good alternative. Start
about 10m right of the diedre at a short steep wall. Climb the wall, then
a small corner on to slabs. Work up and right round a nose to a small
slab immediately above a pinnacle-flake (25m). Surmount the overlap
above at its right end by a crack to gain another small slab. Climb a
steep groove to a slabby terrace. Climb a crack in the left side of a
steep wall directly above (40m). Scramble to the top (45m).

Between Masha and the steep section of the Second Waterfall is a
large area of featureless rock leading up to a number of diedres in the
top tier. Three routes have been recorded here and doubtless many
other parties have wandered about, ususally looking for Fingal. Since
the wall seems to be climbable almost anywhere at about Hard
Severe, only the description for Fingal is quoted. Good luck!

19 Fingal 300m   Severe *   (1962)
"The following route starts up the rocks on the left of the bottom pitch
of the Second Waterfall and follows a virtually direct line up the crags
diverging leftwards from the watercourse, crossing two diagonal fault
lines (the second being The Terrace) and finishing up the right-hand
edge of a large dark V-shaped depression in the uppermost tier of the
crag, easily identified from the lochside". (Presumably Masha) The
start is not quoted but finds a way up to the Terrace probably a little
right of Masha. Once on the Terrace, go to a point directly below "the
huge wet V-shaped amphitheatre". "Climb up on to a flake 40ft up on
the right-hand enclosing wall of the amphitheatre and continue within
the amphitheatre confines to a huge rock fang. Now escape rightwards
from the amphitheatre by a traverse round the exposed edge (crux),
to an inset slab in a corner leading to easier broken rocks, halfway up
the great slabby wall which is to the right of the amphitheatre. The
obvious chimney in the right-hand corner was followed for 50ft. It
narrows above to an overhanging cleft, but one can traverse horizontally leftwards for 30ft over the slabs to emerge with surprising
suddenness at the top of the main face".

Note: If, as guessed, the route goes into the V-chimney of Masha, then escapes right to finish up an obvious corner capped by a small square roof, then there is a line quite close to the Second Waterfall continuing up the top tier by either of two diedres. This might be **Promiscuous Wall** (1975), apparently loose. An ascent of this line would guarantee an adventure, free from the confines of guide books.

20 The Second Icefall (Waterfall) 180m V   (1979)
A winter ascent of the Second Waterfall. Like most waterfalls, its formation of ice depends both on the flow of water and the length of the cold spell. On the first ascent the ice was wide and thick (climbed mostly on its left side, direct being very steep). It is probably rarely in this condition. In colder weather in 1980 it did not form, but in the long cold spell of 1986 it was in excellent condition.

CENTRAL BUTTRESS

21 Boreas 150m Mild Severe *   (1965)
This route lies up the right side of the Second Waterfall, keeping as close to it as practicable and finishing on the Upper Pavement (the summit tier is unclimbed). The rock is better than it appears. Scramble up steps next to the Waterfall until just above the Lower Pavement.
1. 35m Climb straight up the subsequent slab.
2. 20m Go round a ledge to the right, then up a broken groove.
3. 20m Go diagonally left up the groove to the very edge of the Waterfall. Then traverse right across steep rock (crux) to gain another ledge, which slants up right.
4. 25m Continue right along the ledge, then up to the foot of a shallow chimney facing the waterfall.
5. 25m Climb the chimney for 10m, then go diagonally left beneath overhanging rock. When the angle eases, move up onto a rightwards ascending shelf.
6. 25m Continue up the shelf and over a short steep step to arrive at the Upper Pavement and finish up right.

22 The Third Icefall (Waterfall) 150m V   (1986)
In 1979 the Third Waterfall froze from the lip of its roof in a huge icicle. In 1986 this was absent and an improbable alternative line was taken. The lower icefall (below Lower Pavement) was omitted due to thin and hollow ice and the foot of the main fall reached by scrambling up from

the left. Three long pitches led to the top left corner of the ice. From here a short awkward ramp breached the overhangs (this is the second break left of the icicle). A final chockstone led to a finish up a long easy gully (not included in the length).

23 Original Route Moderate   (1950)
Start left of the lower part of the Third Waterfall by a 10m loose chimney to a shelf of heather and ash trees, gaining the Lower Pavement after 60m. Follow this rightwards. Finally, traverse right across broken rock to gain a grassy rake leading to the top.

24 Right-hand Route, Central Buttress 110m Severe (1954)
Start from the top right end of the Lower Pavement. Climb to a water-sprayed ledge and follow it up right to an awkward traverse (crux) round a bulge to a heather ledge. Climb the 20m vertical wall above on good holds. The route now improves. Trend left to a prominent groove bounded on the left by a wall, the edge of which forms a sharp ridge topped by a semi-detached pinnacle. Straddle the groove till one can traverse left on to the exposed arete which leads to the top of the pinnacle. Continue on the crest to easier ground.

25 Three Tier Route 280m Severe   (1968)
This must take a similar line to Central Buttress, Right-hand Route except that it includes the bottom tier (below the Lower Pavement). There is scope for several lines here but the section of cliff is not very attractive. Start between the Third and Fourth Waterfalls on the lower vegetated ramp. Go up and left to gain a right-sloping shelf by various lines. Go up a short distance to a black waterfall chimney. Go up this, then left after a few metres and follow an edge to gain the Lower Pavement to the right of the Third Waterfall. Climb an obvious chimney to finish on the edge of the buttress.

26 The Fourth Waterfall 200m IV   (1986)
There are two tiers separated by the Lower Pavement. The lower one was very thin but on good ice. In summer it is a good route for a foul day, with sound rock (Moderate).

27 North Ridge 300m Very Difficult   (1954)
Start at the lowest rocks beyond a large, highly-coloured outcrop. Climb fairly direct by short walls to the foot of a recess with a tree above. Climb the left wall to the tree and a mossy overhang. Continue up steep rock (much variation possible).

FAR NORTH WALL

28 The Green Knight 100m IV   (1979)
In the centre of this wall, a prominent green icefall forms in a wet recess immediately above a small yellow outcrop. The icefall only forms in very good conditions.

29 Gawain's Chimney 120m III/IV   (1979)
The narrow chimney just left of the wet recess of The Green Knight. It looks like a crack from a distance.

THE DIONARD BUTTRESSES

The Dionard Buttresses line the hillside above the west bank of the Allt an Easain Ghil extending south from Creag Urbhard. The buttresses are named One to Five from right to left (north to south), although they are not well-defined and there has been much confusion in the past. The following detailed identification should prevent future problems. Approaching from the north (as most will) the first place from which all the buttresses are visible is where the Allt an Easain Ghil enters Loch Dionard. The buttresses are described from this vantage point.

The First Buttress is easily identified as the big face with its distinctive band of overhangs facing Creag Urbhard. Seen from the head of the loch the vegetated fault line of Plume is partly in profile on the left edge, running up to a terrace at the top of the buttress. The Second Buttress consists of three tiers each sloping up from left to right. The middle tier is a long low 60m wall. The lower tier is a shorter and more broken wall running up over the top of the First Buttress. The top tier is more rounded and has a distinctive banana-shaped groove in its centre. The Third, Fourth and Fifth Buttresses are set back in a single larger tier and just break the skyline behind and left of the Second Buttress, top tier. Much more obvious from here is the furthest south, and second largest buttress, Creag Alistair. From the valley bottom just short of Creag Alistair, it is seen as dome-shaped with a branched fault line in the centre. The Fifth Buttress is directly uphill from here and has two obvious right-slanting slabby ramp lines with a less continuous ramp between their top ends. A steep heathery slope runs rightwards up underneath the Fourth and Third Buttresses, which are separated by a deep forked gully.

THE FIRST BUTTRESS

The spectacular central section of this buttress offers probably the finest rock climbing on Foinaven. A band of large overhangs dominates the wall; Millenium penetrates these to give the best route. Above and right of the biggest overhang is a separate inverted L-shaped roof taken by Cengalo. Routes are described right to left.

1 Incisor 200m III   (1979)
Right of Cengalo are easy-angled slabs crossed by a stepped ramp line. In good conditions a thin ice smear flows out of the ramp near its left end and down the slabs. Gain the smear by a traverse from the right and follow it for 60m into the ramp. Easier climbing up the ramp and across a heather terrace leads to a series of short corners leading to a skyline notch obvious from the ramp. An undistinguished route.

2 Toothache 200m Difficult   (1959)
The route follows a vague ridge between Cengalo and the ramp line. Approaching uphill, start at the point where the angle of the face relents. Climb an open corner, then up the ridge to the right of the slabs below the Cengalo overhang. Continue up until a traverse left leads back to the ridge, now parallel to a crack line above the Cengalo overhang.

3 Cengalo 210m VS *   (1969)
An excellent route, sustained and exposed but not technically difficult. The highlight is the large inverted L-shaped overhang, passed by a very exposed and unprotected traverse left. Start immediately left of the open corner of Toothache, on slabs below the inverted L-shaped overhang.
1. and 2. 75m Climb the lower slabs to a small stance below the groove leading up to the L-shaped overhang.
3. 35m 4b Climb the left wall for 12m, then make a delicate traverse left to gain smooth frontal slabs.
5. 6. and 7. 100m Continue more or less directly, the line being vague but sustained, over smooth slabby rock. Scramble to the summit ridge.

4 Millennium 305m E2 ***   (1982)
A tremendous route, possibly the best on Foinaven, taking the overhanging wall just right of the centre of the crag for three pitches to the

FOINAVEN

THE FIRST DIONARD BUTTRESS

1. Incisor
2. Toothache
3. Cengalo
4. Millennium
5. Dialectic
7. Plume

central slabs, then the right-slanting fault through the great roof to the upper slabs. Start right of the overhanging central groove.

1. 35m 4c Climb a short wall to a right-trending break. Follow it to a stance, peg belay.

2. 40m 5b Climb to a wet scoop on the left and up through steep walls to a groove. Go right to a stance under an overhang.

3. 45m 5a Climb the overhang above, moving right or direct, then continue more easily to the slabs.

4. 40m 5c Go left and up to a steep groove leading right. Climb with difficulty to a stance.

5. 45m 5b Follow the undercut ramp through the roofs and exit on to grey slabs.

6. and 7. 100m 4b Climb shallow grooves and slabs to finish.

5 Dialectic 250m E2 (aid) **   (1969)

A good climb, despite some potentially dangerous loose rock, which might go free. The steep wall at the base of the cliff below the great roof of Millenium changes aspect just above the lowest rocks. The route climbs just left of this change for 3 pitches, then breaks out left through the main roof system using some aid. Start about 40 metres right of the vegetated fault of Plume.

1. 35m 5a Climb steep walls rightwards to a small flakey stance.

2. 30m 5a Move right, up a groove, then right again under an overlap (peg runner). Climb a wall, step left and climb steeply to a stance.

3. 35m 4c Climb the diedre on the right to a steep exit on to the spacious bower under the huge roofs.

4. 30m 5b (aid) The huge overhang above is split by a fault running across the steep walls to the left towards the extremity of the slabs of the upper buttress. Climb 10m leftwards from the bower to overhangs. Use aid from awkwardly placed nuts and several pegs to continue 12m along the overlapping fault until the angle eases slightly. Cross an overhanging groove to a sloping small stance, using 1 peg to gain the ledge.

5. 20m 5a Climb a delicate wall and easier rock to good stance.

6. 25m 4c Move right and up grey slabs to a spike at the left extremity of the upper overhang of the buttress.

7. 45m 4c Traverse the smooth slab on the right under the overhang to a stance in a crack line.

8. 4b Climb the crack line to easier ground.

Variation Start: 85m   E2   (1984)
This takes the bulging walls to the right of the original start, following
a steep groove at mid-height between the ground and the slabs below
the big overhangs. The route is intricate and difficult to protect, despite
modern equipment.
1. 25m 4c Climb a series of steep walls and slabs to a heather ledge.
2. 25m 5b Take the groove above until an exposed traverse right is
possible (peg runner) to a small stance and poor peg belays.
3. 35m 5b Climb a steep wall above, and a hanging groove, moving
left to join the third pitch of Dialectic near its top.

6 Opportunist 450m HVS   (1969)
This starts up Dialectic, then continues right under the roofs to form a
spiral girdle of the buttress. Follow Dialectic for three pitches to the
spacious bower. Traverse the slabs on the right for two long pitches
(4b). An easy pitch leads to the top of the first section of Cengalo (just
below the inverted L-shaped overhang). Traverse the rib on the right
on to the large expanse of slabs (4b) and climb these diagonally
rightwards for about five pitches (4b).

7 Plume 120m IV   (1979)
In good (possibly unusual) conditions, an impressive icefall forms
down the big vegetated fault on the left of the buttress.

SECOND DIONARD BUTTRESS
Lower Tier

8 Hirsuit 30m E1 5b   (1986)
Towards the left of the Lower Tier is a prominent square area of clean
rock defined by two crack lines. This is the right-hand crack.

Middle Tier

9 Hugsy-Bugsy 60m Very Difficult †   (1967)
The original description has not been checked or located. "Start at the
lower end of the cliff where two converging grass rakes meet. Climb
an obvious broken corner 5m to the first rake. Traverse 3m right and
then climb a series of short walls separated by mossy ledges keeping
left of an obvious crack. At 25m when the angle eases, trend rightwards to gain the crest of the buttress".

10 Marble Corner 65m HVS **   (1973)
This is the big right-facing corner about two-thirds up the middle tier, just right of a yellow undercut area at the base of the cliff. Recommended. Two pitches (4c, 5a).

11 Look North 65m E2   (1986)
Round the left arete of Marble Corner is another corner capped by a roof. This is the line.
1. 25m 5b Climb Marble Corner for 5m, then traverse left round a corner and cross a slab left to better rock. Move up 5m to belay.
2. 20m 5c Climb the corner to a small roof beneath the main roof (peg runner), swing left to gain an easy traverse line beneath the main roof and traverse out left to a good belay.
3. 20m 5b Climb the crack in the arete.

Upper Tier

12 Banana Groove VS   (1986)
The big banana-shaped groove. "Character building".

THIRD, FOURTH, AND FIFTH BUTTRESSES
The numbering of these buttresses, the least explored section of Foinaven, has led to considerable confusion; some of the following routes may be described on the wrong buttress. The buttresses lie in a line above a heathery ramp which rises to the right away from the base of Creag Alistair. The Third is at the top right while the Fifth is next to Creag Alistair.

13 Badile 165m VS †   (1969)
This route could be on either the Third or Fourth Buttress, the latter being more likely. It starts just left of centre. "Climb diagonally left to a platform in a corner (25m). Move right, then go slightly right (hard), then back left to above the stance. Climb directly to peg belay (35m). Traverse right for 25m making little height. Eventually reach a groove and follow this to big overhangs. Belay on jammed blocks under roof (40m). Climb up to the roof, moving right, and keep moving right until a swing round the edge of the overhang leads to a grassy bay (20m). Climb chimneys and walls, first on the left by a slab above the overhangs, then back to the top".

14 Gemelli VS † (1984)
The route would appear to take a line approximating to the crest of the Third Buttress. In this case it might be close to Badile.

15 Mayday 100m Very Difficult † (1965)
"Follows a prominent black slit seen on the left about 400 metres upstream from the head of Loch Dionard. Approach slit by large heathery rake. Climb slit on left wall with occasional excursions to its bed; at fork, take left fork". A long shot might place this in the gully between the Third and Fourth Buttresses.

16 Smick 200m VS † (1973)
This seems very likely to be on the Fifth Buttress. "The crag has two parallel slabby ramps rising from bottom left to top right. The climb follows the first ramp for one pitch, transfers to the second ramp and follows this to the top, avoiding a bulge on the right".

16a Gritstoner's Revenge 170m VS † (1969)
This is presumed to lie on the Fifth Buttress, starting just left of centre. See SMCJ, 1971, p407.

CREAG ALISTAIR

The routes are described from left to right.

17 Left Edge Route 250m Very Difficult (1967)
Takes an inset slab on the edge which forms the left skyline when approaching from Loch Dionard. Start at the left toe of the buttress and climb easy rock for two pitches, then steeper rock to belay in a corner below roofs and left of the slab. Step out right, then up the slab to a terrace. Climb a further slab by a crack 5m left of the arete. Scramble to the summit.
17a *Winter:* IV (1979)
A fine route with much ice in good conditions. In winter take a different start, via an icefall leading up the main (left-hand) gully of the buttress. Then go steeply out left to join the summer route below the slab. The step out right on to the undercut slab is the winter crux, thereafter the route follows the corner and shallow gully at the left edge of the slab.

18 Succuba 230m E1 *   (1973)
This takes the central crest of the crag between the gullies in the lower
reaches and breaks through the overhangs more or less directly to
climb the steep upper walls. Climb messy loose rock right of the left
gully to a small ledge below better rock (45m). Continue for two pitches
on the slabby front of the buttress to reach the overhangs. Climb a
crack on the right to the overhangs. Cross a wall leftwards and swing
round an overlap onto a steep wall which is climbed to gain a V-groove
below a big roof. Move across left and swing round a second overlap
to gain the edge of the overlaps. Go up left to a small stance (40m,
5b). Finish right, then direct to the summit of the main buttress in two
pitches, crossing a crevasse on the second.

19 Alistair Roses 165m HVS **   (1973)
Start just right of Succuba.
1. and 2. 90m 4b Climb slabs diagonally leftwards, keeping the
right-hand gully to the right, to a good stance.
3. 45m 5b Attain a flake on the left and follow it left under overhangs,
crossing Succuba early on.
4. 30m 4c Continue up slabs to join Left Edge Route.

20 The Great Crack 200m HVS   (1984)
The climb starts up solid water-washed quartzite in or just right of the
right-hand gully continuing in the same line beyond the main overhangs (100m, 4b). Above, a big crack breaks through the upper wall;
follow this throughout, passing several bulges (60m, 5b). Easier slabs
follow to the top (50m).

22 Guinevere Gully 300m II   (1979)
The gully bounding Creag Alistair on the right. Mostly snow, with one
low-angled ice pitch which could bank out under heavier conditions.

DIONARD CRAGS
Three small crags face Creag Alistair at Map Ref 365 475. The lower
left crag is distinguished by a prominent grooved arete which gives
the line of the following route.

Beeline 50m HVS   (1987)
Scramble from the left to the foot of a clean white corner.
1. 40m 5a Just to the left of the main corner, a short wall leads to a
slanting crack which is followed leftwards until an awkward bulge gains

FOINAVEN
CREAG ALISTAIR

17. Left Edge Route
17a. Left Edge Route, Winter
18. Succuba
19. Alistair Roses
20. The Great Crack

a slab. From its top step down and right below overhangs before pulling through them, then move left to a corner which leads to a stance. A good pitch.

2. 10m 4a Continue up the corner.

BEN STACK
712m   (Map Ref 270 422)

On the north-east side of this hill, above Loch Stack, are two bands of cliff. The upper band has three short routes (30m, Very Difficult; SMCJ 1959). Two other climbs in the VS and HVS grades have been completed on this crag, but details are not available.

ARKLE
787m   (Map Ref 311 453)

The south rib of this peak gives a pleasant climb (180m, Moderate; SMCJ 1952).

CREAG NA FAOILINN   *(Map Ref 395 528)*

This is the large but scrappy crag at the head of Loch Eriboll overlooking the track up Srath Beag. Its closeness to the road may compensate in part for other deficiencies.

Pellet Wall Severe   (1989)
This climb takes an obvious line up the crag, right of Offside. Starting at a ledge with a birch tree and an ivy patch, it breaks onto the easier upper wall via a prominent short steep chimney.

Offside 115m Very Difficult   (1969)
Start at the right end of the crag, just left of two birch trees and right of a prominent nose.

1. 20m Go up left to a terrace.
2. 35m Climb a V-groove, avoiding the overhang on the right, and go up slabs to belay in a heathery corner.
3. 20m Climb a corner and short crack to belay below overhangs.
4. 40m Climb the overhang on good holds and easy slabs above.

Monkey Gull 175m Severe †   (1971)
Whether this route has anything in common with the previous is left to
future explorers to decide. On the right side of the crag is an obvious
smooth grey wall. The route goes up on the left of this, starting below
and just right of a tree.
1. 20m Go up a loose groove to a ledge below the grey wall.
2. 35m Walk left and climb a quartz groove near the left end of the
ledge. Turn an overhang on the right and go back left to a steep rib;
belay in a heather niche above.
3. 40m Go up to a light-coloured groove and follow this to where its
continuation splits the right end of a belt of overhangs. Turn the
overhangs on the right and go back to less steep cracks. Belay on a
ledge about 10m right of the obvious overhang.
4. 30m Climb up to a ledge and straight on to the foot of a rounded
ice-smoothed rib.
5. 50m Take the crest of the rib and scramble easily to the top.

CREAG SHOMHAIRLE *(Map Ref 382 507)*

This interesting cliff lies some 5km from the head of Loch Eriboll.
Follow a track up Srath Beag to Strabeg Cottage. To get a good view
of the crags it may be better to cross to the west side of the river. The
crags run for about 2km above a pleasant wood, the best climbing
being at the south end. The rock is excellent gneiss.

1 Strabeg's Weep 50m IV   (1986)
This is the small icefall at the extreme left of the crag, opposite Strabeg
Cottage.

At the left end of the crag there is a steep, smooth grey wall left of
a reddish recess.

2 The Row of Trees 65m E1   (1979)
Start near the left end of the terrace below the grey wall.
1. 20m Climb around the lower slabs on vegetation and traverse right
to below an obvious recess.
2. 30m 5b Climb into the recess and through the overhang with
difficulty, on loose rock, and continue up more easily.
3. 15m Take slabs to the top. Descend by a gully on the left.

3 Mistaken Identity 65m E1   (1979)
Start from the right end of the terrace below the grey wall. The climb takes a clean pillar in the lower half, and an obvious diagonal crack in the upper part.
1. 35m 5a Climb a line of clean cracks. Move left near the top of the cracks past loose flakes to a ledge and recess.
2. 30m 5b Climb the obvious left-slanting crack in the upper wall; it has some vegetation but gives good climbing.

4 Crescent-Shaped Chimney 240m VS †   (1953)
This appears to be the chimney in the large red recess. It is loose and not recommended. Start up the wall left of the chimney and after 35m traverse right into it. Move out left again and up a slanting grassy rake. Make a delicate step back right and up into the chimney. Move out left and up a second chimney. Take its right fork, which has a large chockstone forming a window. Climb out from behind the chockstone and up the wall on the left. A further 40m leads to a big grassy terrace. Scramble to the top. (See also SMCJ 1967, p57)

5 The Harrier 270m VS   (1982)
Right of Crescent-Shaped Chimney a tall pink rib rises above overhangs. This route gains the rib from the right then climbs fairly directly to near the summit via three tiers. Good rock and a sustained standard compensate for the vegetated bits.
1. 20m Start up a short vertical crack, right of an overhung corner, to gain a slab and turfy ramp rising left.
2. 25m A gangway continues up left into a groove and corner.
3. 25m Cross the slab on the left to gain the rib by a bulge, then climb direct to detached blocks.
4. 20m The pink rib continues to a heather ledge.
5. 40m Climb a mossy groove on the right and cross a heathery groove to a broken rib on the right, leading to a small cave.
6. 40m Gain the clean rib above and climb left of the crest to a terrace with belay well back.
7. 20m Go straight up the next rock tier to a bigger terrace.
8. 30m An easy way off leads up right, but the summit crag is well worth climbing, so walk up left to a steep open groove.
9. 20m Climb cracks to flakes leading up right to an overhung corner, with a right traverse to a small stance on a nose.
10. 20m Gain the scoop above, then go up left onto a higher slab leading to a terrace.
11. 10m A final wall is followed by a short scramble to the top.

CREAG SHOMHAIRLE

7. Black Gold
8. The Ramp

9. Bardo Thodol
10. Land of the Dancing Dead

11. Tank Top
13. Warm Front

d. Windy Corner Descent

6 The Plinth 45m HVS   (1983)
Below the central part of the crag is a smooth-fronted, semi-detached buttress. Close to its left edge climb steep red rock by a sustained pitch. The grassy groove on the right provides a way off.

The right end of the face gives several excellent climbs on steep, clean rock. From the top of these climbs either continue up broken rocks and heather for 150m to the top of the crag, or, preferably, make a pleasant traverse right across slabs to the top of **Windy Corner**. This is the broken gully to the right of the main face, which provides a convenient descent (60m, Difficult).

7 Black Gold 85m E1 **   (1989)
A fine route which takes the obvious black streak in the wall left of the big left-slanting ramp. Start below a crack at the left end of the wall. There is a diagonal crack to the right.
1. 20m 5a Gain the crack and climb it to a small ramp, step up right and continue to just below a heathery ledge. Move right to the ledge and a holly bush.
2. 35m 5a Follow a ramp up left and across above a roof to the black streak and move up right into the base of a slim corner. Climb this and continue directly up the black streak to a ledge and tree belay.
3. 30m 5a Move right to gain and climb a corner system leading back above the belay to reach a small holly bush. Traverse up right to the arete and climb this in a fine position to the top. Descend by abseil or traverse off right.

8 The Ramp 105m VS   (1969)
This takes the obvious diagonal fault rising up left from a point about 50 metres left of the right end of the face.
1. 30m Climb a slab to belay by a large cracked flake below an overhang.
2. 20m Move left and go up to where a sharp-edged flake juts out from the roof. Follow the fault-line awkwardly to reach a grassy corner below the upper slab.
3. 12m Continue up the left edge of the slab to a good stance.
4. 35m Climb the steepening mossy slab above to near its top where a crack leads left to a good belay.
5. 12m Cross the heather groove rightwards to easy slabs.

9 Bardo Thodol 95m E1 *** (1984)
Above the start of The Ramp is a great slab which is taken by this
route. Start 8 metres left of Land of the Dancing Dead.
1. 40m 5a Climb blocks passing the overhang to gain a slab. Traverse
left and go up and left to a small ledge. Go right, then directly up to a
stance on the great slab at the bottom of its right-bounding corner.
2. 25m 5a Climb the slabby corner, traverse left under the roof until
near the left edge, then go up a short wall to a stance.
3. 30m 5a Climb up to a steep crack and follow this leftwards to the
edge. Go up a short wall in a fine, exposed position to ledges.

10 Land of the Dancing Dead 90m E1 *** (1979)
At the right end of the face there is a clean rib with a very steep wall
to its left. This route takes the corner-crack on the left of the rib. There
is a Damoclean flake about 20m up. Start below the crack.
1. 35m 5a Climb up the crack to a hanging flake, move left and follow
its continuation to a sloping ledge. Traverse back right into the corner
and follow this to a small stance on the left.
2. 25m 5c Climb the corner crack direct (very strenuous but well
protected). Move left to a spike belay.
3. 30m 5a Continue up to a roof and layback round it to easier ground.

11 Tank Top 45m E6 6b *** (1986)
This climbs the impressive thin crack line just right of Land of the
Dancing Dead, which is climbed for 10m. Then move right to a small
stance. Move up and slightly right until moves left can be made
underneath the roof; pull over this and follow the crack to the top.

12 South-West Edge 75m Severe (1967)
The right edge of the main face rises in two steps. The first is climbed
by a crack on the west side and the second by a steep slab just right
of the edge. Escape right is possible.

To the right of this edge the cliff turns a corner. There is an obvious
gully, Windy Corner (60m, Difficult). Right again there is another steep
section of cliff, the South Face.

13 Warm Front 55m E2 (1989)
This climbs the obvious 'bomb-bay' chimney and crack splitting the
top of the south face on the left. Poor rock on the first pitch leads to

better climbing on the second with fine moves to reach the crack in the headwall.

1. 30m 5b Climb up broken ground of the descent gully to the bulging crack line below the 'bomb-bay' chimney. Move up a ramp then pull right into the crack line, step right then up into a niche below a bulge. Pull over the bulge and belay.

2. 25m 5b Climb up into the chimney and move out left and swing round the arete. Airy moves gain the crack in the headwall and this is followed to easier slabby ground.

14 The Roost 60m   Hard Severe ***   (1962)
This is the very obvious crack in the middle of the south face. Start towards the right end of the heather ledge below the face.

1. 30m Trend left up a strenuous curved crack, on magnificent rock, to a second heather ledge with a holly tree.

2. 30m Continue to beneath the main overhangs and make an exposed traverse left round the buttress into an open corner, which is followed to the slabs above. Either traverse left and descend Windy Corner, or scramble another 100m to the top.

15 Hot Pants 55m   E4 **   (1986)
In the centre of the south face is a prominent roof split by two cracks which continue up a short headwall. This climb takes the right-hand crack, rising diagonally right above the roof.

1. 30m The Roost, pitch 1.

2. 25m 6a Move right and climb the crack to below the roof. Surmount the roof and continue up the crack in the headwall to the top.

16 Catwalk Direct 50m   Severe   (1966)
Start at the foot of the shallow gully in the corner on the right of the south face. Climb the slab direct and finish up a small corner. An easier variation (Very Difficult) traverses left across the slab at 30m and follows an exposed corner to a recessed shelf of large blocks.

BEN HOPE
927m   (Map Ref 477 502)

A few climbs have been recorded on this mountain, both summer and winter, but none of great distinction. They lie on the north-west face, overlooking Loch Hope. Seen from the loch the main feature is a wide gully flanked by two rocky ridges. The right-hand, or south, ridge was climbed by J.H.B.Bell in 1933. It gave 240m of climbing with some difficulty in the lower section, then a traverse across the face of the buttress to the right, followed by excellent rock with occasional difficulties to an airy finish. In winter this gives an excellent climb (Grade III, 1985). Right of this climb are a number of pleasant but escapable lines, which can be climbed at Grade II/III.

A line to the left of the wide gully was climbed by H.M.Brown and party in 1969 and considered to be Grade I under normal winter conditions. Right of the ridge of Bell's climb is a steep grassy rake, forming a steep gully at the bottom. **Petticoat Ridge** avoids the steep part on the right, and from about 60m below the grassy saddle at the top of the rake climbs up to a slabby tower on Bell's ridge. Another ridge rises from the grassy saddle to a higher tower on Bell's ridge with a prominent square-cut pinnacle.

BEN LOYAL
764m   (Map Ref 578 488)

This splendid isolated mountain lies a few kilometres south of Tongue. It has potential for good winter climbs but none have been recorded. There are three main tops: Sgor Chaonasaid, An Caisteal (the highest) and Sgor a'Chleirich. The most impressive climbs are on the south-west face of Sgor a'Chleirich, overlooking Loch Fhionnaich. The approach is obvious from the map. From Tongue drive about 3km along the old road to Durness and branch left to Ribigill farm, where cars must be left. Walk along a good track to an old cottage at Cunside. For the climbs on Sgor a'Chleirich walk about 3km south-west below the Coille na Cuile wood then climb steeply up to the col between Sgor a'Chleirich and the small unnamed hill on the right. The huge cliff on the left is in a magnificent setting. Unfortunately the aspiring climber has to contend with extraordinarily steep vegetation, loose rock and a distinct lack of protection. Numerous parties have been repulsed here.

Priest's Rake   250m   VS   (1958)
A rake, ill-defined at first, rises from left to right across the crag, and another fault divides it in a vertical plane. Below the rake this second fault forms a groove, above it a steep, broken, dirty-looking diedre (Marathon Corner). Start below the lowest rib a few feet left of a dirty groove. Traverse right and climb into the groove. Follow the groove

until an escape on the left leads to an overhung grass patch. Exit on the left and climb exposed slabs to a larger grass patch which is the start of the defined section of the rake. Follow the narrow rake easily to its highest point, whence a rib leads directly to the top.

Marathon Corner   280m   E1   (1969)
This is the steep diedre rising above the lower part of Priest's Rake. The initial sections of these routes may overlap.
1. 35m Start below the corner and climb steep grass to it.
2. 30m Traverse left then diagonally right (12m). Climb the corner for 3m, step left to and climb a shallow groove for 15m.
3. 25m Traverse left 3m, then go straight up to a grass rake.
4. 35m Continue left along the rake to a large detached block.
5. 30m Climb the crack behind the block. Traverse 6m left, then delicately up a slab trending slightly right to a runner; traverse down diagonally right for 5m to the bottom of a shallow groove. Climb the groove to a grass ledge.
6. 15m Re-enter the groove above the belay (peg for aid), climb it and continue to a large corner.
7. 20m Climb the corner using the right-hand crack.
8. 20m Move left up an ill-defined groove and where it ends move left to a ledge and belay.
9. 35m Move back into the groove and traverse the slab to the right using a diagonally rising crack. This leads to a ledge giving access to the main corner. Climb this until stopped by overhangs, then traverse right 5m by a diagonal crack to a ledge.
10. 30m Climb the corner to the top.

Gog   280m   E3 †
One of Martin Boysen's 'desert island routes', this rather mysterious climb has fascinated many. The description is a little imprecise and the grade is speculative. In its lower part the climb follows a narrow discontinuous gangway from left to right. The first break in the ramp is crossed by a fierce and acrobatic move. Higher up the climb crosses a fearfully loose chimney and leads into the central bay. Above is a groove with a slanting overhang. Climb it with difficulty on lichen-covered holds and make a hard traverse right under the roof. Finish up 150m of slabs.

A' Chailleach, Cape Wrath (Climbers, Mick Fowler and Guy Muhlemann)

Sgurr a' Bhatain is the name of the twin tors which are below and slightly west of the summit ridge of Ben Loyal, between Sgor Chaonasaid and An Caisteal. There are two climbs.

Cirith Ungol VS †   (1969)
This takes a line up the centre of the lower tor. The buttress is roughly triangular, with a smooth central section. Start at a broken vegetated groove just right of the centre of the crag. Climb towards a prominent overhang and pass it on the left by a groove. Leave this to cross a steep wall and climb a rib to reach a corner. Follow this to a bulge split by a thin crack. Climb this and the prominent overhanging crack above. Finally, climb a pinnacle and the overhanging crack above it using slings for aid.

Rowboat 55m Mild Severe   (1959)
This follows the left-hand bounding ridge of the upper tor. Start just left of the bottom left-hand corner of the crag. Get onto a ledge immediately above and continue up corners until the ridge merges with the gully on the left (35m). Climb onto a prominent ledge crossing the main face and into a corner which is climbed by the 5m left wall; continue up a grassy groove to belay. Move right, step onto a ledge on the arete and continue up easy rocks.

There is a tor at the summit, An Caisteal, offering several short, steep climbs. The only other recorded climb on Ben Loyal is **Navytex Gully** (150m, Very Difficult). It follows the line of a burn on the northern prow of Sgor Chaonasaid and is not recommended.

BEN KLIBRECK
961m (Map Ref 585 299)

On the west flank of this mountain is an area of rock which can be seen from the Altnaharra to Lairg road. The main feature is **Bell's Gully** (150m, Moderate, Grade II) which separates **Eyrie Buttress** (100m, Difficult) to the north from broken slabby rocks to the south. These broken slabby rocks sport an obvious ice smear in winter (Grade II/III, 1984).

Rosamund's Birthday, Rora Head, Hoy
(Climbers, Mark Carnall and Crag Jones)

CNOC AN FHREICEADAIN   *(Map Ref 612 596)*

There is a crag of loose conglomerate near Coldbackie which has attracted some masochists.

The Scoldings   60m   E3   (1984)
A serious climb with poor protection. Towards the right-hand end of the lower tier is an obvious black cleft. Left of this are two crack lines. Climb the right crack for 12m to a steepening, traverse right a few metres and climb a continuation crack past a bulge to easier ground and a stance. Loose moves up and right lead to the finishing arete.

   The rightmost gully of the three dividing the lower crag has also been climbed (30m Difficult, rock 'adequately sound').

The North-West Coast of Sutherland

This whole area is well described in the SMC *Northwest Highlands* District Guide (Scottish Mountaineering Trust, 1990). Here, the climbs are described following the coast in a clockwise direction from Handa to Farr Point (near Bettyhill). For convenience, the inland crag of Creag Riabhach in the Cape Wrath peninsula is also included here.

THE GREAT STACK OF HANDA   *(Map Ref 133 487)*

This impressive 100m stack is just east of the north-west tip of the island of Handa, an RSPB sanctuary. Access is by boat from Tarbet on the mainland opposite. This stack was the scene of a famous early climbing feat in 1876, when a party of Lewis men stretched a rope across the top of the stack from the cliffs on either side and Donald Macdonald climbed across hand over hand, to cull the sea birds. The stakes left by this party were still visible after the last war! For details see the District Guide and SMCJ 1984. Macdonald's route was repeated by Tom Patey and party, using jumars, in 1967. The ascent from sea-level followed two years later.

The Great Arch 115m VS   (1969)
In a calm sea, land on the north face at a steep green wall. Climb to a ledge and belay (12m). Climb the wall on the right to a higher belay ledge. From here follow a steep groove to reach a left traverse line above the Great Arch overhangs. Continue the traverse left into a hidden corner. Surmount the wall and overhang above to peg belays. Scramble 45m to the top. Descend directly by two abseils.

The nearby 'Mini-Stack', Stacan Geodh Brisidh, appears to have been sliced off the cliff-side. It lies 360 metres east of the Great Stack and can be reached by a grassy descent from the cliff top.

Great Corner 60m VS   (1969)
Start in the corner on the landward side. Traverse left to easier but loose rock leading into a great corner crack. Climb this (4 pegs for aid on the first ascent) to belay on a ledge piled with loose blocks (20m).

Climb flakes behind the belay to the crest of the ridge. Traverse right for 10m on a rounded ledge and follow the groove above to the top. Abseil from a bolt on the summit to a ledge 15m below on the north-west face, and then again to the bottom.

SHEIGRA   *(Map Ref 186 605)*

Near the village of Sheigra, just north of Kinlochbervie, a headland of gneiss interrupts the more usual sandstone. The cliffs are not particularly extensive, but there are some steep walls of immaculate rock with a satisfying quota of large incut holds and good protection placements. With quick access and fast-drying rock, Sheigra provides a contrast to the mountaineering of Foinaven and a feasible option in showery weather.

The cliffs were first explored by Paul Nunn and friends, but many of the following descriptions result from visits by teams from Glenmore Lodge. Another team of climbers recorded a number of routes in 1992, but it has not been possible to define precisely how these routes relate to the earlier ones. Therefore they are described in the Addendum.

Access

Take the B801 to Kinlochbervie from Rhiconich on the A838 and, just before the village, turn right for Oldshoremore and Sheigra, which is at the end of this road (8km). At Sheigra turn left to the campsite and sandy beach. Park as near the end of the road as allowed (near a small cemetery). The headland is on the right (north). For the First and Second Geos (Geo being a corruption of the gaelic geodha, an inlet), go to the last gate before the road reaches the beach and follow a fence which traverses the right slope and then turns uphill, soon passing the inland end of the First Geo (hidden from the approach). The fence then cuts back below the horizon and goes over the crest to the Second Geo (for direct access, cut the corner and head straight for the upper part of the fence).

For the Treasure Island Wall, cross the fence and go directly uphill, passing just right of a square block on the near horizon, over the crest right of its summit and down to the opposite side of the headland, looking out for the distinctive promontory (Na Stacain). The First Geo is at Map Ref 180 600 and is 3 minutes from the gate. The other crags are 5 to 10 minutes further.

THE FIRST GEO
Outer Walls

At the seaward end of the south wall, a slab leads easily down beside a crevasse to a 10m vertical wall round a small promontory. From the base of the slab, one can turn right and at low tide traverse into the back of the geo. At high tide, scramble easily on slabs to reach a platform from which three routes start. Above the right end of the platform is a chimney with a hollow back **(Shelob's Lair**, 15m, Very Difficult). Left of this chimney is an overhanging wall. At the left end of this wall is a left-slanting crack leading into a shallower chimney (Severe, but it may be easier starting on the left). Between these two routes and the overhanging central wall of the geo is a right-slanting broken ramp system guarded from the platform by a short bulging wall. Once this is breached (easiest to the right of its base) the ramp can be followed more easily to the top (20m, Very Difficult).

Turning the other direction (away from the geo) at low tide, one can traverse under the small promontory (where there are some short routes of about VS) to pass a very small inlet (which can be jumped) and reach some short square-cut walls beside some huge boulders. These are at the point where the coast changes to face west. They can also be reached directly by scrambling down. A number of short good problems have been climbed here.

Inner Walls

The First Geo is a good choice in windy weather because the walls are enclosed and the back non-tidal, thus escaping high seas (within reason). The south wall is overhanging and contrasts with the less steep north wall. Access is by scrambling down a V-gully on the north side or by abseil. The starts are related to a bank of huge boulders which lie just above high tide mark. The following climbs are on the south wall, which, beside and below the high tide boulders, is overhanging and smooth. Towards the inland end the wall is black and more stepped. Despite a blockier appearance the rock is still good quality.

Blind Faith 25m E2 5b   (1989)
Start beside the largest high tide boulder. Gain a crack line curving right (from the right) and follow it to the base of an obvious deep, pink groove. Move right to a black crack which leads right to finish (right of a high-level roof).

Road to Reform   25m   E3 5c   (1989)
Climb the crack line which leads out of an overhanging niche and
curves left past the left end of the upper roof. Finish up the steep corner
at the right end of the large ledge.

Shiver Me Timbers   25m   E1 5b   (1989)
Continuing left, the smooth overhanging wall changes into blacker
rock with two large steps near the base. Above these steps is an
apparent slab forming a left-facing corner. From the top step, climb
the stepped wall on the right. Steep moves lead to a pull on to the slab.
Traverse left and climb twin cracks in the slab. Move left to finish up a
short steep wall.

Same Old Story   25m   HVS 5a   (1989)
From the top step, the obvious left-slanting crack line in a corner leads
to the same finishing wall.

The Only Way Is Up   20m   HVS 5a   (1989)
Left of and at the same level as the top step is an overhanging wall.
At its left end is an undercut groove slanting right. Climb this to finish
up the same short wall as Same Old Story.

Gneiss Won   20m   Hard Severe   (1989)
Near the back of the geo is a distinctive black and pink-coloured
cracked wall. Climb this through a slot to finish by a wide flake crack.

   The north wall of the Geo is less imposing and contains a number
of buttresses and grooves. Inland from the descent groove the rock is
pink and looks of poorer quality. The following routes are down from
the descent groove.

In the Pink   15m   Very Difficult   (1989)
Beside the largest boulder (opposite Blind Faith) is a crack line in a
slabby buttress with an obvious pink quartz vein. Climb this central
crack and groove.

Blackballed   15m   Severe   (1989)
On the left side of this buttress, between the crest and a roof-topped
V-groove, is a crack. Climb this until it begins to peter out, then step
right on to the buttress crest and climb a short groove to finish.

Original Route   20m   HVS 5a   (1981)
The roof-topped V-groove is perhaps the following route. "From the
boulders at the back of the geo, a steep black crack can be seen on
the left (north) face. Climb the crack to an overhung bay. Traverse right
and escape by a short steep finish".

R & R   15m   Hard Severe   (1989)
Between the roof-capped groove and another groove to the left (with
a tall pedestal at its base) is a blocky pillar with a shallow, square-cut
groove. Climb the groove, move right round a small roof and continue
up and left via a line of blocks.

Blackjack   15m   Difficult   (1989)
The last black groove is followed direct on satisfying rock.

   At the seaward end of the north wall, below high tide mark, is a
diamond-shaped clean wall with three left-slanting crack lines.

Skate   15m   HVS 5a   (1989)
The right-hand crack line, going through a roof low down.

Flounder   15m   VS 4c   (1989)
The left-hand crack line, passing a ledge at 5m.

THE SECOND GEO
This is the highest and possibly most attractive cliff at Sheigra. Geo is
close to a misnomer because the geodha is short, although accessible
to high seas. Far more distinctive is the big north-west facing wall. The
seaward end is undercut by a cave, but above this there are three
distinctive corners of black rock. The right-most and biggest corner is
Shark Crack. The wall to its right has a prominent crack (Fingers) with
a ledge below it. These two routes are usually reached by abseiling
the corner of Shark Crack to the ledge. The two left-hand corners are
close together and the left one (Dark Angel) forms the boundary
between black rock and the red rock which forms the left half of the
cliff. These corners and four associated routes are reached by abseiling down the right-hand corner of the pair (Black Knight) to the Black
Pedestal, a ledge at its base. The Black Pedestal was originally gained
by a traverse from the Shark Crack ledge (5a) but a direct abseil is
better. The landward routes are reached more conventionally from
their base. Routes are described from right (seaward) to left (landward).

Right-Hand Buttress 35m E1 5b   (1989)
A sloping ledge, awash in rough sea or high tide, is reached by abseil.
It is just north of a prominent rock and deep tidal slot standing close
to the cliff which prevents a sea level traverse. From a belay on the
smooth ledge climb a steep wall to a near identical ledge. Escape this
with difficulty up the wall above to an exposed but easier finish.

Fingers 30m HVS 5a   (1970s)
The black wall right of Shark Crack is split by a thin crack. Follow the
crack in an excellent position, with a final steep section.

Shark Crack 30m Hard Severe 4b   (1971)
The route was originally ascended by difficult aid moves from the base
of the geo. Three pitons were used, followed by a few steep awkward
moves to the ledge on the right (HVS 5a and A2). If the ledge is reached
by abseil, the crack above gives excellent climbing.

Lucifer's Link 35m E1 5b   (1983)
From the Black Pedestal, climb the rib on the right, in impressive
surroundings.

Black Knight 30m HVS 5a   (1970s)
Take the smooth groove above the Black Pedestal direct, with an
easier finish on the right above.

Dark Angel 30m HVS 5b   (1983)
From the Black Pedestal, step left and climb the fine groove to the
large upper shelf. Make steep moves up the hanging corner to finish.

Exorcist 40m E1 5b   (1987)
From the Black Pedestal step left into Dark Angel. Traverse across the
lip of the overhang on a quartz band. From its end move up to black
streaks and climb direct to a small ledge underneath a small curving
arch which bends up left to form a groove. Follow black streaks to gain
the groove, crux, and climb direct to the top.

Presumption 40m HVS 5b   (1983)
From the Black Pedestal move left and up Dark Angel for a few metres
to pass the first bulge. Traverse horizontally, crossing the black streaks
of Exorcist and the shallow groove in the face. Climb direct just left of
this groove to finish.

Geriatrics   40m   E2 5c   (1987)
From the Pedestal follow Exorcist to just below the curving arch.
Traverse horizontally left in spectacular position to a ramp at the left
end of the square overhang, then go straight up the wall.

Approach the routes left of here by scrambling down slabby rock.

May Tripper   25m   E1 5b   (1989)
Climb an obvious black streak up the wall starting from the point where
the slabby rock slope meets the cave top. Gain a small ledge; from
here Bloodlust goes up left to a large pocket usually containing a nest
and consequently providing a good landmark. Move up right to a ramp
then follow the black streak up the wall past a pocket to cross Bloodlust
and finish directly.

Bloodlust   25m   HVS 5a   (1978)
Gain the small ledge, as for May Tripper. Go up a shallow corner, then
left up a gangway to the large pocket (possible belay). Make steep
moves right to a small ramp and continue diagonally right to the top
crossing the black streak of May Tripper.
Direct Finish: E2 5b
From the pocket, go diagonally right and back left to finish direct up
the steep wall about 6 metres left of May Tripper.

Juggernaut   25m   E2 5b   (1989)
Start left of Bloodlust and climb the wall, passing the left side of the
pocket. Finish up the arete right of a corner near the top.

Sideline   25m   VS 4c   (1989)
Start at the right end of a low ramp which leads up left. Pull out right
onto the wall and go up to a ledge at the base of the upper corner.
Finish up the wall on the left.

Sideslip   20m   Mild VS 4b   (1989)
Start at the same place as Sideline but take the ramp and a subsequent curving vague crack line.

TREASURE ISLAND WALL
The next section of cliff starts opposite the wall of the Second Geo,
where there is a 3m sandstone block at the top. Beyond the sandstone
block the cliff is short and steep but awkward to reach until, after 100

metres, a shallow stream bed leads to the cliff top opposite a low island. One can descend steeply on big holds on the right (looking down) of the stream at about Difficult. From here rightwards (north-east) the cliff becomes more distinct; The Treasure Island Wall. It extends for about 250 metres to a bouldery beach close to the headland of Na Stacain. The south-west end of Treasure Island Wall, next to the Difficult descent, has excellent juggy rock. The only snag is that the descent may need roping. From the base of the descent move right to a good platform.

The Nook 25m Very Difficult   (1989)
Above and left of the platform (looking up) is a V-groove leading up to a roof, forming a big recess. The Nook climbs the wall between this recess and the descent. Start from the platform. Traverse left and enter the groove. After 5m, take a small ramp leading up right, then climb the steep wall above. Move back left sensationally until above the recess, then go up the wall and a short groove to the top.

Tall Pall 30m Mild Severe   (1975)
Left of the recess is a broad rib, not very obvious from below. This route takes a fine natural line slanting up left to finish on the crest. Start from the platform. Traverse easily left beyond the groove and go up the black slab diagonally left. Continue diagonally left on pink rock and finish directly up the culminating arete.

Plum McNumb 30m VS 4b   (1976)
This good route takes a more direct line. Start from a smaller platform, still above high tide mark but lower and nearer the rib. Traverse left on to the rib, then climb it directly to cross Tall Pall. Climb the steep blunt nose above on remarkable holds. Continue direct to the top.

Further on, steep walls drop into the sea. The routes further north-east are reached by descending a gully (which goes underneath some immense blocks) between the main cliff and a rib with a steep side wall. From the base of the gully, traverse into the back of the geo at mid to low tide. The approach further inland is guarded by very steep though shorter walls. The following route is on the outside wall of the rib formed by the gully.

Spare Rib 15m VS 4c   (1989)
Climb the centre of the wall by a line of left-slanting discontinuous cracks.

At mid to low tide one can cross to the bouldery beach and reach further walls continuing to the back.

Flamingo 25m Severe (1989)
About 15 metres left of Spare Rib is a left-slanting pink ramp with a good crack in the back. This is just to the right of a cave.

Flakey Shakes 20m E2 5c (1989)
Immediately right and parallel to the ramp is a line of deceptively steep booming flakes.

Squeeze to Please 20m Difficult (1989)
Further left, near the neck of the promontory, is an obvious left-slanting chimney. Climb it and the narrow rib on its left. This is a possible descent at higher tide levels but it is difficult to locate from above.

The following two routes lie on the promontory (Na Stacain) on the north-west side of the geo. Descent is by a rib to their left.

Rough Trade 15m HVS 5a (1989)
Opposite Flamingo is a clean gnarled wall. Climb the wall about 2 metres from its left edge with an awkward move left on to a small ramp. Finish up cracks going right.

The Green Channel 15m VS 4c (1989)
The gnarled wall is bounded on the right by a well-defined V-corner. Climb it.

THE NORTH GEO
This is about 400 metres further north and is at the border between the gneiss and larger but more broken sandstone cliffs. It is a long, gloomy slot and the climbs face north.

The Ramp 35m Severe (1970s)
Climb a ramp diagonally right, starting from the high tide line.

Black Rake 45m VS 5a (1982)
Start down to the right. Climb a slippery crack to reach a lower traverse line and follow it by easier but still interesting climbing, moving ever rightwards.

CNOC AN STACA

About 400 metres north of the North Geo, on top of the west end of Cnoc an Staca, there is an unusual series of sandstone obelisks formed by a large slippage. Though merely curious on the landward side, the walls are more impressive on the seaward side. The largest tower (The Cioch) is in the centre of the group and can be reached most easily by a scramble down near the sharp pinnacles to the north. The 40m north-west face of The Cioch is characterised by a steep crack of varying width and relentless appearance.

North-West Eliminate 40m E4 6a   (1987)
Step over a rock crevasse and climb a first crack to below an overhang (peg runner). Move left to the bottom of a long off-width crack. Climb the crack with difficulty and poor protection, step left, go over the roof and finish up a fine hand-jam crack. Descend down a small chimney directly behind.

Un-named 45m HVS 5a   (1987)
Some 15 metres left of North-West Eliminate is a steep crack. Ascend it to a large ledge on the left. Escape up a crack above.

Pinnacle Wall 50m E3 5c   (1987)
About 200 metres north there is a steep south face with shallow cracks facing The Cioch. Take easy ground to a point where the cracks steepen. Climb with difficulty to a pinnacle ledge. Finish up the top wall behind the pinnacle.

Corner Start 50m HVS 5b   (1987)
Just right of Pinnacle Wall, a corner can be reached via a short wall. It leads awkwardly to the pinnacle ledge, which is on the left. Finish as for Pinnacle Wall.

EILEAN NA H-AITEIG (Map Ref 192 583)

This island is well seen from the approach road to Sheigra, lying off the beautiful sandy beach at Oldshoremore. Its undercut left side will attract the climber's eye. It is only an island at high tide. Just east of the linking causeway, and past a sandstone bouldering wall, is a colourful wall of gneiss. About 400 metres beyond the causeway is a gneiss inlet with a clean east-facing wall, well seen from the island. Both these walls would give short climbs (15m) in the lower grades but lack good lines.

Eilean na h-Aiteig itself is composed of a pebbly sandstone. The sandstone itself is reliable but the pebbles can break off, providing a unique uncertainty to the climber. Approach by the east side where a narrow walking ledge leads just above high tide mark to a big open platform. Above the platform a south-facing wall leads to an outer south-west facing wall. This is above a higher platform which is bounded on the left by a gully with a big jammed chockstone at its top. The outer wall can be reached from the top of the rightmost big boulder on the platform, then pulling onto a ledge on the south wall. The ledge leads, with a crawling section, to the higher platform. There is one route on the outer wall and one on the east wall.

Pebble Dash   20m   HVS 5a   (1989)
At the right edge of the outer wall is a corner broken by a roof and an obvious crack leading out right into the easier continuation corner. Well protected.

Hatchet Man   25m   HVS 4c   (1989)
Two-thirds of the way along the walking ledge on the east face, at the first place past the biggest roof, is a bottomless ramp leading out right towards a protruding sod of turf on a ledge at three-quarters height. Pull through the initial roof and traverse right for 3m just above the lip to reach the ramp. Go up the ramp, and just below the dirty ledge traverse left to a cleaner finishing groove.

AM BUACHAILLE *(Map Ref 201 652)*

About 8km north of Kinlochbervie lies the beautiful Sandwood Bay, and 1km west of its south end is this impressive stack. At low tide there is an 8 metre channel between the shore and the stack. In the absence of a Tyrolean rope or ladders, swimming is required. It is important to establish the time of low tide, and to make the ascent fairly quickly, otherwise retreat could be very problematic. Descent is by abseil down the landward face.

Landward Face   65m   VS   (1967)
The grade is 'traditional'. Start just left of centre.
1. 25m Climb overhanging rocks up and onto the prow on the right. Continue straight up until impending rock forces a traverse along a horizontal ledge on the left. Climb the left edge for 4m to a large ledge and belay.

2. 20m From the inset corner of the ledge make an awkward move up and across the wall to a ledge on the right. Continue up to an inset crack of 10m, which is climbed on dubious rock to another left traverse and belay on the left edge.

3. 20m Return to the centre below a deep overhanging crack. From its base traverse left below overhangs until a mantleshelf can be made between two large 'soup-plates'. Cross the slab to rejoin the main crack and pull out awkwardly at the top.

Atlantic Wall 50m E1   (1990)
An intimidating and exposed route on the seaward face, with good rock and protection. The first ascensionists were forced to bivouac at the top, cut-off by the tide and high seas. Start below the south face at the left end of the rock plinth.

1. 15m 5a Climb a small left-facing corner to a roof. Traverse left to the arete and climb this to an exposed stance.

2. 15m 4c Climb the strenuous overhanging flake on the west face above and continue more easily to a large ledge beneath the steep final wall. Belay up right beside a huge detached block.

3. 20m 5a/b Climb the thin crack above the block to a horizontal break. Traverse left to the continuous crack running up the left side of the wall, which leads to easy ground. A fine pitch.

CREAG RIABHACH   *(Map Ref 279 639)*

This steep sandstone crag is situated in the middle of the Parph moor, inland from Cape Wrath. The best approach is to leave the Rhiconich to Durness road at a point about 1km north-east of Gualin House. A straightforward walk of about 8km leads to the crag, which is east-facing. The routes were recommended by the first ascensionists, but have probably not been repeated.

Difficulty in recognising the lines has been experienced even by members of the original parties on later visits, so new visitors may not find the descriptions crystal clear. Nevertheless, given midge-free conditions and an acceptance of vegetation, this crag is worth a visit. In the centre of the crag is a vertical and blank section. A hundred metres left of this is an overhanging, vegetated groove-crack line, taken by the following route.

The Godfather   175m   E2   (1972)
1. 40m   Start right of the gully at a steep vegetated slab. Climb the slab, trending right, to belay in a corner under the steep left wall.
2. 30m   Traverse right to a groove and climb to the top of a pedestal.
3. 40m 5c   The first part of the corner above is blank. Climb a short overhanging chimney on the left wall and make a very hard exit onto a blank slab. Now move back right into the corner and follow this to a stance.
4. 35m   Climb the steep chimney-crack on the left.
5. 30m   An easy gully leads to the top.

Masquerade   180m   HVS   (1976)
1. 45m   Start just left of The Godfather. Climb by chimneys at the left side of the central scoop taken by The Godfather to reach a terrace.
2. 40m 5a   Traverse left on the terrace and climb steep red cracks to a stance below a roof.
3. 35m   Traverse left under the roof and climb cracks, then traverse right (peg for aid) to cracks above the initial line.
4 and 5. 60m 5a, 4c   Finish in two pitches.

Herod's Evil   190m   E1   (1976)
This climbs the centre of the right-hand mass of the crag, following steep cracks and chimneys through overhanging walls. Start at a recess chimney about 75 metres right of the central scoop.
1. 45m 5a   Climb a groove then the right fork into a steep crack, and follow this to terraces with a difficult landing. Belay on the terrace above.
2. 40m 5b   Climb the right-hand groove (several aid pegs), and a block-filled chimney to the midway ledge.
3. 40m 5b   Continue up the chimney to its closure and up by a steep crack to a dangerous landing. Belay higher up on steep vegetation.
4. 40m   Climb with less difficulty in a groove until a short traverse left leads to a ledge right of a hanging slab.
5. 25m   Climb a steep corner right of the slab, then a thin crack on the left and loose blocks to the top.

A'CHAILLEACH   *(Map Ref 249 737)*

South Face   25m   Hard Severe   (1989)
This is a spectacular 25m stack on the west coast about 2km south of
Cape Wrath. It is much easier than appearances suggest. Swim the
short gap to reach the stack and start on the side facing Am Bodach.
Climb up right to reach the arete facing the nearest point of the
mainland. Follow this to the final overhanging wall, which is avoided
by a short traverse right.

AM BODACH

South Face   40m   Difficult   (1989)
The large broad stack next to A'Chailleach can be reached at low tide,
in a calm sea, by stepping over a narrow channel. The south side of
the stack gives an obvious line of steep cracks and good holds.

STACK CLO KEARVAIG   *(Map Ref 295 737)*

This is a superb 40m stack standing at the western end of the Clo Mor
cliffs, easily visible from the road to the Cape Wrath lighthouse. Calm
seas are unusual, and currents can be strong. Approach by boat. The
stack has two summits of equal height; the gap between the two sports
a prominent wedged boulder.

Seaward Stack   55m   HVS   (1989)
Start from a large platform at the north-east end of the stack.
1. 35m Move round the corner onto the seaward face and trend right,
then back left,to gain a short right-angled corner with a crack in the
back. Climb this to a ledge next to the left arete (as seen from the
seaward side). This ledge is level with the highest of the wedged
boulders between the two summits.
2. 20m 5a Move up right to a ledge and follow a short but awkward
open right-slanting groove. Easier ground leads to the top.

Landward Stack   60m   HVS   (1989)
1. 35m Pitch 1, Seaward Stack.
2. 15m 5a Traverse horizontally across the wall to reach the highest
of the wedged boulders. Cross this to the landward stack and climb a
right-angled corner to a ledge.
3. 5m 4c Climb the corner to the top.

CLO MOR *(Map Ref 305 735)*

These great sandstone cliffs lie on the north coast about 6km east of Cape Wrath. They are about 200m high and suffer from loose rock and generally unpleasant weather. Apparently E. Ward-Drummond and T. Proctor spent about 10 days attempting the face, with hanging belays and bivouacs, some time in the early 1970s. However the first complete route was not recorded until 1989.

Clo Mor Crack 175m E3   (1989)
This climbs the prominent, thin straight crack line facing Stack Clo Kearvaig. Approach by boat. The bottom 10m of the crack line is very greasy and overhanging. Start 10 metres left at the foot of a subsidiary crack rising into a chimney which fades out into blank rock at 10m.
1. 35m 5b Climb to the bottom of the chimney and cross the wall on the right to reach a left-slanting flake. Hand traverse right on jams to the arete and continue right for 6m to join the crack line proper. Climb the off-width crack, which forms the right side of a prominent flake at this point, for 6m to a ledge.
2. 15m 5c Follow the thin crack and flying layback flake to a ledge (peg runner).
3. 40m 5b Climb the shallow groove (peg runner) for 12m, then the left wall for 15m and finally the groove again for 12m, to reach a small ledge on the right.
4. 20m 5b The thin steep crack above leads to a good ledge.
5. 35m 5b Move 3m right and climb a corner and prominent right-trending overhanging off-width crack.
6. 30m Climb easily to the top.

Clo Mor Stack 35m Very Difficult and A1   (1989)
This stack lies about 1km east of Stack Clo Kearvair, with a prominent 8m finger of rock forming the highest point. Climb to beneath the rock finger. Lassoo the the top and prussik up to gain the highest point. In good conditions more ethical methods may be successful.

THE SMOO CAVE *(Map Ref 419 673)*

This cave, just east of Durness, has a hole in the roof, formed when The Devil was cornered there by Lord Reay in the seventeenth century. For details see *The Northwest Highlands* District Guide (1990 edition).

In dry weather a 35m Severe climb can be made as follows: Abseil down the highest hole south of the road crossing the cave to gain a ledge 3m above the water. Climb a crack in the corner for 20m, breaking right over a bulge to exit over the back wall of the cave. In the event of failure, retreat seaward by swimming.

WHITEN HEAD *(Map Ref 503 687)*

This is reached by a pleasant 8km walk from the bridge at the outlet of Loch Hope. The cliffs at the headland are 150m, very steep and exceedingly loose. As yet no-one has been attracted to climb on them. Offshore are two quartzite stacks, known collectively as The Maiden, access to which requires a boat. The east stack has a cave through its base. The landing is tricky and is best done on the landward side. There are four routes on this stack and two on the west stack.

WESTERN STACK

Waterfront Wall   55m   Severe   (1988)
A superb route on solid rock up impressive terrain normally reserved for much harder climbs. Start on the north-east (seaward) corner of the stack.
1. 25m Climb up (line variable) on good holds to a depression beneath a steep band, stance on the right.
2. 20m Surmount the small overhang above the stance and move left to a short discontinuous crack line. Climb this for 6m to overhangs and traverse left to a sensational stance on the arete.
3. 10m Easier ground to the top.

Maiden without a Hole   75m   HVS   (1988)
A loose route. Start in the centre of the east face.
1. 30m 4c Climb awkwardly onto a ramp/traverse line. Move left along the ramp for 25m. Belay at the base of a shattered groove.
2. 15m 4c Climb the groove to a large stance.
3. 30m 4c Move right along a ledge and climb a short wall to a further ledge. Cross this to the base of the headwall. Climb up and right (exposed) to the top.

EASTERN STACK

This was the scene of the tragic accident to Tom Patey, abseiling after the ascent of the Original Route. March's Route was taken on a trip to recover the abseil rope left by the original party. It is possible there is some overlap between the four routes described, but they appear to be largely distinct.

Original Route   55m   HVS   (1970)
Start near the cave on the west side.
1. 20m Climb just above sea level across sharp rocks to the left and over bulgy rocks up to a stance on the north side.
2. 20m Move into a steep groove but avoid the overhanging crack by a traverse right onto a limestone-like wall. Climb this for 8m, traverse left into the crack line and continue to a good square ledge.
3. 20m Traverse right over loose blocks to a bay. Climb the left edge to a stance below steep rocks.
4. 20m Move left and climb tottering flakes to the summit.
   The above pitch lengths are as in the original description, although they add up to more than the overall length. Descent is by a single free abseil from the lower edge of the slanting top.

March's Route   65m   HVS   (1970)
From the large platform on the landward side, traverse left along a ledge to an overhang which is climbed on large holds to gain a ledge above the start. Move right and climb the obvious overhanging crack by bridging. Continue to a ledge at 15m. Traverse along the ledge to the seaward side and climb straight up the obvious crack to the summit.

Ode   55m   HVS   (1988)
A fine steep route taking a prominent line up the west face. Start just right of the cave running through the stack, where initial overhangs guard access to a scoop and right-trending ramp.
1. 30m 5a Surmount the overhangs trending left and move back right into the scoop. Follow the prominent right-trending ramp line to capping roofs and move right and up to ledges. Follow these left to belay beneath the prominent central fault cleaving the upper part of the face.
2. 25m 5a Ascend the steep corner line to an exit on the left. The overhanging final wall is circumvented on the left.

Funeral for a Friend   75m   E1   (1988)
This takes the east side of the East Stack. A fine hard first pitch,
followed by easier climbing. Start below the east face at the base of a
pillar to the left of the cave.
1. 20m 5b Climb up the pillar and over a small roof to a niche on the
right. Move up and right and pull over an overhang to climb a short
wall to a ledge.
2. 25m 4a Traverse the ledge rightwards to its end. Move up to a
corner above for 3m to a ledge and belay.
3. 30m 4c Continue up the corner then directly up short walls and
ledges to the top.

FARR POINT   *(Map Ref 725 641)*

This is the peninsula north of the hamlet of Bettyhill. The following
climb can be found close to the remains of Borve Castle, south-east
of the point. Beyond the castle, scramble down and right to the
sea-level; a calm sea and low tide are advisable.

The Farr Side   180m   VS 5a ***   (1992)
This is an interesting and enjoyable traverse through some impressive
scenery. Traverse left to the entrance to a sea arch which runs
underneath the castle. Belay on a ledge just above the sea. Now
traverse photogenically through the arch, never more than 2 metres
above the high tide mark. The next four pitches keep going left, never
more than 6 metres above the water, on steep rock with perfect holds.
Continue to the end of the peninsula (although it is possible to escape
earlier).

The Caithness Coast

The climbing on this coastline is on both sea-cliffs and stacks, mostly developed very recently. The crags on the north coast are described first, then proceeding southwards from John o'Groats.

FORT ROCK *(Map Ref 063 711)*

This stack lies about 5km west of Holborn Head near Thurso. In the apparent absence of any local name it has been christened Fort Rock. It overhangs on all sides and the only real line of weakness is a right-trending groove on the east face. Approach by boat from Scrabster.

East Face 30m HVS (1989)
Land on the landward side and scramble to a large ledge at 8m. From the east end of this ledge (on the arete of the stack) move up into a niche and make a tricky traverse right above overhangs to gain the groove. Follow this to capping overhangs and escape left onto the grassy top.

HOLBORN HEAD *(Map Ref 106 717)*

Clett Rock is a stack on the north side of the head, just north of Scrabster. It provides a superb challenge combining exciting currents, usually rough seas and very steep climbing. It is separated from the mainland by a 25 metre channel. Approach by boat from Scrabster.

North Route 45m E3 (1988)
Start on the seaward side near the centre of the wall at a large flat ledge just above high tide level. This ledge is about 10m long and capped by large overhangs 25m up; it is about 12 metres west of an obvious deep corner-chimney on the face.
1. 25m 4c From the right end of the ledge ascend an obvious right-trending crack system until it is possible to stomach traverse right above overhangs to a ledge on an arete.
2. 20m 5c Move up leftwards into the overhangs and make difficult moves up right onto a projecting ledge. Continue up right-trending cracks to a ledge and finish by grooves above and to the right.

West Route   50m   Severe and A2   (1969)
Start at the north-west corner of the stack.
1. 10m From the extreme end of the landing platform move round a
corner and climb a steep slab for 3m to a ledge. Move left then go up
to the next ledge.
2. 12m Step up and round a corner from the left end of the ledge and
climb a steep slab to an overhanging crack. This was climbed using
pegs. Peg belay.
3. 15m Climb the wall from the left of the ledge for a few feet, then
make an awkward move right onto a small platform. Easy rocks lead
to the next large ledge and peg belay.
4. 12m Climb the prominent crack up the overhanging wall to a ledge
and so to the summit.

DWARWICK HEAD   *(Map Ref 205 715)*

These sandstone cliffs were extensively investigated by the Caithness
Mountaineering Club some 20 years ago. The following descriptions
have not been checked, and it is not known if there have been
significant changes. It seems likely that peg belays mentioned will
have rusted away long ago. Likewise the abseil posts used by the first
ascensionists may no longer be there. It should be borne in mind that
the grades are for climbing standards of twenty years ago. The cliffs
harbour abundant bird life. The sandstone is generally sound in the
lower sections but tends to be unstable higher up.
Access
From a jetty near the Point of Ness (Map Ref 208 712) it is possible
to traverse under the cliffs at low tide. Alternatively walk along the top
of the cliffs beyond Dwarwick Head and scramble down the first big
gully. Then either scramble along the base of the cliffs if the tide is low,
or follow a ledge about 15m above the base, 'The Catwalk'. From a
break in the cliff the base can then be reached by abseil. The climbs
are described from left to right.

Crock's Crawl   15m   Very Difficult   (1969)
The start is the obvious line to the right of the descent from the Catwalk,
where the cliff has not been undercut. Move up to the right end of a
ledge about 4m up. Traverse left along the ledge and climb an obvious
crack to a large ledge and block belay. Scramble up right to reach
abseil posts or traverse left to reach the Catwalk.

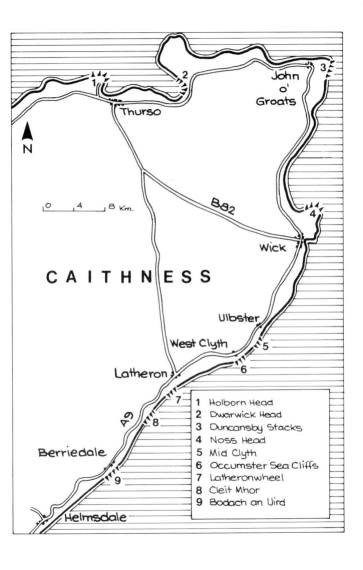

N

0 4 8 Km.

CAITHNESS

Thurso

John o' Groats

B.82

Wick

Ulbster

West Clyth

Latheron

Berriedale

Helmsdale

A.9

1 Holborn Head
2 Dwarwick Head
3 Duncansby Stacks
4 Noss Head
5 Mid Clyth
6 Occumster Sea Cliffs
7 Latheronwheel
8 Cleit Mhor
9 Bodach an Uird

Cluck 15m Severe   (1969)
Start as for Crocks Crawl. Follow the ledge for about 8 feet to the left
and go directly up on delicate holds to the same finishing ledge as for
Crocks Crawl.

Initiation Direct 25m Severe   (1969)
Start just left of the next break in the undercutting of the cliff. Climb
straight up a groove. Move left on good holds beneath an overhang.
Peg belay on a good ledge (15m). Climb straight up moving slightly
right near the top (10m). Belay on the abseil post.

Evening Wall 25m Severe   (1969)
Start as for Initiation Direct. Instead of following the groove go right
round an awkward block to reach a ledge. Move diagonally up right to
reach a large ledge and peg belay (20m). Climb directly to the top
(5m); the belay post is 10m back.

Initiation Corner 25m Very Difficult   (1969)
Start as for Initiation Direct. After 3m, traverse right above the undercut
cliff to a large ledge. Climb up 2m to another ledge and continue along
ledges to a corner. Follow the corner to the top.

Corkscrew 30m Very Difficult   (1969)
Climb Initiation Corner as far as the corner, then continue the traverse
right to a large block belay (15m). Move up and left back into the corner
for a few feet. Climb onto a large ledge overhanging the belay. Move
right to an obvious groove finish.

Cormorant Way 25m VS   (1969)
Start from the base of the cliff just before it turns right into a big cave.
Climb to a ledge about 5m up and just left of the big cave. Make an
awkward move left to another ledge. Go up 2m to a ledge running
along the face of the cliff. Traverse this left to the end and take an
obvious crack to a small ledge beneath an overhang. Peg belay (20m).
Traverse right using a crack at eye level, and after reaching a small
ledge move up to a large ledge and peg belay 5m from the top.

Cormorant Crack 20m VS   (1969)
Start as for Cormorant Way. From the ledge 5m up move right over
an overhang and follow a crack to a good ledge and block belay (12m).
Follow the crack to a large ledge 5m below the top, peg belay (8m).

Diversion 30m VS (1969)
Start 3m right of the big cave and 5m left of Shag Crack. Make an awkward start to surmount a slight overhang and follow a groove to a narrow ledge beneath a triangular nose (10m). Traverse right around the corner and go up the first crack to a ledge and peg belay (10m). Climb the crack directly to the top (10m).

Shag Crack 20m Severe (1969)
Start between the big and little caves where there is an obvious crack running half way up the cliff. Follow the crack to a large ledge and block belay (10m). Move directly up on exposed but good holds to the top. No belay.

Jolly Roger 25m Difficult (1969)
Start just right of Shag Crack. Climb up for 6m then bear left over poor rock to a large ledge and belay (12m). Continue up and left until a natural break leads to the cliff top (12m).

Puke 25m Severe (1969)
Start just right of Jolly Roger. Climb diagonally right to reach a platform and peg belay (10m). Traverse delicately right then go up a corner to a ledge, then climb straight up a steep wall to a pleasant slab finish.

Midge Corner 20m Severe (1969)
Start 5m left of the little cave. Follow a large crack to a niche about half way up. Step right to gain a corner, mantleshelf onto an obvious nose and climb to the top.

Zigzag 40m Severe (1969)
Start at the foot of the first minor headland 12m right of the corner mentioned in Midge Corner. Climb awkwardly up to overhangs and traverse delicately left to a ledge and peg belay (15m). Traverse along the ledge into a corner, climb up 2m and continue left along ledges to the next turn in the cliff line. Climb down to a ledge above the small cave and doubtful belay (15m). Climb directly above the belay and finish up a good slab (10m).

DUNCANSBY STACKS *(Map Ref 400 719)*

Duncansby Head is the north-east corner of Scotland, 3km from John o'Groats. There are several spectacular stacks. The largest, The Great Stack of Duncansby, is the most southerly. Just north of this is Witches'

Hat Stack, an 85m wafer of rock, and 2km further north are two more stacks: The Knee is a very impressive 45m obelisk which overhangs all the way round, while The Little Knee lies just to the north and is rather squat. These two stacks are seriously affected by strong tidal currents. Approach by boat.

The Knee   45m   HVS   (1989)
Start from ledges at the northern end of the seaward face.
1. 30m 5a From the highest ledge a short steep wall on the right leads to another ledge. Climb the steep corner on the left for 6m to a 6m traverse right to a steep corner (just left of a prominent chimney with a huge precariously wedged block.) Ascend this to a ledge system beneath the final overhanging section.
2. 15m 5a Ascend the overhangs in the centre of the face, pulling right onto a projecting ledge. Continue direct to the top. Abseil descent down the seaward face.

Little Knee   30m   Severe   (1989)
Start at the south-east arete of the stack. Climb the arete to the ledge at 8m. Walk along the ledge on the seaward side of the stack to its right end, from where an overhanging wall with good holds leads to the summit.

Witches' Hat Stack   65m   HVS   (1989)
Start at the seaward end.
1. 25m 4b Climb up on the south side to gain the seaward arete at a ledge. A short steep wall leads to a further ledge from where 15m of shallow cracks lead to a belay just below and right of the start of a prominent shallow groove.
2. 40m 4c Move up and left into the groove and follow this past several dubious flakes to gain the arete again just below the top. Follow the arete to the top. Abseil descent down the line of the route.

Great Stack   70m   Very Difficult   (1958)
The rock on this stack is friable and grassy, and its seaward face is "sheer". From the south-west corner of the most southerly stack climb a short wall, sloping grass and broken rock to a belay (35m). A 15m wall on the 'inside' face of the stack, at the south end, leads to a narrow ledge below a 6m wall. Climb this by an exposed crack. Continue up a narrow ridge to the top.

SKIRZA   *(Map Ref 395 680)*

The two most promising areas at Skirza are Wife Geo and Salt Skerry. Wife Geo consists of three massive buttresses situated at the entrance to a long inlet. Salt Skerry is a tidal ledge giving access to a section of cliff. The rock quality varies considerably; at Wife Geo it deteriorates near the top, with loose slate and vegetation. However, the climbing compensates.

   Turn off the A9 about 6km south of John o'Groats, taking the road to Skirza Head, the headland on the north side of Freswick Bay. At weekends this road can be followed until a dirt track takes you to parking at a quarry. Otherwise, park at the pier. About 500 metres north of the Quarry is Salt Skerry, a mainly tidal ledge which gives access to some climbing. A further 500 metres north is the inlet of Wife Geo.

WIFE GEO

Most of the climbs here finish on loose boulder clay and grass, so permanent abseil points have been placed at the top of the Central and South Buttresses.

Superstring   40m   HVS 5a   (1992)
This route takes a large square corner on the south wall of the Central Buttress. Since the route begins above a large cave, it is necessary to place runners during the abseil approach to avoid ending over the sea. The main difficulties are two roofs; the second roof is best passed to the right. Continue up the right wall for the last section.

Quark Soup   45m   Severe 4b   (1992)
There is a broad dry ledge at the bottom of the east face of the South Buttress, which can be reached by abseil. Start on the south corner of the buttress. Follow a distinct line, passing a bulge at 20m. At about half-height, leave the groove and belay on the higher of two ledges on the east side. Continue up a crack line in this wall to finish.

NOSS HEAD   *(Map Ref 385 545)*

This is the headland at the south side of Sinclair Bay, 3km north of Wick. It is the most prominent feature on the Caithness coastline.

   Follow the signs for Wick airport, then take a single track road across the runway and out to Noss lighthouse. If this road is closed, an alternative route is via the village of Staxigoe, on the coast just north of Wick. A few hundred metres before the lighthouse is a large car park for visitors to the castle of Sinclair and Girnegoe. From the car park, follow the large wall south to the coast. The northern boundary of the first area is the deep inlet at the end of the wall. Another inlet marks the southern limit of the climbing. Between this point and the lighthouse there are various walls and corners, most still to be explored.

The rock is reminiscent of Occumster, but much cleaner. On the whole it is very solid, varying between a hard black slate to a lighter, more weathered, sandstone. Belay points are readily available at the top and although tidal, most climbs have dry ledges at the bottom. There are a greater range of grades here than at other Caithness cliffs, with several excellent lower grade routes. The general topography is very rugged, with jutting prows and deep chimneys.

There are two easy scrambles to sea-level; one is on the north side of the south inlet, and the other is a few metres further to the north. The routes are described northwards from the south inlet.

Chun   8m   Hard Severe 4c   (1992)
At the end of the wall on the south side of the inlet is a broken crack, which trends left from an undercut start.

Blue Whin   8m   Hard Severe 4c   (1992)
Climb the vertical crack in the middle of the wall on the south side of the inlet.

Soggy Nine   10m   VS 4c   (1992)
There is a wall at the back of the inlet, left of the cave. Take a central crack to a sloping ledge. Move 2 metres right, then continue up a crack to the top.

The next routes are on the south-facing side of the promontory which forms the south side of the Inlet.

Tsunami   6m   Hard Severe 4b   (1992)
Three metres from the seaward end of the wall lies a short undercut crack. Start two metres to its left. Traverse right into a small cave below the crack and finish on large holds.

Active Front   6m   Severe 4a   (1992)
Left of Tsunami is a flat wall marked by outcrops of calcite. Start right of centre, climb past a projecting band of rock at two-thirds height, and finish where the upper strata change direction slightly.

Moving left again the wall ends in a corner which gives an easy way to the top of the buttress. **Micro Prow** (5m Hard Severe) is the small prow with massive holds. **Won-Yo** (5m Very Difficult) is the undercut short corner 2 metres left of the prow. **Orographic** (6m Severe) takes the wall 2 metres further left, and **Coriolis Crack** is the undercut ill-defined crack just left again. On the north side of the inlet, **Firefly** (8m Very Difficult) takes the square corner, and to its left is **Bug** (6m Very Difficult), which goes up a stepped left-slanting corner.

The next climbs can be reached by walking north out of the inlet, passing under a large overhanging prow. The next moderate section is the easiest descent route via a notch. **Tea Time Problem** (5m VS 4c) is just left of the descent: climb up under a small roof, go right and up the short hanging corner. **Dinner Time Problem** (5m VS 4c) is the short crack to the right of the descent route.

Do-San   6m   Difficult   (1992)
Turn the corner from Dinner Time Problem. Climb the first crack on the wall, passing left of a projecting spike.

Soy Sauce   6m   Difficult   (1992)
Start as for Chicken Supreme. Exit left from below the large roof, and continue up a short crack to easy ground.

Chicken Supreme   8m   Severe 4a   (1992)
Moving right there is a large roof. Climb easily to below the roof, exit right onto a large ledge, then go up the crack above.

Jumper Off   8m   Mild VS   (1992)
Start 3 metres right of Chicken Supreme. Move left from below another large roof and make an awkward mantleshelf move. Finish up the wall above.

Chinese Puzzle   6m   VS 4c   (1992)
Right again is a deep open book corner, capped by a roof. Climb to the roof, move out to the right and finish up the arete.

Dan-Gun   8m   Moderate   (1992)
Climb the large groove right of Chinese Puzzle.

The Panda's Thumb   10m   HVS 5a   (1992)
Right of Chinese Puzzle is a large roof, bounded on the right by a slim
toothed arete. Right again is another roof. Scramble onto a broad
ledge, then start right of the arete, but swing round onto the left wall.
Follow a short thin crack to the top.

Recovery   10m   Severe 4a   (1992)
This is the vertical crack left of the chimney in the bay right of The
Panda's Thumb.

Cosmo's Chimney   10m   Moderate   (1992)
Climb the large chimney.

Rebound Wall   10m   VS 4c   (1992)
Round the corner right of the chimney is a flat wall. Take a line just left
of centre to a broad ledge. Continue more easily.

Keeper's Corner   10m   Severe 4a   (1992)
Climb the square corner right of Rebound Wall.

Hourglass   10m   VS 4c   (1992)
Start from a ledge just right of Keeper's Corner. Make initial hard
moves to reach a small ledge. Negotiate the chimney to reach the
exposed corner directly above. An excellent route.

Time Lapse   10m   Hard Severe 4b   (1992)
Climb the corner right of Hourglass, finishing by the crack line directly
above the start.

About 100 metres north of the wall leading down from the car park
are two small headlands. The first is topped by large flat slabs. The
south side is severely overhung and overlooks a short wall bounded
by a large cave. The end of the second headland is detached and
almost forms a sea stack. The south side of this headland has a broad
ledge at half-height.

Temnoku   5m   VS 4c   (1992)
Halfway along the large ledge is a slightly overhanging, square corner.

Rhonchi   5m   15ft VS 4c   (1992)
Climb the slightly overhanging crack 2 metres left of Temnoku.

Scamble   10m   Moderate   (1992)
Traverse left along the narrow ledge from Rhonchi, then go up the short chimney.

Half Yoking   6m   Very Difficult   (1992)
This is the corner line climbed from sea-level to the seaward end of the ledge.

Jam Butty   6m   HVS 5b   (1992)
This is the continuation of the corner line, a slightly overhanging crack.

Ying Ping   5m   15ft VS 4c   (1992)
Start from the end of the promontory, at the south side of the gap before the stack. Climb the corner.

OCCUMSTER STACK

About 2km north of Lybster harbour (Map Ref 245 350) is a group of stacks. Occumster Stack is the most northerly and most impressive, a slender finger of rock.

Occumster Stack   25m   E1 4c   (1989)
Starting from a ledge on the south-east corner, the route follows a crack on the left side of the seaward face. The rock has very sharp-edged horizontal striations; falling is not recommended. Simultaneous abseil descent, watching out for sharp rock.

OCCUMSTER SEA-CLIFFS

The main feature at Occumster is an impressive square buttress which faces straight up the coast. When seen from the north it appears as a massive castellated block. On the whole the rock is inferior to either Mid Clyth or Latheronwheel, with a predominance of brittle slaty rock. However, protection is often good.

Turn off the A9 about 1km north of Lybster. A single track road leads towards the sea and limited parking at the end. Cross a field to the coast and the main buttress can be found a few hundred metres to the north.

There are several areas of climbing. The most easily found is the main buttress. Immediately to the north is an east-facing vertical brittle slate wall, the Sabbath Wall. At its north end is a descent route to a tidal ledge, which leads to The Lower Wall. The bottom section of this wall is a hard slate but the top is a better quality sandstone. South of the main buttress is a ledge only accessible by abseil. South again is a steeply dipping section of cliff which runs into the sea. If this is followed to sea-level (treacherous when wet), it leads to another sea-level wall, The Roof Area.

THE MAIN AREA

1   Tardis   20m   VS 5a   (1992)
The leftmost crack on the buttress. Climb the crack to a small roof. Follow the crack line after the roof, and finish onto the top of the large block somewhat detached from the main cliff. It is also possible, but less satisfying, to finish onto the same ledge as Raspberry Ripple.

2   Raspberry Ripple   20m   HVS 5a   (1991)
Climb the next crack to the right. The crux is a small roof.

3   Blue Tattoo   15m   VS 4c   (1992)
Climb the next crack right again, finishing on a large triangular ledge beside a flat block.

4   Sonic Screwdriver   15m   VS 5a   (1991)
Climb the two parallel thin cracks which finish on the same large ledge as Blue Tattoo.

5   Time Machine   15m   VS 4c   (1992)
The central line on the buttress. Follow a deep crack to half-height, move left onto a good ledge with a prominent rectangular notch to the right, then move directly up to finish.

6   Klingon   15m   VS 5a   (1992)
Just right of Time Machine is a crack which fades at 6m. Follow this to a ledge and move slightly right. Pull up on small holds to reach a welcome jug above. Finish on easier rock above.

7   Tralfamadorian   15m   VS 4c   (1992)
Climb the vertical crack situated 3 metres left of the right edge of the buttress. Superb protection.

Round the corner to the south is an east-facing wall. This runs for about 15 metres to a corner bordering a short north-facing wall.

OCCUMSTER MAIN BUTTRESS

1. Tardis
2. Raspberry Ripple
3. Blue Tattoo
4. Sonic Screwdriver
5. Time Machine
6. Klingon
7. Tralfamadorian

Strawberry Slider 20m Severe 4b (1991)
Follows the corner between the north and east-facing walls.

Gollach 15m VS 4c (1992)
On the wall to the right of Strawberry Slider is a vertical crack which
starts above a large rock pool. Traverse to the crack from the left or
right, climb until it peters out, and exit left via a small flake.

Nightlife 20m HVS 5a (1992)
The wall ends on the right with a crack which leads to the edge of a
large roof. Climb the crack to the roof and gain the corner with some
difficulty. Follow the corner to the top of the block, and finish on the
wall directly above.

Teuchter 10m VS 4c (1992)
On the wall to the left of Strawberry Slider are two cracks running
parallel to the corner. Climb to a niche, exit left and scramble to the
top.

Tingwall 10m HVS 5a (1992)
Left of Teuchter is a crack system. Climb to beneath a roof, move left
on poor footholds, and pull up to easy rock above.

Duck Soup 10m VS 4c (1991)
Left again a corner line leads under a roof next to the sea. Move out
right from under the roof to finish.

Nocturnal 10m Severe 4a (1992)
Starting from the same point as Duck Soup, move out to the corner
over the sea. From a small ledge climb directly up to finish on top of
a pinnacle.

THE GULLY

The main face of the buttress ends in a large damp gully. Although
slow to dry, the climbs in the gully are worth a visit. Access is easiest
by abseil from the north side, but is also possible from the bottom of
the main buttress. At the back of the gully is an easy but slimy
scramble; not recommended.

Sputnik 10m VS 4c   (1992)
Near the back of the gully, on the landward side, is an open book
corner. Climb this to a platform, then continue to a small ledge and
trend left to finish.

Andromeda 10m HVS 5a   (1992)
Another 8 metres right of Sputnik is a double crack. Climb the left-hand
crack. Surmount a small projection near the top and finish up a short
left-facing corner.
Original Start:
Climb a thin crack 2 metres further left to a ledge and traverse right to
the main crack.
Alternative finish: Hard Severe 4b
Avoid the crux by traversing right near the top into a large bay.
Continue to the top on the right of the arete which forms the left edge
of the bay.

SABBATH WALL
A short distance north of the Main Buttress is an easily accessible wide
ledge which runs south, cutting the cliff at mid-height. Sabbath Wall
lies above this ledge.

Plainchant 10m VS 4c   (1992)
At the south end of the ledge are a few easy rock steps. From the
lowest of these, and before turning a corner, climb the well protected
crack which ends in a square-cut notch.

Saint Andrew's Crack 10m VS 5a   (1992)
Climb the crack line two metres right of Plainchant.

Colour Supplement 8m VS 5a   (1992)
At the south end of the ledge, just before stepping down, there is a
very thin crack which peters out just before it reaches the overhanging
block above. Climb the thin crack to a horizontal crack, move left and
finish up the corner left of the block.

Rum and Raisin 8m Severe 4a   (1992)
Starting close to the south end of the ledge, climb the double crack
which ends just right of a prominent overhanging block.

Mint Chocolate Chip 8m   Severe 4a   (1992)
Five metres right of Rum and Raisin there is another crack system.
Climb this to finish just right of a small north-facing wall.

Stipend Step-up 8m   Mild Severe 4a   (1992)
Climb the double crack just right of Mint Chocolate Chip.

Caramel Crack 8m   Hard Severe 4b   (1992)
Climb the crack line 3 metres right of Chocolate Mint Chip, which ends
between a small shelf and a small south-facing wall.

Post and Mail 8m   Hard Severe 4b   (1992)
Start by a mantleshelf two metres right of Caramel Crack, then move
up the twin cracks to a slightly overhanging finish left of an overhanging
block.

There are a number of short routes further right. **Cleric Crack** (8m
Hard Severe 4c) is the crack two metres right of Post and Mail.
Benediction Corner (10m Very Difficult) is the obvious corner right
again. **Presenter's Problem** (6m Mild VS 5a) takes the next crack to
the right, exiting left of a large overhanging block, and **Presbytery
Problem** (5m Mild Severe 4a) takes a short crack to its right. **Pew Line**
(6m Moderate) follows the V-shaped groove at the back of the corner
further right.

The following routes can be reached either from the gully, or by a
traverse from the south end of the Sabbath Wall.

Pan Drop 15m   VS 4c   (1992)
Traverse round the corner from the left end of the Sabbath Wall to
climb the imposing open book corner.

Heed Bummer 15m   HVS 5a   (1992)
This is the direct route over the large roof to the right of the corner line
of Apollo. Access to the square corner below the roof is difficult. Once
installed (good protection), hand traverse out on a small ledge on the
right wall, pull over the roof and follow easier rock to the top.

Apollo 15m   VS 4c   (1992)
This is best reached by abseil but it can also be reached by traversing
left from Pan Drop. Climb the right-facing corner to a ledge and finish
over easier ground to the top.

Giotto 10m VS 4c (1992)
Climb the left-curving crack 2 metres left of Apollo. Finish left from the platform at the top.

LOWER WALL

Pull the Plug 10m VS 4c (1992)
In the recess which forms the descent route is a pair of thin cracks on the right. Climb the right-hand crack.

Narced 10m VS 4c (1992)
This is the first prominent crack line north of the descent route. Climb into the roofed niche, then climb the crack which splits the small roof above (crux).

Mischief 10m VS 4c (1991)
Right of Narced is a crack line which ends in a notch. The finishing moves are harder than they look.

Manic Gannet 10m VS 4c (1992)
Right of Mischief is a section with a small roof at mid-height. This climb takes the thin crack which splits the roof.

Efflurage 10m HVS 5a (1992)
Three metres right of Manic Gannet is a prominent crack line which extends across the wave-cut platform. Climb the crack past a horizontal crack at mid-height, then climb over a small roof and finish up the crack system above on small holds (crux).

Gazpacho 10m VS 4c (1992)
The prominent crack to the right.

At the top of the next section of wall are two parallel cracks and a corner to the right. **Spotty Dog** (10m Hard Severe 4b) takes the left-hand crack, **Gemini** (Severe 4b) follows the right-hand crack, and **Wotsit** (Severe 4b) is the crack right of Gemini.

Quaver 10m VS 4c (1992)
Climb the corner to the right of Wotsit. Traverse across a ledge near the top and finish as for Wotsit.

Zippy Trousers 10m VS 4c   (1992)
Climb the double crack 2 metres left of Comunn Gaidheil Paislig.

Comunn Gaidheil Paislig 10m Hard Severe 4b   (1992)
Climb the crack in the left side of the shallow cave which forms the start of Nudibranch Procurement.

Nudibranch Procurement 10m Hard Severe 4b   (1992)
Some 5 metres left of the end of the lower ledge is a shallow cave, roofed by a flake. Climb the cave, then trend left to finish at the notch above.

The following climbs are to the left of the descent route. **Jelly Spider** (10m VS 4c) is the first crack, **Soupdragon** (Hard Severe 4b) is the next crack line south, and **Weak Link** (Difficult) is the square-cut corner.

Primeval Soup 10m HVS 5a   (1992)
This takes the left-facing corner immediately right of the large mouth-shaped cave, which is only easily accessible at low tide. Climb to a square ledge below the corner. Move left and go up to the small ledge above the cave. Climb up and right to regain the top of the corner.

CAVE AREA
A couple of hundred metres north of the Main Buttress lies a headland almost separated from the mainland by a large gloup. The south side of this headland slopes into the sea. At low water it is possible to reach the Lower Wall by walking south along the shore. The first routes described end in the large room-shaped cave a short distance south of the headland.

Cave Access 8m Moderate   (1992)
The left-trending stepped ramp left edge of the cave.

Reflections 8m Severe 4a   (1992)
On the wall below the cave lie two well-defined cracks. Start below the right-hand edge of the cave, at a short crack. Climb this, then step left to the twin cracks. Follow these until they fade out a couple of metres short of the cave. Trend left to finish at the right edge of the cave.

Angus the Echinoderm 15m HVS 5a (1992)
Right of Reflections, before the wall changes direction, is a prominent triangular niche at 2m, with a number of calcite streaks above. Climb into the niche, then go up a groove to a small roof. Pass this on the left to reach a vertical crack, then climb this to a larger roof. Move right onto a thin slab (sling for aid) and finish easily.

Wrinkly Semmit 15m Hard Severe 4a (1992)
This route starts 15 metres south of the one metre step in the ramp leading down from the headland. Climb the crack, then trend left to avoid the bulging overhang. Step right again to climb a short vertical crack to an awkward mantelshelf. Continue up the wall above to finish at a small corner.

Heavily Starched 15m Severe 4a (1992)
Start just left of a vertical calcite stripe. Climb the rib, trending right to the bulge of Wrinkly Semmit. Trend left, following a crack line to finish up the wall to the left.

Steam Iron 15m Hard Severe 4a (1992)
Two metres right of Wrinkly Semmit is a fading crack line which leads to a large loose open corner. Climb the corner, finishing right of a large roof.

ROOF AREA
The roof in question is at the south end of the ledge, just where it slopes into the water, about 100 metres south of the Main Area. The ledge dips steeply to the south and is very slippery when damp.

Hang Ten 8m E2 5c (1992)
At the left end of the roof is a crack which runs up the wall across the roof and continues above. Climb the crack to the edge of the roof where hard moves lead to the wall above.

Near Horizons 8m VS 4c (1992)
Right of the large roof is a wall ending in a left-facing corner. Climb the middle of the wall on thin protection.

The Conjurer 8m VS 4c (1992)
Climb the wall right of the left-facing corner to a horizontal break. Traverse right and finish more easily.

Heedbanger 8m   HVS 5a   (1992)
Move up the ledge until a large cave topped by a roof is reached. Climb
the right-hand rear corner to the roof, bridge across and move out.
Finish up a short crack.

Dances with Fulmars 8m   Difficult   (1992)
From the top of the Ramp, or by traversing round from Heedbanger,
it is possible to reach a ledge. This climb takes the gently sloping crack
at its left end.

THE RAMP
This is the ledge which leads to the roof area. There are two points on
the Ramp where care must be taken while traversing round a corner,
especiallly if the rock is damp.

Percy the Owl 8m   Difficult   (1992)
Just beyond the first bad step going down the Ramp, climb a series
of large steps to a corner, where an awkward mantelshelf leads to
easier ground.

Bowmore 10m   Hard Severe 4b   (1992)
Climb the first crack on the right wall of the small bay with the green
pool.

Catwalk 8m   HVS 5a   (1992)
There is a large roof above a slimy green pool set back from the edge
of the ledge. Climb the back of the bay to the roof, bridge across the
drop to move out to the edge of the roof, then climb up on great holds.

Ardbeg 6m   Hard Severe 4b   (1992)
Climb the corner which terminates the left wall of the bay.

Bruichladdich 6m   Severe 4a   (1992)
Two metres left of the bay, round the second bad corner, lies the first
crack on this section of the wall. Mantleshelf onto a large block, then
climb the rightmost crack.

Music Boat 8m   Severe 4b   (1992)
Starting 6 metres down the ramp from Catwalk, climb a left-facing
corner to reach a crack and follow this to the top.

Bunnahabhain 8m   VS 4c   (1992)
There are two large overhanging blocks on this wall. This route climbs
the first of these directly.

Lagavulin Severe 4a   (1992)
Start below the second large overhanging block. Climb a short crack
and move left below the block, then go straight up, passing right of
another overhanging block. Finish up a well-defined undercut crack.

Caol Ila 10m   Severe 4a   (1992)
Starting 5 metres down the Ramp from Lagavulin, climb the deep
groove with the undercut start.

MID CLYTH

The four climbing areas here include the large wall immediately
beneath the Mid Clyth lighthouse, The Shelf (just south of the lighthouse), The Stack Area and The Overhanging Wall (which lies south
again). Unlike the majority of the Caithness cliffs, the rock is compact
solid sandstone divided by a band of brittle slate. At the Stack Area
this comprises the first few metres and poses no problems, but it can
occur in the middle of routes elsewhere. The approach to all the
climbing areas starts at the lighthouse (private). There is ample
parking in the car park on the main road.

LIGHTHOUSE WALL
Walk 100 metres north from the lighthouse and go down onto a broad
terrace halfway down the main wall. At the south end of this terrace
scramble down a corner, using the *in situ* fishing rope. The Lighthouse
Wall runs south from this point. The most noticeable feature is a
buttress directly below the lighthouse itself.

Aqualung 15m   Severe 4b   (1992)
About 6 metres left of the descent is a left-facing corner. Climb this to
a ledge, then another corner to a second ledge, and so to the top.

Rapture of the Deep 25m   HVS 4c   (1992)
On the north side of the buttress is a well-defined corner. Climb to a
roof and exit left onto a good ledge. Move up a ramp to the right and
step out onto the face (crux; sparse protection). Climb to a horizontal
ledge just below the top, then finish easily up a delightful layback crack.

An Ataireachd Ard   25m   VS 4c   (1992)
Another 6 metres south of the buttress lies a shallow groove with a
small plinth at its base. Climb the groove on the right, then go up a
series of small ledges to a more prominent ledge (crux). Traverse a
few metres right along the ledge, then climb to the top on large holds,
passing a large roof on the right.

THE SHELF
Walking south from the Lighthouse there is an area of boulders close
to the cliff edge. There is a shelf of rock below, the north end of which
is permanently above water. The south end of the shelf is bounded by
a small bay and a south-facing cave. Approach by abseil.

Circle Line   20m   VS 4c   (1992)
At the south end of the shelf there is a ledge at 15m which can be
reached by an easy scramble. Start at a right-facing corner which
crosses the slate band via a notch. Finish up two large obvious steps.

THE STACK AREA (Skerry Mor)
The stack is barely separate from the coastline and is easily missed.
A partially tidal ledge starts just south of the stack from which most of
the following climbs start. There is no simple descent; the easiest
abseil is from a platform 2m below the top. The climbs are described
from north to south.

Strange Attractor   20m   E1 5b   (1992)
Right of the north wall there are two obvious and impressive lines. This
climb is the chimney-crack immediately right of the layback crack. Start
below the overhanging open chimney. Climb to the right under the roof
to a crack. Swing across strenuously to the spike below the chimney
and pull up into the notch. Climb the crack line trending right and finish
strenuously to the right of the dog-leg crack.

Giant   15m   VS 4c   (1990)
This route takes the layback crack, which starts after a scramble over
the slate band to reach a ledge at 5m. Climb the crack (large gear
useful) and finish direct past a precarious block, or exit leftwards.

Maelstrom   15m   HVS 4c   (1991)
The recessed crack line curving gently left, which lies left of Giant,
gives a strenuous but well protected climb.

Raccoon Kicker 20m HVS   (1990)
Climb the first corner at the south end of the north wall (at the start of a series of corners and aretes).

Sprockletop 15m Severe   (1990)
The corner behind the obvious overhanging spikes. The aretes to each side give good problems, as yet unled.

Captain Sensible 15m HVS 4c   (1991)
Left of Sprockletop is an unclimbed corner line which moves right under a small roof. This ill-defined route lies 5 metres left again, and reaches a small corner at 8m, then trends right to finish strenuously.

Criticality 12m Severe   (1990)
Climb a direct line to the abseil platform via a crack to a ledge, then go up a corner.

Comedy of Thirst 12m E2 5b   (1991)
An obvious feature is a very large block, whose top forms a ledge at 6m. Start up the corner at the north end of the block. From the ledge, climb the crack strenuously for two moves before exiting onto a ledge on the right.

John's Peel 15m Severe   (1991)
Climb the corner at the south end of the block. Gain a groove and continue to the top.

Shallow Chimney 15m VS   (1990)
The shallow depression in an otherwise blank section gives a pleasant technical climb. The crux is a mantleshelf at the top.

Silverfish 15m E1 5b   (1991)
The thin crack 3 metres right of Layback Crack. The difficult move from the slate onto the sandstone is marked by a calcite fish shape. Step off a block left of a large niche, move right after 2m and follow a groove to the top.

Layback Crack 15m VS 4c   (1991)
The obvious corner. A chockstone at the top eases entry into the notch.

The next four climbs are on the Inset Wall, which lies between Layback Crack and a small buttress.

Diagonal   15m   Severe   (1990)
Start 3 metres left of Layback Crack below a strenuous direct line.
Trend right to a ledge, then join Layback Crack.

Mug's Game   15m   HVS 5a   (1992)
Start as for Diagonal. Climb to the ledge at 5m, then follow the corner
line directly to the top.

Theatre of Cruelty   15m   E2 5b   (1992)
Climb the central line up the juggy wall, moving through the overhang
via a small groove.

Frog Stroker   15m   HVS 5a   (1992)
With apologies to Richie Gunn. There is a corner where the small
buttress meets the inset wall. Climb this, using the wall and crack to
the right to overcome the overhanging crux. Sustained.

SOUTH BAY
To climb here requires low tide. It is a sheltered corner and its right
side (Knuckle) offers probably the easiest and least strenuous route
here.

Steerpike   10m   HVS 5a   (1992)
Just north of South Bay is a corner below a small roof. Climb the crack
directly below the roof. It can also be reached less strenuously by
following the corner to the roof and moving left to make the same
finishing moves.

Knuckle   15m   Very Difficult   (1990)
Meander up the right side of the bay, not quite in the corner.

Small North European Mammal   10m   Severe   (1991)
Start on the ledge in the centre of the bay then move right via ledges
to a niche. Exit left to an easier finish.

Adagio   12m   VS 4c   (1991)
Start at the same ledge as the previous route, then overcome the small
roof and finish at the same ledge as Oxter.

Allegro   12m   VS 4c   (1991)
Climb the crack midway between Oxter and Adagio.

Oxter   15m   Severe   (1990)
Climb the scoop on the left side of the bay to a platform. Step right at the top for the easiest finish.

OVER THE WATER
The cliff turns through a right-angle after Oxter and the next section has very little in the way of a ledge at the bottom. Some of the climbs may require a hanging belay.

Velvet Scooter   15m   Severe 4a   (1991)
Traverse round the corner from Oxter to the corner, at the back of which is a deep chimney capped by a roof. Start immediately right of this, trend right and finish with an awkward move onto a broad ledge.

Mac-attacked   15m   Severe 4b   (1991)
The deep chimney left of Velvet Scooter, exiting right under the roof past a loose block.

Electric Aardvark   12m   VS 4c   (1991)
Overcome an awkward holdless mantleshelf at the start, then follow a corner to the top.

Crispy Aromatic Duck   10m   Very Difficult   (1991)
The easy-angled line on the left.

   South of this section is a pillar with a slightly overhanging top. A heavily birdlimed chimney goes up left of the pillar. Further south is a short wall bounded on the left by a sea-cave.

Drawbridge   15m   Severe 4b   (1992)
Starting at the right end of the wall, climb an offwidth crack which leads to a roof.

D.I.Y.   10m   VS 4c   (1992)
Climb the obvious crack line to the left of the previous route.

Keystone   10m   Severe 4a   (1992)
Climb the leftmost crack on the wall next to the cave entrance.

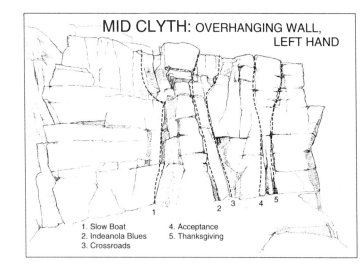

MID CLYTH: OVERHANGING WALL, LEFT HAND

1. Slow Boat
2. Indeanola Blues
3. Crossroads
4. Acceptance
5. Thanksgiving

OVERHANGING WALL SECTION

From the stack area, walk 100 metres south around a small inlet. Scramble down a corner to reach a tidal ledge.

1 Slow Boat 10m Very Difficult (1991)
Climb the obvious large corner.

2 Indeanola Blues 10m Severe 4b (1991)
The left-hand corner, 2 metres right of Slow Boat.

3 Crossroads 10m HVS 5a (1992)
Start in the corner right of Indeanola Blues, and continue up the flake above.

4 Acceptance 10m E1 5b (1992)
This is the wall and hanging crack right of Crossroads.

5 Thanksgiving 10m E1 5b (1992)
Climb the steep crack a few metres away from the platform edge.

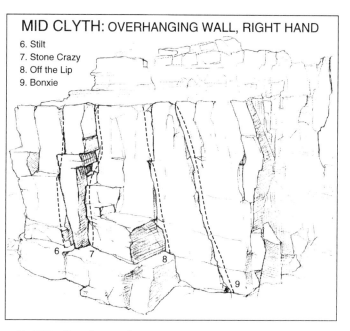

MID CLYTH: OVERHANGING WALL, RIGHT HAND

6. Stilt
7. Stone Crazy
8. Off the Lip
9. Bonxie

6 Stilt 10m Severe 4b   (1991)
Traverse right around the arete above the sea. Where the ledge
widens, climb a crack to a ledge then continue to the top.

7 Stone Crazy 10m VS 4c   (1991)
Just right of Stilt a corner leads to a roof, where a step right and up
gains a square corner. Follow this to the top.

8 Off The Lip 10m VS 4c   (1991)
Continue the traverse to where the ledge finishes, climb a crack line
to a tiny roof then finish straight up.

9 Bonxie 10m Very Difficult   (1991)
From the end of the ledge, traverse a further 2 metres right to a large
crack which trends left. Climb this to the top.

LATHERONWHEEL

This area, although not as extensive or as high as Mid Clyth, provides some excellent climbing in a sheltered and picturesque setting. The sandstone is of good quality, with little evidence of the slate. Approach by turning off the A9 into Latheronwheel village and follow the main road down to the harbour, then walk south down the coast for 500 metres. The easiest descent is a scramble down a stepped chimney on the north side of the stack, which leads to the base of Little Flat Wall. The Big Flat Wall (which lies to the north) and The Stack may also be reached from here. The climbs on the South Corner are reached by a scramble down the back corner of the bay. The climbs are described starting at the north end.

PINNACLE AREA

The climbs in this area can be approached by walking south from the harbour to a small bay with a distinctive group of four stacks. The bay is separated from the Big Flat Wall by a short peninsula which is penetrated by a sea cave. Descend a gully at the back of the bay.

Sticky Fingers   10m   VS 4c   (1992)
On the extreme end of the peninsula, directly facing the outermost stack, is a dog-leg crack. Climb to a roof, move left and continue by a crack to the top.

Fancy Free   10m   VS 4c   (1992)
Some 5 metres south of Sticky Fingers is a thin crack on an outside corner of the face.

Forgotten Corner   10m   Severe 4b   (1992)
Climb the corner left of Fancy Free.

Footloose   15m   Severe 4a   (1992)
Further south round the corner is a cave, and about 6 metres north of the cave is a corner. Climb the corner to the roof, then exit right.

Coprolyte   15m   HVS 4c   (1992)
Follow the ledge south as far as the sea cave. On the wall immediately to the right is a pair of cracks which converge at 10m. Climb the left-hand crack to the junction, then move up and left to a ledge. Loose at the top.

North of the Big Flat Wall are three parallel corners, of which the leftmost is Primary Corner. On the frontal wall further north are two prominent cracks; the following route takes the one to the right. Access at high tide is by abseil down the left-hand (vegetated) crack.

Freaker's Crack 15m HVS 5a   (1991)
Start from an obvious narrow alcove. Chimney out of the alcove to an airy position at the base of the crack, then follow the impending crack with difficulty and increasing exposure.

Angel of Sleep 15m HVS 5a   (1992)
This follows the arete immediately right of Eye of the Storm. Start up left of the arete, then move back right as soon as possible. Continue up the right side to finish up a short hanging corner, bounding a detached but seemingly solid block.

Eye of the Storm 20m Hard Severe   (1991)
Climb the central of the three parallel corners by bridging past an awkward bulge.

Primary Corner 15m Severe   (1991)
The leftmost of the three corners, reached by abseil except at low tide. Climb to a ledge and finish up a crack.

THE BIG FLAT WALL

1 The Other Landscape 20m VS 4c   (1991)
This climb takes the left-hand of two central cracks on the Big Flat Wall. Start at low tide on the boulder beach. Climb the right edge of a cave then traverse left into the main crack, which is climbed direct with good protection.

2 Gervasutti's Wall 15m E1 5b   (1991)
The most continuous thin crack 3 metres right of the large niche. Start from the end of a ledge below high tide level, move round the initial bulge and climb the crack and final wall direct.

3 Free Fall 12m VS 4c   (1991)
Start in the large niche at the left end of the wall. Climb the right corner in the rear of the niche then exit onto the wall above. Poorly protected.

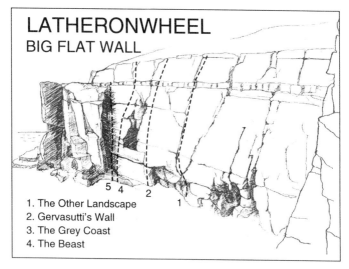

LATHERONWHEEL
BIG FLAT WALL

1. The Other Landscape
2. Gervasutti's Wall
3. The Grey Coast
4. The Beast

4 The Grey Coast 15m VS 4b (1992)
Start in the smaller niche at the far left of the wall. Bridge up the niche and pull onto the wall above. Climb the wall trending slightly right, then finish up a diagonal crack.

5 The Beast 15m VS 4c (1991)
Climb the strenuous black off-width crack defining the left end of the Big Flat Wall.

The next five climbs are on The Little Flat Wall. **Sunspot** (15m VS 4c) takes two parallel cracks in the wall right of Little Flat Wall to a notch belay. **Two Bit Ram** (Severe 4a) is the corner at the north end of the wall. **Pistachio** (Severe 4b) takes the crack above a large triangular notch. **Wallnut** (Severe 4a) is the crack 2 metres left of the triangular notch, and **Stoneware** (Severe 4a) is the crack 2 metres left of Wallnut.

THE STACK AREA

Flight from Sadness 15m E3 5c   (1992)
This takes a line on the very steep north face of the stack, which overlooks the Little Flat Wall. Start up the easy arete on the left. From the end of the roof, launch right onto the wall and continue up and right until hard moves gain the large ledge. Finish straight up.

Stepping Out 15m Severe 4b   (1990)
Start immediately below a right-angled corner. Climb to a ledge, step into the corner and continue to a large block at the top.

Laphroaig 15m HVS 5a   (1990)
Start as for Stepping Out but continue over the overhang (instead of stepping onto the ledge) and continue direct.

   Left (south) of the Stack descent is possible via ledges. The next obvious feature is an arete which is at the boundary of an overhanging section. North of the arete is a 6m wall with an obvious notch.

Coaster 10m Severe 4b   (1991)
Climb out of the notch and continue to the top.

Puffin Attack 10m VS 4c   (1992)
Follow a line up the centre of the slabby wall midway between Shocket and Coaster.

Shocket 10m Severe 4a   (1990)
Start right of the arete by balancy moves, traverse left to the arete and follow a large flake to the top. An alternative start takes the overhanging crack directly below the arete (4c).

The Serpent 10m E2/3 5b   (1992)
This route climbs the narrow face right of the Guillemot Crack. Start centrally below the break. Climb past the break, move right a little, then go left to the prominent crack. Follow this to a ledge just below the top. Finish easily.

Guillemot Crack 10m E1 5a   (1990)
Climb the large continuously overhanging arete south of the obvious arete at the boundary of the overhanging section mentioned above.

Summer Days Left-Hand 10m E1/2 5b (1992)
Climb the left side of the wall right of Fallout to the break, then finish straight up.

Summer Days Right-Hand 10m E1/2 5b (1992)
Hand traverse right at the break, then go up at the end of the ledge.

Fall Out 8m HVS 5a (1991)
The corner 5 metres south of Guillemot Crack.

Free Wheeler 8m HVS 5a (1990)
Start at the foot of the corner of Fall Out, then trend left.
Direct start: 10m HVS 5b (1992)
Climb a crack directly to join the parent route.

BEDROCK
From Guillemot Crack scramble down to sea-level just to the south. The Bedrock area extends to a small inlet which prevents any further progress.

First Ascent 15m Very Difficult (1991)
Climb a triangular slab below a roof. Step round the roof to the right, then trend left to the top.

Fred Flintstone 15m Very Difficult (1992)
Just south of the moderate section there is a small recess. Climb the left corner.

Bam Bam 15m Severe 4a (1992)
Left of Fred Flintstone a crack leads to a corner.

Bully For Brontosaurous 15m VS 4b (1992)
Climb the notch and crack line just left of Bam Bam.

Sorry Scorry 15m VS 4b (1992)
Climb the crack line just left again.

Thinking of Wilma 10m VS 4b (1992)
Climb the corner arete of the inlet.

Bouldermobile 15m VS 4c (1992)
From the arete traverse 2 metres into the inlet along a narrow ledge.
Climb direct up the crack line to the right of a large bird-limed chimney.

CRUSTY WALL
This wall can be seen from Bedrock as the lichen-encrusted wall which
faces north across the inlet. The rock is surprisingly sound and dry.
Access is by abseil down the south side of the inlet and an easy
traverse out to a ledge at the bottom of the wall.

Dog on a String 10m VS 4c (1992)
Start in the centre of the wall, climb an obvious crack to a horizontal
break, move left and follow the crack to the top.

SOUTH CORNER
The South Corner is a small roughly square bay just south of the inlet.
A broad ledge to the south leads to the area, which can be reached
by scrambling down a chimney in the back of the bay or down some
moderate rock on the less steep right wall.

Dream 10m VS 4c (1992)
Probably best reached by abseil, this is a sustained vertical crack
starting at sea-level 2 metres north of the bay.

Night Sweat 15m VS 4c (1992)
Climb the exposed arete at the north corner of the bay.

Somnambulist 10m VS 4c (1992)
The north end of the back wall of the bay has an overhanging corner.
Climb into the notch and move out under the roof. Finish straight up
a crack line.

Night Shift 8m Hard Severe 4b (1992)
Follow a crack line to the left of the back wall, trending right at the top.

Thief's Fork 8m Severe 4a (1991)
This takes the first bifurcated chimney on the right after scrambling
down the back of the bay.

Gym Jam 8m VS 4c (1992)
The hanging crack just to the left of Thief's Fork.

Left of Gym Jam is a deep easy chimney. Left again is a short section of wall split by three crack lines.

The Morning Line 8m HVS 5a   (1992)
The central crack is quite strenuous but well protected.

Shearwater 8m HVS 5a   (1991)
Traverse out of the bay to the south to an obvious slightly overhanging crack. Follow this strenuously to the top.

Therapy 8m Very Difficult   (1991)
Climb the corner to the left of Shearwater.

CLEIT MHOR   *(Map Ref 173 300)*

About 2km north of Dunbeath (on the Helmsdale to Wick road) there are three stacks marked on the OS Map as Cleit Mhor. The central stack, Cleit Bheag, is the most appealing.

Cleit Bheag 35m E1   (1989)
The obvious crack on the seaward face is harder than it looks.
1. 25m 5b Climb easily to overhangs at 15m. A difficult section then leads to a chimney and a stance on the right.
2. 10m 4c Move left and climb the wall to the top.

Cleit Ruadh 15m HVS   (1989)
The northern stack is climbed up its seaward face. A short technical wall at 6m provides the crux.

BODACH AN UIRD   *(Map Ref 118 217)*

This fine 30m stack lies 2km south of the village of Berriedale, which is about 18km north-east of Helmsdale. Approach by boat. It had been climbed before the ascents recorded here, probably via the Landward Face or Bird Poo Wall.

South Route 35m HVS   (1989)
A good route taking a series of grooves on the south side of the stack. Start at the left of two obvious grooves.
1. 10m 5a Climb easily up into the chimney in the back of the groove. Traverse the left wall to a stance on the arete.

2. 15m 5a Climb straight above the belay for 3m and move right to climb a groove to overhangs. Traverse left to the left arete of the groove above the stance, and climb the wall above the overhang, trending right to a good stance.

3. 10m 4c Trend left on dubious rock to a shallow groove leading to the top.

Landward Face   30m   VS 5a   (1989)
From the landing site on the seaward side of the stack, follow ledges up and round the north side to reach a good stance in the centre of the landward face, about 10m above the sea. Climb the steep wall just right of a wide crack to a steep crack line that leads to a horizontal break. Continue up the wall to the top.

North Arete   40m   E1   (1989)
The north edge of the stack is characterised by a large hanging flake at 25m. Start directly below the flake.

1. 15m 5a Climb a steep corner, making a detour left then right to reach a good stance on the landward side of the arete.

2. 10m 5b Follow the crack in the hanging pillar above to the right to an overhang, then hand traverse left in a spectacular position and make a difficult exit onto a good ledge on top of the hanging flake.

3. 15m Continue up the stepped ridge to the top.

Bird Poo Wall   35m   VS   (1989)
The obvious line on the seaward face.

1. 20m 4c Climb the left-facing line of corners and cracks on the right side of the wall to reach a large overhung ledge.

2. 15m 4b From the left end of the ledge follow the vague crack line up and right to the top.

Orkney

Most of the climbing on the Orkney Islands is on Hoy, just south of Orkney Mainland, although there is some outcrop climbing near the south tip of the Mainland and numerous stacks around the coastline. Access to Orkney is by P & O Ferries who operate a daily service (except Sundays) between Scrabster near Thurso and Stromness on Orkney Mainland. A weekly service also operates between Aberdeen, Orkney, and Shetland. Full details of these services can be obtained from P & O Ferries (tel. Aberdeen 572615, or Stromness 850655).

ORKNEY MAINLAND

The rugged coastline of Orkney Mainland provides numerous stacks. Several of these have been climbed although only two are fully described here. Both are situated just off the west coast, north of Stromness. They are easily approached by driving to an old army base at Yesnaby on the west coast and walking south (about 15 minutes for Castle of Yesnaby).

Castle of Yesnaby 35m E1 5b   (1967)
Approach by abseil; at least one extra rope will be required. Swim to the base, and climb the south face. An excellent route.

North Gaulton Castle 50m HVS   (1970)
An elaborate rope technique similar to Patey's method for reaching the top of The Great Stack of Handa (a huge Tyrolean traverse) was used to reach the base of the stack on the first ascent. The stack can then be climbed in two pitches.

  Stack o'Roo lies just north of the Bay of Skaill and provides a loose and dirty climb of Severe standard. Other stacks which have been climbed include Standard Rock off Costa Head at the north tip of the island and Stackabank and Clett of Crura on South Ronaldsay.

SOUTH RONALDSAY

Clett of Crura 25m HVS   (1990)
The landward face of this stack (which has also been climbed on the seaward face) offers a rather green route, with difficulty concentrated

into a short section. Swim to the base. From ledges on the landward side gain and climb ledges in a depression left of centre. At 20m a short overhanging crack has to be climbed to gain a few metres of easier climbing to the top.

HOY

Hoy is the second largest island in The Orkneys and offers perhaps the highest sea-cliff in the British Isles, the 346m St. John's Head. Climbs have been made on this huge face, including a recent very hard and impressive line, but most of the climbing lies on the much televised Old Man of Hoy. The most convenient transport to the island is via a small passenger ferry run daily from Stromness to Moaness Pier in North Hoy (contact Mr S. Mowat tel. 0856 850624). The island can also be reached via a ferry run by the Orkney Islands Shipping Company. It runs from Houton on the Orkney Mainland to Lyness and Longhope on Hoy. (tel. Kirkwall 2044). In addition it is worth a mention that the taxis on Hoy provide a very useful means of getting about.

OLD MAN OF HOY

From Rackwick Bay on the west side of the island a path goes diagonally left up the hillside to the cliffs above the Old Man, which can be reached in about 45 minutes.

East Face (Original Route) 135m E1 (1966)
The landward face of the stack. Aid was used on the first ascent. Care must be taken to leave a doubled rope on pitch 2 to avoid a bottomless abseil during descent! Start at the end of the boulder ridge linking the stack to the mainland. Very large Friends are useful, and although the climbing may be only technically HVS the grade is justified by epics experienced by some experienced parties!
1. 20m 4b Climb a shattered pillar to a large ledge, The Gallery.
2. 30m 5b Traverse right to gain the foot of the great crack. Climb this past roofs at 10m and 20m. Step right at the top to a triangular alcove.
3. 20m Step right and move back left over loose easy ledges to regain the crack line which is followed for 8m to a large ledge.
4. 45m 4b Near the right-hand end of the ledge climb up a few metres and traverse delicately left to another ledge. Climb the chimney in the corner, then wriggle right along a horizontal ledge until easy ledges lead to grass below the final crack.
5. 20m 4c Climb the sensational terminal crack on excellent rock.

A Fistful of Dollars   140m   E5   (1984)

This climbs the south-east arete, which was first climbed in 1967 using considerable aid. The free ascent was made for the BBC live spectacular.

1. 20m 4b As for the Original Route.

2. 40m 6a Climb the corner on the left to the top of a pinnacle at 10m. Step right onto a steep wall and go up to a flake on the left side of an overhang. Pull up left and follow the groove-flake system above to its top. Traverse right to a thin crack near the arete, then up to a long narrow ledge on the right.

3. 25m 5c Climb the arete, step right to a crack in an overhang and pull up to a good ledge on the right. Step up to ledges on the right side of the arete, then climb a thin crack through an overhang and up to a square ledge.

4. 25m 5c Move up for a few feet and traverse onto the left wall of the arete. Move up and left to reach a good crack and follow this to a big ledge on the arete (the pitch can be split here). Climb up a short crack on the right, move left onto fragile ledges, then go up the wall to a small overhang. Pull over and move left to the arete. Go up this for 6m to ledges and belays.

5. 30m 5c/6a Continue up the arete to a ledge below an overhang. Take the overhang on its left and pull up to a niche. Climb the thin finger crack above to small ledges on the headwall. Make an ascending traverse right across the wall and up cracks to finish on the arete.

South Face   140m   E2   (1967)

A fine sunny route on acceptable rock, low in the grade. Large Friends are useful.

1. 20m 4b As for the Original Route to the Gallery.

2. 30m 5b Climb the corner on the left, go up the steep wall above (bold) to a flake on the left. Climb this to a ledge, then walk 15m left to belay on blocks below a shallow chimney-crack.

3. 20m 5b Climb the shallow chimney to a ledge below a roof.

4. 25m 5b Surmount the roof (strenuous) and continue up the crack to belay at the top of the grassy Haven.

5. 45m 4c Traverse right to join the Original Route at the base of a corner. Finish up the corner. On the first ascent the summit was reached directly from The Haven via a loose chimney to the left of a huge block, followed by a final groove to the top.

Ancient Mariner   165m   E2   (1982)
The obvious chimney-crack in the upper half of the west face is
reached by a devious entry starting on the south face. Start 12 metres
right of the arete forming the junction of the south and west faces. The
rock requires care in places.
1. 45m 5b/c Climb the wall for 10m to reach the start of a groove. Go
up this (old peg runners) until about 3m from its top, then traverse left
along an obvious break into the centre of the wall. Move up a few feet
and continue traversing to the arete. Climb up the arete to a ledge and
a huge detached block.
2. 45m 5b Climb a short groove on the left and traverse steeply
leftwards into the main crack line. Follow the crack passing numerous
ledges to reach a belay.
3. 45m 5a Continue in the same crack line.
4. 30m 4c Climb up and slightly rightwards to gain the huge grassy
terrace. From its top climb the left wall and then the obvious corner
crack to emerge on the summit.

A Few Dollars More   145m   E3   (1984)
This route takes the prominent crack line in the centre of the north face
and provides a fine climb. From platforms below the south face
traverse an obvious break across the west face to gain access to the
introductory buttress on the north face.
1. 10m Scramble up to a belay.
2. 45m 4c Climb an open groove for 10m, then a chimney in the right
wall to its top. Traverse a ledge left to the main groove and up to a
belay ledge at the top of the introductory buttress.
3. 30m 5c Move right onto the wall and up a groove-flake to its top.
Climb steeply to a break in the overlap and follow the crack line above
to reach a large cave and belay.
4. 30m 5b Climb the steep crack out of the left side of the cave. Follow
the crack for 20m to ledges near the left arete. Go up short walls
rightwards to a grassy ledge below the middle of the headwall.
5. 30m 5b Climb thin cracks in the wall leading to a bottomless
groove-corner and up this to a ledge on the left. A short crack and wall
leads to the top.

ST. JOHN'S HEAD

This immense cliff, about 3km north of the Old Man of Hoy, is breached
by three routes. The first two in 1969 and 1970 were multi-day ascents
while the more recent Big John was climbed in eleven hours. St. John's

Head has two main faces (north and north-west) both of which are vertical, more than 300m high and with precarious vegetation. The original route on the cliff climbs a pillar between the north and north-west faces while Longhope Route and Big John scale the north face. The descent is by a grassy slope and a short rock step about 350 metres north of St. John's Head. This is not the same descent used in 1969 and 1970 which required numerous abseils and Tyrolean techniques.

Original Route   400m   "Extremely Severe"   (1969)
Start at the foot of the main face and climb grassy slabs to a small cave under roofs at the top of the grass. (This section is very serious with no protection and is extremely precarious grass.) Traverse horizontally right along the grassy ledge for 15m and then up a crack using two pegs for aid near the top (4c). Follow the ledge to the right for belays. Traverse a few metres right, then go up onto the firm wall. Follow a line of flakes for a few metres, then break right and continue up and slightly to the right on superb rock to reach an excellent ledge (4c). From the right end of the ledge go straight up to another good ledge (4b). On the first ascent a bivouac was taken here in hammocks.

Climb the chimney on the right to a good platform. Step left and follow the overhanging chimney past a loose block to belays a few feet after the chimney (4c). Up easily then traverse delicately right above loose blocks to a ledge system (4b). Follow the ledges to belay in a corner after 6m. Step right and move up to a prominent crack (4b). Step down right from the foot of this and move up to belay at the foot of a prominent corner (4b). Climb the corner for 6m until a hand traverse left can be made to a good ledge (4c). Climb the awkward corner behind the belay, then traverse left to the end of the ledges (4b). (Second bivouac).

Traverse to the right end of the ledge. Climb the crack then move left for 12m to good belays (4b). Move back right and climb the awkward corner to exit right with a poor peg for aid (4c). Move easily back left. Traverse to the right extremity of the terrace. Up the loose corner until a smooth niche below an overhanging block can be reached by stepping to the right (4b). Climb up the niche using a nut for aid, then peg up the steep crack for 12m until it is possible to reach good belays under a huge roof (4c, A2). Traverse right with ease, then make a difficult move up a scooped wall, then layback a small roof (4c). Belay under a roof. Climb the obvious chimney exit through the summit overhangs (4b).

Longhope Route   450m   "Extremely Severe"   (1970)
This climb was named in memory of the local lifeboat which went down
in 1969 killing all eight of its crew. The first and only ascent to date
took seven days to complete and anyone attempting this route should
be prepared for anything. The left (north) side of St. John's Head is
steep grass for the first 150m. Longhope Route takes the wall on the
right of the grass, moves left to the top of the grass, and climbs a series
of grooves in the first part of the headwall to a prominent band of
overhangs. It traverses up leftwards below these overhangs eventually gaining the left arete (Big John), and then heads back right to
climb the headwall via a thin peg crack.

 Start at the foot of the red sandstone wall to the right of the grass.
About 4 pitches lead up the wall and then escape leftwards about 30
to 40m below the top of the grass. Climb in two pitches to reach a large
ledge beneath a rock roof (5b). Climb up (some aid was used to get
over a roof at the start of pitch 3) and after a right-slanting ramp (5c)
there follows a memorable horizontal traverse left (rurp for a handhold)
"a classic limbo dance through overhanging red sand dunes" (two
pitches, 5c). Climb the grass to rock (35m). A slab followed by a groove
leads to ledges, an excellent pitch (35m, 5a). (Big John gains these
ledges from below and to the left and then heads off left).

A chimney on the right leads to a stance below a prominent groove
with a wide crack in the back (20m, 4b). The "Vile Crack" (5c) leads to
a ledge on the left, move left along this to beneath a large right-trending
flake (35m, 5c). Layback the flake (5a), climb up (5a), and then up
right (5c) to gain a grass ledge on the right. The fourth bivouac was
taken here. Move left to beneath an overhang. Surmount the overhang
with a few pegs for aid and continue up and left to a stance below giant
steps leading back right (5b/A1). Climb the steps and follow a stomach
traverse line (The Vice) to the left arete (Big John) (5b/A1).

Climb just right of the arete towards a horizontal finger of rock
projecting from the right (The Guillotine). Stand on this and move up
left to a stance on the arete (crux; 12m, A2). Move up just right of the
arete to a ledge, then make a 5a hand traverse right to reach a 25m
crack. Climb the crack (aid) to a spectacular stance, The Crows Nest.
Move right for 5m (peg in place, some aid), and climb a 12m (4c)
layback crack to the top.

Big John   435m   "Extremely Severe"   (1988)
This takes the soaring arete to the left of Longhope Route. "Not many
routes compare". Start on the left side of the grass slope at the base
of the cliff.
1. to 4. 135m Climb grass to a tangle of ropes beneath the centre of
the upper wall. Belay at the top of a rope hanging down a rock wall.
5. 40m 5b Climb the slabby wall trending right to a ledge, then go
back left to grassy ledges level with the base of the 4b chimney on
Longhope Route.
6. 45m 5c Traverse horizontally left for 25m and climb up and back
slightly right for 20m to a stance 20m below the prominent overhanging
flake crack leading up left to the arete.
7. 20m 4c Climb to a ledge at the start of the flake crack.
8. 25m 5c Layback the overhanging flake and struggle sensationally
up the upper flake to a small corner ledge.
9. 15m 5b Continue in the same line up the corner to a ledge on the
arete beneath a prominent overhang.
10. 35m 5b Trend left round the overhang and follow a vague fault
line to a ledge after 25m. Move right along this to the arete, surmount
an overhang and gain a ledge.
11. 25m 6a Climb a difficult but well protected crack on the right side
of the arete to a ledge. Traverse this round to the left side of the arete
to belay where two large blocks have dropped from the overhang
above about 12m left of the arete.
12. 30m 5c Pull over the overhang and climb direct for 6m to a traverse
crack. Follow this rightwards to a ledge just left of the arete. Move up
via two dubious undercut flakes and use a very poor peg in a poorly
protected position to gain a ledge. Crux.
13. 30m 5b Climb a delicate wall on the left to gain a shallow groove
leading to a ledge. Climb the short chimney above to a further ledge
and belay below an overhang on the left.
14. Surmount the overhang in the fault line, then continue more easily
to the top.

RORA HEAD

This fine headland, located just south of the Old Man of Hoy, presents
some spectacular sandstone cliffs some 70 metres north of its highest
point. The rock is generally of good quality, but it takes two or three
fine days to dry and clean up after rain. A route was climbed here by
the now famous Remy brothers in 1970, but the following routes are

recent, very much in the modern idiom. Descent to all the routes is by a 60m abseil from an *in situ* peg in a small gully just south of the wall. The rope should be left in place and jumars should be carried. A wide selection of gear, particularly Friends, is also essential.

Roring Forties   80m   E3 **   (1991)
The easiest route on the wall, following an excellent line based on the obvious towering arete and crack system to its left.
1. 25m 5c Start beneath the seaward arete and the right-hand corner crack. Climb to a small roof, continue up the crack then step up left and traverse to the arete. Climb this to a good belay.
2. 20m 5c Make some bold moves up the left edge of the arete, step left and go up the obvious crack to a ledge where the crack widens.
3. 35m 5b Climb the wide crack to a ledge beneath a roof. Swing left below this and continue to the top, bearing left and finishing just right of a short corner.

Mucklehouse Wall   100m   E5 ***   (1991)
This route climbs the wall right of the arete, which, since it overhangs by some 15m, is somewhat strenuous. Low in the grade.
1. 30m 5c Climb Roring Forties pitch 1, but continue up the arete above the belay before swinging onto the overhanging face. Belay just above a small roof.
2. 35m 5c A tremendous fist-jamming pitch up the slanting crack in the centre of the face. From the belay, hand traverse right along a break to dubious flakes at the base of the crack. Pull into the crack and climb it on excellent jams before moving left to the arete. Continue up to a large ledge.
3. 10m 5b Traverse right along a foot-ledge to belay on a block beside a small stepped groove.
4. 25m 6a Climb directly up the dark red streak and pull up into a cave (The Fairy Grotto). Slither out left via a block to an excellent layback finish. An impressive pitch.

Rats Stole My Toothbrush   20m   E5 6a **   (1991)
An alternative bold start to Mucklehouse Wall. Scramble up easy ledges on the right of the face to a ledge in the corner (also approachable by abseil). Climb the obvious flake above, then traverse left across the left wall on flat holds until it is possible to move up to a semi-rest in a corner under a roof. Swing out left (even harder for the short) and climb to the belay at the top of pitch 1 of Mucklehouse Wall.

Two Little Boys 85m E6 ***   (1991)
A stunning, sustained and strenuous route taking the main challenge
of the wall.
1. 25m 6b Start up Roring Forties then move up to twin overhanging
cracks right of the arete. Fix good protection then climb the cracks on
finger locks, past an *in situ* Hex 3, and continue up the overhanging
wall to a belay just above the roof. A desperate pitch.
2. 35m 5c Mucklehouse Wall, pitch 2.
3. 25m 6b A brilliant and photogenic pitch, sustained and deceptively
overhanging, up the dark red wall. Climb gently up the obvious
right-trending line of white flakes then finish up the headwall.

The following routes are also on Rora Head. Approaching from
Rackwick, after passing the high point, the coast pulls away and drops
to the left from the path, then begins to flatten out. Four distinctive
gullies indent this section, numbered 1 to 4. Gully 4 is the furthest away
from Rackwick and provides an easy descent to a non-tidal beach.
The section of crag with the routes described below extends from Gully
4 back towards Rackwick to the far side of Gully 3 (which has a
prominent vegetated pillar forming its base). The routes are described
from left to right, looking in.

Fillet of Soul 30m E1 5b   (1992)
This route climbs the prominent slabby arete of the right wall of Gully
4. Start on the left of the overhangs at its base. Climb out right through
the overhang, traverse right, then climb diagonally to the arete proper.
Follow this to the top.

Back Bone 40m E4   (1992)
This route starts about halfway between gullies 4 and 3, below
prominent vertical twin cracks which run the full height of the black
pillar. Scramble or climb awkwardly rightwards through lush grass to
belay at the foot of the cracks.
1. 25m 6a Climb the cracks steeply past two small roofs (crux) to a
ledge. Continue with difficulty to belay on the last ledge below the
headwall.
2. 15m 5c A sensational pitch. Gain the niche above the overhanging
block and exit leftwards. Belay with care well back.

The Eternal Optometrist 50m E3   (1992)
You'll see why! This route starts from the rightmost earth shelf below
a shiny black wall at the top of the crag.
1. 25m 5c Climb the central red sandy recess with a difficult move out
right. Traverse right, then climb the airy right arete to ledges and good
belays.
2. 25m 5c Climb up and right through a broken corner. Swing back
left onto the precarious rib which bounds the right side of the black
wall, then climb it and belay just below the top.

Rosamund's Birthday 40m E4   (1992)
This superb route climbs the outer edge of the right wall of Gully 3. It
is best approached by a free abseil down the line of the route to the
bog atop the pillar at its base. The difficult first pitch could be avoided
via the seaward face of the pillar, thus reducing the grade to E3.
1. 10m 6a Climb the initial cracks with difficulty to the first ledge.
2. 15m 5c Climb up until it is possible to traverse above the lip of the
roof on the right arete, then continue to the next ledge.
3. 15m 5c Continue directly to the final steepening where the crack
closes, then finish with hard moves up and left.

THE NEEDLE

The Needle is marked as such on OS maps and is the obvious stack
on the south end of the cliffs forming the western seaboard of Hoy. An
excellent adventure. A grassy promontory juts out from the main cliffs
almost level with the top of the stack. The promontory forms the south
side of a deep narrow chasm or geo biting into the cliffs. An abseil stake
is in place at the end of this promontory.

The Needle 55m "Extremely Severe"   (1990)
Abseil for 60m directly into the sea in the geo. Swim across to ledges
on the far side and traverse round to opposite the stack. Swim across
to ledges on the south side.
1. 15m From the landward corner of the south side trend up leftwards
and then back right above overhangs to a good ledge.
2. 25m 5c Climb through the band of overhangs above at the obvious
place near the centre of the south face (crux) and trend right to a
shallow depression which leads to another good ledge.
3. 15m Move round onto the seaward face and climb to the summit.
Jumar back up to the cliff top or swim off to the south.

Shetland

Shetland has about 2000km of coastline, most of it wild and rugged with beautiful unspoilt scenery. The geology is very varied, with granite, diorite, andesite, gneiss, schist, serpentine and sandstone all represented. Despite this, areas suitable for climbing are surprisingly few as many of the sea-cliffs are shattered and very loose. There are a few inland outcrops, but while these are more sound they are very limited. Nevertheless, some of the crags have plenty of potential, and they are also remarkably free of the loathsome maalie, or fulmar. However, despite a recent catastrophic decline in Shetland's sea-bird population (perhaps the result of overfishing of sand eels), great skuas, arctic skuas and gulls all attempt to decapitate the climber while approaching the cliffs. Given the difficulties the sea-birds find themselves in, the visiting climber should, in spite of the provocation, avoid disturbing their colonies.

Most of the cliffs face west, and are thus exposed to the monumental gales which frequently sweep the islands. Approaches can also be a problem, since the foot of most climbs (except at the Grind of the Navir and at Pundsar) can only be reached by abseil. The crags described are mostly on Mainland, but there are plenty of crags on the other islands (accessible by ferry) which may repay exploration by the adventurous. In addition, the many impressive stacks (though not on the same scale as The Old Man of Hoy) have provided some serious climbing with hazardous approaches.

In case of accident, the local rescue services are efficient and equipped for cliff rescue. There is also a coastguard rescue helicopter based at Sumburgh. Although this was very rapidly on the scene of the only climbing accident so far in Shetland, it would be wise to take spare ropes and jumars and have some knowledge of self-rescue techniques.

THE ESHA NESS AREA

The Esha Ness peninsula of North-West Mainland has a huge potential for climbing. Andesitic tuffs and lavas form impressive 45m cliffs near the lighthouse, and rise to about 80m at the Faither. Bright red rhyolite outcrops at the Grind of the Navir provide more accessible and less austere climbing.

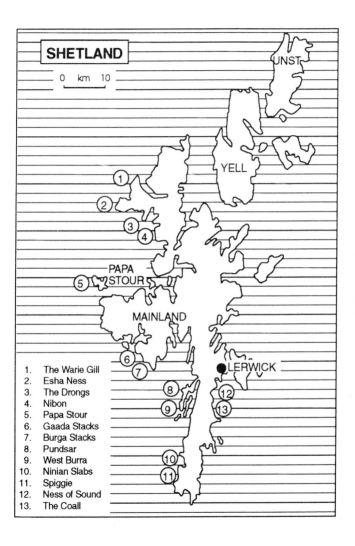

SHETLAND

0 km 10

UNST

YELL

PAPA STOUR

MAINLAND

LERWICK

1. The Warie Gill
2. Esha Ness
3. The Drongs
4. Nibon
5. Papa Stour
6. Gaada Stacks
7. Burga Stacks
8. Pundsar
9. West Burra
10. Ninian Slabs
11. Spiggie
12. Ness of Sound
13. The Coall

THE GRIND OF THE NAVIR   *(Map Ref 212 804)*

This peculiar little twin-towered headland has a complicated layout, giving 20m faces which are covered in good lines. The rhyolite is sound and very rough, sometimes excessively so near the top of the crag; the corruscated surface can crumble alarmingly at first touch. The cliffs take no drainage and have little vegetation, and the climbs are accessible in all but the highest tides by scrambling. Thus this is one of the most pleasant places to climb in Shetland, with routes ranging from Difficult to E4. Protection can sometimes be difficult to arrange; Friends and small wires should be carried. The quality of the climbing here is potentially the equal of any crag of its size in the country.

The quickest approach is from the cattle grid at Leascole (10 minutes). A slightly longer but less boggy approach is along the coast from Esha Ness lighthouse, past some ancient remains and the splendidly-named Hole of the Scraada. The routes are described from north to south.

CRYSTALOCEAN WALL

Spray   12m   Mild Severe   (1988)
Climb the grooves on the left edge to finish awkwardly up the steep corner.

Pickpocket   10m   E1 5a   (1989)
Follow Crystalocean to the blocks below the start of the crack, then break left to follow a line of pockets to the jutting block on the skyline.

Crystalocean   10m   E1 5c   (1988)
The fine, obvious and well protected finger-jamming crack up the centre.

Grindstone   10m   Severe   (1988)
Climb the right edge of the buttress to a niche, then move right and continue up the thin crack.

THE NORTH FACE

Restless Flame   20m   Severe   (1988)
At the centre of the north-facing wall is a short slab. Climb this then the wall above on small holds. A good but poorly protected route.

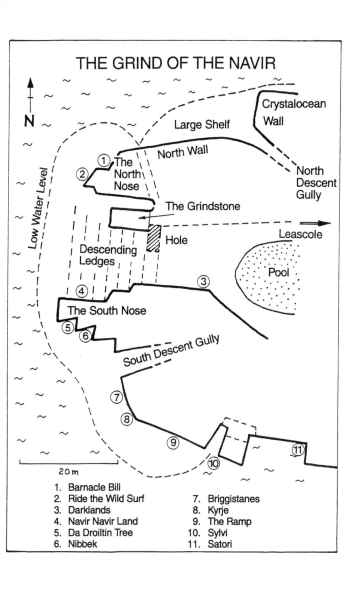

THE GRIND OF THE NAVIR

N

Crystalocean Wall

Large Shelf

North Wall

North Descent Gully

Low Water Level

① The North Nose
②

The Grindstone

Hole

Descending Ledges

Leascole

Pool

③ Darklands

④ ④

The South Nose

⑤ ⑥

South Descent Gully

⑦

⑧

⑨

⑩

⑪

20 m

1. Barnacle Bill
2. Ride the Wild Surf
3. Darklands
4. Navir Navir Land
5. Da Droiltin Tree
6. Nibbek

7. Briggistanes
8. Kyrje
9. The Ramp
10. Sylvi
11. Satori

Tenderness on the Block   20m   Severe   (1988)
Right of Restless Flame is a small slab at the bottom of the main face.
Climb the groove on its left front, then the blocky bay to a loose finish.
Not recommended.

THE NORTH NOSE

1   Barnacle Bill   15m   HVS 5b   (1988)
The obvious smooth corner on the north side of the North Nose. The
crux at 3m is poorly protected; above it the climbing is easier and
pleasant.

2   Ride the Wild Surf   20m   E1 5c   (1988)
Start up the pillar right of Tenderness on the Block and make a
problematic move to gain a ledge. Move right and follow the arete to
a slab, then climb its left edge to finish.

The Raven Banner   20m   HVS 5a   (1988)
Start just around the corner from Ride the Wild Surf. Climb the line of
shallow grooves until it is possible to move left onto the obvious square
protruding block. Finish up the slab.

THE GRINDSTONE
This is the obvious square pinnacle on the north side of the Grind itself;
not to be confused with the route of the same name on the Crystalocean Wall.

Piltock   15m   Severe   (1988)
The obvious crack up the gully wall of The Grindstone. Chimney up
between the crack and the wall until a shelf on the other side can be
gained. Lean back across and follow the crack to the top.

The Grindstone   15m   Difficult   (1986)
A good route up the slabby rib on the seaward side. Descend by
reversing, by abseil, or by a terrifying leap from suspect handholds on
the short side of the pinnacle.

Streams of Whiskey   15m   E3 5c   (1988)
The excellent crack up the south-west face of The Grindstone, above
the triangular niche, is strenuous and well protected.

Black Hole   10m   E1 5a   (1988)
The stepped line up the rib over the hole. Poorly protected.

THE SOUTH SIDE OF THE GRIND

3   Darklands   10m   Severe   (1988)
The short crack at the left (east) end of the face, finishing up the juggy
rib directly above.

Crack n'Up   15m   VS 4c   (1988)
A few metres right of Black Hole, just before this slabby wall falls back
into a series of corners, is a jam crack. Climb this until it is possible to
move right onto the arete. Climb the corner and finish up the wall
above. This route can also be started from the lower corner on the
right.

Pockets of Excellence   15m   VS 4b   (1988)
The left-bounding arete of The Groove of the Navir gives good but
unprotected climbing.

The Groove of the Navir   10m   VS 4b   (1988)
The obvious clean-cut groove. Well protected.

4   Navir-Navir Land   25m   E4 6a   (1988)
The magnificent north wall of the south nose has a crack running up
from a niche at one-third height. Start at the foot of The Groove of the
Navir. Climb the pocketed wall rightwards to a ledge. Place a nut
runner in the niche then climb pockets to its left to clip a peg runner
with difficulty. Traverse right on superb pockets to a large bowl-hold,
then gain a crack and follow it to the top. Superb and very sustained.

THE SOUTH DESCENT GULLY AREA
The area around the descent gully is the highest part of the crag and,
as most of the routes start from sea-level, it is more affected by tides
and weather. Note that the descent gully itself is about Very Difficult
in standard. The steep wall between it and the South Nose is dominated by two fine deep corners.

5   Da Droiltin Tree   20m   HVS 5a   (1989)
An excellent, sustained and well protected route up the left-hand
corner.

6   Nibbek   20m   E1 5b   (1989)
The overhanging right-hand corner. An awkward start leads to fine
jamming and bridging up to the obvious block on the right rib. Move
up into the little niche and finish directly up the bulge on excellent holds.
A superb, well protected route.

7   Briggistanes   20m   Severe   (1988)
This climb wanders up the slabby wall immediately right of the descent
gully. Follow a line of good holds more or less straight up, and where
the wall steepens move up into the scoop using the thin crack on the
right. Traverse right into the corner and finish up it.

8   Kyrje   20m   E2 5c   (1991)
The wall is bounded to its right by a blunt rib. This fine climb takes the
thin crack immediately left of the rib.

Northern Soul   20m   VS 4c   (1989)
This climbs the left-hand of the two obvious cracks to the right of the
rib. From the junction with the ramp continue up the obvious crack and
smooth groove.

The Stile   20m   HVS 5b   (1988)
Climb the right-hand crack to its junction with the ramp. Ignore the
easier lines to the left and right and launch boldly up the blocky nose
above. Excellent climbing, but a bit contrived.

9   The Ramp   25m   Very Difficult   (1988)
A pleasant route which follows the line of good holds up the wall right
of The Stile. Where it steepens, head left up the slabby ramp to a
variety of finishes. The short steep corner on the right of the rib of The
Stile gives a direct finish; Mild Severe. It is also possible to finish by
moving right at the steepening, then around back left; Very Difficult.

The platform beneath these routes peters out just before the large
semi-detached pillar. The next route starts from the ledge on the
south-west corner of the pillar, which is reached by abseil.

10   Sylvi   15m   VS 4b   (1991)
Climb up a few metres then move left across the slab and round the
corner. Move up and left across the wall to a ledge, then follow the thin
crack to the top.

Further on is the South Wing, which is reached by abseil or by descending Rib Tickler. A good view can be had from the little promontory to the south. At its left end is the semi-detached pillar described above; right of this is a bay bounded on its right by the fine corner up which Satori starts.

The Udge   20m   E1 5b   (1991)
The obvious crack just left of the corner gives excellent climbing which is spoilt by the ease of escape. Climb the crack in its entirety to the right end of the glacis of Satori. From here a horrible "udge" move over the block on the right leads to the finish.

11   Satori   25m   VS 5a   (1991)
Climb the corner until it starts to overhang, then exit left across The Udge and up to a little glacis which leads off left.

Rib Tickler   10m   Very Difficult   (1989)
The left-hand of the two ribs at the right end of the wall, finishing nicely up the little juggy nose.

ESHA NESS LIGHTHOUSE   *(Map Ref 204 784)*

A line of magnificent cliffs, about 45m high, lies just south-west of the lighthouse, with the nearest routes just 100 metres from the car park. Stunning lines abound, and the rock is mostly just on the right side of vertical with an abundance of big pockets and knobs. Some of the rock is clean and sound, and although the climbs look ridiculously hard, the routes follow crack lines with good holds and protection. The lack of ledges at the foot of the cliffs and the heavy swell of the boiling sea makes for an intimidating atmosphere on first aquaintance. Approach from the lighthouse and find a hole leading down to the sea where the rock has been stained white by discarded carbide from the lighthouse. White Noise takes the obvious corner just south-west of this and is a useful landmark.

Mary   35m   VS 4c   (1988)
A few metres north of White Noise an exposed rib descends to the sea from a shallow bay at the top of the cliff. Abseil from this to a ledge about 3m above the sea. Follow the rib to half-height, then move right and climb the scoop. The rock requires care on the upper section.

White Noise   25m   VS 4c   (1988)
The obvious clean-cut corner. Abseil to a small ledge left of the corner,
by a cave below a rock scar. Climb the chimney to reach the corner,
then follow this to the top.

Cruel Sea   25m   VS 4c   (1988)
The obvious elegant small right-facing corner just right of White Noise.
Abseil to good small ledges about 15m above the sea and just right
of the corner. Move into the corner and climb it to the top.

   The next routes lie about 50 metres further south-west, close to an
obvious slabby chimney-diedre which is split by a diagonal crack.

Atlantic City   35m   Hard Severe   (1988)
The slabby chimney-diedre. Abseil to ledges just above seaweed level,
then climb the excellent diedre to the top on good rock.

Black Watch   30m   HVS 4c   (1988)
Abseil to a good ledge below and left of the stunning diagonal crack.
Ascend 3m then hand traverse into the crack; climb it to the top. The
rock requires care, but protection is quite good.

Mhairi   35m   Hard Severe   (1989)
About 15 metres further south is a fine rib, identified by a short
left-facing corner at the top. The climb starts from a tiny ledge just
above the sea (belay to the abseil rope). Climb the rib for 15m, then
move right and back left to finish up the left-facing corner.

   South again is a slabby north-facing wall with some overhangs in
its centre. The next route takes the crack at its right-hand end.

Bubblebox   35m   Mild Severe or E3   (1990)
Abseil down the route to lodge in a slimy slit just above the sea. The
route proper starts from the ledge above, which can be gained by any
means that seem appropriate. From here the line is obvious and on
deteriorating rock.

THE WARIE GILL   *(Map Ref 238 833)*

This is a scenic spot where the Burn of Tingon falls into the sea. The
routes lie just south of the Falls, above a large platform, which is

perhaps best reached by abseil (although it is possible to scramble down the short wall and steps at the south end). Most routes are on fine rock but are poorly protected.

Vampire 10m Severe (1988)
Descend an easy rib just left of Silly Arete and go over to climb the thin corner-crack, the furthest line left on the wall before it curves round to face the sea.

Silly Arete 5m Difficult (1988)
The hanging arete suspended above the arch. Descend the chimney on its right, step across onto the bottom foothold, then climb the arete on large holds.

Jet 20m Hard Severe (1988)
The fine obvious corner, gained from the south. Finish straight up the slab above on large pockets.

Bosse-Cat 20m Hard Severe (1988)
A good steep line with big holds. The bulging corner slants right to a pedestal. Step left to climb the final short hanging corner.

Grot-Ville 15m Very Difficult (1988)
A poor route up the right-hand of the twin faults which split the crag.

Wall of Sound 15m E1 5a (1988)
The fine wall with well-spaced protection. Start just left of a funny grey hole. Climb the wall directly, past a peg runner, to finish up a short vague corner.

Lost Volcano 15m VS 4b (1988)
A line of right-trending scoops right of Wall of Sound.

Orange Utang 10m Hard Severe (1988)
Climb directly up the left side of the orange oblong, then go up the wall above.

Purple Haze 10m VS 4b (1988)
Climb over two small overlaps, then the wall directly.

Rock Lobster 10m Very Difficult (1988)
The stepped crack just left of the descent.

The north side of Warie Gill is a small headland with an arch through it; its northern side has some fine corners at its right-hand end. Access is by abseil to the large slabby buttress which divides the wall.

Duckbreaker   30m   Mild VS   (1990)
A worthwhile climb up the obvious narrowing chimney. After a poorly protected start, fine bridging leads to a large rock alcove. Continue to an exposed finish on suspect rock with only just adequate protection.

Serpent's Kiss   30m   Mild VS 4b   (1988)
This takes the big obvious corner on the impressive west-facing wall a little further north. Abseil from a block to a ledge below and left of the corner. Go up right to a ledge then climb the corner to the top, passing another small ledge at half-height.

About 200 metres south of Rock Lobster is an area of slab and south-facing corners, which give easy, well protected climbs on good rock. The area is best identified as being immediately south of a north-west to south-east trending gash in the cliffs. Access is by abseil to a ledge at the bottom, or descend Bol.

Bol   15m   Difficult   (1990)
Traverse left from the ledge and climb the large corner on the left.

Crocus   15m   Very Difficult   (1990)
Start up the short crack in the wall at the left end of the ledge, then continue up left to to the crack up the middle of the slab.

Spring Fever   15m   Severe   (1990)
The corner above the start of Crocus.

Blocky Rib   15m   Very Difficult   (1990)
From the foot of Spring Fever, move diagonally right to gain and climb the blocky rib.

NIBON   *(Map Ref 299 722)*

The coast between Gunnister and Mangaster Voes contains some impressive 60m cliffs of diorite with red microgranite intrusions. Whilst the diorite is fairly sound, the microgranite is very loose, so the routes try to avoid it. The development so far has only scratched the surface and many excellent lines remain unclimbed. The climbing area begins after the second burn after leaving the road end at Nibon. An aid to orientation is the obvious protuding buttress, which is visible from Nibon, and is part of the geo containing Slice of Life. The routes are described from north to south.

Off the Spike   15m   Severe   (1988)
The north-bounding corner of the grey pillar.

Lapdog   15m   E1 5b   (1988)
The next wall immediately right has a left-slanting crack which passes through two small overlaps. This gives good well protected but escapable climbing. From the foot of Off the Spike, traverse right across the slab to below the first overlap, then move up and round it. Move left and then up and right over the second overlap. Follow the crack leftwards and finish by the block just right of Off the Spike.

There is an easy descent route down the south-bounding corner of the pillar, which leads to routes on the next wall south.

Gunnister Rib   10m   Severe   (1986)
The rib right of the short left-facing corner near the left end of the wall. Zigzag up the wall below until it is possible to step left onto the rib proper.

The Flakes   10m   VS 4c   (1987)
The obvious line 10 metres right of Gunnister Rib gives a strenuous but well protected climb.

Borderline   10m   VS 4b   (1987)
Just right of The Flakes is a right-facing groove at the junction of two rock types. Traverse right to gain it, then continue (avoiding touching the red granite as much as possible).

Jerome   15m   Difficult   (1987)
This climb spirals up from left to right on the front of the pillar at the end (south) of the wall.

Empire of the Sun   15m   E2 5c   (1988)
This bold climb takes thin blind grooves up the centre of the wall left of Thule Groove. Fine but escapable climbing.

Thule Groove   15m   VS 4c   (1987)
This fine and well protected route takes the obvious corner bounding
the south side of the bay south of the pillar of Jerome.

Black Magic   15m   E2 5c   (1988)
Climb Thule Groove to a ledge, then step right and climb the thin crack
and rib to the top. Good climbing, but protection is widely-spaced.

Bootie   15m   Hard Severe   (1987)
The 'mirror image' corner of Thule Groove, right of the pillar.

   The next feature south is a large geo, whose south side consists of
a 45m steep slab above a glacis. Access is by abseil, either down the
centre of the slab or down Puissance.

Puissance   45m   VS 4c   (1989)
An excellent varied route up the slabby corner bounding the left side
of the slab. Climb the corner for a few metres until it is possible to
traverse delicately left to a small ledge. Continue up to a large ledge,
and from its left end swing up right on good holds. Continue to a niche
below a prominent crack. Now climb the corner, moving left on superb
holds below the overhang. Continue up the general line of the corner,
keeping to the right wall to avoid dubious rock.

Celandine   45m   HVS 5b   (1990)
A fine climb on good rock, with a serious and unobvious middle section.
Start at the left side of a pillar which reaches down to the glacis, right
of the undercut section of slab. Climb the short left-sloping groove
(crux) to a ledge. Continue up the crack until it is possible to traverse
right to a ledge below a short pink wall. Climb this on good holds, then
move right and up to a ledge on the rib (junction with JLS). The obvious
corner-crack above provides a good and well protected finish.

JLS   45m   Severe   (1988)
The line of least resistance up the middle of the slab, with the traditional
benefits of loose rock, poor protection and resident fulmars. Start up
the right-facing corner right of the pillar, then move left onto the rib at
about 10m. Continue to a belay on the right, then trend up and left
over two sets of large perched blocks to a ledge. Finish straight up.

Spaelimenninir 45m   VS 4b   (1988)
Climb JLS to a belay above the corner, then continue up the obvious
wide crack line; not well protected.

Slice of Life 40m   HVS 4c   (1988)
Around to the right of the slab is a large (unclimbed) groove which
faces out to sea; right again is another geo, the south side of which
comprises the prominent buttress seen from Nibon. This route lies on
the south-facing side of this geo, which has a prominent pink band
near the top. Approach by abseil. Start just left of centre and climb the
overhang on big holds. Continue up the obvious line until a 3m traverse
leads to a crack. Follow this and go slightly left to finish up a corner.
The upper half is rather loose and poorly protected.

About 200 metres south, below the highest point of the cliff at Map
Ref 301 718, is another geo with an impressive back wall. This
provides the best routes at Nibon. Whilst the rock is the soundest
hereabouts, it still requires some care. Approach by abseil down the
corner at the south side of the geo.

Nibon Crack 30m   HVS 5b   (1992)
The north wall of the geo is smooth and overhanging, and is bounded
towards its seaward side by a steep crack. Abseil to its foot on the right
(looking down). Climb the crack with a brief venture onto the steep
wall on the right to pass an awkward section at two-thirds height.

Cattle Rustler 40m   E1   (1992)
Start roughly in the centre of the back wall of the geo.
1. 15m 5b Climb an overhanging right-slanting crack to ledges.
2. 25m 4c Traverse easily right, then climb a left-facing corner. Pull
out right at its capping roof and finish straight up.

Atlantic Hits 45m   E2   (1992)
Start between Cattle Rustler and Quiet City, just left of a corner.
1. 25m 5b Climb up to reach a spectacular flake line which leads left
across the overhanging wall. Pull awkwardly out left to join Cattle
Rustler. Leave it to climb the right side of the pedestal.
2. 20m 5c It is now possible to go diagonally right to rejoin Cattle
Rustler (5a). Instead, climb straight up the slab of Quiet City, then
continue up a big right-facing corner to its top. Traverse out left to pass
the capping roof (crux) and finish more easily.

Quiet City 50m HVS 4c (1991)
Start at the bottom right of the geo, and climb up and left towards a pedestal in the middle of the wall (below a blunt rib). Traverse left below the pedestal, then up right to a belay on its top. Climb straight up the steep slab to the overlap, then move left onto the rib and follow it to the top.

Hermless 60m VS 4b (1992)
This climbs the right-bounding corner of the geo. Start at the left-facing corner of Atlantic Hits, climb this and continue to easier rocks. Go up and right to join the main corner at a large sloping ledge, then follow the corner to the top.

Mincing with Charlie 25m HVS 5a (1992)
This crosses the black wall bounding the right side of the geo. From the right edge of the large sloping ledge of Hermless, step right onto the wall, follow the crack for a few feet, then traverse right and out to the rib. Step round this to belay in a bay below a dodgy-looking overhang. Climb round this to the left, quickly.

PUNDSAR *(Map Ref 365 353)*

This little peninsula, just south of Hamnavoe on Burra-Isle, sports a complex of short faces up to 6m high made of perfect rough granite. Accessible, beautifully situated and quick-drying, they have been covered with routes of all standards up to 6b which the visitor will enjoy rediscovering.

NINIAN SLABS *(Map Ref 374 196)*

These metamorphic slabs provide interesting middle-grade routes, which are approached by abseil to a sea-swept ledge at their foot.

Windward 25m Severe (1988)
The prominent open corner at the north end of the slabs is initially easy, but is delicate to finish.

Black Heart 25m Hard Severe (1988)
Climb the prominent blank section, mid-way along the slabs, to reach a shallow groove. Follow this to a short steep wall which is climbed on good holds to the top.

Atlantic Dance 30m VS 4c   (1988)
Start as for Black Heart, then make a long traverse from the groove
out to the edge of the slabs, stepping down at the quartzite band.
Surmount the overlap then continue easily to the top.

SPIGGIE AREA

Between the Corbie Geo and Fora Ness is a line of pink granite cliffs
which reach a maximum height of 80m. The following climbs have
been recorded on the north side of Corbie Geo (Map Ref 357 172).
Unfortunately, although the situations are superb the rock is frighten-
ingly loose; it seems best to avoid the holds and pad up on friction.

Future Shock 65m VS   (1988)
From the large boulder at the west end of the cliff abseil 50m to a small
ledge. Now traverse 30m right to a poor stance at the base of a
prominent corner. Climb the corner, then follow a thin crack to another
poor stance. Now climb a shallow corner and loose blocks to the top.

Etive Enui 60m VS   (1988)
An extended diagonal abseil from the same boulder leads to an
obvious large ledge about 45m above the sea. From here climb more
or less straight up to the base of the corner of Future Shock. Move
right to the arete then climb straight up to the top.

Push, Don't Pull 60m VS   (1988)
Start from the ledge of Etive Enui. Traverse diagonally right to below
a right-facing corner (poor belay on the ramp on the right). Continue
to the top by the line of least resistance.

FAIR ISLE

This is an excellent place to spend a few days, with beautiful scenery,
interesting birdlife and friendly people. Generally the rock is of limited
interest to the climber, although new route possibilities exist on Sheep
Craig's seaward slab and the offshore slab on the south-west edge of
the island. Elsewhere, the rock is generally poor, although sea-level
traverses are available, particularly just south of Sheep Craig. The
following worthwhile route climbs the steep south-west face of Sheep
Craig, and takes you to its rarely visited summit.

The Good Shepherd   170m   E3   (1991)

An exciting climb with something of an expedition air. The rock is surprisingly solid, but care should be taken and pegs carried. From the mainland opposite Sheep Craig, make a 110m abseil from a rabbit hole (or bring your own stake). It is also possible, but worrying, to scramble down. Depending on the state of the tide, cross the boulder beach and belay on a ramp in a short corner which leads past bird colonies.

1. 45m 4b Climb the short wall which avoids the birds and walk up the easy-angled slope diagonally right to belay behind a large boulder.
2. 50m 4a Climb easy slabby rock diagonally right, passing a constriction of the slab and heading for the base of an obvious corner-groove. Nut and peg belay.
3. 20m 5a Make a bold swing over the bulge above the belay, then move up the groove with interest to a large ledge. Step left and climb the short wall to a smaller ledge at the base of a wide flake crack 5m left of the dirty corner.
4. 20m 5b Climb the flake crack for 15m to a spike, then traverse 5m left to a ledge and nut belay. A good pitch.
5. 35m 5a Climb the obvious slabby groove rightwards to a small ledge and good runners. Now move up left to the top, taking care with the rock. Watch out for vomiting fulmars.

QUARFF TO FLADDABISTER

The coast between these two hamlets, about 8km south of Lerwick, includes a hill called The Coall. There are some interesting-looking cliffs here, up to 30m high, as well as two fine stacks. The more northerly of these has been climbed at Mild VS on rather friable and bird-infested rock. Just north of Easter Quarff, at Map Ref 435 534, is a rather squat schist stack. The north-east arete of this gives **Distant Storm**, 25m Hard Severe.

BURRA

The west coast of West Burra has a large extent of interesting metamorphic cliffs, with some easy slabby routes just south of Banna Minn (The Womni Geo; Map Ref 360 305). There is scope for harder climbs both here and further north, around Whale Wick and the Ramna Geo.

LERWICK

The sandstone cliffs on the west side of the Knab, though variable in quality, offer some delightful short routes, suitable as a fine evening playground. One area, distinguishable by its extraordinary calcite crystals, offers longer routes of up to 25m and up to VS in difficulty. The Sletts, just below Lerwick Hotel, gives some interesting soloing on sound rock (but with nasty landings).

NESS OF SOUND *(Map Ref 470 387)*

This peninsula, which lies just outside Lerwick, sports a number cliffs of variable sandstone, the best of which is Dainaberg. It is 30m high, faces south-east and consists of two facets, the left one vertical with a blunt rib on its right side. This separates it from the right facet, which consists of an area of overhangs surmounted by a steep slab. The rock is generally good and sometimes superb. Approach is by abseil from two bolts at the top, but it is also possible to scramble in unpleasantly from the left. The following route starts about 10 metres right of the rib.

The New Squids on the Block   30m   E5 6a   (1991)
An excellent pitch offering bold and unusual climbing, strangely reminiscent of gritstone. It is fairly low in the grade. Step across the channel and move up on pebbles to a niche below the first overhang. Weave up through a further three sets of ramps and overhangs, eventually pulling out left to a slab. Climb this more or less direct to the top, with dubious protection.

Feeler Gauge   30m   VS 4b   (1991)
At the left end of the left section of the crag is a large bay with a diedre at its back. Enter the bay via the blocky crack at bottom left. From the right corner of the bay move up round the right rib, then climb diagonally up right to a line of cracks. Climb these, then traverse left and up over loose blocks to finish. A good though slightly worrying climb.

HURDA FIELD *(Map Ref 339 697)*

The small granite outcrops on the east side of the road just north of Mavis Grind provide some fun bouldering.

THE STANES OF STOFAST   *(Map Ref 508 716)*

These comprise a collection of large gneiss erratics in a fine situation. There are plenty of problems of up to 6m, usually with good landings, but they would benefit from some cleaning. The whole of the Lunna Peninsula, and also Lunning to the south, contain many boulder-size outcrops which are fun to explore on a summer's evening when you get fed up with the sea.

SHETLAND SEA-STACKS

The sea-stacks of Shetland provide some exciting and serious adventures, usually approached by boat. It is worth noting that Shetland waters are rather notorious, and that the first ascensionists are experienced hands at the art of inflatable-aided stack de-flowering. Due to the difficulty of fitting this type of expedition into the normal rock climbing grading system, some of the harder climbs have been given "Fowler" grades, which indicate that technical proficiency and determination are not the only requirements for a safe and successful ascent.

PAPA STOER

The Foot (The Spindle)   35m   XS 5c   (1992)
This superb stack, which is narrower at its base than at the top, is situated at Map Ref 144 612. The climb takes the south side, that facing away from Lyra Skerry. Start near the left side of the face. A short crack and step right leads to a small ledge and stance. Trend rightwards up the overhanging wall to gain a shallow groove which leads to the top. Several peg runners were used.

Lyra Skerry   Mild Severe   (1992)
Climb this by the only line not overhanging or vertical, up the ramp opposite The Foot.

Lyra Stack   35m   HVS 5a   (1992)
The route goes up the right side of the wall facing Lyra Skerry. A series of steps lead leftwards into a steep crack, which is left of a wider corner crack on the right edge of the wall. Several Friends 2 to 3 were used.

THE DRONGS

This is the well-known and spectacular set of stacks off the Ness of Hillswick, Map Ref 260 755.

Main Drong   60m   Mild XS   (1992)
Evidence of a previous abseil descent indicated that this had been climbed previously by a route unknown. This route takes the north-east face via an obvious left-rising line. Start just right of the gap which separates the main summit from a slightly lower one.
1. 50m 5b   Easy steps lead to an awkward corner. Continue to the crest of the ridge and follow this easily to the lower summit.
2. 10m 4c   Descend into the gap, then climb the summit tower on its right side.

Slender Drong   30m   XS 5b/c   (1992)
A fine climb up the south face. Start at the extreme left end of the south face at a sea-washed greasy groove. Climb the groove, then trend right under large overhangs to reach a shallow cave. Escape left through the overhang, then climb a steep crack to a ledge. Move out left and ascend the final wall on surprisingly good rock.

Slim Drong   15m   VS 5a   (1992)
Climb a shallow corner on the landward (east) side.

Stumpy Drong   15m   Severe   (1992)
Climb the obvious line on the seaward (left) side.

OTHER STACKS

The following assorted stacks are identified by their map references.

Muckle Roe Stack   25m   HVS 4c   (1992)
Map Ref 299 659
This is a fine stack at the outer end of an inlet of the Hamms of Roe. Approach by abseil and swimming. Climb the landward side by a series of steps and a flake, then move right at the top. It is possible to fix a Tyrolean to return.

The Runk   45m   HVS   (1992)
Map Ref 254 774
1. 30m 4c   Start at the north-west end on the seaward side. Climb a right-slanting groove to a col.
2. 15m 5a   Cross to the landward side, then climb a shallow corner to the top.

Harry's Pund   35m   Hard Severe   (1992)
Map Ref 266 772
Start up the south-west arete, then traverse the seaward side leftwards
to gain the top of the south-east arete.

S.P. Stack   25m   Very Difficult   (1992)
Map Ref 263 767
Climb the bizarre leaning slender stack by its low-angled side.

Gaada Stacks
Map Ref 237 453
All five have been climbed, the most notable being the stack
nearest the land, and another with an obvious tall block on its top.
Both are Severe. The largest stack provides a traverse over an arch
(Very Difficult). The other two stacks are easier.

Burga Stacks
Map Ref 255 442
There are three stacks here. The most landward can be climbed by
its north-west arete (Difficult). The south arete of the central stack is
Severe, and the seaward stack with an arch can be climbed by a line
at its east end, traversed, then descended to the west (Severe).

Westwick Stacks
Map Ref 277 420
The more westerly of these two flat-topped stacks can be climbed by
its north side (Very Difficult). The other is Severe via its north-west
side.

The Cutter   30m   HVS 4c   (1992)
Map Ref 273 422
This is a knife-edged stack between the island of Giltarump and the
mainland. Climb a groove just left of the south-east arete.

Stack of the Ship   80m   Very Difficult   (1992)
Map Ref 359 210
On the west coast of St. Ninian's Isle, opposite the island of Hich
Home, lies a stack which is linked to the mainland by a knife-edged
arete. Traverse the exposed arete, then climb a short steep wall to the
top. Beware of fulmars.

List of First Ascents

The first ascensionists are listed, where known, area by area in the order of the preceding chapters.

Sgurr na Lapaich

W 1978 25 Feb	Deer-Grass Gully	J.R.Mackenzie, D.Langudge
W 1989 22 Dec	Lapland Buttress	J.Lyall, A.Nisbet

An Riabhachan

W 1969 12 Apr	Spindrift Gully	D.Smith, J.G.Stewart

Coire Toll a'Mhuic

W 1978 22 Jan	Sea Pink Gully	T.Anderson, J.R.Mackenzie
W 1978 15 Feb	Red Campion	J.R.Mackenzie
W 1978 15 Feb	Enchanters Nightshade	J.R.Mackenzie
W 1978 18 Feb	Streaky	J.Smith, J.R.Mackenzie
W 1978 19 Feb	Trotters Gully	J.R.Mackenzie, T.Anderson
W 1978 19 Mar	Pigsty Gully	J.R.Mackenzie, C.Norman
W 1979 18 Feb	Best Back	J.R.Mackenzie, D.McCallum

Glenmarksie Crag

S 1970s	Greased Lightning	I. Ruscoe and Inverness MC
S 1979 4 Jun	Dog Leg	M.Birch, D.Gilbert, J.R.Mackenzie
S 1979 18 Jun	Wild Mint	D.Butterfield, J.R.Mackenzie, D.McCallum
S 1979 30 Jun	Six Trees, Walk on By	J.R.Mackenzie, D.McCallum.
S 1979 3 Jul	The Juggler	M.Birch, J.R.Mackenzie
S 1979 23 Sep	Small Wall Thins	J.R.Mackenzie, D.Gilbert
	Two Step	D.Gilbert, J.R.Mackenzie
	Staircase	D.Gilbert, J.R.Mackenzie
	Kojak	J.R.Mackenzie
S 1979 27 Oct	Dog Mantle	M.Birch, J.R.Mackenzie
S 1979	Clutch and Thrutch	J.R.Mackenzie
S 1979	A Touch of Class	J.R.Mackenzie
S 1980 26 Apr	Hiroshima Grooves	J.R.Mackenzie, D.Butterfield
	Proteus	J.R.Mackenzie
	Trade Route	D.Butterfield, J.R.Mackenzie
	Central Groove	J.R.Mackenzie, D.Butterfield
S 1982	Callisto	B.McDermott, D.Butterfield
	Variant: Polish Peacemaker R.Brown, C.White 10 June 1989	
S 1982	An Feur Ghorta	B.McDermott, D.Butterfield

Variant: Sickle Moon J.R.Mackenzie, G.Cullen 25 November 1989
S 1982   An Fear Feusagach   B.McDermott, D.Butterfield
Variant: Selene G.Cullen, J.R.Mackenzie 25 November 1989

S 1989 19 Jun	Phobos	J.R.Mackenzie, R.Brown
S 1989 26 Aug	Strategic Arms Limitation	J.R.Mackenzie, R.Brown
S 1989 10 Sep	Deimos	J.R.Mackenzie, R.Brown

Direct version: 24 August 1990

S 1989 30 Sep	Gritstone Corner	J.R.Mackenzie, P.Figg
S 1990 12 Mar	Sea of Tranquillity	J.R.Mackenzie, G.Cullen
S 1990 22 Apr	Dynamite	R.Brown, J.R.Mackenzie
S 1990 3 Jun	Little Teaser	J.R.Mackenzie, R.Brown
S 1990 10 Jun	Dogg'Edd	G.Cullen, P.Whitefield

Direct version: G.Cullen, J.R.Mackenzie, R.Brown 17 July 1990

S 1990 16 Sep	A Bit on the Side	J.R.Mackenzie, R.Brown
	Powder Monkey	J.R.Mackenzie, R.Brown
S 1990 10 Oct	Pom	J.R.Mackenzie, G.Cullen
S 1991 14 Apr	Right Unprintable	J.R.Mackenzie, R.Brown

Scatwell River Slabs

Most lines were climbed by M.Birch, D.Butterfield and B.McDermott in the 1980s.

Scatwell Upper Slabs

S 1990 18 Mar	Stranger than Friction	R.Brown, J.R.Mackenzie
S 1990 Summer	Early Learning Centre	G.Cullen, J.R.MacKenzie
S 1990 23 Sep	Bushwackers Slab	J.R.Mackenzie, A.Walker
	Walkers Farewell	A.Walker, J.R.Mackenzie
	Bonzai Wall	J.R.Mackenzie, A.Walker
S 1992 1 Aug	Legless Lizard	M.Hind, S.Lockhard
	Slow Worm	
S 1992 2 Aug	Strawberry Ripple	M.Hind
	Coffin Slab	
	Ready and Waiting	
	Alive and Kicking	
	Easy Going	
S 1992 4 Aug	Pipestrelle Cracks	M.Hind, S.Lockhard
S 1992 10 Aug	Gardener's Question Time	J.R.MacKenzie, C.Fox
S 1992 14 Aug	Friction with Strangers	J.R.MacKenzie, R.Brown
	Stretch	R.Brown, J.R.MacKenzie

Meig Crag

S 1979 30 Jun	Meig Corner	J.R.Mackenzie, D.McCallum
	The Balance	J.R.Mackenzie, D.McCallum
	Shy Brides Crack	D.McCallum, J.R.Mackenzie
S 1991 23 May	The Birch	J.R.Mackenzie, M.Hind
S 1991 23 May	Limited Liability	M.Hind, J.R.Mackenzie
S 1991 21 Aug	Erection Crack	J.R.Mackenzie, G.Cullen, M.Hind
S 1991 1 Sep	Correction	R.Brown, T.W.Brown
S 1991 11 Sep	Nicked In Time	M.Hind
S 1991 Summer	The Rake	M.Hind
S 1992 19 Jan	Angst Arete	J.R.Mackenzie, R.Brown, G.Cullen
S 1992 28 Jan	Lone Pine Groove	G.Cullen, J.R.Mackenzie
S 1992 13 May	Sidewinder	M.Hind
S 1992 13 May	The Go-Between	M.Hind, R.Scott
S 1992 10 Jun	Yellow Streak	M.Hind, R.Brown
S 1992 11 Jun	Gabbro Slab	J.R.Mackenzie, G.Cullen
S 1992 14 Jun	The Wee Nibble	M.Hind, J.R.Mackenzie
S 1992 2 Jul	The Promenade	M.Hind
S 1992 3 Jul	Dancing in the Rain	M.Hind, J.R.Mackenzie
S 1992 Jul	Sidestep	M.Hind
S 1992 31 Jul	Blueberry Hill	M.Hind, S.Lockhart

Aspen Crag

S 1991 23 Jun	Meridian, The Aspen	J.R.Mackenzie, G.Cullen
S 1991 23 Jun	Burlesque Crack	G.Cullen, J.R.Mackenzie
S 1991 28 Jun	Icturus	R.Brown, J.R.Mackenzie
S 1991 3 Jul	Tantalus Groove	M.Hind, J.R.Mackenzie
S 1991 3 Jul	Shadow Grasper	J.R.Mackenzie, M.Hind
S 1991 17 Jul	Mac The Knife	M.Hind, J.R.Mackenzie
S 1991 17 Jul	Creeping Stealth, Mid-Flight Crisis	J.R.Mackenzie, M.Hind
S 1991 Aug	Chocks Away	M.Hind
S 1991 8 Sep	Underneath the Arches	M.Hind
S 1991 8 Sep	Jumping Jack Flash, Rock and Roll Suicide	M.Hind
S 1991 21 Sep	Uncertain Voyage	J.R.Mackenzie, R.Brown
S 1992 29 Apr	Sloshed in Action	J.R.Mackenzie, M.Hind
S 1992 29 Apr	Licking the Lip	R.Brown, J.R.Mackenzie
S 1992 16 May	Gobstopper	R.Brown, J.R.Mackenzie
S 1992 22 Aug	The Dark Side of the Moon	M.Hind, R.Brown
	Woolly Jumper	

Dam Crag

S	1991 15 May	Simple Delights	G.Cullen, J.R.Mackenzie
S	1991 17 May	The Gulf Crisis	M.Hind, J.R.Mackenzie
S	1992 Summer	Thick as a Brick	M.Hind

Sgurr a'Mhuilinn, Creag Ghlas

S	1967 Aug	Oh Dear	J.Renny, M.Strong
S	1967 Aug	The Lizard	D.Bathgate, R.N.Campbell
		The Loop Pitch: M.Selwood, J.R.Mackenzie 28 July 1990	
S	1978 28 May	Boulder and Bolder	M.Birch, J.R.Mackenzie
S	1979 2 Oct	Spare Rib	R.McHardy, J.R.Mackenzie
S	1980 15 May	Sweet Charity	J.R.Mackenzie, D.Butterfield
S	1991 25 Aug	Whoops	G.Cullen, J.R.Mackenzie
S	1992 20 May	Evening Arete	R.Brown, J.R.Mackenzie
S	1992 7 Jun	Wandering Minstrel	M.Hind
S	1992 7 Jun	Glass Slipper	R.Brown, J.R.Mackenzie, M.Hind
S	1992 Jul	The Big Trundle	M.Hind, R.Brown

Sgurr a' Ghlas Leathaid

W	1971 5 Jan	Lady's Gully	Mrs N.Tennent, J.R.Mackenzie

Creag a' Ghlastail

S	1989 24 Sep	The Curate's Egg	J.R.Mackenzie, R.Brown
W	1990 16 Feb	Ghlastail GTX	G.Cullen, J.R.Mackenzie
W	1991 17 Feb	Three Stroke Gully	G.Cullen, J.R.Mackenzie, M.Hind

Raven's Rock and Raven's Rock Quarry

S	1970 22 Jun	Ravens Squawk	J.R.Mackenzie, A.Finlay-Sherris
S	1970	Pad Slab	J.R.Mackenzie, R.Richard
S	1971 18 Sep	Scorpion	J.R.Mackenzie, A.Ross
S	1971	Rejector	J.R.Mackenzie
S	1978 14 Jan	The Chimney	J.R.Mackenzie, T.Anderson
S	1978 23 Apr	Tombstone Buttress	J.R.Mackenzie, M.Birch
S	1978 May	Cavalcade Wall	J.Smith, T.Anderson, R.Brown, C.Fraser, J.R.Mackenzie
S	1978 2 Jul	Zigzag	J.R.Mackenzie
S	1978 7 Jul	The Croak	J.R.Mackenzie, M.Birch
S	1978 16 Jul	The Sting	J.R.Mackenzie, M.Birch
S	1978 12 Aug	Ravens Horror	J.R.Mackenzie
S	1978 8 Sep	Raspberry Traverse	R.Brown, J.R.Mackenzie
S	1978 16 Sep	Archenemy	J.R.Mackenzie, M.Birch
		The Corner	M.Birch, J.R.Mackenzie

S 1978 23 Sep	Kingfisher	J.R.Mackenzie, F.Adams
	Black Crack	F.Adams, J.R.Mackenzie
	Black Wall	J.R.Mackenzie
	Midgit Corner	F.Adams, J.R.Mackenzie
S 1978 17 Nov	Roots	R.Brown, J.R.Mackenzie
S 1978	Acceptor	J.R.Mackenzie
W 1978	Centre Fall	R.Brown, J.R.Mackenzie
S 1979 27 Jul	Jacobite Wall	J.R.Mackenzie, P.Goodwin
S 1979 29 Jul	Shorty	P.Goodwin, J.R.Mackenzie
S 1980 13 May	Close to the Edge	J.R.Mackenzie, M.Birch
S 1980 9 Aug	Bone Idle	J.R.Mackenzie, R.Brown
S 1980 Summer	Fancy Tickler	C.Roylance, J.R.Mackenzie
S 1980 Summer	Obituary	D.McCallum, D.Butterfield
S 1981 27 Jun	Ejector	J.R.Mackenzie

Red Rock

S 1978 21 Apr	Red Wall Grooves	J.R.Mackenzie, M.Birch

Moy Rock

S 1972 29 Apr	Harderthanitlookscrack	J.R.Mackenzie
	Slanting Crack	J.R.Mackenzie
S 1978 2 May	Boggle	J.R.Mackenzie, M.Birch
S 1978 6 May	Speleological Nightmare	M.Birch, J.R.Mackenzie
	Peregrination	M.Birch, J.R.Mackenzie
S 1978 31 May	Magnificrack	J.R.Mackenzie, R.McHardy, M.Birch

Ben Wyvis

S 1970 20 Jun	Klettershoe	J.R.Mackenzie
W 1982 31 Dec	Caberfeidh	J.R.Mackenzie, G.Gorner
S 1984 7 Jul	Rubbers	J.R.Mackenzie
W 1986 19 Feb	Wyvis Waterfall	A.Winton, D.Bond
	Probably first climbed in the 1960s	
W 1986 20 Feb	Slab Smear Left-Hand	A.Winton, D.Bond
W 1992 29 Dec	Discovery Buttress	D.Broadhead, J.R.Mackenzie
W 1993 31 Jan	Gael Force Grooves	J.R.Mackenzie, M.Hind

An Coileachan: Garbh Coire Mor

W	Central Gully	N.S.Tennant and party
W 1976	Dandelion	C.Rowland and party
W 1976 Dec	Burdock	C.Rowland, S.Rowland, D.Scott
W 1976	Primrose (left fork)	C.Rowland, M.Anthoine
W 1979	Primrose (right fork)	D.Butterfield, C.Frazer, D.McCallum, J.R.Mackenzie

W 1979	13 Jan	Echo Face	J.R.Mackenzie, D.McCallum
W 1979	27 Jan	Short Shrift	J.R.Mackenzie, R.Brown
W 1979	10 Feb	Plumline	J.R.Mackenzie, R.Brown
W 1979	11 Feb	Prune Buttress	R.Butler, D.Howard, D.McCallum, C.Roylance
W 1979	17 Feb	Crystal Tripper	J.R.Mackenzie, D.McCallum
W 1979	5 May	Sage Corner	J.R.Mackenzie, D.Butterfield
W 1981	28 Feb	Ravenshead	D.McCallum, A.Russell
W 1984		Moonflower Direct	D.Butterfield, A.Hayward
W 1984		Shadows and Light	D.Butterfield, A.Hayward
W 1985	19 Jan	The Ramp Tramp	C.Maclean, A.Nisbet
W 1986	28 Feb	Venus Fly-Trap	D.Dinwoodie, D.Hawthorn
W 1987	9 Dec	The Turf Accountant	S.Jenkins, M.E.Moran
W 1991	17 Nov	Sideshow	G.Cullen, J.R.Mackenzie

Beinn Liath Mhor Fannaich, Sgurr Mor, Carn na Criche

W 1967	9 Apr	Wot Gully	R.Graham, R.Warrack
W 1967	10 Apr	Easter Gully	B.Brand, O.Bruskeland
W 1967	11 Apr	East Face	R.Graham, R.Warrack
W 1980	19 Jan	Downward Bound	J.R.Mackenzie, D.Gilbert
W 1980	14 Mar	The Resurrection	J.R.Mackenzie, D.Butterfield
W 1983	19 Feb	The Boundary	D.Rubens, D.J.Broadhead
W 1990	12 Jan	Brumous Buttress	G.Cullen, J.R.Mackenzie
W 1991	27 Jan	Gelid Groove	J.R.Mackenzie, G.Cullen
W 1991	14 Feb	Grand Illusion	G.E.Little, J.M.G.Findlay
W 1991	21 Dec	Intro The Groove	J.M.G.Finlay, G.E.Little

Sgurr nan Clach Geala

S 1961	3 Apr	Skyscraper Buttress	T.W.Patey, J.M.Taylor, J.White, G.K.Annand
S 1961	16 Apr	Sellers Buttress	T.W.Patey, R.Harper

First ascent probably made in 1960 by R.H.Sellers and J.Smith. No details are available. Buttress named after Sellers who was killed later that year.

W 1965	6 Mar	Alpha Gully	P.Baker, D.S.B.Wright
W 1965	6 Mar	Gamma Gully	P.N.L.Tranter, I.G.Rowe
W 1970	28 Feb	Beta Gully	P.F.Macdonald, J.Porteous (centre fork) I.G.Rowe, W.Sproul (right fork)
W 1972	19 Feb	Sellers Buttress	G.S.Strange, D.Stuart
W 1972	Mar	Delta Gully	D.Dinwoodie, M.Freeman
W 1974	16 Mar	Epsilon Gully	M.Freeman, N.Keir
W 1978	18 Feb	Skyscraper Buttress	R.J.Archbold, M.Freeman, J.C.Higham, R.A.Smith

Direct Start: D.Dinwoodie, C.Jamieson, K.Murphy 9 February 1986
Right-Hand Start: D.Dinwoodie, D.Hawthorn 26 February 1986

W1978	18 Feb	Sunrise Buttress	P.R.Baines, D.M.Nichols
W1982	2 Jan	First Footing	N.Halls, A.Kimber, R.Townshend
W1983	13 Feb	Cuileag Buttress	R.Arnott, A.Nisbet
W1985	18 Jan	Cuileag Corner	C.Maclean, A.Nisbet
W1986	19 Feb	Destitution Road	D.Dinwoodie, K.Murphy

Sgurr Breac

W1991	16 Feb	Neverending Story	J.M.G.Findlay, J.G.Findlay, G.E.Little
W1991	16 Feb	Ptarmigan Corner	J.M.G.Findlay, G.E.Little

Beinn Dearg and Cona'Mheall

S 1946	Jun	Bell's Route	Dr.and Mrs.J.H.B.Bell
S 1962	Apr	The Tower of Babel	T.W.Patey
S 1962	Apr	The West Buttress	T.W.Patey
W1963	Jan	Inverlael Gully	J.M.Taylor, A.G.Nicol, T.W.Patey
W1964	29 Mar	Penguin Gully	T.W.Patey, W.H.Murray, N.S.Tennent
W1967	14 Jan	Gastronome's Gully	A.W.Ewing, J.Brumfitt, I.G.Rowe, W.Sproul
W1967	25 Mar	Whatawaytospendeaster	W.Sproul, A.McKeith
W1967	25 Mar	Rev.Ian Paisley Memorial Gully	W.Sproul, A.McKeith
W1967		Spaghetti Gully	I.J.Butson and party
W1968	10 Mar	Orangeman's Gully	T.W.Patey
W1968	10 Mar	Papist's Passage	T.W.Patey
W1968	11 Mar	Fenian Gully	T.W.Patey
W1968	11 Mar	The Silken Ladder	T.W.Patey
W1969	2 Mar	Yon Spoot	D.W.Duncan, M.Rennie
W1969	18 Mar	Eigerwanderer	T.W.Patey, J.Cleare
W1969	18 Mar	Vanishing Shelf	J.Bower, D.W.Duncan
W1970	Mar	Emerald Gully	B.Fuller, P.Nunn, A.Riley
W1976	Jan	Bonus	A.McHardy, C Rowland
W1976	31 Jan	Pickwick	M.Freeman, G.Stephen
W1976	1 Feb	Wee Freeze Gully	D.M.Jenkins, P.F.Macdonald
W1979	7 Apr	The Ice Hose	I.Dalley, D.Nichols, G.Strange
W1981	28 Dec	The Centre Party	P.Barrass, A.Nisbet
W1981	28 Dec	The Wall of Retribution	A.Nisbet
W1986	22 Feb	Body Freeze	M.Fowler, C.Watts
W1986	Mar	Emerald Edge	S.Falconer, R.Robb
W1987	1 Feb	Grotto Gully	G.Cohen, S.Cohen
W1987	11 Apr	Snort Trail	M.Fowler, C.Watts
W1987	11 Apr	Traumatic Interference	S.Venables, J.English
W1988	7 Feb	Archway	R.Everett, S.Richardson

W 1988	12 Mar	Ice Bomb	M.Fowler, D.Wilkinson
W 1989	18 Feb	White Settler's Gully	S.Aisthorpe, J.Lyall
W 1989	22 Feb	The Tower of Babel	S.Aisthorpe, J.Lyall
S 1990	8 Apr	Tower of Enchantment	D.Rubens, G.Cohen
W 1991	6 Jan	Jewel in the Crown	S.Richardson, C.Cartwright

Cadha Dearg

| W 1986 | 8 Feb | Geddes's Gully | B.Hall, A.Rouse |

Long sought after by Mike Geddes, whose knowledge of remote corners of the Northern Highlands was unrivalled, the secret of this climb was passed on after Geddes's untimely death to G.Cohen and A.Rouse. Rouse got there first!

| W 1986 | 2 Mar | Captain Patience | C.Downer, D.Scott |

Strone Nea, Royal Hotel Buttress

S 1962	June	The Shaft, Nick-Nack Wall	T.W.Patey
S 1988	Summer	Yellow Edge, Morse Crack	P.Cairns, F.Fotheringham, D.Neville
S 1988	Summer	Telegraph Road, Telstar	P.Cairns, F.Fotheringham, D.Neville
S 1991	9 Mar	Beached Whale, The Linesmen	G.Cullen, J.R.Mackenzie

Seana Bhraigh, Meall nan Fuaran, Bodach Beag

W 1963	4 Apr	Pomegranate Gully	P.N.L.Tranter, J.C.Wedderburn, D.S.B Wright
W 1963	5 Apr	Sham Gully	D.S.B. Wright, P.N.L.Tranter, J.Wedderburn
W 1963	6 Apr	Bealach Gully	W.D.Fraser, J.Wedderburn
		The Chute	J.Wedderburn, I.D.M.Chalmers, W.D.Fraser
W 1963	7 Apr	Sunday Post	W.D.Fraser, J.C.I.Wedderburn
		Press-On Gully	D.S.B.Wright, P.N.L.Tranter, I.A.Campbell
W 1963	8 Apr	Monday Post	W.D.Fraser, P.N.L.Tranter
		Query Cleft	P.N.L.Tranter, W.D.Fraser
W 1964	14 Feb	Pelican Gully	C.S.M.Doake, P.N.L.Tranter, J.C.I.Wedderburn
W 1965	19 Feb	Diamond Diedre	J.C.I.Wedderburn, J.Kowalska
		Far West Buttress	J.C.I.Wedderburn, J.Kowalska
W 1971	2 Jan	The Rough Diamond	P.F.Macdonald, I.G.Rowe
W 1978	21 Jan	Pineapple Gully	P.F.Macdonald, C.Rowland

W1978 15 Feb	Eagle Gully	D.Dinwoodie, A.McIvor, P.Devlin, G.Thompson	
W1978 16 Feb	Flowerpot Buttress	P.Devlin, D.Dinwoodie	
W1978 15 Apr	Diamond Edge	D.Dinwoodie, R.Robb, R.A.Smith	
W1983 2 Jan	Sagittarius	A.Kimber, J.Mount, R.Townsend	
W1983 7 Apr	Y Gully Buttress	I.Rae, J.Wilson	
W1983 8 Apr	Toll Gate	I.Rae, J.Wilson	
W1986 3 Apr	Freevater Gully	I.Rae, J.Wilson	
W1986 4 Apr	Campsite Cleft	I.Rae, J.Wilson	

Glenbeg

S 1962 Oct	Deanaich Slabs	T.W.Patey	
S 1962 14 Oct	Rowan Chimney	T.W.Patey	
S 1962 14 Oct	The Madonna	T.W.Patey	
S 1966 5 Jun	Cottage Slabs	Corriemulzie MC party	
S 1966 5 Jun	Niagra Slab	D.J.Wilson, A.W.Beveridge	
S 1975 19 Jun	Unnamed Wall	P.Whillance, J.Lamb	
S 1975 29 Jul	Campiglio	R.Morrow, K.Schwartz	

Alladale

S 1962 26 Jun	Whigmaleerie	T.W.Patey	
S 1963 11 May	Jug Rib	W.D.Fraser, P.N.L.Tranter	
S 1963 11 May	East Route, West Face	C.S.M.Doake, J.C.I.Wedderburn, J.K.McLean	
S 1963 12 May	Indecision	W.D.Fraser, J.C.I.Wedderburn	
	Direct Start: D.S.B.Wright, C.N.B.Martin, 11 July 1963		
S 1963 11 Jul	Tane	A.R.M.Park, W.D.Fraser	
S 1963 11 Jul	Tother	P.N.L.Tranter, N.Travers	
S 1963 11 Jul	The Gully	P.N.L.Tranter, N.Travers, D.Martin	
S 1963 12 Jul	Gully Buttress	W.D.Fraser, A.R.M.Park	
S 1966 15 May	Bang	P.N.L.Tranter, P.F.Macdonald	
S 1967 Apr	Snowdrop	A.Fyffe, J.Inglis	
S 1968 Jul	Rumble	K.Spence, P.F.Macdonald	
S 1975 20 Jun	Narcissus	J.Lamb, P.Whillance	
S 1977 15 Jun	Guano Slabs	N.Muir, A.Paul	

Rhue

The cliffs here have been developed over a short space of time, mainly by Glenmore Lodge parties including F.Fotheringham, A.Fyffe, A.Cunningham, R.Mansfield, J.Fincham, M.Burrows-Smith, J.Hepburn and S.Blagborough.

Ardmair

S	1986 Summer	Friends Retrieval	A.Taylor, F.Fotheringham
		Totem Pole Crack	A.Taylor, F.Fotheringham
S	1988 2 Apr	Summer Isles City	I.Taylor, D.Meldrum
S	1988 12 Apr	Market Day	I.Taylor, S.Ryan
S	1989 19 May	Primitive Dance	A.Fyffe, J.Hepburn
		Town without Pity	J.Hepburn, A.Fyffe
		Just Add Lib	L.Healey, R.Mansfield
		Unleash the Beast	R.Mansfield, L.Healey
S	1989 20 May	Sculptress	L.Healey, R.Mansfield
		Carved from Stone	R.Mansfield, L.Healey
		A Spot of Deception	A.Liddell, A.Fyffe
		The Friendly Groove	A.Fyffe, A.Liddell
		Skeletons	A.Liddell, A.Fyffe
S	1989 26 May	Moondance	R.Mansfield, A.Fyffe
S	1989 27 May	Breakfast Corner	A.Fyffe, R.Mansfield
		Little Monster	R.Mansfield, A.Fyffe
		Microlight	A.Fyffe, R.Mansfield
		Terrace Crack	A.Fyffe, R.Mansfield
		Space Monkey	R.Mansfield, A.Fyffe
		Buried Treasure	A.Fyffe, R.Mansfield
		Acrimonious Acrobat	R.Anderson, C.Greaves
		Bolshie Ballerina	R.Anderson, C.Greaves
		Dangerous Dancer	R.Anderson, C.Greaves
S	1989 28 May	Exasperated Escapologist	R.Anderson, C.Greaves
		Convoluted Contortionist	R.Anderson, C.Greaves
S	1989 3 Jun	First Fruits	C.Greaves, R.Anderson
		Furious Fiddler	R.Anderson, C.Greaves
		Relax and Swing	A.Cunningham, R.Mansfield
		Cruel World	R.Mansfield, A.Cunningham
		Colour Co-ordinated	A.Cunningham, R.Mansfield
		Burning Desire	R.Mansfield, A.Cunningham
S	1989 4 Jun	Grumpy Groper	R.Anderson, C.Greaves
		Tunnel Vision	C.Greaves, R.Anderson
S	1989 9 Jun	Spider Jive	A.Fyffe, A.Cunningham
		A Bit on the Side	A.Fyffe, A.Cunningham
S	1989 10 Jun	Dawn Patrol	A.Cunningham, A.Fyffe
		From Rags to Ritches	A.Cunningham, A.Fyffe
		Alliteration Alternative	A.Fyffe, A.Cunningham
		The Parapente	A.Cunningham, A.Fyffe
S	1989 17 Jun	99, Les Rosbif	T.Prentice, R.Anderson
		Ignorant Iguana	R.Anderson, C.Greaves
		Shaker Loops	T.Prentice, R.Anderson, C.Greaves

			Twisting Twitcher	R.Anderson, T.Prentice
			Muscle Hustle	R.Anderson, T.Prentice
			Small is Possible	L.Healey, J.Pickering
			Diamond White	A.Cunningham, A.Fyffe, L.Healey
			Small is Beautiful	L.Healey, J.Pickering
			The Way It Is	J.Pickering, L.Healey
			Siesta	A.Fyffe, A.Cunningham
			Still Waters	A.Fyffe, A.Cunningham
S 1989	July		Gravity's Rainbow	A.Fyffe, A.Cunningham
			Big Foot	A.Cunningham, A.Fyffe
			The Raingoose	A.Fyffe, A.Cunningham
			Stone Canyon	A.Fyffe, A.Cunningham
			Thorn in My Side	A.Cunningham, A.Fyffe
			Let it Bleed	A.Fyffe, A.Cunningham
S 1989	Aug		Comedy Waltz	R.Mansfield, L.Healey
			Mandolin Rain	A.Cunningham, J.Pickering
			Neart nan Gaidheal	A.Cunningham (unseconded)
			Sunstroke	A.Fyffe, M.Burrows-Smith
			Turn Turtle	A.Cunningham, J.Pickering
S 1989	3	Sep	The Fish Business	R.Anderson, C.Anderson
			Loan Shark	R.Anderson, C.Anderson
S 1989	Sep		The Brahan Seer	A.Cunningham, A.Fyffe
			Common Ground	A.Cunningham, A.Fyffe
			Skinhead Violence	A.Fyffe, A.Cunningham
			On the Western Skyline	A.Cunningham, A.Fyffe
S 1989	Oct		Biological Warfare	A.Cunningham, A.Fyffe
S 1989	Nov		Le Pontif	A.Cunningham, A.Nisbet
S 1990			Antipodean Cruise	A.Cunningham, P.Thompson
S 1990			Rock-a-Bye-Bye	A.Cunningham, P.Thompson
S 1990			Blanka	G.Suzca, G.Lawrie
S 1991			Hammerhead	G.Ettle, C.Forrest
S 1991			Laggavoulin	K.Geddes, A.Fyffe
S 1991			Little Red Rooster	K.Geddes, A.Fyffe

Sgurr an Fhidhleir

S 1962	May		Direct Nose Route	N.Drasdo, C.M.Dixon

The scene of a remarkable early attempt by Ling and Sang. Later, such redoubtable names as Baird, Parker and Young were forced into making long detours to the right. Ancient ironmongery from these early attempts can still be found on the lower half.

Tower Finish: J.R.Mackenzie, D.Gilbert 10 June l979 (1PA). Climbed in mistake for the Direct, D.Gilbert thought he was in for "an easy old fashioned classic."

S 1967	1	Jun	The Magic Bow	M.Boysen, T.W.Patey

S 1968 11 Jun   The Phantom Fiddler   T.W.Patey
    Magic Line link: R.Everett, D.Gaffney 10 Sept 1989
S 1975   May   Fidelio   D.M.Jenkins, P.F.Macdonald,
    R.McHardy
S 1977   G-String   R.McHardy, P.Thomas
W 1979 20 Jan   North West Face   A.Nisbet
W 1979 20 Jan   South Gully   J.Barmby, B.Sprunt
W 1979   Feb   West Face   P.F.Macdonald, C.Rowland
W 1979   Feb   Nose Route   N.D.Keir, R.A.Smith
    Unusually good winter conditions
W 1987 17 Jan   Direct Nose Route   W.Moir, C.Forrest
    1PA on the 3rd Pale Slab. FFA: R.Everett, S.Richardson, Jan 1991.

Conmheall

S 1955   Aug   Acheninver Pinnacle   D.Niven, G.F.Webster
S 1962   May   Middle Crag   T.W.Patey
S 1978 11 Nov   Levitation Towers   J.R.Mackenzie, D.McCallum

Stac Pollaidh

S 1906   West Buttress   Dr, Mrs and Miss Inglis Clark,
    C.W.Walker
S 1953 8 Nov   November Groove   D.Stewart, G.Cairns
S 1956 2 Apr   No.2 Buttress   G.S.Johnstone, M.Johnstone
S 1957 7 Jul   Virgin and Child   I.Clough, D.Pipes (aid)
    Pinnacle
    FFA Royal Marines, May 1964
S 1957 Summer Baird's Pinnacle   RAF Kinloss (aid)
    FFA T.W.Patey 12 June 1968
S 1959 18 May   South Rib   A.Zaluski, J.Whitrow
S 1959 18 May   Anyways   J.G.Wright, J.Ryman
S 1959 21 May   South Face Route   A.Zaluski, J.Whitrow
S 1962   Jun   North-west Corner   T.W.Patey
S 1964 26 Aug   Jack the Ripper   M.G.Anderson, G.Mair
    The original route traversed into November Groove before the present
    final pitch. First ascent of this pitch unknown.
S 1965   Aug   Enigma Grooves   T.W.Patey, R.Barclay
    A corner on the right avoided the final chimney. Described finish:
    J.R.Mackenzie, P.Goodwin 18 August 1979.
S 1969   Jul   Felo de Se   R.Carrington, J.MacLean
    1PA, 1NA: FFA T.Prentice, R.Anderson, 10 September 1989.
S 1974   Jul   Summer Isles Arete   Mr and Mrs J.R.Mackenzie
S 1977   Jun   Cuckoo Crack   I.Dalley, D.McCallum
S 1985 5 May   Release the Bats   G.Leslie, A.Fraser
S 1985 14 May   Party on the Patio   A.Fraser, J.Dickson (1NA)
S 1985 29 Sep   Vlad the Impaler   A.Fraser, J.Dickson

S 1987 22 Jun	The Irascible Porcupine	A.Fraser, J.Dickson
S 1987 27 Sep	Nosferatu	A.Fraser, Ms W.Faulkner
S 1988 14 May	The Moine Thrutch	A.Tibbs, A.Mathewson
S 1988 14 May	Black Riders	S.Richardson, T.Prentice
S 1988 14 May	Stakeout	T.Prentice, S.Richardson
S 1988 14 May	Pretty Bourgeois Crack	T.Prentice, S.Richardson
S 1988 15 May	Coigach's Burning	T.Prentice, S.Richardson
S 1988 15 May	Bloodsucker	S.Richardson, T.Prentice
S 1988 30 May	Expecting To Fly	T.Prentice (unseconded)
S 1988 15 Oct	Angus The Arsonist	G.Robb, A.Fraser
W1989 Mar	November Groove	G.Thomas, N.Wilson
S 1989 26 Aug	Walking on Air	T.Prentice, R.Anderson
S 1989 2 Sep	Mid-Flight Crisis	R.Anderson, C.Anderson
S 1989 9 Sep	Plane Sailing	R.Anderson, C.Anderson, T.Prentice
S 1989 9 Sep	Wingless Warlock	R.Everett, D.Gaffney
S 1989 10 Sep	Shadow on the Wall	R.Anderson, T.Prentice
S 1991 11 May	Bats in the Belfry	A.Fraser, J.Thomson
S 1991 11 May	The Cheshire Cat	A.Fraser, J.Thomson
S 1992 8 Aug	Calum the Clansman	I.Hartley, J.Lyall

Cul Beag

S 1958 11 Aug	Lurgainn Edge	Dr and Mrs J.H.B.Bell
S 1959 17 May	Quelle Delicatesse	J.G.Wright, A.Zaluski
S 1959 17 May	Curving Chimney	J.G.Wright, A.Zaluski
S 1979 10 Jul	Lickerish Quarter	R.Gatehouse, C.Smith
S 1979 10 Jul	Kveldro Ridge	R.Gatehouse, C.Smith
S 1990 Jun	Tant Pis	H.Irvine, A.Keith

Cul Mor

S 1979 12 Jul	Buffalo Ballet	R.Gatehouse, C.Smith
W1991 13 Jan	The Cul	S.Richardson, R.Everett

Suilven

S 1935	Gray's Route	Robin Gray
S 1947	Portcullis Route	A.Parker, S.Paterson
S 1957 18 Jul	Rose Route	A.Smart, A.Mitchell
S 1968	Heatwave	H.MacInnes, M.C.MacInnes
W1992 15 Mar	Western Approach Route	A.Matthewson, J.Maclaurin

Quinag,   Beinn an Fhurain

S 1961 3 Aug	Tenement Ridge	G.R.Ambler, J.R.Sutcliffe
S 1962 May	Mild	T.W.Patey

S 1963		Bitter	T.W.Patey, A.G.Nicol
W 1965	Mar	The Waste Pipe	T.W.Patey, R.Ford
S 1968	12 Jun	The Pillar of Assynt	T.W.Patey, H.MacInnes
S 1968	28 Jun	Ricketty Ridge	T.W.Patey
W 1969	17 Mar	The Wind Pipe	T.W.Patey, J.Cleare
S 1971	3 Jul	The Family Way	B.Dunn, J.R.Houston

Direct start: J.R.Sutcliffe, J.R.Myers 5 June 1982

S 1977	9 Jul	Toby	D.Gardner, A.Paul
W 1979	21 Jan	Y Gully (right fork)	J.Barmby, B.Sprunt

The left fork taken in descent by J.Anderson, A.Nisbet

W 1979	21 Jan	Cave Gully	J.Anderson, A.Nisbet
W 1979	13 Feb	Y Buttress	A.Nisbet, N.Spinks
W 1979	13 Feb	Cooper's Gully	B.Clough, J.Elliott, R.MacGregor
W 1986	20 Feb	The Gully of Nedd	D.Dinwoodie, K.Murphy
W 1986	21 Feb	Eas Coulin	A.Cunningham, A.Nisbet
W 1991	9 Feb	Beinn an Fhurain icefall	B.Davison, A.Nisbet
W 1991	10 Feb	Noggin the Nog	B.Davison, A.Nisbet

Old Man of Stoer

S 1966	Jun	Original Route	T.W.Patey, B.Robertson, B.Henderson, P.Nunn
S 1987	Jun	Ring of Bright Water	S.Yates, I.Halliday
S 1987	29 Aug	North-west Corner	M.Fowler, C.Newcombe

Reiff

Precise details of the first ascents of climbs on the Reiff sea cliffs are not available. Many of the shorter routes were first soloed by B.Lawrie. Large numbers of the other routes have been done by Aberdeen and Glenmore Lodge parties, and other individuals including A.Cunningham, A.Nisbet, D.Dinwoodie, D.Hawthorn, K.Murphy, N.Morrison, W.Moir, M.Hamilton and R.Anderson.

Foinaven

Cnoc a'Mhadaidh

S 1971	2 Jun	Quergang	P.Nunn, R.Toogood
S 1973	Jun	Pilastre	M.Boysen, P.Nunn
S 1975	Jun	East Slabs	T.Lewis, R.Toogood
S 1975	Jun	The Great Roof	P.Burke, R.S.Dearman
S 1976	Jun	West Slabs	R.S.Dearman, D.Moorhouse
S 1976	Jun	Star Turn	B.Griffiths, P.Nunn, R.Toogood
S 1978	May	Wrath	P.Nunn, T.Lewis, C.Bonington
S 1983	May	Familiar	P.Nunn, R.Toogood

Coire Duail; Creag Dubh

S	1968 27 Aug	Red Grooves	M.G.Bond, I.G.Clough
S	1969 Jul	Coire Duail Grooves	G.N.Hunter, D.F.Lang
S	1971 Jul	Gualin Wall	J.A.Brooder, M.Simkins
S	1975 27 May	Sava	P.W.Green, P.A.Haigh

Named by D.Gardner and A.Paul in 1977, who were unaware of the first ascent.

S	1977 11 Aug	Seers Corner	D.Gardner, A.Paul
W	1986 28 Feb	Windfall	B.Hall, A.Rouse
W	1986 1 Mar	North-east Buttress	B.Hall, A.Rouse
S	1989 4 Oct	Promised Land	S.Blagborough, A.Nisbet

The first half had been climbed by R.A.Croft and J.R.Sutcliffe in May 1975.

W	1992 29 Dec	Overseer	C.Cartwright, N.Wilson

A'Cheir Ghorm

S	1954 17 Jun	North Ridge	L.S.Lovat, T.Weir, A.D.S.Macpherson
S	1954 17 Jun	South Ridge	L.S.Lovat, T.Weir
S	1959 Jul	Cave Ridge	I.G.Cumming, Miss H.Rose

Coire na Lice; Lord Reay's Seat

S	1964 28 Aug	Original Route	T.W.Patey, A.S.Russell, D Bull, N.Bull
S	1964 12 Sep	Fishmonger	W.D.Fraser, P.N.L.Tranter
S	1971 8 May	Pobble	P.Macdonald, R.A.North

Direct Finish: E.Jackson, S.N.Smith July 1983

S	1976 13 Aug	Breakaway	B.Dunn, A.Paul

Creag Coire na Lice

S	1958 21 Jun	Cantilever Climb	B.Halpin, J.Bradley, I.Clough
S	1966 2 Apr	Rhino Buttress	P.N.L.Tranter, D.B.Martin

Creag Urbhard

S	1910 May	South Ridge	G.T.Glover, W.N.Ling

This climb may have been on the far (south) side of the First Dionard Buttress. The rocks were said to rival the Dolomites in steepness.

S	1950 6 Jul	Original Route	A.Parker, J.Young
S	1951 May	Fourth Waterfall	T.Weir, A.D.S.Macpherson
S	1954 15 Jun	Right-hand Route, Central Buttress.	L.S.Lovat, T.Weir, A.D.S.Macpherson
S	1954 18 Jun	North Ridge	L.S.Lovat, T.Weir
S	1959 26 Apr	Pantagruel	T.Sullivan, T.Abbey
S	1959 26 Apr	Gargantua	T.Sullivan, M.Denton

S 1962 12 Jun	Fingal	T.W.Patey
S 1962	Zigzag	N.Drasdo, C.M.Dixon
S 1965 25 Apr	Boreas	A.R.M.Park, P.F.Macdonald
S 1965 25 Apr	Chicken Run	I.G.Rowe, P.N.L.Tranter
S 1966 14 May	KWH	M.Galbraith A.McKeith
S 1967 8 Jul	Crawlie Mouzie	D.Bathgate, W.Pryde
S 1968	Three Tier Route	H.MacInnes, M.MacInnes
S 1969 Jun	Tortoise	P.Nunn, C.Rowland
S 1969 Jun	The Veterans	T.Howard, P.Phipps

A complete description is given in the SMCJ, 1970.

| S 1972   May | Masha | D.Marshall, C.Rowland |

Right-hand finish: E.Jackson, S.N.Smith July 1983

| S 1975 | Promiscuous Wall | C.Ogilvie, M.Searle |

The description has not been published, but see SMCJ 1977, p.152.

S 1976 11 Aug	Whitewash	B.Dunn, A.Paul
W1979 8 Feb	The Terrace	B.Clough, A.Nisbet
W1979 9 Feb	Second Waterfall	A.Nisbet, N.Spinks
W1979 10 Feb	Flyover	B.Clough, A.Nisbet
W1979 11 Feb	The Green Knight	A.Nisbet
W1979 11 Feb	Gawain's Chimney	B.Clough, J.Elliott, A.Nisbet
W1979 12 Feb	The Fly	R.MacGregor, A.Nisbet
S 1979 13 Jul	Iolaire	D.Broadhead, D.Rubens
W1980 7 Feb	First Waterfall	J.McKeown, C.Mcleod, B.Sprunt
W1980 8 Feb	Thawr	A.Nisbet, N.Spinks
S 1983 Jul	Foxtrot	E.Jackson, S.N.Smith
W1986 28 Feb	Third Waterfall	A.Cunningham, A.Nisbet
W1986 28 Feb	Fourth Waterfall	W.Todd
S 1986 Jul	Fiscal's Rib	G.Mitchell, J.Dunn
S 1987 25 May	Mad Mink	S.Richardson, T.Prentice

Dionard Buttresses and Creag Alistair

S 1959 25 Apr	Toothache	E.Buckley, G.Lee
S 1965 23 May	Mayday	J.W.Highet, N.D.Smith
S 1967 May	Hugsy-Bugsy	Dr and Mrs A.W.Ewing
S 1967 20 May	Left Edge Route	J.Brumfitt, B.Sproul
S 1969 Jun	Opportunist	P.Nunn, C.Rowland
S 1969 Jun	Cengalo	T.E.Howard, C.Rowland
S 1969 Jun	Dialectic	P.Nunn, C.Rowland, R.Toogood

The ascent took two days. The Variation Start was climbed in 1984.

S 1969 Jun	Badile	T.E.Howard, P.Phipps
S 1969 Jun	Gritstoner's Revenge	T.E.Howard, P.Phipps
S 1973 Jun	Smick	C.Rowland, J.Smith
S 1973 Jun	Succuba	P.Nunn, J.Smith, T.Briggs
S 1973 Jun	Marble Corner	P.Nunn, M.Boysen

Originally named Double Corner.

| S 1973   Jun | Alistair Roses | M.Boysen, M.Richardson |

W 1979	9 Feb	Left Edge Route	B.Clough, R.MacGregor
W 1979	10 Feb	Guinevere Gully	B.Clough, J.Elliott
W 1979	10 Feb	Incisor	R.MacGregor, A.Nisbet
W 1979	11 Feb	Plume	R.MacGregor, N.Spinks
S 1982	31 May	Millennium	A.Livesey, P.Nunn
S 1984	Jun	Gemelli	P.Nunn, M.Richardson
S 1984	Jun	The Great Crack	A.Parkin, P.Swainson
S 1986	Jul	Hirsuit	B.Mattock, R.Webb
S 1986	Jul	Look North	R.Webb, B.Mattock
S 1986	Jul	Banana Groove	G.Mitchell, J.Dunn
S 1987	23 May	Beeline	S.Richardson, T.Prentice

Creag Shomhairle and Creag na Faoilinn

S 1953	28 Jun	Crescent-shaped Chimney	D.Haworth, J.Tester
S 1962		Windy Corner The Catwalk The Roost	Caithness MC

Modestly graded Severe, this climb was to experience severe inflation. By 1986, on the first ascent of Hot Pants, it was considered 5a!

S 1966	18 Aug	Catwalk Direct	J.R.Sutcliffe, D.Chapman
S 1967	21 May	The Cage	J.Brumfitt, B.Sproul
S 1967	31 May	South-West Edge	J.R.Sutcliffe, D.Chapman
S 1969	28 May	The Ramp	R.How, J.R.Sutcliffe
S 1969	23 Aug	Offside	C.Stead, M.Stead
S 1971	5 Aug	Monkey Gull	M.Horsburgh, K.Schwartz
S 1971	21 Aug	Land of the Dancing Dead	C.Jackson, T.Proctor
S 1979	11 Aug	The Row of Trees	K.Spence, G.Cohen
S 1979	11 Aug	Mistaken Identity	D.Jamieson, G.Nicoll
S 1982	1 Jun	The Harrier	J.R.Sutcliffe, J.R.Myers
S 1983	3 Jun	The Plinth	J.R.Myers, J.R.Sutcliffe
S 1984	1 Aug	Bardo Thodol	G.Cohen, G.Macnair
W 1986	1 Mar	Strabeg's Weep	A.Cunningham, A.Nisbet, W.Todd
S 1986	28 Jun	Tank Top	M.Hamilton, R.Anderson
S 1986	28 Jun	Hot Pants	M.Hamilton, R.Anderson

A fine day's work by Murray Hamilton

S 1989	21 May	Warm Front	R.Anderson, C.Greaves
S 1989	21 May	Black Gold	R.Anderson, C.Greaves
S 1989	18 Jul	Pellet Wall	S.Steer, A.Tibbs

Ben Hope, Ben Loyal and Ben Klibreck

S 1933		Bell's Gully Eagle Buttress	J.H.B.Bell, D.Myles
S 1956	1 Apr	Petticoat Ridge	G.S.Johnstone, M.Johnstone
S 1958	8 Jul	Priest's Rake	D.D.Stewart, R.Tombs

S 1959 25 Jun	Rowboat	K.Richardson, D.Dewell
S 1968 3 Jun	Navytex Gully	H.M.Brown
S 1969 Jun	Cirith Ungol	L.Brown, R.G.Wilson
S 1969 14 Jun	Marathon Corner	L.Brown, A.P.Turnbull
W1969 23 Dec	Bell's Gully, Ben Klibreck	H.M.Brown, D.McNab
S 1970s	Gog	M.Boysen, M.Kosterlitz
S 1984 1 Aug	The Scoldings	M.Wilkinson, C.Plant
W1984 Winter	The Ice Smear	C.Fenton, N.Wilson
W1985 30 Dec	Bell's Ridge	I.Stewart, N. Wilson

Great Stack of Handa

S 1876		Donald Macdonald
S 1969 Jul	The Great Arch	G.N.Hunter, D.F.Lang, H.MacInnes
S 1969 Jul	Great Corner	G.N.Hunter, D.F.Lang

Sheigra

S 1971 Jun	Shark Crack	R.Dearman, K.Bridges, P.Nunn
S 1975 Jun	Tall Pall	P.Nunn
Formerly known as The Rib		
S 1976 Jun	Plumb McNumb	P.Nunn, R.Toogood
Formerly known as Steep Start		
S 1970s	Fingers, Black Knight The Ramp	R.Toogood R.Toogood
S 1978 May	Bloodlust	P.Nunn, P.Fearnehough
S 1981 Summer	Original Route	G.Cooper
S 1982 29 May	Black Rake	P.Nunn, R.Toogood
S 1983 May	Dark Angel	P.Nunn, R.Toogood
S 1983 May	Presumption	P.Nunn, R.Toogood
S 1983 Jul	Lucifer's Link	P.Nunn, P.Kershaw
S 1987 May	North-West Eliminate	M.Boysen, R.Carrington
"See what that does to their tights" - M.Boysen		
S 1987 May	Pinnacle Wall, Corner Start	M.Boysen, R.Carrington, G.Birtles
S 1987 May	Geriatrics, Exorcist	R.Carrington, M.Boysen
S 1987 May	Unnamed	P.Swainson, J.Given
S 1989 22 May	Sideline, Sideslip May Tripper, Juggernaut	R.Anderson, C.Greaves

Am Buachaille

| S 1967 23 Jul | Landward Face | T.W.Patey, J.Cleare, I.Clough |
| S 1990 15 Sep | Atlantic Wall | S.Richardson, R.Clothier |

Creag Riabhach

S 1972	May	The Godfather	D.Marshall, C.Rowland
S 1976	Jun	Masquerade	T.Howard, A.Maskery
S 1976	Jun	Herod's Evil	B.Griffiths, P.Nunn, R.Toogood

Cape Wrath

S 1989 27 May	Am Bodach	G.Muhlemann, S.Macintyre, S.Richardson
S 1989 17 Jun	A'Chailleach	S.Richardson, G.Muhlemann, M.Fowler, N.Dugan
S 1989 18 Jun	Stack Clo Kearvair, Seaward Stack.	M.Fowler, C.Watts
	Landward Stack	G.Muhlemann, S.Richardson
S 1989 18 Jun	Clo Mor Crack	M.Fowler, C.Watts
S 1989 19 Jun	Clo Mor Stack	M.Fowler, C.Watts, G.Muhlemann, S.Richardson

Whiten Head: The Maiden

S 1970	Jun	Eastern Stack, Original Route.	P.Nunn, T.W.Patey, B.Fuller, C.Goodwin, C.Rowland.
		Tom Patey tragically died descending the stack	
S 1970		Eastern Stack, March's Route	W.March, J.Cunningham
S 1988 28 May		Eastern Stack, Ode	M.Fowler, C.Newcombe
S 1988 28 May		Funeral for a Friend	C.Watts, J.Lincoln
S 1988 28 May		Waterfront Wall	M.Fowler, C.Newcombe
S 1988 28 May		Maiden without a Hole	C.Watts, J.Lincoln
S 1992	Sep	The Farr Side	S.Campbell, J.Walker, N.Wilson

Holborn Head

S 1969 14 Jun	Clett Rock: West Route	R.Jolly, M.Willis, D.Young
S 1988 29 May	Fort Rock	M.Fowler, J.Lincoln, C.Newcombe, C.Watts
S 1988 28 Aug	Clett Rock: North Route	M.Fowler, J.Lincoln, J.Cuthbert, N.Dugan

Dwarwick Head

S 1969	May	Initiation Direct	A.P.Turnbull, M.Willis
S 1969	May	Evening Wall	D.Young, A.P.Turnbull
S 1969	May	Initiation Corner	D.Young, S.Scadden
S 1969	May	Corkscrew	D.Young, S.Scadden
S 1969 5 Jun		Crocks Crawl	D.Young, S.Scadden
S 1969 25 Jun		Cluck	S.Scadden, A.P.Turnbull
S 1969	Jun	Jolly Roger	R.Jolly, J.Johnston

S 1969	2 Aug	Midge Corner	D.Young
S 1969	13 Aug	Zigzag	D.Young, S.Scadden
S 1969	27 Sep	Shag Crack	S.Scadden, A.P.Turnbull
S 1969	27 Sep	Puke	D.Young, J.Johnston
S 1969	18 Oct	Cormorant Way	S.Scadden, A.P.Turnbull
S 1969	9 Nov	Cormorant Crack	S.Scadden, A.P.Turnbull
S 1969	9 Nov	Diversion	S.Scadden, A.P.Turnbull

Duncansby Head

S 1958	Sep	Great Stack	J.K.Butler, J.A.McLeish, J.D.Porter
S 1989	27 May	The Knee	M.Fowler, P.Allison, N.Dugan, J.Lincoln
S 1989	27 May	Witches Hat Stack	M.Fowler, N.Dugan, P.Allison, J.Lincoln
S 1989	27 May	The Little Knee	M.Fowler

East Caithness Coast

S 1989	26 May	Occumster Stack	M.Fowler, N.Dugan, P.Allison, J.Lincoln
S 1989	Jul	Noss Head Stack	C.Dale, A.Dale
S 1989	1 Oct	Bodach an Uird: Landward Face	G.Muhlemann, S.Richardson
		North Arete	S.Richardson, G.Muhlemann
		Bird Poo Wall	C.Watts, S.Richardson, G.Muhlemann
		South Route	M.Fowler, C.Watts
S 1989	2 Oct	Dunbeath: Cleit Mhor	M.Fowler, C.Watts, N.Dugan
		Cleit Ruadh	C.Watts, S.Sheridan, N.Dugan, M.Fowler

Skirza

S 1992	20 Jun	Superstring	G.Milne, R.Christie, J.Mackenzie-Ross
S 1992	28 Jun	Quark Soup	J.Perry, J.Mackenzie-Ross

Noss Head

The climbs here were all pioneered during August and September 1992 variously by R.Christie, J.Mackenzie-Ross, G.Milne, M.McNally and J.Perry.

Occumster

The first ascents here were again accomplished during a short period of time in 1991 and 1992. The pioneers were:
J.Mackenzie-Ross: (Strawberry Slider, Time Machine, Apollo, Mischief, Gemini, Soupdragon, The Conjurer, Music Boat)

R.Christie: (Duck Soup, Tardis, Blue Tattoo, Sonic Screwdriver, Klingon, Tralfamadorian, Gollach, Teuchter, Tingwall, Heed Bummer, Pull the Plug, Manic Gannet, Gazpacho, Spotty Dog, Hang Ten, Heedbanger, Catwalk)
J.Macintosh: (Rasberry Ripple)
J.Perry: (Nightlife, Nocturnal, Sputnik, Pan Drop, Giotto, Wotsit, Quaver, Primeval Soup, Heavily Starched)
G.Milne: (Andromeda, Plainchant, St. Andrew's Crack, Colour Supplement, Rum and Raisin, Mint Chocolate Chip, Stipend Step-up, Caramel Crack, Post and Mail, Cleric Crack, Benediction Corner, Presenter's Problem, Presbytery Problem, Efflurage, Narced, Zippy Trousers, Comunn Gaidheil Paislig, Nudibranch Procurement, Jelly Spider, Weak Link, Reflections, Angus the Echinoderm, Wrinkly Semmit, Steam Iron, Bowmore, Ardbeg, Bruichladdich, Bunnahabhain, Lagavulin, Caol Ila)
M.McNally: (Pew Line, Percy the Owl)
J.Grove: (Near Horizons)
H.Jones: (Dances with Fulmars)

Mid Clyth

S 1990 Summer	Raccoon Kicker, Oxter	G.Milne
S 1990 Summer	Criticality	R.Gunn
S 1990 Summer	Shallow Chimney	R.Christie
S 1990 Summer	Knuckle	D.Sinclair
S 1991 Summer	Giant	J.Grove
S 1991 Summer	Maelstrom, Silverfish	R.Christie
S 1991 Summer	Lay-back Crack	R.Christie
S 1991 Summer	Crispy Aromatic Duck	R.Christie
S 1991 Summer	Indeanola Blues	R.Christie
S 1991 Summer	Stone Crazy, Off the Lip	R.Christie
S 1991 Summer	Captain Sensible, John's Peel	J.Mcintosh
S 1991 Summer	Adagio, Allegro	J.Macintosh
S 1991 Summer	Comedy of Thirst	S.Clark
S 1991 Summer	Diagonal, Velvet Scooter	J.Mackenzie-Ross
S 1991 Summer	Slow Boat, Stilt, Bonxie	J.Mackenzie-Ross
S 1991 Summer	Small North European Mammal	G.Milne
S 1991 Summer	Mac-attacked	J.Perry
S 1991 Summer	Electric Aardvark	R.Gunn
S 1992 6 Jun	Strange Attractor, Steerpike	R.Christie
S 1992 6 Jun	Crossroads	R.Christie
S 1992 10 Jun	Theatre of Cruelty	S.Clark
S 1992 10 Jun	Drawbridge	J.Mackenzie-Ross
S 1992 11 Jun	Mug's Game	R.Christie

S 1992 11 Jun D.I.Y.   J.Perry
S 1992 11 Jun Keystone   J.Mackenzie-Ross
S 1992 14 Jun Acceptance,   S.Clark
               Thanksgiving
S 1992 5 Jul   Rapture of the Deep   R.Christie
S 1992 5 Jul   An Ataireachd Ard,   G.Milne
               Frog Stoker
S 1992 22 Aug Aqualung   J.Mackenzie-Ross
S 1992 22 Aug Circle Line   R.Christie, J.Mackenzie-Ross

Latheronwheel

S 1990 Summer Free Fall   J.Macintosh
S 1990 Summer Two Bit Ram, Stepping   R.Gunn
               Out
S 1990 Summer Fall Out   R.Gunn
S 1990 Summer Freewheeler   J.Grove
S 1990 Summer Laphroaig   G.Milne
S 1990 Summer Pistachio, Wall Nut   R.Christie
S 1990 Summer Stone Ware, Coaster   R.Christie
S 1990 Summer Shocket, Guillemot   R.Christie
               Crack
S 1991 26 Sep The Other Landscape   S.Clark
S 1991 26 Sep Gervasutti's Wall   S.Clark
S 1991 28 Sep Primary Corner   K.Wallace
S 1991 29 Sep Freaker's Crack, The   K.Wallace
               Beast
S 1991 29 Sep Eye of the Storm   K.Wallace
S 1991 Summer Thief's Fork   J.Perry
S 1991 Summer Shear Water   R.Christie
S 1991 Summer Therapy   J.Mackenzie-Ross
S 1992 9 May   Sunspot   R.Christie
S 1992 9 May   Fred Flintstone,   J.Mackenzie-Ross
               BamBam
S 1992 13 May The Grey Coast   S.Clark
S 1992 17 May Summer Days   S.Clark, I.Lawson
S 1992 22 May Angel of Sleep   S.Clark
S 1992 30 May The Serpent   S.Clark
S 1992 1 Jun   Bully for Brontosaurus   J.Mackenzie-Ross
S 1992 1 Jun   Sory Scorry, Dog on a   R.Christie
               String
S 1992 1 Jun   Dream   R.Christie
S 1992 4 Jun   Night Sweat, Gym Jam   R.Christie
S 1992 4 Jun   Somnambulist   J.Mackenzie-Ross
S 1992 4 Jun   Night Shift   J.Perry
S 1992 1 Jun   Thinking of Wilma   R.Christie
S 1992 18 Jun Bouldermobile   J.Mackenzie-Ross

S 1992 10 Jul   Sticky Fingers   R.Christie
S 1992 10 Jul   Fancy Free, Footloose   J.Perry
S 1992 10 Jul   Coprolyte   J.Mackenzie-Ross
S 1992 20 Jul   The Morning Line   R.Christie
S 1992 18 Aug   Flight From Sadness   S.Clark
S 1992 Summer Puffin Attack,   S.Clark
                Freewheeler Direct

Orkney Mainland

S 1967   Jul   Castle of Yesnaby   J.Brown & party
S 1970 Easter   North Gaulton Castle   P.Minks, C.Phillips
S 1970   May   Stack o'Roo   J.Upton, E.Sweeney, A.Harris,
                                        K.Toms
S 1990 Summer Clett of Crura   S.Sustad, N.Dugan, M.Fowler

Old Man of Hoy

S 1966 18 Jul   East Face (Original   R.Baillie, C.Bonnington, T.Patey
                Route)
S 1967 8-9Jul   South Face   J.Brown, I.McNaught Davis
S 1967 8-9Jul   South-East Arete   P.Crew, D.Haston
          Originally climbed at A4, this climb is now superceded by the free climb
          "A Fistful of Dollars"
S 1982 Easter Ancient Mariner   A.Strapcans, G.Jenkin
S 1984 28 Jun   A Fistful of Dollars   P.Whillance, M.Hamilton
S 1984   Aug   A Few Dollars More   M.Hamilton, P.Whillance,
                                        P.Braithwaite

Other Hoy Cliffs

S 1969 6-8Apr   Original Route   E.Ward-Drummond, A.Evans,
                                        J.Street, L.Dickinson,
                                        B.Campbell-Kelly
          A film was made of this ascent, which required two bivouacs.
S 1970   Jul   Longhope Route   E.Ward-Drummond, O.Hill
          An epic seven day ascent.
S 1988 20 Jun   Big John   M.Fowler, J.Lincoln
S 1990 27 May   The Needle   M.Fowler, S.Sustad, N.Dugan
S 1991 20 May   Roring Forties   D.Turnbull, A.Donson
S 1991 23 May   Rats Stole my   A.Donson, D.Turnbull
                Toothbrush
S 1991 25 May   Mucklehouse Wall   D.Turnbull, A.Donson
S 1991 14 Jun   Two Little Boys   D.Turnbull, C.Rees
S 1992 4 Jun   The Eternal Optometrist C.Jones, M.Carnall, A.McNae
S 1992 5 Jun   Fillet of Soul   C.Jones, A.McNae
S 1992 5 Jun   Back Bone   M.Carnall, C.Jones
S 1992 6 Jun   Rosamund's Birthday   M.Carnall, C.Jones

Shetland

In this section, in some instances the names of the first ascensionists are given at the end of a group of climbs with the same given date.

S	1986	20 Jun	The Grindstone	A.Long
S		1986	Gunnister Rib	A.Long
S	1987	28 May	The Flakes, Borderline	A.Long, J.Grunberg
S	1987	4 Jun	Jerome, Thule Groove	A.Long, J.Grunberg
			Bootie	A.Long, R.Long
S	1987	Jun	Off The Spike	A.Long, I.Leask
S	1988	Apr	The Ramp	A.Long

Direct Finish: A.Long I.Leask, April 1990;
Right-hand Finish: A.Long May 1988

S	1988	28 May	Barnacle Bill, The Stile	
			The Groove Of The	A.Long, M.Sanderson
			Navir	
S	1988	13 May	JLS	A.Long
S	1988	May	Darklands	A.Long
S	1988	11 Jun	The Raven Banner	
			Spaelimenninir	A.Long, R.Cookson
			Briggistanes	A.Long
S	1988	18 Jun	Spray, Grindstone	
			Restless Flame	I.Davidson, R Cookson
			Crack n'Up	A.Long, I.Davidson
S	1988	Jun	Windward, Black Heart	
			Future Shock	
			Atlantic Dance	I.Davidson, R.Cookson
S	1988	Aug	Crystalocean, Cruel	
			Sea, Serpent's Kiss	C.Stewart, W.Moir
S	1988	Aug	Streams of Whiskey	
			Pockets of Excellence	
			Navir-Navir Land	
			White Noise, Wall of	
			Sound, Black Watch	
			Orange Utang	
			Empire of the Sun	
			Slice of Life	
			Black Hole, Black	W.Moir, C.Stewart
			Magic	
S	1988	Aug	Tenderness on the	A.Long
			Block	
S	1988	Aug	Ride The Wild Surf	
			Atlantic City, Jet,	
			Silly Arete, Bosse-Cat	
			Grot-Ville, Lost Volcano	
			Purple Haze	
			Piltock, Vampire	W.Moir

S 1988	Aug	Etive Ennui, Push Don't Pull	R.Cookson, A.Long
S 1988	Aug	Rock Lobster	C.Stewart
S 1988	29 Aug	Lapdog	A.Long, M.Sandison
S 1989	16 Apr	Da Droiltin Tree Rib Tickler	A.Long, F.Palmer F.Palmer, A.Long
S 1989	29 Apr	Mary, Mhairi	A.Long, M.Sandison
S 1989	3 May	Pickpocket	M.Sandison, A.Long
S 1989	4 Jun	Nibbek Northern Soul	A.Long, F.Palmer F.Palmer, A.Long
S 1989	17 Jun	Puissance	A.Long, J.Lee
S 1990	Apr	Bol, Crocus, Blocky Rib Spring Fever	A.Long A.Long, J.Lee
S 1990	May	Bubblebox	A.Long, J.Lee
S 1990	27 May	Duckbreaker	A.Long, J.Lee
S 1990	16 Jun	Celandine	A.Long, I.Leask
S 1991	27 Apr	The Udge	M.Sandison, A.Long
S 1991	27 May	Kyrje, Satori	A.Long, D.George
S 1991	31 May	The Good Shepherd	A.Donson, D.Turnbull
S 1991	2 Jun	The New Squids On The Block	A.Donson, D.Turnbull
S 1991	27 Jun	Feeler Gauge	A.Long, D.Absalom
S 1991	29 Jun	Sylvi	A.Long, D.Absolom, S.Wakefield
S 1991	3 Jul	Quiet City	A.Long, D.Absalom
S 1992	10 May	The Runk	A.Nisbet, C.Jones, J.Lincoln, M.Fowler
S 1992	13 May	Main Drong, Slender Drong	M.Fowler, A.Nisbet, J.Lincoln, C.Jones
S 1992	15 May	The Foot	M.Fowler, C.Jones, A.Nisbet, J.Lincoln
S 1992	17 May	Muckle Roe Stack	C.Jones, J.Lincoln, A.Nisbet, M.Fowler
S 1992	19 May	The Cutter	A.Nisbet, J.Lincoln, C.Jones, M.Fowler
S 1992	20 May	Slim Drong, Stumpy Drong	M.Fowler, A.Nisbet, J.Lincoln
S 1992	20 May	Harry's Pund	A.Nisbet, J.Lincoln, M.Fowler
S 1992	20 May	S.P. Stack	J.Lincoln, N.Dugan, A.Nisbet, M.Fowler
S 1992	21 May	Nibon Crack	M.Fowler, J.Lincoln
S 1992	21 May	Cattle Rustler	M.Fowler, C.Jones, J.Lincoln, A.Nisbet
S 1992	21 May	Atlantic Hits	C.Jones, A.Nisbet
S 1992	22 May	Lyra Stack	A.Nisbet, J.Lincoln, C.Jones, M.Fowler
S 1992	23 May	Hermless	D.George, A.Long
S 1992	23 May	Mincing with Charlie	A.Long, D.George

A Proposed Extension To The Scottish Winter Grading System

Since the introduction of the numerical system for the grading of Scottish winter climbs more than two decades ago, several developments have taken place in equipment, technique and attitude. These developments have placed such a strain on the grading system that the leading activists have agreed that it must be extended to take these changes into account. In particular, the new modern mixed routes must be graded so as to indicate their high levels of technical difficulty, while taking into consideration the frequently greater seriousness of the older-style ice routes. The elements of this extended system can be summarised as follows:

(i) Nearly all grades up to and including grade IV will remain unaltered.

(ii) Climbs of grade V and above will have two grades, an overall grade in roman numerals, and a technical grade in arabic numerals. Some hard technical mixed grade IV routes have also been given a technical grade.

(iii) The overall grade will take into account all factors affecting the difficulty of reaching the top of the climb, including its technical difficulty, seriousness (frequency of protection and reliability of belays) and sustainedness (length of hard sections of climbing and number of hard pitches).

(iv) The technical grade will reflect the actual difficulty of the hardest section(s) of climbing, without reference to seriousness. It is not intended to be used as a technical pitch-by-pitch grading. A technical grade of 5 indicates relatively straightforward, steep ice climbing; a technical grade of 6 would generally indicate more technical mixed climbing; technical grades of 7 and 8 would indicate much more intricate and harder snowed-up rock moves.

(v) The technical grade will normally vary not more than two below or two above the overall grade. Thus V,5 can be taken as an average grade V route of the old system. A higher technical grade than the overall grade would indicate greater technical difficulty, offset by better protection (as frequently found on mixed routes); a lower technical grade would indicate greater seriousness. Thus the system has some parallels with the E-grade system for summer rock climbs.

(vi) The previous artificial ceiling of grade V (and reluctant VI) has been removed, so as to reflect more realistically the differences between the old classic climbs of grade V and the current state-of-the-art routes.

Some degree of variability will undoubtedly occur, but the grading has to take account of what is thought to be average conditions. These proposals should be a great improvement over the ridiculous cramming of the grades that had developed. It should also be noted that, while this list has been compiled after consultation with many of the leading figures in Scottish winter climbing, despite broad overall agreement it is possible that the use of this system in practice may lead to a revision of the boundaries between the overall grades. It is hoped that publication of this list will not only be useful to the higher grade winter climber, but that it will also lead to lively debate and exchange of information so that it can be progressively refined and improved. Where recent information has not been available, it has not been possible to give a technical grade; in the list that follows these climbs have been given only their existing overall grade. The climbs in this Volume of the Northern Highlands guide have probably had fewer repeats than those elsewhere in Scotland, so the two-tier grade information is rather scanty. Reports of repeat ascents with suggested two-tier grades will be very welcome.

A complete list of the suggested new grades for all the harder Scottish winter climbs (where information is available) has been published in the 1992 SMC Journal.

Creag a' Ghlastail		Ice Bomb	VI,7
Ghlastail GTX	V	Geddes's Gully	V
The Fannaichs		Captain Patience	V
Ravenshead	V	**Coigach**	
Crystal Tripper	V	Nose Route	V
Shadow and Light	V	Direct Nose Route	VII,8
Venus Fly Trap	V	The Cul	V,5
The Boundary	IV/V	Fhurain Icefall	V,5
Grand Illusion	V	Eas Coulin	IV/V
Destitution Road	V		
Cuileag Corner	V,5	**Foinaven**	
Skyscraper Buttress	V	Overseer	V,5
Beinn Dearg and Cadha Dearg		The Second Icefall	V
Jewel in the Crown	VI,5	The Third Icefall	V

Addendum

Northern Highlands Volume 1.

The following information and new climb descriptions were received after Northern Highlands Volume 1 went to press.

SGURR A' CHOIRE GHAIRBH
See Volume 1, page 49.

Fisherman's Blues 180m III/IV
S.Kennedy, M.Macleod, D.Richie. 17 Nov 1992.
A short distance east of Hunter's Pass at the head of the corrie are two prominent slabby buttresses separated by a narrow gully. Tropical Buttress lies on the right-hand buttress. This route lies on the larger left-hand buttress, starting a short distance up the gully at the first obvious ramp line. Climb leftwards up the ramp over some steep steps to reach the crest of the buttress. Continue up the crest by a series of grooves to reach a large detached block on the right. A further series of grooves and steps lead to easier ground.

FUAR THOLL, SOUTH-EAST CLIFF
See Volume 1, page 62.

Sandstorm 170m VII,7
M. Moran, A.Nisbet 23rd March 1993.
This route aims directly for the steep groove which cuts the walls midway between Tholl Gate and The Fuhrer. The steep and compact rock makes this a demanding climb which requires liberal snow as well as frost. Start 20 metres left of Tholl Gate.
1. 45m Follow a vague left-trending ramp, then go back right to an easement. Continue direct to a blank wall just below an obvious cracked corner. Avoid this by a dogleg to the right to reach good belays at the corner.
2. 30m Climb the corner to a ledge, then go direct up a very steep groove (peg for aid) and swing left to moss ledges. Further strenuous moves lead up and right to a small stance just left of the main groove.
3. 45m Swing up to the exit of the groove, then go direct up the walls to a stance in the right-facing corner where the cliff steepens.

4. 30m   Go up right on flakes, then move back left to the crest of the buttress and a hard exit to easier ground.
5. 20m   Short steps lead to the top.

BEINN BHAN, COIRE NA FEOLA
See Volume 1, page 81.
Recent information suggests that route 15, In XS, is incorrectly located. It probably takes a concealed corner line to the right of Y-Gully, rather than to the left as described in the text and marked on the diagram.

Indigenous   170m   IV,6
P.Mynch, M.Moran 14th January 1993.
This is the obvious right-rising diagonal line which starts from the bottom of Y-Gully. Start up an easy chimney, then follow mixed ground to the foot of the ramp. (In XS probably goes straight up from here.) Climb the ramp, which on this ascent gave one turfy and one iced pitch, with an evil chockstone slit to finish. Easy steps then lead to the top of the A'Chioch ridge.

SGURR A' CHAORACHAIN, NORTH BUTTRESSES
See Volume 1, page 102.

Totem   150m   IV,5
A.Nisbet, D.Coburn, R.McFaddeen, R.Peak. 3 Mar 1993.
This is a winter version of the summer climb, taking a series of steep blocky grooves just left of the crest and finishing past the right side of the Totem pinnacle. Easier options further left were avoided.

MEALL GORM
See Volume 1, page 110

Gorm Gully   150m   II
This good wee route holds snow better than the other climbs on this face. Climb the deep narrow gully left of the three-tiered buttress (the third gully left of Blue Pillar) via easy snow to a final ice pitch.

LIATHACH, COIRE NA CAIME
See Volume 1, page 126.

The Shining Path   160m   IV,6
M.Moran, S.Birch. 3 Mar 1993.
A big ice fall forms right of Toll Dubh Chimney to the left of the edge of Twisting Gully. Start just left of the gully at a slanting groove. Climb thin awkward ice up the groove, then trend more easily left up iced steps until a short steep ice corner leads to the foot of the main wall. On the first ascent, the wall was split by a diagonal right-slanting weakness which gave a fine 40m pitch. Climb turfy corners above to the top.

The Andes Couloir, Variation   180m   V,6
S.Birch, C.Collin, M.Moran
This takes a line right of the original climb, incorporating two icefalls of which the second is short but vertical. Above, a right-facing turfy corner leads to the upper couloir.

Fat Man's Folly   170m   IV
D.Broadhead, D.Rubens. 30 Jan 1993.
This climb starts up a deep gully about 40 metres left of Valentine Buttress, then breaks right to follow a line of weakness.
1. 40m   Climb easily up the gully to belay beneath an obvious short slot.
2. 30m   Climb directly to belay at the slot.
3. 30m   Climb the slot and the pitch above.
4 and 5. 60m   Continue to a slanting corner.
6. 10m   Climb the slanting corner.

Last Orders   230m   IV
S.Pearson, G.Cohen. 23 Jan 1993.
This is the left-hand of two gully lines on the right side of Bell's Buttress.
1. 40m   Climb easy snow.
2. 40m   Climb two icy steepenings to below large roofs, then move right and climb the right wall via difficult moves to reach a crack above the overhang. Move back left into the main gully line and continue to a belay.
3, 4 and 5. 150m   The gully gradually eases, and after 20m gives straightforward climbing to the top.

BEINN EIGHE, COIRE MHIC FHEARCHAIR

CENTRAL WALL
See Volume 1, page 162.

Assegai   120m   V,6
M.Moran, A.Nisbet. 29 Jan 1993.
This winter ascent was based on the summer line. Start 5 metres right of Cool Cleft.
1. 35m   Climb a wide steep chimney, then go right to belay below the chimney of the summer route.
2. 40m   Move left into a corner, then into cracks just to the right, before moving back right to the summer line above its chimney.
3. and 4. 45m   Follow the summer line.

WEST BUTTRESS
See Volume 1, page 170.
The Upper Girdle crosses West Buttress using both of two parallel ledges, but the most recent route descriptions refer only to the upper ledge. Maelstrom starts from the Second Terrace.

Blood, Sweat and Frozen Tears   100m   VII,8
M.Moran, A.Nisbet. 26 Mar 1993.
This is an outstanding and very sustained route up the big vegetated groove right of Earth, Wind and Fire. Above the Upper Girdle, the groove continues between the inset slab of Earth, Wind and Fire and the arete of Shoot the Breeze. The route can be approached via West Central Gully (II), or via two 50m abseils. The line can be seen from the top of Central Buttress (although the groove is less obvious from here than from below) and the first abseil is from a point 6 metres right of a big perched block. The second is from the belay at the end of pitch 2. On this ascent the groove was heavily verglassed, but it may become easier under heavy icing.
1. 30m   Climb the groove, at times on the right wall, to belay on the lower ledge of the Upper Girdle.
2. 20m   Continue up the groove, then move left onto a steep slab to reach the upper ledge of the Upper Girdle. Pull through the overhangs above the ledge (at the same point as Earth, Wind and Fire), then immediately swing right into the continuation corner. Climb this and move left to a block belay.
3. 50m   Go left and climb a big corner past a difficult overhang.

BEINN ALLIGIN
See Volume 1, page 184.

Hatchet Man   80m   III
A.Nisbet, S.Chiles, H.Davies, P.Worthington. 27 Jan 1993.
Midway up the long right wall of the Eag Dubh is the only easy break,
a slabby ramp. Climb this in three pitches.

Under the Hammer   110m   V,6
A.Nisbet, G.Ollerhead. 27 Feb 1993.
The left side of the final gully of the Eag Dubh is a buttress which is
both steeper and larger than it appears. This route is based on a central
corner system, with frequent deviations onto the right wall. It can be
approached via a shallow gully on the left (II).

SLIOCH

Skyline Highway   205m   VI,7
R.Webb, N.Wilson. 23 Jan 1993.
This is a winter ascent of the summer line, as described in Volume 1
page 219.
1. 30m   Climb the steep parallel cracks (crux).
2. 20m   Move left, then go up past a small roof and continue to the
first terrace.
3. 35m   Traverse left along the terrace.
4. 40m   Climb a right-trending groove, hard at the top, to the next
terrace.
5. 40m   Traverse back right to the edge of the buttress.
6. 40m   Continue to easy ground at the start of the easy connecting
ridge which leads to the summit.

AN TEALLACH, COIRE A' GHLAS THUILL
See Volume 1, page 320.

The Magnificent Seven   200m   III
*N.Kekus, A.Andrew, D.Taylor, C.Brook, T.Wagg, I.Forth, P.Buck. 25
Mar 1993.*
This takes the leftmost of the narrow buttresses left of Major Rib (the
third buttress left of Fourth Prong). Climb the obvious line up the
buttress, with an easy first pitch onto the buttress proper, and a narrow
rock chimney and vertical corner on the penultimate pitch.

Northern Highlands, Volume 2.

The following descriptions were received too late for inclusion in the main body of the guide.

STRATHCONON

HIDDEN CRAG   (Map Ref 372 562)

This south-facing 13m crag has a flat grassy base and a pleasant atmosphere. It is set at about 80 degrees with several left-slanting crack lines, and has a profusion of small positive holds. The rock is affected by drainage, and takes a day or two to dry out. There are two *in situ* belay stakes at the top, one near the centre and the other nearer the right end.

To approach, either take the minor road along Strathconon and park at the first large layby on the left after the Meig dam, or leave the A832 just beyond Contin and follow the minor road (that eventually leads to Loch Achilty and Glenmarksie) to the same layby. Leave the road at a gate opposite the layby, and follow a forestry track through trees. Exit through a gate up on the right; the crag lies down to the left, about 10 minutes from the road. The routes are described from right to left.

Hoist by one's own Bullshit   13m   HVS 5b *
R. Brown, J.R. MacKenzie, G.Cullen. 7 Feb 1993.
A quick drying route with a well protected crux. Towards the right end of the main crag is a flat-topped pedestal below a left-slanting crack. Start immediately right of the pedestal and climb straight up via fingery flakes, then step right to a ledge and finish up pleasant rock.

Chinese Eyes   25m   E1 5b *
R.Brown, J.R.Mackenzie. 7 Mar 1993.
This fingery climb takes the left-slanting crack. Start right of the pedestal, climb to the crack and follow it with decreasing difficulty to an exit up the wall.

Shield Bug   13m   E1 5b
M.Hind. 9 Feb 1993.
Climb a shield of flakes left of the left-slanting crack, then finish up the wall above.

The Barker 13m E2 5c **
J.R.Mackenzie, R.Scott, R.Brown. 7 Mar 1993.
A climb with considerable bite, with sustained and interesting climbing. Left of the flakes of Shield Bug is a narrow crack. Climb this, using holds mostly on the wall on the left.

Pledge 13m E1 5b *
M.Hind. 9 Feb 1993.
Well left of The Barker is a smooth wall with a small overlap and ledge above at one-third height. Climb the smooth wall to the ledge and finish direct; sustained.

Creepy Crawly 12m E1 5b
M.Hind. 9 Feb 1993.
Climb the wall right of the slanting crack near the left end of the crag.

SCOOP CRAG *(Map Ref 374 565)*

This narrow crag of particularly smooth schist has a curving scoop with steep walls both above and to its left. It is a south-facing sun trap and dries quickly.

The approach starts from the same layby described in the approach to Hidden Crag, above. Follow the same track to the gate; the crag lies up and right (about 15 minutes from the road). The routes are described from left to right.

The Spike 20m VS 4c
R.Brown, J.R.Mackenzie. 23 Feb 1993.
This takes a good line on the left of the main crag. Start below a lobe of slab which lies right of a tree and right of a slanting corner. Climb the slab to the scoop, then follow a left-slanting break on hidden holds to finish up the left arete.

Fleetstreet Hack 20m E1 5b *
R.Brown, J.R.Mackenzie, R.Scott. 7 Mar 1993.
Climb the short steep wall left of The Scoop via an inset corner, then continue more easily to the headwall. Step right to its centre and climb the thin wall to a recess and the top. A high side runner in the crack of The Scoop provides the only protection below the recess.

The Scoop   25m   HVS 5a **
J.R.Mackenzie, R.Scott, R.Brown. 7 Mar 1993.
This fine delicate climb takes the line of the scoop, starting by delicate padding to a horizontal break. Traverse left along the break to the easier slab above, then follow this up left to below a crack. Finish up the crack.

Brass Monkey   20m   E3 6a
M.Hind, R.Scott. 14 Mar 1993.
This is the very bold and thinly protected wall right of Fleetstreet Hack. Climb the scoop of The Scoop, then continue ever thinly up the slab to the wall. The grade assumes prior knowledge of the obscure gear placements, a smattering of small RPs.

Confectionary Arete   20m   Very Difficult
J.R.Mackenzie, R.Brown. 12 Mar 1993.
The right arete of the crag is much easier than it appears. Start at a break a few metres up, level with the top of the lower scoop. If started from the base, the climb provides an unprotected slither.

BEN WYVIS AND THE FANNICH FOREST

COIRE NA FEOLA

Walking on Air   190m   IV/V **
G.Cullen, J.R.Mackenzie. 28 Feb 1993
Towards the right end of the main buttress is a hanging corner which forms an icefall. This is left of a much shorter icy corner. The first two pitches are serious.
1. 40m   Climb the steepening corner to a recess on the left (Friend 2 and 2 runners), then step right to climb a ramp to rock belays.
2. 50m   Climb the steepening icefall above to rock belays on the right below a watertight cave.
3. 35m   Climb past the cave to a shelf below a steep barrier wall, then traverse left to a slanting crack left of the centre of the wall. Climb the crack and ice groove above to rock belays above the crest.
4. 35m   Climb the snow field to the summit rocks. Belay near a groove at their right end.
5. 30m   Climb the pleasant groove to the plateau.

SGURR MOR

Several recent repeat ascents of The Resurrection have been made. The route was found to have a fine Alpine atmosphere, with the final belay being the summit cairn, but after the initial 10m the difficulty drops to grade II. An initial optional icefall forms just right of a short *cul-de-sac* gully left of the initial steep band. This may be avoided by the easy gully on the right. Either way, gain the large snowfields which lead to the final rock band. Although the route is technically straight-forward, snow belays and other doubtful forms of security may be required. The overall grade is III,4 if the harder start is taken.

CARN NA CRICHE

A Saucer Full of Secrets   240m   IV
J.Finlay, G.E.Little. 31 Jan 1993.
A surprisingly good route which starts at an obvious icefall halfway up the ramp that divides the main crag from the lower right-hand wall. It continues up the open groove above in the same general line.
1. 45m   Climb a zigzag line up the initial icefall to a belay on the left.
2. 40m   Continue to a wide snow ramp. Climb this to a belay at a short rock wall on its upper side.
3. 45m   A little further on, an open icy groove runs up right from a snow bay. Climb this and belay on the left.
4. 40m   Continue up the groove to a belay on the right.
5. 45m   Climb to the top of the groove, exiting onto a small snowfield. Belay on the right.
6. 25m   Easy snow leads to the top.

COIGACH AND ASSYNT

THE RHUE SEA-CLIFFS

Noggin the Nogg   25m   E3 6a
A.Cunningham, M.Burrows-Smith. Jun 1992.
This takes a line near the edge of the right wall of Rhue Corner. Move right along the first crack and go up into a recess. Gain the crack on the left and climb this to the next break, then finish up and right onto an easy slab.

Rhue Morgue   25m   E4 5c
M.Burrows-Smith, A.Cunningham. Jun 1992.
From halfway up Rhue Corner, hand traverse the huge break left for
6m to the thin crack which splits the headwall. Climb this in a sensational position to the top. A Cad 9 was used to protect the hand
traverse; apply at Glenmore Lodge for hire!

ARDMAIR

FISH FARM WALLS

M.V.Braer   35m   E2 5c
A.Cunningham, G.Reid. Aug 1992.
This takes the right-hand crack. Climb through the lowest rocks to the
base of a short right-angled corner below the crack. Belay here, or
walk round to the same point. Climb the corner and crack to the
heathery break, then finish as for Loan Shark.

MONSTER BUTTRESS

The Raven   30m   Severe
G.Reid, A.Cunningham. Aug 1992.
Climb the huge left-slanting diagonal fault, which is sometimes occu-
pied by a big black bird.

ARAPILES WALL
The horn on Antipodean Cruise has mysteriously disappeared.

BEAST BUTTRESS

Beastmaster   25m   E6 6b
M.Burrows-Smith. Sep 1992.
The first ascent was red pointed, but the grade is for an on-sight lead.
Climb the thin crack right of Neart nan Gaidheal to reach Unleash the
Beast. From here, swing out right and go up the flakey wall to the large
break. Move right round a block and finish up the easy crack.

AIRS ROCK

The Parapente
A harder start (5c) may be made by starting 2 metres right of the left-hand arete at an inset recess which leads to a right-slanting crack.

Zigzag Line   15m   HVS 5a/b
A. and R. Wallace. Jul 1992.
Some 2 metres right of the direct start to Parapente is a reddish flaky corner above a short slab. Climb the corner to the slab and finish up the groove on the left.

Underpants Arete   10m   Mild VS 4b
A. and R. Wallace. Jul 1992.
Right of The Way It Is the rock bulges out and is cut by horizontal breaks. Climb a vague edge through the breaks to the top.

THE NORTH-WEST COAST OF SUTHERLAND

SHEIGRA

The following climbs are thought to be distinct from those described in the main text, but they have been included here because it was uncertain exactly how they related to the previous climbs.

From Sheigra, walk west for 500 metres to a shallow saddle overlooking the sea, then walk up the hill northwards (following the coast) to a drystone wall. Just beyond the wall is an easy descent gully; Easter Buttress appears as the obvious wall on the left. Directly to the north is a taller buttress crowned by a free-standing pinnacle on its seaward prow; Pinnacle Buttress. About 50 metres further north is a squat cubic block, The Di, with an obvious flat overhanging roof jutting from its east face. It is overshadowed by an enormous free-standing 50m tower.

EASTER BUTTRESS
The routes are described from left to right. All the climbs here, and those on The Di, were first ascended by M.Wright, H.Adamson and R.Chapman during April 1992.

Cracked Egg   10m   Mild Severe
Climb the wide crack to the left edge of the buttress, passing jumbled blocks at one-third height.

Taniwha   10m   Severe *
Climb the crack 2 metres right of Cracked Egg.

Codswallop   10m   HVS 5a
Climb the poorly protected wall directly between the preceeding two climbs.

Creme Egg   10m   Severe **
A good climb which takes the curving crack splitting the centre of the face.

THE DI

Franks Planks   10m   E1 5b ***
The east face is split by an overhang at half-height. Towards the right end a leaning crack runs up past the end of the overhang and is capped by three giant roofs. Climb the leaning corner to reach the crack between the centre and left-hand roofs, then traverse along the wall and go round the end of the left-hand roof to finish by manteling up its left edge.

Little Tinker   7m   HVS 5a **
Climb the curving crack up the centre of the east face.

Above the mainland cliff, about 500 metres north of the gully that descends to Easter Buttress, is a small lochan that lies in a shallow saddle above the sea. Looking seawards there are two free-standing pinnacles; the right-hand one is just 2 metres thick. Cross the drystone wall and walk south-west beneath the mainland cliff for about 200 metres until opposite the left-hand and larger of the two pinnacles. The mainland cliff is about 20m high at this point and provides a good route.

Friends at a Funeral   30m   E1 5b **
M.Wright, R.Chapman, H.Adamson. 20 Apr 1992
This route takes the shallow corner and hand crack which runs almost from the bottom to the top, and which is the most obvious feature on this part of the mainland cliff. Climb a staircase to the bottom of the

crack, then climb this in three progressively more difficult stages, passing two ledges. Belay well back.

The routes on The Cioch, described in the main body of the text, are thought to lie on a group of towers south of the pinnacles described above.

SANDWOOD BAY

The large buttress on the mainland cliff opposite Am Buachaille contains the following route:

Just Deserts   115m   HVS 5b
P.Nunn, M.Richardson. 27 May 1984.
Just right of the square arete of the buttress the cliff is split by a corner.
1. 40m   Climb the corner, passing an overhang at mid-height, to a square ledge.
2. 35m   Traverse right round a rib and belay on a slab.
3. 40m   Ascend the slab and the crack above, passing a small roof. Continue up an open wall to finish.

Beyond Am Buachaille are two pinnacles, one squat and the other blade-like. The seaward face of the squat pinnacle gives the following climb, which takes a yellow crack and groove at its right end.

Howard's End   30m   E2 5b
M.Richardson, P.Nunn. 24 May 1992.
   1. 15m   Climb the jamming crack to a square shelf.
   2. 15m   Climb the steep crack to an overhang. Pass this by a step onto the rib on the left, then layback the upper crack to the top. Abseil descent from an *in situ* sling at the back of the pinnacle.

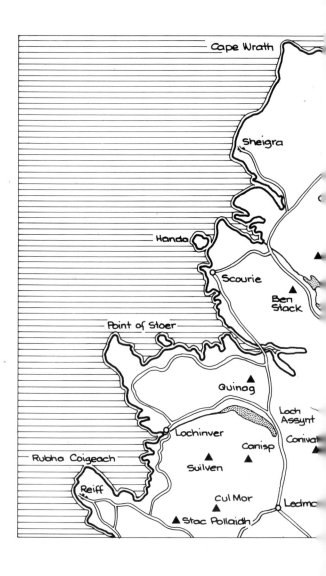